Minna Wagner

Ernst Benedikt Kietz: *Minna Wagner*, drawing, 1840. Nationalarchiv der Richard-Wagner-Stiftung, Bayreuth.

Minna Wagner: A Life, with Richard Wagner

Eva Rieger

Translated by Chris Walton

UNIVERSITY OF ROCHESTER PRESS

The University of Rochester Press gratefully acknowledges support from the Mariann Steegmann Foundation.

Translation copyright © 2022 Chris Walton

First published 2022
Reprinted in paperback 2023

Original German-language edition: Eva Rieger, *Minna und Richard Wagner: Stationen einer Liebe* © Georg Olms Verlag AG, 2., überarbeitete Auflage Hildesheim 2019, Germany.

University of Rochester Press
668 Mt. Hope Avenue, Rochester, NY 14620, USA
www.urpress.com
and Boydell & Brewer Limited
PO Box 9, Woodbridge, Suffolk IP12 3DF, UK
www.boydellandbrewer.com

ISBN-13: 978-1-64825-045-3 (hardcover); ISBN-13: 978-1-64825-047-7 (paperback)
ISSN: 1071-9989 ; v. 185

Library of Congress Cataloging-in-Publication Data
Names: Rieger, Eva, author. | Walton, Chris, 1963– translator.
Title: Minna Wagner: a life, with Richard Wagner / Eva Rieger; translated by Chris Walton.
Other titles: Minna und Richard Wagner. English
Description: Rochester: University of Rochester Press, 2022. | Series: Eastman studies in music, 1071-9989; 185 | Includes bibliographical references and index
Identifiers: LCCN 2022002074 (print) | LCCN 2022002075 (ebook) | ISBN 9781648250453 (hardback) | ISBN 9781800106079 (ebook other) | ISBN 9781800106086 (epub)
Subjects: LCSH: Wagner, Richard, 1813-1883—Marriage. | Wagner, Minna, 1809–1866—Marriage. | Composers—Germany—Biography. | Composers' spouses—Germany—Biography.
Classification: LCC ML410.W11 R5413 2022 (print) | LCC ML410.W11 (ebook) | DDC 782.1092/2 [B]—dc23
LC record available at https://lccn.loc.gov/2022002074
LC ebook record available at https://lccn.loc.gov/2022002075

Contents

Illustrations

Abbreviations

BB   Richard Wagner. *Das braune Buch. Tagebuchaufzeichnungen 1865–1882*. Edited by Joachim Bergfeld, first published 1975. Munich and Zurich: Atlantis Musikbuch Verlag, 1988.

Burrell   Richard Wagner. *Letters of Richard Wagner. The Burrell Collection*. Edited by John N. Burk. New York: The Macmillan Company, 1951.

CWT   Cosima Wagner. *Die Tagebücher*. Edited by Martin Gregor-Dellin and Dietrich Mack. 2 vols. Munich and Zurich: Piper, 1976–77.

ML   Richard Wagner. *My Life*. Translated by Andrew Gray, edited by Mary Whittall, first published 1983. Cambridge, New York etc.: Cambridge University Press, 2009.

RWA   Richard Wagner Archive, Nationalarchiv der Richard-Wagner-Stiftung, Bayreuth.

SB   Richard Wagner. *Sämtliche Briefe*. 26– vols. Vols. 1–9 edited by Hans-Joachim Bauer, Klaus Burmeister, Johannes Forner, Gertrud Strobel, and Werner Wolf. Leipzig: Deutscher Verlag für Musik, 1967–2000. Vols. 10–25 and 27 edited by Martin Dürrer, Margret Jestremski, Isabel Kraft, Andreas Mielke, and Angela Steinsiek. Wiesbaden: Breitkopf & Härtel, 1999–.

SSD   Richard Wagner. *Sämtliche Schriften und Dichtungen*. 6th edition (Volksausgabe). 16 vols. Leipzig: Breitkopf & Härtel, [1911].

Notes on this Translation

This is a translation of Eva Rieger's *Minna und Richard Wagner: Stationen einer Liebe* (second, expanded edition), published by Georg Olms AG, Hildesheim, 2019. The author has slightly revised the text of her book for this English edition. We have made use of existing English translations in the case of Wagner's autobiography *My Life* and the letters of the Burrell Collection (for their bibliographical details, see the abbreviations above; for bibliographical details of the original editions, see the bibliography at the end of this book). We have, however, standardized the spelling and punctuation as in US English without further comment (using double quotation marks for quotations, writing "Zurich" instead of "Zürich" as is given in the English edition of the Burrell letters, etc.). On those few occasions where we have also amended existing translations to bring them closer into line with the German original, we have added a corresponding remark to the relevant footnote.

Minna Wagner's frequently unorthodox, dialect-influenced orthography (e.g., "schlegt" for "schlecht" in her letter to Mathilde Schiffner of July 18, 1854) has been neither copied nor mimicked in the English translations given here, though we have kept her occasional misspellings of names (e.g., "Bethhofen" for "Beethoven" in her letter to Mathilde Schiffner of March 22, 1852).

All measurements are given in imperial units; distances are given as a straight line (for example, the distance between Zurich and Brestenberg is given as 15 miles, though anyone driving there today will find that they have to cover over twice that on winding alpine roads).

Introduction

"He could not breathe without her"

In March 1872, Cosima Wagner, Richard's second wife, wrote in her diary: "Richard calls to me: What's the difference between Wotan and Siegfried? Wotan married Minna, but Siegfried married Cosima."[1] In Wagner's *Der Ring des Nibelungen*, Fricka is Wotan's nagging wife, constantly reminding him of his obligations and needling him with barbed comments. By contrast, Siegfried's love for Brünnhilde is an ecstatic passion that overwhelms them both like a force of nature. Wagner used comparisons like this to encourage what became the stereotypical image of his first wife Minna, one that has dominated her reception down to the present day.

But Minna Wagner saw her relationship with Richard from a different perspective, one that seems more realistic. In 1855, when they were living in Zurich, she declined a joint invitation from friends by writing: "My lord and master is still unwell, so we were unable to come and hear Mrs. Hoffmann sing [...] I simply had to stay and take care of my child."[2] Describing Richard as both "lord and master" and "child" in the same sentence offers us a succinct summing-up of their respective roles in their marriage, as Minna saw things. She was the lover-cum-mother, while Richard, the supposed patriarch, was in fact emotionally dependent on her. In the years when they lived together, Minna washed and mended his clothes, massaged him with olive oil, and heated his bathwater; but she also listened patiently to his plans and ideas, and let him play his operas to her as he wrote them. She shielded him from outside disturbances, haggled with servants, and even took on the lowliest chores when servants were beyond their means, sewing his underwear and his dressing gowns. In short: she ran the whole household and provided him with his creature comforts. It was Richard who was always running up debts, not her; but when these became so great that illicit escape was the

---

1   CWT I, 495 (March 1, 1872).
2   Fehr 1934, 333 (January 25, 1855).

only option, she joined him in moonlight flits across fields on all fours and endured perilous storms at sea by his side, though the strain of it stretched her sanity to its breaking point. She even on occasion resumed her pre-marital career as an actor in order to keep them financially afloat.

Nor were Minna's domestic duties solely practical in nature. For some twenty years she was vital for Richard's mental and erotic well-being. His letters to her from the early years of their relationship reveal an unparalleled passion and a near-neurotic degree of dependence on her. Later, this dependence mutated into a sense of deep familiarity; but even then, he could not cope without her. He wrote to her about his future plans and current performances and would often end his letters by adding "more by word of mouth." His love affairs are laid out before us in the assorted biographies published about him, though it is often overlooked that he repeatedly begged Minna to come back to him once those affairs were over. For the first two decades of their marriage, she was the only person able to provide him with the inner quiet he needed to compose. Minna's first biographer, Friedrich Herzfeld, did not hesitate to criticize her harshly, but was nevertheless convinced that:

> In their first twenty years of marriage, [Richard] suffered almost unbearably whenever he did not have Minna by his side. She was an indispensable ingredient in his life. He could not breathe without her. On all his travels, he could never wait to return home to her embrace. As well as she could, Minna provided him with a real home.[3]

If Wagner was away and had no news of her, he could be overcome by a sense of panic. In letters to Franz Liszt in 1849 he admitted that without her, he was "often the most piteous weakling." But "once I've got my wife back again, I can get on with work, happily and joyfully."[4] By this time, they had been married for thirteen years. Despite Richard's later insistence that she had neither understood nor supported his mission as an artist, she could justifiably claim that she had in fact played a significant role in the co-creation of his works.

Richard's willingness to equate himself variously with Wotan and Siegfried demonstrates just how much he regarded his art as being intertwined with his personal life. In the 19th century, the Romantics had increasingly turned music into a means of spiritual confession. As with any other composer of significance, Wagner did not express his direct experiences through his

---

3   Herzfeld 1938, 133.
4   SB III, 75 and 81 (June 5 and 18, 1849).

music, but the ideas, emotional needs, and convictions that those experiences prompted in him. For him, life was a stage, but the stage was also life; the two overlapped. Music enabled him to depict both feelings and ideas as a reflection of inner, subjective experiences.[5] Then there was the element of theater. Through the power of his imagination and his creative drive, Wagner's music dramas succeeded in channeling his emotional world into works of art that became qualitative milestones in music history. But when applied to his own life, such methods were doomed to failure, because the world of his imagination conjured up ideas and images that did not correspond to the lived truth. It was those who were closest to him who suffered on account of this; and during the most important years of his life, it was naturally Minna who suffered most.

The marriage of Richard and Minna Wagner was not without its tragic aspects. This was largely because the 19th century had erected norms of marital behavior to which Richard was unable or unwilling to conform. Marriage was a social and economic partnership in which the respective roles of man and woman had been fixed. The division of labor that had emerged as a structural principle in industrial societies existed also between the sexes, assigning the woman primarily to the domestic arena, while the man's responsibility was to go out and earn a wage. Richard often regarded himself as unbeholden to bourgeois norms, but he never expressed any objections to this specific allocation of roles. He would rage when Minna took ill, leaving him to cope with extra household chores that he saw as woman's work. Conversely, however, he consistently refused to adhere to "male" norms by going out to earn a regular wage. And as already mentioned above, he was constantly in debt during the years when he lived with Minna, which made it impossible for her to run a normal bourgeois household. They often lacked even the basic monies to get by. And when they begged others for it, she felt ashamed while he did not. "To be dependent solely on the amity of friends is a sad way for a woman to live," she wrote when Richard asked her to follow him into Swiss exile in 1849.[6] Wagner became a virtuoso in scrounging and borrowing from others, because money to him was first and foremost a means of supporting his work—and this took precedence before everything else. But such attitudes gradually eroded all of Minna's faith in him, and chronic skepticism took the place of trust as the years went on.

---

5   See Bekker 1924.

6   July 18, 1849 (RWA).

How are we to imagine Minna Wagner? The posthumous assessments to which she was subjected could hardly be more contradictory. All too often, facts have been distorted, discounted, or downright denied. She has been depicted as a somewhat frivolous, unsophisticated actress—and a bad one at that—who was unworthy of her husband and made his life even harder than it needed to be. Martin Gregor-Dellin has claimed that "she was both demure and flirtatious, the very model of a heartbreaker,"[7] though the facts fail to support any such claim. Others, by contrast, have described her as "down-to-earth and dowdy,"[8] which rather seems the very opposite. Wagner and other contemporaries are in fact on record as praising her acting prowess, her humor, graciousness, and beauty—though their assessment has most often been turned on its head by later commentators. Wagner himself once remarked that she was "devoid of any coquetry,"[9] and there is proof enough that he was repelled by women who came across as effusive and artificial. "She stood conspicuously apart from all the unpleasant impressions that the theater offered," he wrote of her, adding that she possessed "a friendly calm and serenity that had something almost motherly about it and by no means suggested frivolity or heartlessness."[10]

Minna is often accused of having failed to understand Wagner's works, and his infidelity in their marriage is frequently excused as being a result of the supposed intellectual and spiritual gap between them.[11] It is true that Minna assumed a limited period of viability for any opera, and she also judged it by the income it earned. But this was a stance she shared with innumerable artists' wives who were tasked with running a household. She inwardly wrote off *Tannhäuser* once it had been performed at a large number of opera houses. In fact, Wagner himself thought along not dissimilar lines. In a letter to his publisher Breitkopf & Härtel, he once expressed a desire that the third act of *Lohengrin* "will hopefully still be played for a while after my death."[12] But Minna never made a secret of her enthusiasm for his works. She even wrote to Richard on occasion to assure him that she adored

---

7 Gregor-Dellin 1980, 107.

8 Fehr 1933, 33.

9 ML, 129.

10 ML, 90.

11 Robert Gutman claims that the opposite was the case: "his numerous [...] affairs, especially during those vigorous days in Biebrich, brought him no female Nietzsches." Gutman 1968, 110.

12 SB VIII, 106 (July 10, 1856).

his music. In 1854, she attended a performance of *Tannhäuser* in Frankfurt am Main and wrote of how she was "quite spellbound with delight and rapture. I cried continually, such that the newspapers the next day even wrote of how I was so visibly moved."[13] As an experienced actor, she was also able to offer Richard practical insights into stagecraft in his early years in the business. But *Tristan und Isolde* went beyond her understanding. It seemed to her to be an aberration, the expression of an adulterous ecstasy that she could never condone. Nor could she find any reason to learn to like it: "I don't want to know about his triumph and this opera, which I cannot stand in any case because I know what brought it about. The text is disgusting, almost immorally open in its fiery passion."[14]

So it was by no means the complexity of its musical language that prompted Minna to reject *Tristan*. In any case, just how far removed Wagner's musical ideas were from those of his circle of friends and colleagues is often ignored. Minna's acquaintances included Ferdinand Heine, Wilhelm Fischer, Joseph Tichatschek, Anton Pusinelli, and Wagner's sisters, none of whom were able to comprehend why he refused to continue writing operas in the style of say, *Rienzi, Tannhäuser,* or *Lohengrin*, given that these were popular and brought in money. Wagner's brother Albert was an actor and a singer with ample experience of the stage himself, and he begged his younger sibling to compose works with a more practical bent that would make things easier for his singers. Even a contemporary as gifted as Robert Schumann, who had always been open to musical innovation, was unable to get to grips properly with Wagner's music and ended up offering crass misjudgments: "He is truly unable to think and write four nice measures one after the other."[15] Clara Schumann's opinions of Wagner's music are as emotional and negative as those expressed by Luise Büchner, Elisabet von Herzogenberg, and other women intellectuals of the day. Felix Mendelssohn Bartholdy, Joseph Joachim, and Johannes Brahms all found Wagner's music difficult to grasp (though the last of these did revise his opinion, as did Schumann). And yet it is always only Minna who is singled out for her supposed enduring incomprehension of it.

Minna's sense of estrangement set in when Wagner embarked on the composition of the *Ring* cycle, though it had little to do with any lack of

---

13 May 8, 1850; November 7, 1854 (RWA).

14 Fehr 1953, 149 (letter to Jakob Sulzer, December 15, 1858).

15 Letter from Robert Schumann to Felix Mendelssohn Bartholdy of October 22, 1845, quoted in SB II, 25.

understanding on her part, and was more because of the emotional distance that Richard began erecting between them. This in turn was because the woman he now regarded as his muse was not his wife, but Mathilde Wesendonck. We have the proof of this in the many annotations that he made on the compositional sketch of the first act of *Die Walküre*, which are easy enough to decipher (such as "L.d.m.M.?" = "Liebst du mich Mathilde?" / "Do you love me, Mathilde?"), and show just how much he identified himself and Mathilde with the lovers Siegmund and Sieglinde. Wagner had once been accustomed to reading, playing, and singing everything he wrote to Minna. But her presence could now only be a disruption, so he placed his compositional process at one remove from her. The increasing sense of alienation that she felt was thus occasioned by a realignment in Richard's erotic interests, not by her purported musical limitations.

Despite the many differences between them, the letters that Wagner wrote to Minna remain the most authentic he ever wrote, because "he could write to her on the basis of a matter-of-fact stability."[16] But Wagner was only able to offer his wife a secure existence for a short space of time. Their years of marriage were characterized by repeated removals, selling off furniture, setting up home anew, tumult, money shortages, and debt. His dream of being able to afford a two-wheeled, horse-drawn carriage was something he spoke of even before marrying Minna, and one he mentioned to her time and again. But it was Cosima, his partner in Tribschen and Bayreuth, who was the beneficiary when he could finally afford it. It was not an incompatibility of character between Wagner and Minna that led to her disappointment, demoralization, and ultimate rejection, but Richard's insistence on making promises that he could not keep, and on forging plans for a future that seemed destined to remain a chimera.

In the late 19th century, it was almost impossible for women to combine having a family with achieving self-fulfillment in their chosen career. But Minna loved her work. She had always earned enough as an actor and was sought-after in her time. It was Richard who urged her to leave it all behind her—though not in any homage to bourgeois norms, but because he became jealous when she went on stage. After he fled Dresden in 1849, Minna pondered whether or not she should leave him and return to the

---

16　Dahlhaus/Deathridge 1984, 89. However, this applies only to the time up to the Wesendonck crisis. Afterwards, Richard endeavored more and more to keep Minna pacified, and ceased to tell her his innermost thoughts and feelings.

stage, because she feared that they would be plunged back into a period of penury. Nine years later, shortly after the Wesendonck crisis, she once again considered returning to her former profession. This time, her sister-in-law Clara Wolfram advised against it, pointing out that many theaters were in dire financial straits, that Minna no longer owned a costume wardrobe, and that others had remained in the profession and gained further experience while she had spent the intervening years away.[17] So it would be wrong to claim that Minna had given up the theater with any sense of satisfaction.

Many of Minna's contemporaries offer us descriptions of her. "She was so beautiful that she alone would have sufficed to make that married couple interesting,"[18] wrote the painter Friedrich Pecht. The musician Ferdinand Praeger, whose reminiscences have admittedly proven to be in part unreliable, praised her gazelle-like eyes and her good-natured friendliness: "Her appearance was at one with her gentle speech, which entranced everyone. In their home, it was she who read the eyes of everyone and knew what would please them, and who did everything—without the slightest fuss—to keep everyone happy."[19] Richard's niece Johanna Jachmann-Wagner described her as a strikingly pretty, gracious, trusting woman, with a sound notion of what was practical, and a healthy dose of common sense.[20] This was confirmed by Gustav Kietz, who described her as an "unusually beautiful, highly sympathetic woman, full of heartfelt kindness and amiability [...] fully involved in the work of her husband."[21] To be sure, however, Pecht did add: "No one actually saw the beautiful woman or the former actress, let alone the lady artist—instead they saw just the kind-hearted, inwardly pedestrian, sober character who clung to her husband with all her soul, following him everywhere with her head bowed, yet essentially clueless about his importance and who yearned for a regular bourgeois existence and so stood in irreconcilable, inner opposition to him, despite all her love and fidelity."[22]

Probably the most discriminating description of Minna comes from the pen of her close, trusted friend Emma Herwegh, who was the wife of the famous revolutionary Georg:

---

17   Burrell, 373 (June 3, 1858).
18   Quoted in Glasenapp 1977, I, 347.
19   Praeger 1892, 56.
20   Kapp/Jachmann 1927, 125.
21   Quoted in Glasenapp 1977, I, 361.
22   Quoted in Glasenapp 1977, I, 361.

In around 1850, Mrs. Minna Wagner was comely and pretty in appearance. She did not have the same level of education as her husband, but in her disposition and true kind-heartedness she nevertheless possessed many predominant characteristics in which she was far superior to him, and for which you had to love and honor her. She was not at all notable for especially brilliant conversation, but more importantly: in the most difficult of times, when they both lacked what they needed the most, she knew superbly how to keep her adored husband as far as possible away from all worries about their daily bread and the bitter prose of her everyday hours.

What poetic understanding she possessed she endeavored to explore in practical terms. Where others would gush, or express themselves in bad verses, she chose action. There are few women who have been through such a tough "schooling" as Minna, and who passed their final exams as efficiently as she. To be sure, you couldn't demand subtle diplomacy of her. She was too passionate for that, too unable to restrain her inadequately educated nature. But whoever appealed to her excellent heart could be sure of being understood and of finding a sympathetic ear.

When she married Wagner, she was a beautiful, celebrated, tragic actress, while he was an unassuming, relatively unknown musician, constantly in debt. Vanity thus had no part in her choice of husband. However, she would have needed a multitude of natural gifts and ample ebullience to be able to keep up with him later in their life of struggle, deprivations, and dreadful routine. And those were qualities she probably never possessed, or at least she never had the leisure to cultivate them. But at her core, she was admirable.[23]

"We nowhere else find as many banalities or superficialities as in the letters that Wagner wrote to his wife," claimed the editors of his complete letters.[24] To Liszt he wrote detailed reports of his problems when composing, Mathilde Wesendonck remained the *grande seigneuse* to whom he wrote in a lofty, ennobling tone, but Minna was his correspondent for everyday business. Yet when commentators claim that "he ignored Minna when it came to his real problems, especially concerning his creative work,"[25] they are themselves ignoring the fact that he conceived almost all his most important works during the period when he and Minna lived together—even if we discount their final years, after their marriage had become dysfunctional. With the exception of *Parsifal* and *Tristan*, Wagner's mature works were planned in Dresden or in the years before—even the ideas behind *Der Ring des Nibelungen* emerged in the late 1840s. Back then, he seems to have had

---

23   Emma Herwegh in *Das Forum* 1/31 (1914), 142f.
24   SB VI, 25.
25   Ibid.

little need for ecstatic, idealized love affairs such as he experienced later with Jessie Laussot, Mathilde Wesendonck, and Cosima von Bülow. He needed a female partner sound of heart and mind with enough tact to give him the support he needed to get through the worst hardships. In this, Minna fitted the bill perfectly.

When Minna went on a trip through Germany in the autumn of 1854, Wagner willingly assigned her all authority to act on his behalf in her efforts to procure the amnesty that they hoped might facilitate a move to Weimar: "Rest assured that I have complete trust in your discretion!" he wrote as he placed his fate in her hands.[26] His letters address her with all manner of endearments, humorous diminutives, superlatives, word-plays, and animal names in several languages from Italian and French to cod-Latin (from "good bunny" to "Carissima Minna," "Chère épouse," and many more), but they also include precise reports about preparations for operatic performances and about the respective merits of singers both male and female. If he received letters praising his works, he would sometimes copy them out for her, or simply include them with his own, full of pride. So we are surely justified in asking whether Wagner would ever have managed to achieve what he did in the creative realm were it not for the devotion and active support of his first spouse. Early on in their relationship, in autumn 1835, Wagner wrote of his feelings for her to his then-bosom friend Theodor Apel: "More than any concept of morality, love makes me powerful; a high-flying, sentimental love would unnerve me now—but mine makes me happy and cheerful."[27] Two decades later, he was indeed ripe for a "high-flying," sentimental love when he encountered Mathilde Wesendonck, though it brought him torment and joy in equal measure. In these initial, turbulent years of his career, however, it was Minna he needed.

If we cannot trust Wagner's biographers in their opinion of Minna, what about Wagner himself? When he began to dictate his autobiography *My Life* to Cosima von Bülow in 1865, he was confronted with the problem of explaining to his new partner and his select readership[28] both why he had recently separated from Minna, and what had made him marry her in the first place against the wishes of his family, despite all manner of hindrances. To provide a convincing account of the latter, he had to list her merits—for

---

26   SB VI, 267 (October 1854).

27   SB I, 221 (September 22, 1835).

28   Wagner had his autobiography *My Life* printed in just over a dozen copies for perusal by only a few friends.

any criticism could be twisted around to make him appear foolish instead. The result is a strange mixture of contradictory statements. His account of his flight from Dresden in 1849 may suffice here as an example. For several weeks after fleeing the city, he remained without any word from his wife. His tone in *My Life* is business-like and neutral: "I inquired about her sympathetically of one of her relatives."[29] But a letter he wrote in July 1849 tells a different story. He reached out to Minna's daughter Natalie, begging her to convince Minna to come to him straightaway. He pulled out all the rhetorical stops, ending with a hefty dose of emotional blackmail:

> Oh God, if only Minna were with me! [...] Oh, if only the blessed spirit of love were to visit Minna again soon: if these noblest, purest feelings for me do not overpower her soon, I fear that she will never again be able to love me: then she should tell me that she never wants to see me again, that she cannot love me any more,—and then—fare well, art and everything that makes my life what it is! Then I shall take up my walking staff and go out into the wide world so that none shall ever find a trace of me![30]

She joined him, but in less than a year he was planning to quit Europe and run away with Jessie Laussot instead. He wrote a farewell letter to Minna that offered a devastating assessment of their relationship, listing every criticism that came to mind: "The utter differences between us in the depths of our being have become a torment to me, as also to you, and have been ever since we have known each other; sometimes they have proven to be milder, at others more glaring."[31] His planned elopement failed, he returned to Minna, and five years later, he could still write to her: "Believe me, dear Minna, even if in some things we don't really think the same and let off steam about this or that: neither of us can look back on our life without seeing the great proof of love and endurance in how we have stayed close to each other, even in the most difficult, often terrible situations."[32] Three years after this, they separated for good.

As we can see, Wagner was constantly vacillating, his letters a reflection of his momentary whims and circumstances. His consciously convoluted utterances, reassurances, and lies are intended to bend reality to suit him. This was all deeply rooted in his histrionic nature, and it impedes us from being

---

29   ML, 427.
30   SB III, 96 (July 10, 1849).
31   SB III, 276 (April 16, 1850).
32   SB VII, 44 (March 6, 1855).

able to interpret what he says as any source of objective truth. By contrast, Minna's letters are almost insistent in repeating the same opinions time and again. In itself, this suggests that they may be regarded as the more trustworthy documents. She did once threaten Richard that she would write her own memoirs[33]—though since her perspective of things was at times diametrically opposed to that of her husband, it would only have heightened the overall confusion. It is thus our task to interpret events in the light of how they occurred, treating all our sources with due caution, in hopes that by gathering together letters, reminiscences, contemporary utterances and historical facts, we might seek out and find what comes closest to what was real and true.

---

33   CWT I, 797 (March 1, 1874).

Chapter One

"I have become her despot"

From Love to Marriage

> God knows, my wonderful girl, if an hour ever escapes me in which I do
> not remember you a thousand times! It's delight and agony at the same
> time, because to think of you is joy, and to see you so vividly before me
> and yet to know that you are so far away is agony! [...] We have to get
> out of these sordid theatrical conditions that we have experienced up to
> now; as a married couple we have to enter further into the echelons of
> a bourgeois, higher life; and look, my sweet child, I have the sure faith
> and the firm hope that when we are married, happiness will come and
> abide with us.[1]

Richard Wagner wrote this to his lover Minna Planer at a time when she
was far away from him. Throughout his life, he always strove to improve his
circumstances. So it is all the more astonishing that he should have married
a woman without a dowry. The decisive factor was his passionate love for
her, which overcame him when he was just 21 years old, and which became
a constant obsession. At first, to be sure, he had imagined that he might keep
the upper hand in their relationship and drop his lover whenever he saw fit.
But things turned out differently.

The woman he loved was Christiane Wilhelmine Planer, known to all as
Minna. She was born on September 5, 1809, into a poor family in Oederan,
a little town in the Erzgebirge some 20 miles to the southwest of Dresden, in
the kingdom of Saxony. As her birth-cum-baptismal certificate in the church
of Oederan confirms, she was four years older than Richard. Minna's parents were Johanna Christiana, née Meyer (1782–1856), and Gotthelf Planer
(1770–1855), who had married on September 25, 1802. Gotthelf was a

---

1   SB I, 297 (June 10, 1836).

trumpeter in the Saxon Army, in which capacity he served under Napoleon in the renowned Battle of Wagram against the Austrians in July 1809, just a few miles outside Vienna. His cavalry regiment from Oederan, the so-called Elector's regiment, suffered heavy losses, and afterwards returned home to Saxony. Johanna Planer gave birth to ten children, some of whom died in infancy. Minna's eldest sister was Charlotte, who went on to marry a doctor named Adam Tröger; she died in 1864. She was followed by Henriette-Wilhelmine (called Jette), then came Minna in 1809, Amalie in 1811 (a singer who later married a Russian cavalry captain by the name of von Meck), then Karl Eduard in 1818, who died in 1843 at the age of 25. Minna did not grow up in comfortable times. Her birth certificate states that her father was a "toolmaker [mechanicus] hereabouts." The profession of "mechanici" was situated between craftsmanship and industry, responsible for making tools and machines. After Gotthelf was unable to find any more work as a trumpeter, he started making iron hooks for the carding combs that were used in the wool industry. The Napoleonic Wars caused immense material damage to Saxony, and as a former ally of France it found itself compelled to accept a peace treaty with Russia and Prussia in 1815 that resulted in the loss of over half of its land and 42 percent of its remaining inhabitants. To make matters worse, 1816 and 1817 saw two bad harvests in Saxony that exacerbated the poverty there.

The business of Minna's father initially went quite well. But misfortune came when a manufacturer in Chemnitz ordered a large number of comb hooks in 1819. Gotthelf was delighted at the prospect of a lucrative contract, and so spent the last of his money on buying the necessary materials. His children had to help out with production because their small, flexible fingers were particularly well suited for the job. They worked hard, day and night, and were promised ample Christmas presents by their father as their future reward. But when he went to deliver the goods, Gotthelf learned that his client's business had collapsed. That bankruptcy in turn brought about his own ruin.

Gotthelf Planer never recovered from this blow. His later mental confusion might have been connected to this trauma, and Minna's own lifelong fear of poverty could well have been a result of the shock she too had endured. Even if she had not fully understood the dimensions of poverty as a child, this fateful blow will nevertheless have been imprinted deeply on her mind.

But what were they to do with the large quantities of the special fine wire that was used to make the wool combs and was now superfluous? 10-year-old Minna was sent out to sell it to the milliners who could use it to make artificial bouquets. She left home with heavy baskets full of wire. Whether thanks to an early display of her acting skills or to childish earnestness, she managed to promote her wares so skillfully that she was able to sell every-thing. For the first time, she was able to experience the pleasure of having accomplished something truly useful. This experience also had a lasting impact on her, and awakened in her a desire both to alleviate her family's poverty and to learn a profession of her own.

The Planer family meanwhile moved to Dresden. Even though the Napoleonic Wars were some years past, their consequences could still be seen in the city. A contemporary reported seeing crumbling churchyard walls, rubble, and debris in many places. The Zwinger also presented a picture of decay. The building itself was damaged, and grass had begun to sprout in the floors.[2] Gotthelf Planer even tried his hand at making pianos. But the middle classes were finding it difficult enough to feed themselves, let alone make music, and he was hardly able to sell anything. The destitution of the Planer family, and the fact that education cost money, meant that Minna was only allowed to get the most basic schooling. She learnt no more than the rudiments of reading, writing, and arithmetic, as the spelling mistakes in her later letters prove. Besides, Gotthelf was convinced that nothing more was necessary for his daughter anyway—and her later husband was clearly of the same opinion: "Your father was quite correct in not wanting you to learn how to write,"[3] remarked Richard on one occasion.

Perhaps it was a desire to escape poverty that in spring 1825 led the 15-year-old Minna to engage in intimate relations with a royal Saxon captain of the guard by the name of Ernst Rudolph von Einsiedel. If she did so of her own free will, then it is likely that she was lured primarily by the prospect of prosperity, since marriage to a man from a wealthy family would have lifted her out of poverty for good and brought considerable relief to her suffer-ing family. The aristocratic "von" and the dashing uniform presumably con-tributed to the favorable impression he made. At this time, all army officers were from noble or patrician families. The few members of the bourgeoisie who made their career in the military belonged to the so-called "Amtsadel" or "nobility of office," whose titles originated in their function in the state rather than in anything hereditary.[4] As Richard Wagner later recorded the

---

2   Gustav Klemm, quoted in Becker 1962, 15f.

3   SB XI, 80 (May 12, 1859).

4   The von Einsiedel family is mentioned in the "Gotha" almanac of Germany's aristocratic lineages.

events in *My Life*, "a certain Herr von Einsiedel fell desperately in love with her and in an unguarded moment succeeded in ruining the inexperienced girl."[5] This suggests that Minna was actually a victim of rape.

Whatever the circumstances might have been, the consequences for her were disastrous: she became pregnant. Von Einsiedel promptly left, never to be seen again. Minna was right to despair, because to be "dishonored" thus would have been a huge blow to her father, who had already lost everything else. She was terrified of her father's wrath, but her horror at the absence of any options seems to have led her to unburden herself to her mother and her sister Charlotte. They decided that there was only one solution: concealment. All three of them agreed to convince Gotthelf that it was his wife, Minna's mother, who was expecting a child. It was a clumsy trick, but it worked. The child, called Natalie, was born on February 22, 1826 in a maternity hospital in Dresden—a public institution that served as a place of refuge for women in the last period of pregnancy, during childbirth, and in the days after delivery. It also served as a training school for midwives. Perhaps Minna's mother told her husband that she was going to give birth there, and that she was taking Minna along to help. Wagner later recounted how "in circumstances perilous enough to threaten her life, she had brought a daughter into the world,"[6] which suggests that there were complications resulting from her compulsion to conceal the truth.

Minna's father suspected nothing to the day he died. Even her daughter Natalie seems to have remained in ignorance of her true origins. The Wagner bibliographer Nikolaus Oesterlein visited her in around 1880 when she was already 54 years old, and she told him, too, that she was Minna's sister. This lifelong lie led to repeated friction between mother and daughter. Minna regarded Natalie as her daughter and treated her accordingly, while Natalie refused to be dominated by a woman who was supposed to be her sister, and so defended herself as she saw fit.

Natalie's baptism took place in the Kreuzkirche in Dresden. Minna and her mother did not dare to lie to the ecclesiastical authorities, and so declared Natalie to be the natural daughter of Minna Planer and Ernst Rudolph von Einsiedel. Minna's sister Charlotte acted as godmother. Thus a phalanx of women was formed against the father, who was presumably delighted about the birth of another daughter, so long after his other children. This episode, comingled with resultant feelings of guilt towards her mother, might also

---

5   ML, 128.
6   ML, 129.

explain why Minna helped to look after her parents until they died, why she did everything in her power to persuade Richard to send money to them, and why she maintained a good relationship with Charlotte throughout her life. It is also noteworthy that her child's full name was "Ernestine Natalie," thus including the name of the father: did Minna perhaps suppose that he might still marry her at some point in the future? Years later, against his will, Minna persuaded Richard to accompany her to the regional court in Dresden in order to initiate alimony proceedings against Einsiedel for Natalie.[7] It is not known when this took place, but her efforts were in any case unsuccessful. Richard considered it tactless (he spoke of a "lack of delicacy" on her part), though the procedure was surely intended by Minna both to provide for her daughter and to grant herself some sense of belated satisfaction and thereby fulfil an inner need of her own.

Minna learned two things from this brutal experience, and they became second nature to her: You could believe men's promises only if they were linked to a concrete proposal of marriage, and only if their finances were on a firm footing. A reliable income was to her synonymous with one's general standing. She also learned how to put up a bourgeois façade. This explains her later fear of dishonor and ridicule when her husband had to flee from Dresden after his role in the uprising of 1849. She attached great importance to maintaining at least an outward semblance of normality. This, however, was something that Richard was unable to comprehend, and he often mocked her in his letters for her proclivity to pretend for the sake of others.

What profession could Minna now learn? The guilds still maintained a monopoly of trade in Saxony, and women were excluded from them. Minna was aware that she was considered attractive, and she knew she was not untalented. Her family clearly had an artistic streak—her father had been a musician, one of her sisters became a singer, and Minna had proved herself adept at improvising a second part to songs they sang. For middle-class women—to whose number Minna believed she belonged, despite her parents' poverty—there were essentially just two professions available: that of governess, and that of artist. But while governesses were still dependent on male authority and were liable to be humiliated by parents and children alike, the career of a stage artist could enable a woman to gain recognition equal to that of men.

The writer Fanny Lewald (1811–89) was especially impressed by women stage artists because they presented her with an image of the independence

---

7   CWT II, 148f. (July 29, 1878).

that she herself desired: "I could spend hours sewing and knitting while imagining what a joy it would be for me to be independent and have a profession of my own, like these women."[8] Perhaps it was this aspect of acting that fascinated Minna. But there was another, darker side to the profession.

The theater director and historian Eduard Devrient was of the opinion that the introduction of women on stage had meant that "the judgment of the male audience—the audience whose opinions counted—became clouded by sexual interests."[9] Women thus had to act with extreme caution if they did not wish to be seen as creatures of lust, indulging their sensuality. The acting profession enabled women of the lower classes to rise up and win fame and prestige, but it also harbored the danger of a loss of honor. They were courted by the playboys of the day and often liable to be seduced, which could in turn mean being compelled give up their chosen career in disgrace. Such "indiscretions" were naturally blamed on the victims, not on the men (who were generally well situated and often regarded actresses as little more than upmarket prostitutes). Inevitably, it was usually those female artists who earned poorly who were dependent on such "cavaliers," since they could supplement their meagre salaries by providing sexual favors. In the eyes of society, however, actresses were a class of women generally teetering on the brink of debauchery.

The "costume paragraph" was an additional burden on the time and finances of actresses, as it meant that they were responsible for their own stage clothes. In his study of actresses published in 1905, Heinrich Stümcke described a situation typical of his day: "While the actor recovers from his exertions in the pub, drinking beer and playing cards, the unfortunate comedienne sits bent over her sewing with needle and scissors, struggling to adapt her only robe of state to suit the character of a new role by means of ornaments, folds, or a different decolletage."[10]

The process of commercialization meant that the problems inherent in the acting profession changed over the course of the 19th century. Actors had hitherto tried to gain the respect of the bourgeoisie, but the situation of the theater and its status now shifted in the direction of commercial speculation. It was usually the actresses who were the first to fall victim to these changes. An acting proletariat emerged whose career progression became ever more dependent on bowing to the whims of the theater directors. Women

---

8   Rheinberg 1990, 151.
9   Quoted in Stümcke 1905, 30.
10   Ibid., 60.

accordingly often resorted to the time-honored practices of surreptitious prostitution, using sex in order to survive. In the second half of the 19th century, a social chasm opened up among actresses. Some succeeded in establishing a career in their own right, which in turn brought them the respect of the bourgeoisie, while others ended up among the extras or the chorus where they were much worse off financially. Some even landed on the streets, with little left for them except to engage in begging and prostitution.

Despite everything, Minna decided to become an actress. At the age of 22, she began training with Else Mevius, an actor who worked at the Court Theater in Dresden from 1828 to 1833. Minna soon began getting her first roles, which secured her an income. She was acting in the theater on the Freiberger Platz in Dresden when she enjoyed a stroke of luck: the director of the Dessau Court Theater happened to be in the audience, and promptly offered her a contract. It was almost certainly not just a matter of good fortune or good looks on her part: Minna was clearly a convincing actor.

It will surely have been a sublime, exhilarating feeling for Minna to captivate an audience and to feel able to achieve an effect by virtue of her own ability. To receive the homage of an audience and to acknowledge their enthusiastic applause will have made rehearsals on freezing stages and the endless stitching and sewing of stage costumes seem worthwhile. But acting on stage harbored specific professional dangers to which Minna was particularly exposed as an attractive young woman. Men frequently stalked her, though there is no indication that she ever prostituted herself to alleviate financial hardship. In 1854, Franz Brendel wrote that "a woman singer must know as a woman how to captivate the world of men. She has to know how to flirt and to dress well."[11] Minna was well aware of the dangers that came with her profession, but she also knew how to avoid them.

We have Minna's draft reply to an admirer who had sent her two letters asking for an answer. She wrote:

> As I have assured you by word of mouth, I shall enjoy your feelings of friendship for me and now I can only repeat this in writing. But if the mysterious intimations in your letters, which I fail to understand, should have a different meaning I would sincerely regret it, since my position and my circumstances do not allow me to enter into any other relationship.[12]

---

11   Brendel 1854, 46.
12   Burrell, 29.

The back of this draft bears a note in Richard Wagner's hand from the year 1835, which suggests that Minna must have still been fending off admirers when she was already in a relationship with him.

Minna had to provide for herself, and also had to send money to her parents to enable her brother to go to university in Leipzig. Several years later, she put pen to paper to record her experience of life in poverty: "There were times when I was often short of the 4 groschen I needed for lunch due to the dire cash situation of the theater management; I then pawned my earrings and the like, which were often indispensable to me on stage, and sent the money to my brother, who was supposed to use it to help him study. I only kept back 3 pfennige in order to buy myself a bread roll that I ate for my lunch as I walked around the city, while pretending to my landlord that I was invited to eat out somewhere."[13] Besides sheer fraternal solicitude, this willingness to support her brother might also have served to compensate for feelings of guilt, because Minna's mother was still looking after Natalie while she was little.

Minna met her future husband in August 1834, when he was just 21 years old. Richard Wagner was born on May 22, 1813. His artistic talent had been emphatically encouraged by his stepfather Ludwig Geyer, who was also his role model. Four of Richard's six older siblings chose a career on stage. His older brother Albert became a tenor, Rosalie and Luise worked as actors, Clara as a singer. Even as a child, Richard played small roles with enthusiasm. Later, he recalled "figuring in a tableau vivant as an angel, entirely sewn up in tights and with wings on my back, in a graceful, though laboriously learned, pose."[14] During his school days, he also took part in a performance of Weber's opera *Der Freischütz* with self-made costumes and masks.

Richard was a deeply sensitive child and easily excitable. Visits to the theater stimulated the boy's imagination to the point of distress. His relationships with friends were also highly emotional. At school he would be passionately attached to some or other chosen one amongst his peers, with their friendship determined by the degree of his friend's commitment to Richard's own fantastical notions. He never knew his biological father, his stepfather died when he was just 8 years old, and so he grew up amongst his sisters and half-sister Cäcilie. The eldest sister Rosalie was given the task of caring for her younger siblings. Richard's letters reveal his affectionate, almost rapturous, infatuation with her. "Despite the fact that, as I have mentioned,

---

13   SB I, 420 (Minna writing to Theodor Apel, November 17, 1849).
14   ML, 5.

there was little tenderness in our family, particularly as expressed in caresses," he later wrote in *My Life*, "the predominantly feminine element in my surroundings must have had a strong impact on my emotional development."[15] Wagner's family relationships were thus primarily with women, and he harbored a deep love for his mother and sisters. When he was 22, he wrote a few lines to his mother that reveal a heartfelt intimacy, despite their florid style: "Is not the love of a mother far, far more unsullied than any other? [...] Everything comes from your heart, from your dear, good heart, which God willing will always be inclined to me, for I know that if everything else abandoned me, it would always be my last, dearest refuge." With her he had experienced the warmth, fidelity, and love that he so desperately needed. Women who are prepared to love steadfastly in all circumstances would later become a basic topic in his operas. His mother seems to have corresponded to this ideal. After once falling out with his family because of his dissolute episodes, Richard wrote to his friend Theodor Apel in tears: "A mother who loves me dearly is all that I still have—nothing more!"[16]

After a rather wild phase as a student, Richard began to pursue more serious relationships with women. We find references to amorous adventures in diary-like notes that he made from 1829 to 1832: "Becoming dissolute. A dissolute time in the summer."[17] He took some time before he finally plucked up the courage to approach women properly, and he soon had his first sexual experiences, probably with the help of alcohol and in cahoots with his male friends. In 1832, he fell in love with one or both daughters of one Count Pachta near Prague, whom he had met through his sister Rosalie (who was working at a theater in Prague at the time). He was rejected, however, which hurt him deeply, and for the moment he concentrated on building up his self-confidence among his male peers. His ebullient manner helped him to gain self-assurance among his friends, and he later wrote in *My Life* of how "I acquired [...] the first inkling that I could amount to something not only among men but also among women."[18]

Wagner began his theatrical career as a chorus master in Würzburg in 1833. In 1834, at the age of 21, he was offered the position of music director at the Magdeburg Theater Company that was about to give its annual summer performances as a guest ensemble in Bad Lauchstädt. Richard found

---

15   Ibid., 14.
16   SB I, 210 und 214 (July 25 and August 21, 1835).
17   SB 1, 81.
18   ML, 77.

everything about it so mediocre that he decided to turn it down—until he met Minna Planer, whose generic role in the troupe was that of "first youthful lover." Right from the very first moment he was captivated by both her beauty and her character. He praised her kindness and her graceful, fresh appearance, which was complemented by a self-confidence in how she moved and behaved. It is striking how frequently Richard emphasizes her purity in the midst of a supposed cesspool of thespian sin. He was so taken with her that he decided on the spot to accept the post offered to him, and rented an apartment in the same building as her. When she was on stage: "In the midst of this dust cloud of frivolity and vulgarity, she seemed to me always like a fairy [...]. This lovely actress differed wholly from those around her by her unblemished sobriety and elegant tidiness, as well as the absence of all theatrical affection or comical stiltedness."[19]

Richard's assessment of her ability is contradictory. He writes of how Minna is "a very respected actress"—a statement that naturally makes one sit up and take notice—but then he promptly denies her any talent as an artist, adding: "I cannot judge whether or not the routine she will acquire over time will succeed in making her a 'good' actress." Since he does not exclude this possibility from the outset, he must at least have assumed that her talents were not entirely limited. Given the uncompromising critical faculties that Wagner cultivated throughout his life in matters pertaining to his art, it seems highly unlikely that he would have fallen in love with an actress who was incompetent. Moreover, he himself wrote several times of the disgust he felt when Minna's talent and intellectual abilities were criticized.[20]

At first, Minna did not take much notice of him, and he found her cold and inaccessible. But they soon became closer. He was touched by her utter unconcern at the erysipelas that periodically disfigured his face, and instead continued to visit him and look after him. On one occasion he apologized for his appearance—he was still suffering from a rash on his mouth—and was convinced that she would be unwilling to kiss him in such a state. Instead, she promptly did so to prove he was wrong. He wrote of how all this happened in an atmosphere of friendly calm and composure, and that her actions were neither frivolous nor unfeeling, but radiated a caring nature.

Their theatrical troupe moved from Bad Lauchstädt to Rudolstadt in order to continue its series of summer guest performances. Richard's feelings for Minna now intensified. In addition to her sexual allure, it was her

---

19   Ibid., 89.
20   E.g., ibid., 95 and 101.

motherly nature that especially attracted him. He longed for security, and instinctively felt that she was someone who could provide it. But as his love grew, so did his feelings of jealousy. He learned that Minna was friends with a young aristocrat who was affectionate towards her, but whose social position and lack of any personal fortune ultimately compelled him to enter into a marriage of convenience with another woman. Wagner understood that achieving the goal of his desire would be no easy task, since Minna was not like the frivolous women she sometimes played on stage. It would require a demonstration of serious intent on Richard's part before she would allow further boundaries to be crossed. For his part, Richard found these hurdles irksome, and so began whiling away his evenings in Rudolstadt with friends, drinking beer, eating bratwurst, and gambling away his salary at dice and the roulette tables that were set up in the open-air market of the town. Contact with Minna ceased for a while.

There is a somewhat flippant letter from Richard to his friend Theodor Apel from this period in which he claims to have achieved sexual consummation with Minna. Marriage was not in his thoughts. On the contrary, he rather envisioned a life of freedom surrounded by his (male) friends, and his description of Minna is accordingly nonchalant, and punctuated by breathless dashes:

> You ought to have Planer too—she has quite transfigured me sensually a few times—it was really magnificent. At present, I am quite without any love interest—I have no time for it—I'm still inclined to Toni a little—oh, dear God, that's all—I am living at present in sweet rapture, because tomorrow I get my wages;—but my God, that's all too prosaic! [...] When I asked her why she granted me all these favors, since she did not love me, and could not love at all, Minna replied—'What can I do, if you have more strength [than] me and kiss me half to death?'"[21]

This crude, cocky offer to Apel was influenced by what Wagner was reading about free love at the time. In reality, he would never have coped with any promiscuity on Minna's part. Perhaps he was also embarrassed to admit to Apel that he had fallen seriously in love—after all, Wilhelm Heinse's novel *Ardinghello* and Heinrich Laube's *Das junge Europa* had made it fashionable to claim that superficial, sensual pleasure was the measure of all things. Wagner was writing from Rudolstadt, but his later reminiscences make no mention of any intimate contact having come about there. We can thus

---

21   SB I, 164f. (September 13, 1834).

Figure 1.1. Richard Wagner, silhouette, 1835. Nationalarchiv der Richard-Wagner-Stiftung, Bayreuth.

assume that he was simply engaging in empty boasts to a friend. Minna had bestowed her favors in the form of flirting and kissing, but nothing more. Another unplanned pregnancy would have meant the end of her career. For her at this point, marriage was the only option.

After the end of the summer season in Rudolstadt, the troupe returned home to the garrison city of Magdeburg. Their repertoire at the city theater was an ambitious one. Richard had made great progress since his first appearance as the troupe's conductor in August 1834, and his reputation grew accordingly. Minna had meanwhile become a recognized actor. She allowed some of her admirers to visit her, though Wagner's memoirs insist that her behavior was always decent and her reputation remained unsullied.[22] All the same, he was annoyed about his apparent rivals. After Minna's death, a poem by an unknown admirer was found in her papers, the first stanza of which describes her appearance at the time: slender, with luxuriant brown hair, dark eyebrows, and a "noble brow." This ode in her honor ends with the following lines: "The noble figure [is] as slender and light as the Graces, swift gliding as a Vestal priestess, yet hardly touching the ground!"[23]

Richard had to cope with the fact that the woman he loved also aroused the desires of competitors, even though she herself was supposedly unaware of it (if we are to believe her anonymous poetic admirer). Wagner became angry and confronted Minna about her gentlemen callers. She assured him that they were from the upper classes and thus behaved more discreetly and more modestly than theater lovers from the bourgeoisie. But this only intensified the bitterness of his accusations. These incidents reminded him of his experiences in the Pachta household near Prague, three years earlier, when he had been humiliated to see how gentlemen of rank were given priority access to the daughters of the family. Richard found it intolerable to come off second-best in matters of the heart. So he and Minna separated for three months at the end of 1834, during which time, as he later recalled, "I pretended in half-despairing self-abandonment to enjoy the company of a motley crew and behaved in every way with such blatant frivolity that Minna, as she later told me, was moved to sympathetic concern for me."[24]

Richard could not bear to be rejected sexually while at the same time be compelled to watch how others were entertaining higher hopes than him. Minna thought it wise to make friends with the stage director, the theater

---

22 ML, 94–95.
23 Burrell, 20.
24 ML, 93.

director, and the most important members of her ensemble, and she found it better to yield than to fight—something that was alien to Richard, who often quarreled with his colleagues in the troupe because he was convinced of the rightness of his own artistic and aesthetic views. He was unable to comprehend Minna's reasons for remaining compliant. But this was her chance to earn money; if she lost it, she would have had few alternatives. Richard's spirit of adventure was quite foreign to her. He was happy to travel from one place to the next, gaining experience along the way, but this was in any case hardly an option for women at the time. Minna's sole concern was her earnings, which she needed for both herself and her family. She felt no compulsion to establish any kind of artistic legacy like Richard, who was driven to prove his talents to the world.

Minna understood that Richard suffered on her account, and she pitied him the more for it. She was still better known than he was. Her name appeared on theatrical posters, she was praised in verse, courted by admirers, and was the recipient of numerous offers to appear elsewhere, as is proven by her extant correspondence with theater directors between 1832 and 1836: "Dear Miss! In answer to your letter, I am asking whether you would be willing or able to obtain a release from your present contract for the month of February or a little later, in which case I should like to sign an agreement with you for a longer term" (letter from Dessau of November 26, 1832). "Should you still be of the same opinion, I would consider myself fortunate if you were to support my institution with your splendid talent" (Brandenburg, January 16, 1834). "Your talent, known to me, leaves me no doubt that that you will be successful with the public here, since it is a cultivated one" (Lübeck, September 16, 1834).[25] And so it went on, with inquiries from Berlin, Coburg, Gotha, Dessau and Königsberg (Kaliningrad today). She took roles in all manner of plays, from comedy to farce and tragedy. In the Eumorphia Theater in Dresden alone, she played the following roles: Elvira in *Die Schuld* by Adolph Müllner, Julie in *Die Schweizerhütte am Rheinfall* by Johanna Franul von Weissenthum, Fanny in *Die Engländerin*, also by von Weissenthum, the dancer Gambasuella in the farce *Die Benefiz-Vorstellung*, and the Widow Dahl in the play *Die Erbschaft* by August von Kotzebue. None of this could be described as high literature that would have required much acting finesse, and it was closer to fleapit fare. But such roles still required a lot of preparation, self-assurance, and professional skill.

---

25 Burrell, 450 and 457.

Enduring the artistic success of the woman he loved was a challenge for Wagner—a young composer who was ambitious, but still unknown. And the thought of being rejected by Minna was unbearable to him. But she finally offered an open reciprocation of his feelings on New Year's Eve 1834. His initial attempts, accompanied by champagne, were still rebuffed; but by the time the punch bowl came around, the shackles of convention fell away. Minna did not abandon her composure, but nevertheless returned Richard's demonstrations of affection in a manner that made it clear to the others present that they were now a couple.[26]

One evening, Wagner had arranged to meet Minna at her apartment. He played whist with friends beforehand, and arrived late and completely drunk. She could hardly send him home, and so he stayed the night. "She provided me with everything I needed, and as I soon sank into the deepest sleep, she unhesitatingly surrendered her bed to me." The following morning, as he later recorded in his memoirs, "illuminated for me with glowing clarity what was to become a long and boundlessly fateful lifetime relationship."[27] This account was committed to paper several decades afterwards. In it, he downplays his feelings, presenting things as if his henceforth permanent relationship with Minna had somehow overwhelmed him unawares. But Minna had created a new identity for herself as an actor that relied on her being independent and appreciated by her audience. This was not something she was going to abandon in a fit of impetuousness. It was Richard who had pushed for their relationship to become intimate; it was he who sought to be close to her at all times; and yet he remained loath to enter into any obligations himself.

Despite her misgivings, Minna no longer put up any resistance to his wooing. Over thirty years later, Richard visited Magdeburg with his second wife, Cosima. He showed her the street where Minna had lived at the time and told her how he had spent whole days there.[28] Looking back, Richard claimed that in reality she had never truly felt any love for him and had lacked passion. Her prime concern, he claimed, had been a desire to ensure his well-being.

She obviously thought highly of my talent and was surprised and captivated by my unexpectedly quick string of successes; my eccentric nature, which

---

26 ML, 94.

27 Ibid., 95.

28 CWT I, 611 (December 10, 1872).

she knew so well how to humor by genial moderation, stimulated her to continual exercise of this power, so flattering to her self-esteem, and without ever evincing any desire or real ardor herself, she never requited my impetuous advances with any coldness.[29]

Wagner here implies that he had never experienced the bliss of real passion from his former partner. Ironically, he dictated these lines to Cosima, who was not much inclined to sexual delights herself ("all the passion of love has departed from me, though with R. it still prevails," she confided to her diary in the year of their marriage).[30] What's more, by the time Cosima committed Richard's words to paper, Minna was already dead, and so hardly in a position to contradict anything. Had Minna not kept his letters, we might have the impression that their early love affair was tepid, even borderline asexual. But Minna was perfectly capable of showing passion, as Richard boasted to Theodor Apel in 1835: "You should read [her] letters—they burn with fire, and we both know that this is not something innate to her."[31]

After the end of the theater season in Magdeburg in spring 1835, Richard traveled to Leipzig to see his family, while Minna went to her parents and Natalie to Dresden. The Magdeburg theater was bankrupt. Towards the end, its director had handed out tickets for boxes in the theater in lieu of paying wages to his troupe. They were useless to Richard, but Minna—who always lived frugally—was actually able to convert them into a small amount of money. She had already honed her sales talents as a child, and now brought them to bear again in order to persuade others to buy the tickets.

Minna visited Richard in Leipzig, where she was invited to tea with his mother and sister Rosalie. He was barely able to hide his infatuation, it seems. It became clear to him, he later recalled, "that my days of patriarchal family dependence were over,"[32] and that his future was with Minna. That summer, he traveled together with her and one of her sisters to Saxon Switzerland, a mountainous region to the southeast of Dresden that remains popular with holidaymakers to this day. Their youthful high spirits were interrupted, however, by a fit of jealousy on Richard's part, "for which there was in fact no pretext, but which nourished itself on past memories as well as premonitions

---

29 ML, 94.
30 CWT I, 311 (November 11, 1870).
31 SB I, 207 (June 6, 1835).
32 ML, 100.

based on the experience I had already gained with women."[33] This confession reveals Richard's deep-seated fears of being slighted or abandoned. He was able to take a determining role in matters pertaining to his professional career, but when it came to women, he was dependent on their affection and acceptance. This in turn fed his latent aggression and led to unfounded scenes of jealousy. But this outburst was an exception that summer, which remained otherwise enjoyable. He always retained happy memories of a night they spent awake together in Bad Schandau in beautiful weather.

Director Bethmann now managed to procure subsidies from the king that were enough for him to re-engage Richard. With this renewed sense of certainty, Richard borrowed money and set off forthwith on his own to hunt out artists in Bohemia, Nuremberg, Würzburg, and Frankfurt who might be suitable for the Magdeburg theater. His happiness at the moment knew no bounds, with Minna the "central point" of his life; it was she, he claimed, who provided him with "consistency and warmth."[34] He wrote to Apel in high spirits that he had made of her "a soft, devoted woman." He went on: "She loves me to the point of illness, I have become her despot; no one crosses her threshold of whom I do not approve; she sacrifices everything to me." He now even claimed that her stage presence exuded "life, warmth, passion."[35] But then something unexpected happened that for the moment shattered his dreams: Minna left Magdeburg. Bethmann had reneged on a promise to give her a leading role, which he gave instead to a rival of hers by the name of Grabowsky. She felt deeply wounded by this. What was more: Wagner did not have any kind of permanent contract in Magdeburg. Minna's fear of slipping down the social ladder, coupled with her anger at having been undeservedly rejected, now prompted her to seek an engagement at the Königsstadt Theater in Berlin. Theaters were keen to get her, and the stage world was her oyster—a fact that will have rightly bolstered her pride. She did not want to leave Richard; she just wanted to live and work somewhere else for a while. Richard's brother-in-law Wolfram worked in the same ensemble in Berlin, but it seems he took delight in relaying the latest gossip to him, according to which Minna was dabbling in unsavory company. When Richard wrote in desperation asking for more information, Wolfram sheepishly admitted that he had been party to idle chatter.

---

33   Ibid., 102.
34   SB I, 227 (October 26, 1835).
35   SB I, 222 (October 2, 1835).

Wagner had originally gone to Magdeburg to be near Minna. Her sudden departure from the city now had a disastrous impact on him. Decades later, he could still recall the "utter alarm" that seized him. From November 4 to 11, 1835, he wrote long, daily letters, urging her to return home. Richard's yearning, passionate invocations are also masterpieces of persuasion.[36]

The first letter was written immediately after Minna's departure.

In the morning, 8:30—

Minna, my state of mind can't be described—you are gone and my heart is broken, I'm sitting here hardly able to think and crying and sobbing like a child. Great God, what shall I do? How and where may I find consolation and peace! When I saw you leaving, all my feelings and sensations painfully broke loose in me; the morning mist in which I saw you drive away trembled through my tears; Minna, Minna, all at once I felt the terrible certainty that the coach was bearing you away from me for good. My dearest girl in doing this you are doing a terrible wrong—I am bound to you by chains a hundred thousand strong, and now I feel as if you would throw them around my neck and would strangle me with them. Minna, Minna, how you have changed me! I'm sitting now in my quarters, thoughts are whirling around me; a ghastly void—nothing but tears, pity and misery. [...] Even to face the thought of a twelve days' separation is enough to shake me to the depths of my soul, and—good God—to you a separation for a full half-year is some slight affair that you slip into without any emotion. [...] Do you have a human heart? Have you *any* feeling for sublime love and fidelity? Minna, Minna, does not this voice penetrate your heart? My God, my God, what else can I tell you, my heart is breaking![37]

The flood of letters seems never-ending. Richard wrote that he was hobbling around like a shadow and would never compose again if she left him. She was his focal point, one in which all his strivings and actions were concentrated. Grief and sorrow were eating him up, he claimed, he was unable to suppress his tears in public, and his heart was broken (again). "You are my fiancée and I have a right to you; we are due to marry already at Easter—why do you have to go to Berlin?"[38] We already find here an insistence on a reality of his own—something that would have such a fatal impact on Richard's plans in later life. He loved Minna, so she simply had to love him back. Anything else was unthinkable. His letter crossed with one from Minna in

---

36   These letters are given here in highly abbreviated form.

37   Burrell, 31–33.

38   SB I, 236 (November 6, 1835).

which she wrote that she would not be returning to Magdeburg and would tell him the reasons by word of mouth. Richard slipped into a complete panic. He now grasped that Minna was not going to give up her career for him, but instead wanted to continue with it alongside their relationship. For him as a man, pursuing a career was utterly natural; but for a woman he loved to think that way was inconceivable:

> You will sacrifice to me your life but not your theatrical CAREER, which I would tread upon to keep it from separating us. I swear to you, Minna, I don't care for your stage life at all, and before sacrificing our love to it I would rather remove you instantly and entirely from the theater, marrying you on the spot, with 600 thaler salary, to which I can add 200 thaler for a few years [...] Open your heart, Minna, if you don't I am going to compel you; by God, I shall come to Berlin and tear you away by force, and if that should pain you, tell me that you don't love me any longer, and so give me the death blow! My girl, my girl, no one was ever loved as much as you! I will prove my love to you by renewing now with unceasing strength my offers for our union; if you reject this union there will be other ways to convince you of the power of my love. This is sworn by your Richard.[39]
>
> I would sooner become accustomed to the thought of an early death than to that of a separation from you. But I will play this chord no more today. What is there left to say after my previous letters, to the girl whose heart has not been touched by these entreaties, by these presentations, these offers? This girl would no longer be touched in her heart—only by a sharp knife. [...] you often saw my tears, kissed them away from my eyes. Do I no longer move you? I am working hard to conquer my pain; as early as seven in the morning I sit down to write to you; then I work continuously until one o'clock at my opera, which now is reviving in me in its full power, and is closely connected with the possession of you. [...] Never let yourself imagine that time will soothe and lessen this pain. Time affects me in a quite different way—instead of gradually diminishing my love for you as a habit and dulling it, your absence has only made it stronger and more durable, and the same would happen with my agony of separation. I can already feel how it begins to gnaw at my heart.[40]

Richard's alternate threats of violence, offers of unconditional submission, fervent crying, and begging did the trick. Minna replied that she was unhappy with the frivolousness of the theater and wanted to return to him. His pleading reassured her that he was serious. And he was! He was

---

39   Wagner to Minna, November 7, 1835, in Burrell, 37 (slightly amended).
40   Wagner to Minna, November 8, 1835, in Burrell, 38 (slightly amended).

overjoyed—and especially impressed that she had turned down four roles that had been offered to her in Berlin. He now went before the theater committee in Magdeburg and insisted passionately that she be recalled. Since she was in fact urgently needed, the Magdeburg management immediately agreed—which in itself is further proof of her talent. On a stormy, pitch-black winter's night, he traveled to meet her by special mail coach, greeting her with tears of joy and accompanying her back to the same Magdeburg apartment of which he had become so fond.

These letters are not just tokens of an impetuous, youthful love affair, for they also reveal traits on Richard's part that remained typical of him throughout his life. His violent fantasies were later transferred into the artistic world, which he on occasion claimed he wanted to destroy utterly. His notion of a sharp knife penetrating Minna's heart was an expression of a compulsive desire to possess her that was in utter disregard of her own overriding desire to continue with her career. This tone of voice continued in the letters that he wrote to her from Berlin when he was himself visiting the city six months later. There is also a striking reversal of roles when he writes that he no longer wants to appear "so soft." She was presumably the more emotionally robust of the two of them, at least for as long as his reputation in the musical world remained so tenuous. When he points out that she has the theater as her purpose in life, whereas he only has *her*, this in effect signifies a reversal of the traditional gender roles.

What had begun as an infatuation had turned into a powerful sense of dependence that Wagner could no longer deny. He wrote to Apel: "Let someone come along and turn up his nose at my love for Minna, and I'll punch that nose for him. God knows what or how I would be without her now! Let this simple hint suffice for you, and go and imagine the rest!"[41]

In March 1836, the premiere of Wagner's opera *Das Liebesverbot* took place in Magdeburg. Minna still believed his assurances that the work would bring him a lot of money. The first performance was undistinguished because the company's financial situation precluded adequate rehearsal time; and on the second day, several singers got into a brawl backstage that ended in the cancellation of the performance. But Minna even forgave him his easygoing way with money. When Richard found a court summons nailed to his front door, he fled straight to her, and found her sympathetic, providing highly

---

41   SB I, 253 (December 27, 1835).

soothing respite, "with truly comforting assurance and steadfastness in every aspect of her manner towards me."[42]

Wagner's bourgeois-minded family was opposed to his marriage, which they regarded as unsuitable along class lines. His mother in particular implored him to leave Minna, but this was inconceivable to him. His mind was made up. Minna continued to insist on having an independent career, and began negotiating with the management of the theater in Königsberg. Wagner joined her in this, and although no post as a kapellmeister was vacant at this time, the Königsberg company dangled the prospect of his succeeding to such a post in the near future. It was decided that Minna should travel ahead. Wagner was aghast at the thought of being without her, and now, more than ever, he actively sought her proximity in Magdeburg, hardly ever leaving her side.

Wagner traveled to Berlin in hopes of organizing a production of his *Das Liebesverbot*, and once more fired off a series of passionate love letters to Minna. He was helpless and abandoned, he claimed, and painted a glowing picture of the sheer unending magnitude of his desire, waiting for her return letters in trepidation and emotional anguish.

> My Minna, Minna, Minna! I weep without restraint, and really I'm not ashamed of my tears. It is no usual state I am in, all the misery of my life culminates in the thought: There is a good, dear, wonderful girl who is suffering for my sake! Minna, my poor child, give me some comfort, some reassurance.[43]

He describes to her his successful negotiations with Karl Friedrich Cerf, the director of the Königsstadt Theater in Berlin, who had supposedly offered him the prospect of a production of *Das Liebesverbot*. When Cerf asked him to take over the position of his conductor Franz Glaeser, who happened to be on leave, this glimmer of hope was sufficient for Richard to construct a whole edifice of castles in the air:

> If I can't start with my job in Königsberg right away, I'll stay here in Gläser's place for the time being and will personally conduct my opera [...] and maybe some time come to Berlin with my dear wife and a fine youngster, to take Gläser's position; at that time you need no longer be at the theater [...] And now nothing, nothing in this world must separate me from you, by God and Eternity, nothing, nothing my Minna, can tear you from your Richard.[44]

---

42   ML, 120.
43   Burrell, 44 (Wagner to Minna, May 21, 1836).
44   Burrell, 44–45.

When Wagner happened to read in the papers that Minna had indeed accepted an engagement at the theater in Königsberg and was thus leaving Magdeburg, he suffered under the notion that "crude" strangers would be able to see her in person, while he had to remain far away. He was afraid that she might not need him anymore, and every possible trifle made his fears flare up. He wrote to her of how his passion consumed him, of the agonies he was enduring, the pain and the anxiety—and time and again, his sexual desire shimmers through, coupled with a yearning for her maternal protection.

Wagner believed that the woman he loved ought to follow his lead, steadfastly and lovingly. This was neither an acquired philosophy, nor some political or nationalistic conviction or an artistic credo. It was the emotional fundament of his very being, and accordingly also forms the bedrock of his artistic oeuvre. Richard hoped that marrying Minna would enable him to exercise even more rights over her. He was determined to talk her out of pursuing her acting career, which would remove her from the gaze of potential rivals and thus negate any necessity for jealousy on his part. His doubts about Minna's intentions were hardly unfounded, for she was from the very start uncertain as to whether Richard would be able to support her. As a result, she hesitated to commit herself to him. But Richard's impetuous courtship won her over. In July 1836, he followed her to Königsberg, and on November 24 of that same year, Richard married Christine Wilhelmine Planer, four years his senior, the third daughter of Gotthelf Planer, a handyman from Dresden, and his wife [Johanna] Christiana. The wedding took place in the Tragheim Church in Königsberg.

Wagner's family was worried, partly because Richard was too young to marry according to the bourgeois norms of the day, but also because his bride came from an impoverished milieu. Only Richard's sister Rosalie stood by him when news reached his family of his willful marriage. Minna's parents were also afraid that Richard, as an artist, would be unable to support their daughter properly. But he did not let any of that concern him. Although 23, he was still a minor according to Prussian law, so he simply added a year to his official age.[45] Richard would never pay much attention to obeying authority. In fact, Minna also lied about her age—though she, by contrast, made herself out to be younger than she was. Not a single date was correct on the marriage certificate that the officiating pastor presented to them.

---

45   Marriage from the age of 21 was legally permitted in Germany only from 1900 onwards.

An Fräulein

Minna Planer

bei ihrem

Vermählungs-Feste

mit dem

Musikdirector Herrn

Richard Wagner.

Wenn Dir die Kunst auch holde Blumen windet
Zum Kranze, der Dein Haupt so freundlich schmückt,
Wenn Deine Leistung Anerkennung findet,
Und ungetheilter Beifall Dich entzückt! —
So welkt der Lorbeer; Ruhm und Schönheit schwindet;
Nur Liebe ist's, die ewig uns beglückt:
   Darf erst zum Lorbeer sich die Rose neigen,
   Dann nennst Du wahres Glück mit Recht Dein eigen.

Wohl Dir! — Du hast den treuen Freund gefunden,
Der Lust und Leid mit Dir von Herzen theilt;
Und nahen Deinem Leben trübe Stunden,
Als Trost und Schirm an Deiner Seite weilt.
Wenn Neid und Undank je Dein Herz verwunden,
Führt Liebe Dich, die alle Schmerzen heilt;
   Doch wollen Freundeswünsche auch begleiten
   Den Herzensbund, und Segen Euch bereiten.

So wandle, holde Künstlerin durch's Leben,
Indem Dir Kunst und Liebe Blumen streu'n;
Recht lang' mögst Du, die Grazien umschweben,
Noch Königsberg durch Dein Talent erfreu'n.
Du kannst dem Bild des Dichters Leben geben,
Wir müssen selbst, als „Stumme" Dank Dir weih'n:
   So mög' uns Deines Geistes schönes Walten
   In mancher Blüthe herrlich sich entfalten.

Wenn dann Dein Gatte hier im Reich der Töne
Uns leitet in der Harmonien Land;
So stellst Du uns des hohen Dichters Schöne
Lebendig dar im Bild', das er erfand.
Daß manchen Dichter auch der Lorbeer kröne,
Reicht ihm der Künstler gern die Bruderhand;
   Was Schiller, Göthe, Lessing Hohes sangen,
   Mög' est durch Dich als Wahrheit uns umfangen.

Königsberg, den 24. November 1836.

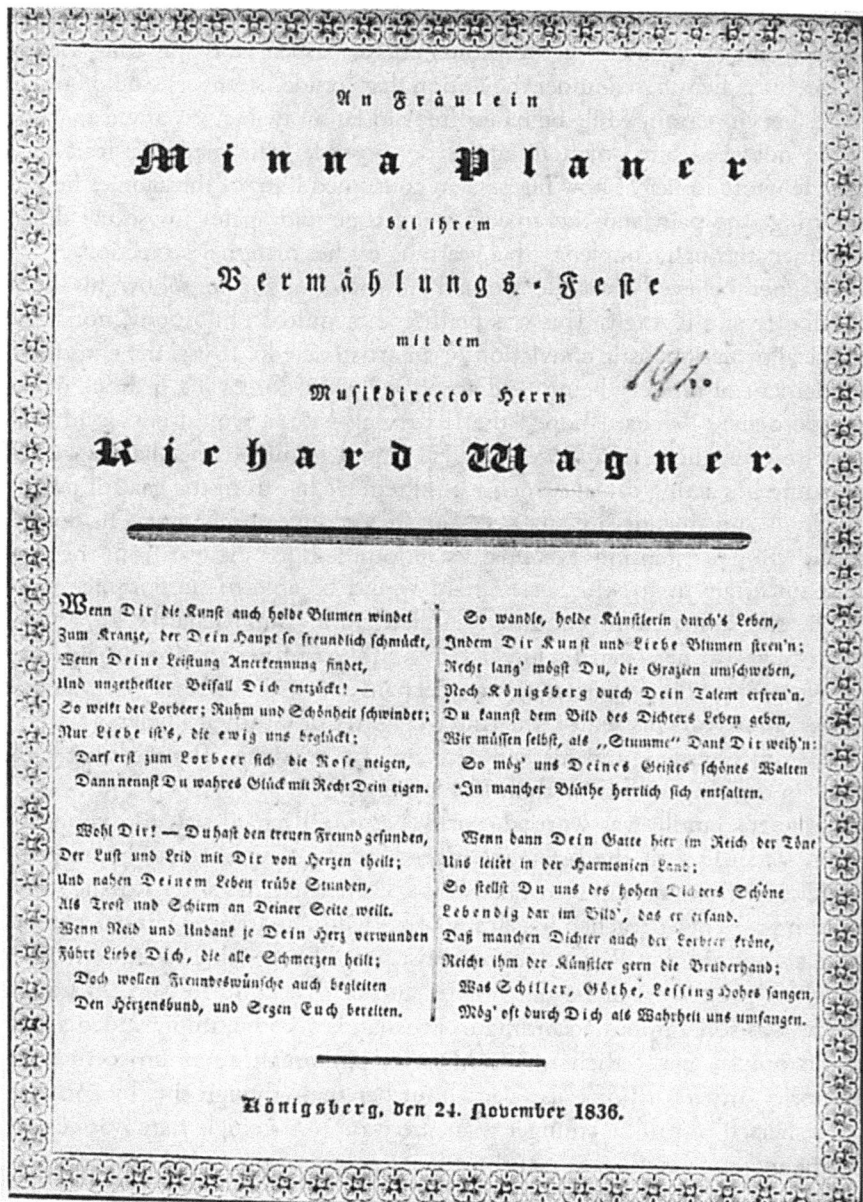

Figure 1.2. Marriage announcement of Richard Wagner and Minna Planer. Eva Rieger Collection.

Richard and Minna had to report to the pastor one day before their wedding ceremony. Afterwards, Minna was supposed to play the pantomime role of Fenella in Auber's opera *La muette de Portici* (The Mute Girl of Portici) in a benefit performance whose proceeds were intended for the happy couple. But she had not yet been able to finish her costume and became nervous when the pastor kept them waiting for a long time. This tense situation led to an exchange of unpleasantries between the groom and the bride, culminating in an open argument. They had finally agreed that Minna ought to go when the priest opened the door to invite them in.

The takings were good at the benefit performance. After the party on the eve of their wedding, however, Richard had to spend the night freezing on a hard sofa because the bridal bed was as yet off-limits. At the wedding ceremony the next day, he wore a dark blue tailcoat with gold buttons, while Minna wore a splendid dress that he had chosen. "She greeted me with real warmth and a sparkle in the eyes."[46] The church was crowded, and everyone in high spirits. In retrospect, however, Richard claimed that the 23-year-old groom was already harboring doubts:

> At this moment it suddenly became clear to me as if by a vision that my nature was caught in two cross-currents dragging me in entirely different directions: the upper one, facing the sun, bore me forward as if in a trance, while the lower one gripped me in some deep and inexplicable anxiety. The extraordinary levity with which I knew how to dispel the conviction surging repeatedly upward in me of committing a two-fold sin against my own nature was absolved and supported by the truly warm affection with which I looked upon the young girl, so exceptional in her way and so uncharacteristic of her surroundings, who had now thus bound herself so unconditionally to a young man.[47]

Wagner dictated these words to his second wife several decades later, so we are justified in placing a question mark over them. At the time, however, he clearly did not perceive his marriage as any kind of "two-fold sin," but wanted it to bind Minna fast to him.

As was the custom, Minna's parents had to provide the groom with a declaration of consent, and it demonstrates that they were happy for their daughter, despite their misgivings:

---

46 ML, 132.
47 Ibid., 133.

It is with heartfelt pleasure that we give our full consent to your matrimonial union with our beloved daughter Minna, and hereby offer our parental blessing from afar. We have every confidence in you that you will surely make our good daughter happy through your true and faithful love. We also cordially ask and admonish her, always and in all circumstances of life, to fulfil the duties that she will assume before Almighty God in the hour when she receives the marital blessing.[48]

After the wedding ceremony, there was a sumptuous meal and a merry celebration in which their colleagues from the theater took part. The couple was presented with a silver sugar bowl and a silver cake basket, and each guest was given a pink silken handkerchief on which a poem was printed to "Miss Minna Planer on the occasion of her wedding celebration with Music Director Mr. Richard Wagner." The poem itself offers further proof of how popular Minna was on the Königsberg stage:

> So wandle, holde Künstlerin durch's Leben,
> Indem Dir Kunst und Liebe Blumen streun;
> Recht lang' mögst Du, die Grazien umschweben,
> Noch Königsberg durch Dein Talent erfreu'n.

> [Wander through life, fair artist, while Art and Love strew flowers before thee; mayest thou still long delight Königsberg by thy talent while the Graces hover over thee.[49]]

Minna was well aware that she was taking a great economic risk by marrying Wagner. Thirteen years later, she recalled:

> What were you, after all, when I married you? I'm sorry to have to tell you: you were a poor, neglected, unknown, unemployed musical conductor; and what prospects did I have to look forward to at that time? [...] Everything that kept me busy and active in our home was intended only to please you, and from the earliest times I did everything out of love; even my independence, which I valued so highly, I gave up gladly to be able to belong to you completely.[50]

Giving up her financial independence had been difficult for Minna. Nevertheless, she held on to Wagner out of love. More importantly: she

---

48 *Königsberger Hartungsche Zeitung,* November 30, 1906.
49 Burrell, 459 (slightly amended).
50 Draft of letter from Minna Wagner, May 8, 1850, in Burrell, 290–91.

believed in him. But she had fallen in love with a man who was as yet insignificant, making debts everywhere, contemptuous of bourgeois order, and full of dreams for the future that never seemed to materialize—and in the course of time, this would be the undoing of them both. Many years later, after Richard had long since married Cosima, he pondered all of this, and Cosima recorded the following in her diary: "Over coffee we talked a lot about Minna, acknowledging her beauty and how a true instinct had led R. to her. 'It meant that I was cut off from all foolishness, and thought only of my work.' He regrets the fact that she married him."[51]

---

51   CWT II, 797 (September 21, 1881).

Chapter Two

"Deprived of incipient motherhood"

Riga, London, Paris, 1836–42

Richard had followed Minna to Königsberg, but now spent weeks on end without any source of income. Not until April 1, 1837, did he finally get a job. Yet he paid no regard to his past creditors in Magdeburg, nor to the imperative to restrict his spending in the present. Minna soon had to come to terms with his penchant for costly furnishings, and the resultant frustrations often led to fierce quarrels occasioned by his need for special comforts. He required a luxurious ambience around him in order both to feel at home and to be inspired in his creative work. Minna, by contrast, preferred to purchase only what was actually affordable. Over the course of 1836 and 1837, Richard's purchases included 24 meters of silk and satin, 18 meters of damask, 35 meters of muslin, four pairs of kid gloves, silk scarves, and green Florentine (a type of smooth, shiny silk). He spent so much beyond his means that legal proceedings were instituted against him.[1]

Worst of all for Minna were his absurd accusations of her supposed infidelity. Richard's jealousy remained excessive even after their marriage, and in 1836 the then 10-year-old Natalie—who had joined them in Königsberg—witnessed something that she remembered even into old age. Minna was due to play the role of the mute Fenella in Auber's *La muette de Portici* (the same she had played in the benefit performance before their marriage), but it was cancelled. On the way home, she led the way in a fashionable red and black plaid coat. Richard followed her, with Natalie pattering along behind them. Natalie later recalled the incident thus:

---

1   Busch-Salmen 1991, 217.

A soldier said: "There goes a pretty girl: she could be my sweetheart." Now Richard pounced on Minna and she had to drag him home, still raging. I said: "Minna, your Richard is naughty, you must unmarry him." I was a little girl and didn't yet know the word "divorce." At that point, he gave me some sweets to pacify me.[2]

It is also to Natalie that we owe an account of the extremely cold winter of 1836–37, when Minna used to get up very early in the morning to do the household chores before hurrying off to rehearsal. She then had to rush home at noon to prepare lunch, after which she had to sew her costumes for the evening performance, often while memorizing a new role at the same time.

> As the sewing machine was not yet known at that time every stitch had to be done by hand. She did not dare sit near the window because of Richard's mad jealousy. Then she had to bundle her repaired wardrobe together and hurry for the evening performance; I always accompanied her so as to be able to help her dress and make her quick changes without delay. The dressing rooms were very far from the stage. Then she came home, quivering with cold, for the big theater was not and could not be heated; she had to appear in white satin shoes and with bare neck and arms for a summer scene, while the audience sat in the pit and galleries wrapped in thick furs and bulging muffs. Even on her way home, if she had been applauded and called back many times, Richard would make a scene in senseless jealousy, rave all night long, and treat Minna in the most brutal way. When at last he got tired of raging and fuming, Minna, crying bitterly, would sit down to memorize a new role for the next morning's rehearsal; but it often happened that she lay for hours shaken by convulsions on account of Richard's outrageous treatment. As she lay there, he would fall on his knees before her, crying and begging for pardon like a baby. But the peace lasted only a few hours at the most, so he would soon start again to torment Minna with his degrading rough treatment.[3]

Richard later confirmed this description in *My Life*: "It was the bitterness and violence of language and behavior in which I indulged myself. These scenes frequently sent my wife into paroxysms."[4] On another occasion he writes of the "raging vehemence of my tone and diction, through which the target of it all felt herself so deeply wounded that I [...] had to rely on admission of my

---

2   Burrell, 73 (amended).

3   Burrell, 74.

4   ML, 137.

own guilt to pacify the injured party and beg her forgiveness."[5] Before their marriage, Richard had promised her that he would refrain from all spiteful words and would never quarrel with her, though this merely confirms that his unjust reproaches had tormented her from the very beginning.[6]

Richard's compulsive jealousy presumably led to feelings of guilt on his part that in turn erupted into renewed aggression. Minna could do nothing to counter these agonizing, obsessive scenes. When she could bear no more in late May 1837 she decided to flee, and took an opportunity offered by the attentions of an admirer by the name of Dietrich. Richard had already noted with annoyance the man's increasing intimacy with Minna. For her part, it seems she had no desire to embark on a new love affair, but merely wanted to return to her parents. One day, after returning home, Richard discovered that the closet had been emptied. He remembered that Minna and 11-year-old Natalie had said goodbye to him in tears earlier in the day—something that had failed to strike him as odd because he was so wrapped up in his own excess of work. Not even their maid had known of Minna's travel plans.

Richard rushed out of their apartment, only to find that they had both left by express mail coach. He immediately followed on after them. But by the time he reached Elbing (today Elbląg in Poland), some 60 miles from Königsberg, his finances were exhausted, and he had to turn back. Fortunately, he had their silver wedding gifts with him in his pocket—the sugar bowl and the cake basket—so he sold them and returned home to Königsberg on the proceeds. This return trip remained for him one of the saddest memories of his early life. He finally learned from a friend that Minna had let Dietrich accompany her for a while in the direction of Dresden, where she had stopped and sought rest and recuperation with her parents. It thus seems that she had not succumbed to the advances of Richard's rival, but had merely used his gender as a means of protection for the journey. Since Dietrich was in love with her, he might also have tried to persuade her along the way to leave Richard for good. Either way, this was hardly a pleasant situation for a woman in Minna's anxious state, for her nerves were already shattered.

Richard was meanwhile reproaching himself for his intemperate behavior. He traveled back to Dresden and met her in the meagre apartment she was sharing with her parents. They had been taken aback at Minna's condition and received him coldly, afraid that his arrival would prompt further commotion. He ignored their unfriendly reception, as his only concern was

---

5   Ibid., 130.
6   SB I, 236 (letter of November 6, 1835).

Minna, whom he wanted back at any price. As he recalled in *My Life*: "It turned out that Minna had indeed felt herself ill-treated by me and declared that she had been forced to take this drastic step solely because of our untenable situation, to which she thought me both blind and deaf."[7] It was his emotional outbursts and the lack of money that had led her to flee in despair.

Richard talked to her for days on end in Dresden, begging her to return. He now dangled before her the prospect of his getting a music director's position with a good salary in Riga, "which offered me the possibility of setting up house in such a way that Minna could withdraw from the theater entirely and thereby be in a position to spare me humiliation and anxiety in future."[8] This was a difficult decision for her, as she had only recently established an independent existence for herself. She was initially at a loss as to what she should do, and asked Richard not to pressure her with his requests and suggestions. She had reasons to be skeptical, because she was by now familiar with his tendency to conjure up enticing prospects for jobs, money, and performances that inevitably all turned out to be illusory. But Richard now traveled to Berlin in order to negotiate a contract with the director of the opera house in Riga, who happened to be visiting the city. On June 20, 1837, just before his return to Dresden, Richard wrote to Minna to admit that she had been right to complain about his behavior:

> You are right, my wife, and God knows that I heartily repent it. But you punished me cruelly for this, and consider whether your behavior has not offset a great part of my guilt. [...] If you charge me to "Be a man," I answer, "Be a wife." [...] Minna, become my wife again, cast away all your evil thoughts, be entirely mine once more![9]

Not even these entreaties were able to alleviate Minna's fear of his fierce outbursts. After returning from Berlin, he organized quarters for them in a modest guest house by the banks of the Elbe in the Dresden suburb of Blasewitz. When Minna surprised him by announcing that she wanted to go on a little trip with some friends, he accompanied her to her parents' apartment in Dresden, then went back to Blasewitz to await her return there.

But then Minna's elder sister Charlotte appeared at his apartment and asked him to provide written permission for a passport for Minna. Richard immediately sensed a renewed danger of losing his wife, and once more went

---

7   ML, 140.

8   Ibid., 141.

9   Burrell, 77 (letter of June 20, 1837).

to see her parents. This time they accused him of being unable to support their daughter properly. They refused to tell him where she was, fearing that his rhetorical skills would once more make her weak. Finally, he learned through a friend that the ominous Herr Dietrich had arrived and was doing all he could to convince Minna to run away with him after all. His persuasive words were proving increasingly effective, given that her doubts were growing as to whether marriage to Richard made any sense at all. She had decided to put financial security above love.

Richard was devastated. Time and again he had overcome hurdles in order to win over Minna, but now he had reached a point at which no way out seemed possible. He had to accept that it was simply impossible to ascertain her whereabouts. He sought comfort and help from his sister Ottilie Brockhaus and her husband Hermann, who were living with their two children in a lovely summer house outside Dresden, and took him in. Ottilie tried to distract him from his pain by getting him to read. This worked, and despite his dejected state he was still able to make the first draft for the libretto of his next opera, *Rienzi*—the work that would in just a few years bring him his first major success. Richard remained in Dresden until the fall of 1837, when he was due to take up the post of first music director in Riga's newly opened theater—the job about which he had already boasted to Minna.

Since Minna was still untraceable, he invited her sister Amalie to accompany him to Riga. She was a talented singer, had sung under his direction in Magdeburg two years before, and he wanted her to strengthen the ensemble at his disposal. He succeeded in procuring her a position as the *prima donna* in Riga, and she took on the role of Romeo in Bellini's opera *I Capuleti e i Montecchi*. One of the Riga newspapers even wrote of her soulful, moving performance.[10] Amalie was also upset by Minna's sudden disappearance. She knew how difficult it had been for her sister to leave, and how painful her disappearance had been to Richard. When she and Richard attended a performance of *Fidelio* and witnessed the unwavering love of Beethoven's Leonore for her husband Florestan, they were both moved to tears by thoughts of Minna, who had seemingly diverged so far from the ideal they saw portrayed on stage before them.

Minna meanwhile had been compelled to admit that she had been fooled by the character of her Mr. Dietrich, who had lied to her merely to entice her into what for him was just a fleeting affair. This realization led to a nervous

---

10   Quoted in Glasenapp 1977, I, 291.

breakdown on her part, and she fell seriously ill. Inwardly crushed and miserable, she wrote a "truly shattering letter" to Richard, openly admitting her infidelity and begging him to forgive her for how she had behaved. Wagner later wrote in his memoirs: "Just as she had been driven to [unfaithfulness] by despair, so had she now been brought back from this path by despair over the misery into which she had plunged herself."[11]

Richard was at this time fully occupied with his conducting duties in Riga, which also entailed writing additional arias for operas by other composers in the local repertoire. But he did not hesitate for long. He had actually begun steps to initiate divorce proceedings in the Königsberg courts, but he was instinctively moved by her remorse and asked her to come to him immediately. He admitted that he blamed himself most of all, because it was his jealous scenes that had finally driven her to flee. He told her that he never again wanted to speak about what had happened, and was overjoyed at the prospect of their reunion. He assured her that she should sweep aside any lingering hesitation and just come to him.

> Forget everything, my poor wife, I take no heed of the past, no heed of the present, nothing—nothing any more—only *one* burning desire, one longing is still alive in my heart; I count every minute until I can hold you in my arms. [...] You found me worthy of your limitless good favor, you smoothed out every wrinkle of care, which hid so much misery and pain, and do I deserve it? No: in return I can give you limitless faithfulness, nothing more. [...] I am quite crazy; Minna's coming back, Minna's coming back! And what a wonderful letter she wrote to me! How true, frank, just, and, my God, how unhappy![12]

When Wagner later wrote his autobiography, he placed the blame for their problems completely on Minna. But things were far from being so one-sided. She had also heard tales from third parties of his own exploits, and this had fortified her earlier resolve to separate. As we can see, Richard had to pull out all the rhetorical stops to change her mind and get her back.

Minna felt a considerable sense of relief. Richard now had a permanent job and she could turn her attention to domestic tasks. From now on, she only appeared rarely on stage, which meant that she no longer had to endure the torment of Richard's jealous scenes. It was Amalie who went to fetch her in Dresden and accompanied her on the long journey to Riga, so we may assume that she will have listened to her complaints and her remorse,

---

11   ML, 146.
12   Burrell, 79–81, here 80.

and reported in turn on Richard's steadfast love. It was now Minna's turn to demonstrate gratitude by means of perfect housekeeping. Amalie had an apartment in the same building, and Richard was looking forward to evenings with the two of them: "So she will be close by if we ever want to stuff ourselves." He conjured up meals of bratwurst, pancakes, and Saxon cheese pancakes, all of which Minna knew how to cook. On better days there would be Russian salad, salmon, and even fresh caviar in the evening, he claimed. Richard wrote to her that he had bought two black poodles for them as a temporary substitute for children; but once children came, he wrote, the poodles would have to be given away. The sisters often sang folk songs together, with Minna quite adept at singing the lower, accompanying line. "Happiness restored," Richard confided to his diary.

Why did Richard allow a "dishonored" woman—in the traditional, 19th-century sense—to return to him? He had been cuckolded. Infidelity on the part of women was considered a well-nigh unforgivable offense at this time. Members of the Riga Theater had written letters to him, ridiculing him for his behavior, and teasing him as a husband betrayed.[13] "Manly" behavior was expected of a man, and he was also supposed to demonstrate this to the outside world. The proper thing was to challenge one's opponent to a duel, or at least to ostracize one's wife. By refusing to do either, Wagner had behaved uncharacteristically and in an "unmasculine" fashion. Ultimately, what won him over had been Minna's assurance that she had "only now come to a true realization of her love for me." This, as he himself admitted, had moved him deeply and had changed his mind about her.

Decades later, Wagner returned to this episode, and it is revealing to see how he evaluated it in retrospect. On one occasion, Minna stumbled upon an unflattering description of their marriage in an autobiographical note he had published.[14] She was hurt by it, but he soothed her with a remarkable explanation in a letter of 1859:

> If anyone should speak to you in the future about this passage [in the autobiography] with a questionable look about him, then laugh in his face and say: Well, of course, he was so mad that he danced with me out of jealousy, and then in order to allow no one to come too close to me, he insisted on marriage under such unfavorable, beggarly circumstances that on calm reflection I sensed what misery we would have to go through. But what was I to do? I loved

---

13 SB XI, 93 (letter to Minna of May 18, 1859).

14 This must have been either Wagner's "Autobiographical Sketch" of 1843 or "A Communication to My Friends" of 1851. See Chapter 9 below.

him too, and so the two of us, young as we were, tumbled into woes that were soon enough so fierce and sorrowful that I myself believed I would be unable to endure it. That's why I ran away one day from my rash, passionate young husband, who plagued me with the strongest possible outbursts of an intolerable jealousy despite being himself crushed by debts, with the prospect before us of a summer without any wages.[15]

Richard's self-criticism here makes his account seem credible. He felt able to take Minna back, in contravention of the reigning social norms, because he could see how his excessive behavior had wounded her, and he understood her flight from him as an act of desperation. This ability on Wagner's part to put aside past sufferings and to transform them into something artistically productive was one of his most remarkable qualities. Minna had not left him because of any real affection for another man, but because of Richard's jealous fits (which now fortunately subsided) and because she believed that he was incapable of providing her with a regular household income. And she had long learned the bitter lesson that money was the basic prerequisite of existence. Moreover, when a woman married in the 19th century, it meant giving up her civil and political rights. She was henceforth forbidden from owning property and from entering into gainful employment. Minna was still helping to support an illegitimate daughter, and her parents lived in poverty. All these responsibilities weighed heavily on her. When a supposedly rich man—that Mr. Dietrich—professed his love for her and promised a life of prosperity, it seemed reasonable to her to join him, despite not being in love with him. The weeks and months that followed must have been more than agonizing for her. It is notable that she refrained from ever mentioning this episode again. Instead, she did her best to expunge it, probably also out of shame. She had let herself be seduced by a liar, whereas she felt that Richard, despite his emotional outbursts, was in fact devoted to her with every fiber of his being. This touched her, and ultimately made her regret what she had done. Richard later wrote in *My Life* that "my family had also received reports of my wife's positive qualities, and this was particularly beneficial as it spared me the painful and difficult necessity of defending her dubious conduct towards me."[16]

Richard's continuing dependence on her was the determining factor. In an undated letter to her from the summer of 1837, he wrote: "I am so full of you, my poor angel, I carry you so close and warm in my breast; o come

---

15   SB XI, 91 (May 18, 1859).
16   ML, 151 (slightly amended).

to my arms, let us protect and care for each other, and we shall never die, we shall live united in eternity."[17] Such sentiments are not merely proof of his continuing love for her, but also an expression of a deeply rooted bond between them.

After a while, Riga began to pall on Wagner. He had long ceased to get on with Holtei, the director of the theater where he worked, and he even discovered that the man had been stalking Minna (albeit unsuccessfully) under the pretext of wanting to engage her as an actor. Wagner was in any case convinced that Holtei was gay, though "he found it advantageous to provoke gossip about his relations with women in order to distract the attention of the public from other and far more disreputable vagaries."[18]

Richard was also annoyed with his colleague Heinrich Dorn, whose opera *Der Schöffe von Paris* he had conducted. Richard's contract was not extended, and Dorn was hired instead—apparently after having exploited Wagner's hostile relationship with Holtei. When Wagner confronted him, Dorn defended himself by claiming that Wagner would in any case never have extended his contract on account of the low wages it offered, especially given his debts to assorted creditors. But as Wagner pointed out, it would have been the third year of his contract, which would have brought with it a much-needed increase in salary. He also insisted that Holtei had not intended to sack him. But Dorn showed no willingness to go back on his own contract, so Wagner began to suspect intrigues against him. Minna was similarly furious about what seemed an act of betrayal by a friend. Richard and Dorn had often played whist together and eaten salmon at the Society House on Schwarzhäupterplatz, and she had got on well with Dorn's wife, too. Richard decided to use their current circumstances to effect a major change of scenery: "Not without some skill, I played upon my wife's indignation at the treachery I had suffered to induce her to accede to my rather eccentric plan to go to Paris."[19] He knew well enough that it would otherwise have been difficult to convince Minna to agree to such a move. But he was desperate to escape theatrical life in the provinces and wanted to realize his grand artistic goals in a world-class city.

Minna acknowledged the situation in which they found themselves, but remained skeptical. "She had never harbored any passionate hopes and

---

17 SB I, 339ff. (undated, but before September 21, 1837).
18 ML, 153.
19 Ibid., 156.

anticipated the misery that lay before us, but acquiesced out of love for me."[20] Her lack of worldliness prevented her from realizing just how illusory were Wagner's notions from the outset. Not for the first time, Richard was deluded about the true extent of their mounting problems, and was also convinced that a newcomer such as he could truly succeed in Paris, Europe's capital city of opera. But in these first years of marriage, Minna still tended to bow to his judgment, even when she was not completely convinced by his predictions of success. The only document that he could produce as proof of Parisian prospects was confirmation of having sent an elaborated draft of an opera text to the famous Parisian opera librettist Eugène Scribe with a request that he turn it into a full-scale libretto. Since he had initially got no reply, Richard decided to approach Eduard Avenarius, who was married to his half-sister Cäcilie and was working in Paris as a bookseller for the Brockhaus company. Richard asked Eduard to go and see Scribe on his behalf, which he duly did. Scribe subsequently wrote back to Wagner to offer several meagre comments on the draft he had sent. Wagner suspected that Scribe had only read his first act, and thus had no further interest in the project. But this was not going to get in the way of his grand plans, and Scribe's letter had a positive impact on Minna, who had no means of properly assessing its import: it "had such a significant effect on the otherwise by no means sanguine outlook of my wife that she found herself increasingly able to overcome the terrors of setting out with me on the Parisian adventure."[21]

An old friend from Königsberg, one Abraham Möller, now came to visit the Wagners in Riga. Richard complained to him about how they were finding it impossible to save up money for their trip to Paris because their creditors were eating it up as it came in. Möller did not think twice and advised them that there was just one way out: they must simply run away. He suggested that Wagner should wait to pay off his debts until he was successful in Paris and his finances had recovered. Wagner immediately thought it a grand idea. Möller's plan was to first take them across the Russian border in his carriage, then bring them to a port city in eastern Prussia. Once they were on the Prussian side, a friend of his could help with their escape. All this would have to be done without passports, because Richard's creditors had made sure to have these confiscated to prevent them executing just such a plan. They would have to cross the border in secret.

20   SB I, 408 (letter to Theodor Apel, September 9, 1840).
21   ML, 157.

Wagner agreed. His penchant for evading conflict as quickly as possible matched his restless nature and was in contrast to that of his wife, who preferred stability. This time, however, she too was blind to the risks involved, and was as keen as he was to make a new start. It is possible that she felt drawn to Paris because Cäcilie and Eduard Avenarius lived there. Richard was in any case about to lose his job in Riga. He made sure, however, to keep Minna in the dark about the true extent of the dangers involved in their illegal flit. Before they could leave, it remained for Minna to sell some of their furniture and household items—a procedure with which she was to become familiar over the course of her marriage. The contents of the bedroom were sold off, as were the grand piano, a mahogany dresser, a mirror wardrobe, a clothes trunk, curtains, kitchenware, and several pictures. They only took with them what was absolutely necessary.[22]

Minna gave a few more guest performances in order to supplement their funds for the trip. A benefit concert for Richard included Beethoven's Symphony No. 5 and Mendelssohn's *Calm Sea and Prosperous Voyage*, while Minna recited the monologue of Beatrice from Schiller's *Bride of Messina*. She was also granted a guest performance in which she appeared as both Preziosa and Maria Stuart, and bade farewell to the Riga audience in the title role of Theodor Hell's *Christinen's Liebe und Entsagung*. This was a demanding program, but the critics gave her a favorable reception: "Her highly attractive appearance, gracefulness of posture, and facial expressions make her a very appealing presence on stage. Only her otherwise very expressive speech sounds unfamiliar and at times somewhat incomprehensible, which may be partly due to the fact that Mme. Wagner has not set foot on the stage in a long time, and has perhaps got a little out of practice."[23]

It was Minna's misfortune that the last of her four evening performances coincided with a guest performance by an Italian bass, which meant that the auditorium held almost only those with subscription tickets. In order to get all the money she had expected, Minna also sold off most of her theater wardrobe, though this also meant burying her dreams of ever performing again. Her identity as an actor was thus extinguished, and what little she took with her to Paris was probably merely a sentimental memory of better times.

On a sunny day in July 1839, Minna and Richard rode through the beautiful Riga countryside with their luggage and Robber, their Newfoundland

---

22 Burrell, 463.
23 Quoted here as in Glasenapp 1977, I, 322.

dog whose touching devotion had endeared him to them, and whom Richard was determined to take along. He trotted alongside their carriage in the sweltering heat until they could no longer bear to treat him thus, and Richard managed to rearrange their luggage to make space for him. When they arrived at the Russian–Prussian border, they met Möller's friend as prearranged. He picked them up and then drove away from the main road, taking various detours to reach an inn where they met the guide who was to take them across the border after sundown. The border guards were Cossacks who were under orders to fire. So Richard and Minna had to wait for the moment when the guards were relieved by others, as this would give them a few minutes during which the soldiers were distracted from their border duty. After waiting for several hours, their time came. Robber luckily remained calm during their escape, keeping close to Richard as if he sensed the danger they were in. Möller was waiting for them in a Prussian inn on the other side of the border in a state of high anxiety. Minna was completely exhausted and was probably also in a state of shock. Running away at the risk of one's life, like a criminal on the run, was hardly something to which any of them was accustomed.

Once they were safely across, Richard began planning their onward journey with Möller. They would first sail to London on a ship that was to depart from the Prussian port of Pillau. They decided on a boat because taking Robber on a journey of many days by coach from Königsberg would have been quite impractical (the railways had not yet reached this part of Prussia). After spending a few days at an inn, recovering from the mental and physical strain they had endured, Minna and Richard continued onto Pillau. They were seated in a country-style wagon that was akin to a handcart and was unsafe. To make matters worse, it tipped over, and Minna was so badly injured in the fall that she only managed to reach a nearby farmhouse with the greatest of effort. She was near paralyzed from the shock and pain, so Richard had to half-carry her. He got a farmhand to lead him to the nearest inn while Minna remained in agony overnight at the farm. The farmers were sullen, their home unpleasantly unhygienic. Natalie later added more intimate details to the story that she apparently heard from Minna herself. Wagner had supposedly been catapulted from their wagon and had landed in a cesspool, and the farmers initially didn't want to let him in because he stank so infernally. But this comical part of the story was compounded by tragedy. As Natalie recalled the accident, "Minna was caught beneath the vehicle in such a way that she, severely injured, was deprived of an incipient motherhood, the greatest happiness of a young wife."[24]

It thus seems that Minna had been pregnant, but had lost the baby on account of the accident. Worse still, her injuries made her unable to bear children thereafter. Motherhood was regarded as the ideal form of life for a bourgeois woman in the 19th century. Indeed, it was supposedly the ultimate expression of femininity, so there is an especially tragic aspect to Minna's childlessness. Wagner really wanted children. *My Life* contains no mention of this miscarriage, presumably since he did not wish to be seen as having been responsible for it—after all, it was his debts that had made it necessary to flee Riga in the first place. Thus we must picture one of the most famous composers in the history of music, standing at the door of a filthy farmhouse, his clothes drenched in manure, his wife writhing in pain from a miscarriage.

Given Minna's weak state, the onward journey to the coast must have been torturous to her. But her agonies were far from over. The couple again had to hide in an inn near the harbor before sneaking out to board their ship:

> The whole long way to the boat they had to creep on the ground, through high wet grass, so that none of the watching beach guards would notice them. Arrived at the boat at last, they were quickly concealed by the captain, who had waited for them. They were hidden in the very lowest hold, behind barrels, crates, and bales of goods, so as not to be found when the ship was inspected. In this terrible position they had to remain for many agonizing hours, until they reached the open sea and the captain could free them.[25]

Once they were let out of the hold, they were put up in the captain's small cabin—though the bed was too small for two people.

We might think that Minna had by now been tested enough: badly injured, terrified, her life in danger time and again—but the worst was still to come. The ship was manned by a crew of just seven men. If the weather had been favorable, then the crossing to England would have taken just over a week. But it turned out to be a dreadful ordeal taking three times as long. They arrived at the port of Copenhagen after one week. They replenished their food supplies, then continued through the Danish Straits via Elsinore towards the Skagerrak, the stretch of water to the northwest of Denmark where the North Sea begins. But then the wind shifted, and a storm set in that lasted for several days. Minna and Richard promptly got seasick, and

24 Burrell, 83.
25 Ibid., 84.

their misery continued until the captain finally headed for the Norwegian port of Sandwike near Arendal, where they were able to go ashore. They had just two days of rest before the captain ordered them all to sail on, despite the storm not having abated, and against the advice of the ship's pilot. Once they were back at sea, they suddenly heard the crew cursing and shouting: the ship was heading for a reef, though luckily only grazed it. But it still meant returning to land to have the ship's hull checked.

Two days later, on August 1, 1839, they resumed their voyage. All was calm for a few days until another violent storm hit them on August 6. They now endured a full seven days in fear of their lives. They panicked all the more when they saw the despair of the crew, who seemed to have given up on the ship, and whose malign glances gave the impression that Minna and Richard were somehow responsible for the dreadful state they were all in. Minna felt an indescribable fear, and was quite expecting to be drowned. When the rain and wind were joined by a thunderstorm, Minna felt she would rather be struck by lightning from above than drown in the waters below. In her panic, she begged Richard to let her tie herself to him so that they would not be separated when they sank into the deep.[26]

The next night was similarly spent in mortal agony until the storm finally abated in the morning. But the captain now lost his way because dense fog meant he could not determine their current location. Finally, they saw a ship sailing in the same direction, and he followed it until he saw it driven onto a sandbank. It took another harrowing twenty-four hours before they could land, because another storm developed around the offshore sandbanks. Minna's nerves were so strained that she spent the whole night awake, watching the little bright red bells on various guard ships nearby and pointing them animatedly out to the crew, while Richard by contrast slept soundly, feeling reassured that land could not be far away. On the night of August 12, the ship headed into the Thames Estuary and docked in London. What a relief it was to feel solid ground beneath their feet again! Three terrible, never-to-be-forgotten weeks were finally over.

Minna liked London more than Richard did. She praised the calmness and good manners of the English, but Richard missed a sense of coziness and found the politeness of the locals somewhat forced.[27] Both marveled at the many ships that crowded the River Thames, the wide streets, the hubbub, and the busy life of a highly cosmopolitan city. They took a hackney carriage

---

26   ML, 163.
27   Praeger 1892, 75.

to the West End where the cultured and fashionable classes lived, with Robber lying across their laps and his head hanging out of the window since he was otherwise too big to fit. They found a place to stay there, and the next day Richard hired a carriage to take them on a tour through the city according to a route he himself had sketched out on a map. Minna's astonishment knew no bounds at everything they saw. One special event was a visit they made to a session of the House of Lords, for which they managed to procure tickets by sheer good luck.

There followed further forays through the streets of London, many on foot and to the point of exhaustion. Robber went missing for a while, which occasioned much agitation. Money was tight and they had to leave soon, because the French metropolis was their real destination. Having had enough of sailing ships, they took a steamboat this time.

Richard decided that they should spend a few days in Boulogne so that he might finally complete the orchestration of Act 2 of his new opera *Rienzi*. They took out a short-term lease on an apartment with two near-empty rooms that they "proceeded to furnish sparsely enough but adequately for our purposes, a task in which Minna excelled."[28] She managed to procure a bed, two chairs, and a table that served both as Richard's workplace and as a dining table for the meals that she prepared over the fire—skills she had learned from an early age. They wrote from Boulogne to ask Eduard Avenarius to find them a one-room apartment with an alcove in Paris. It had to be furnished, though they would themselves provide beds, bedding, tableware, candlesticks, and other utensils. Minna would be doing the housekeeping herself, added Wagner, as she was determined to manage on as little money as possible. So they would need no domestic staff except a maid to do the most menial tasks.

In mid-September, Richard and Minna finally set off for Paris itself, with Robber once again awkwardly squeezed into their carriage. Minna will have marveled at this new metropolis just as she had in London. The wide boulevards, elegant carriages, and fancy fashions were striking, though the cabarets and cafés of the bohemian quarter were less suitable for women like her. For the moment, Eduard had procured them a modest, cheap room in a hotel. It had no cooking facilities, which meant they had to dine out in restaurants. Wagner promptly paid a visit to the composer Giacomo Meyerbeer, who was at the height of his fame, and who welcomed him warmly. He also went to see the famous piano virtuoso Leopoldine Blahetka. Both she and

28 ML, 168.

Meyerbeer organized musical soirées, and we may assume that Minna and Richard attended them together.

Their money was completely spent not long after arriving in Paris. So Richard had to pawn Minna's jewelry, their wedding gifts, their silverware, and finally even their wedding rings. Minna also pawned the last, precious remnants of her theater wardrobe, including a blue trailing skirt embroidered with silver that had once been owned by the Duchess of Dessau. Thus, piece by piece, the insignia of her career as an actor were lost. After a few weeks, they also lost Robber in the crowded streets, which upset them both. Even worse for Richard: he later saw him on the street, but because Richard had earlier chastised him several times, Robber now fled from him and refused to be caught again. This made his former master even more depressed, and he took it as a bad omen.

About two months after their arrival in Paris, Richard's sister Luise came to visit them with her husband, the bookseller Friedrich Brockhaus. In his memoirs, Richard was insistent that he had not asked his brother-in-law for money. But if true, it was presumably at Minna's insistence, for she was simply delighted to see them and was in any case always anxious to keep up bourgeois appearances. Given Wagner's customary lack of inhibition in borrowing from others, we can probably chalk up this instance as Minna's success. She was even happy to accompany Luise when she went shopping for luxuries, when Minna managed to pretend that they had similar financial means at their disposal.

During this time in Paris, the Dresden-born artist Ernst Benedikt Kietz became one of Minna's dearest friends. He was amiable and unworldly by nature, and although he had come to Paris to continue his training, he generally took so long to complete the portraits for which he was commissioned that these mostly remained unfinished, and his buyers had to leave without them. So he was just as much in need of money as the Wagners. This helped to cement the bonds of friendship between them, as did the fact that he willingly subordinated himself and played the part of a surrogate son. Minna found this mother-and-son relationship immediately to her liking, and she continued to mother him in her letters and communications of later years. Richard liked guests who let him dominate the conversation, so he happily accepted Kietz into the family circle for their evening gatherings. And Kietz was able to have a calming influence on Richard when circumstances and repeated failure made him desperate. Their evenings together thus generally ended on a cheerful note, despite all their worries. The librarian Gottfried Anders and the translator and editor Samuel Lehrs also became friends of the Wagners in Paris. Since frugality necessitated socializing at home, this meant Minna assumed an important role. She became respected and loved by those around her, which made her feel valued and gave her strength. All three of these men were bachelors, so Minna probably extended her hospitality to mending and patching their clothes too. Richard's half-sister Cäcilie Avenarius and her husband Eduard also often joined them on an evening. Heinrich Laube and his wife Iduna paid them visits too, and he in turn introduced Richard to Heinrich Heine, whose works would provide him with material for his next two operas, *Der fliegende Holländer* and *Tannhäuser*.

Laube took an interest in Wagner's future, and persuaded his wealthy Leipzig family and other acquaintances to provide Richard with a regular income for a few months. Wagner now decided it was time to leave their furnished room and move into their own apartment:

> My prudent and careful wife had already become anxious and nervous as a result of the careless manner in which I treated the more mundane aspects of life and was only persuaded to this step by the assumption that she would be able to run an independent household at less expense than the hotel and restaurant existence was costing us.[29]

The rent for their new, cozy quarters was 1,200 francs a year, to be paid in quarterly installments. The furniture they still lacked was now acquired on installments as well. But how were they going to finance running a household? Richard was having nothing but bad luck despite all his efforts to earn a living. Everywhere seemed to be turning him down. The score of his overture *Rule Britannia* was returned by the Philharmonic Society in London (when Richard found he would have to pay seven francs to cover the postage costs of sending it back, he refused and abandoned the package). And when a theater in Paris finally gave him a commission, it promptly went bankrupt. Richard went on long walks with Minna on which he would fantasize about emigrating to South America, for he was convinced that no one there knew anything about opera or music, and that it was a place where he might make a living through honest, diligent work. Minna was used to his exalted outbursts, but admonished him when she felt he was letting himself be overly influenced by reading the novel *The Founding of Maryland* by Heinrich Zschokke, in which a group of emigrants from the Old World achieve happiness and freedom in the New. There was at present no alternative, she insisted, to staying the course in Paris.

---

29 ML, 181.

Figure 2.1. Ernst Benedikt Kietz: *Wagners Land und Luft Sitz* (Wagner's Air and Country Seat), drawing, caricature of the Wagners' domestic life when they lived in penury in Paris, 1839. Kietz draws Minna as the dominant partner. Nationalarchiv der Richard-Wagner-Stiftung, Bayreuth.

While Richard was out and about in search of work and an income, Minna stayed at home. He admitted in his memoirs that this had been a lonely time for her. But Ferdinand Praeger later insisted that Wagner was well aware of his wife's merits:

> The hitherto quiet and gentle housewife was transformed into a heroine. Her placid disposition was healing comfort to the disappointed, wearied musician. The whole of the Paris period is "a gem of purest ray serene" in the diadem of Minna Wagner. Thoughts of what the self-denying, devoted little woman did then has many a time brought tears to Wagner's eyes. The most menial house duties were performed by her with willing cheerfulness. She cleaned the house, stood at the washtub, did the mending and the cooking. She hid from the husband as much of the discomforts attaching to their poor home as was possible. She never complained, and always strove to present a bright, cheerful face, consoling and upholding him at all times.[30]

It is not documented just what Minna actually did in the household. Given the many times they had to move apartments, we can hardly assume that she busied herself with storing potatoes in a root cellar, preserving fruit or peeling and preparing it to be dried by the local baker. It also seems unlikely that she would have engaged in other tasks that were common in households at the time, such as baking bread, curing and smoking meat, or filling barrels with cucumbers, turnips, sauerkraut, and suchlike for the winter months. Neither Minna nor Richard mentions any such chores in their letters, nor was Richard one to plan ahead for the household.

Richard had to look for new sources of income while finding the means to pay off existing debts. He frequently begged Kietz for money ("for heaven's sake, let your tailor wait for these 14 days or 3 weeks, and help me out until then"), and it was now Kietz who had a good idea. An older, wealthy lady from Leipzig, one Miss Leplay, was looking for a place to stay for two months for herself and an acquaintance. Since the Wagners had rented a rather spacious apartment, they offered bed and breakfast to the two of them. Minna served them a breakfast similar to what they would have got in a hotel, and was happy with the few sous that she earned in the process. The two ladies brought upheaval to their household, but the Wagners needed the money so badly that they immediately took on a new lodger once the ladies had departed. Miss Leplay later visited Minna in Dresden, which suggests that

---

30   Praeger 1892, 87–88.

they had enjoyed a good relationship. Her successor was a painter by the name of Brix, who also became friends with them.

Wagner continued his tireless search for money-earning opportunities. He wrote several songs and offered them to the publisher Maurice Schlesinger. When Schlesinger suggested that he should write articles for the *Gazette musicale* that he published, Richard agreed, though he was given only half of the usual fee because the other half was spent translating his German into French. But he was at least successful in this particular endeavor, and people read what he wrote. Schlesinger now suggested that he should write an instructional work for the valved cornet (the "cornet à piston"). When Wagner asked how he should proceed, Schlesinger sent him five tutors for the instrument that had already been published—it was one of the most popular instruments played by men in Paris at the time. Wagner's task was to put together a sixth volume. The commission ended up being fulfilled by someone else, so Schlesinger charged him instead with writing fourteen "suites" for the instrument, and sent him sixty vocal scores of operas from which he might choose suitable melodies. "I marked the appropriate places in each volume with slips of paper, and constructed from the sixty volumes an odd edifice around my desk, in order to have the maximum amount of melodious material within my immediate reach,"[31] he recalled in *My Life*. But Schlesinger withdrew this monotonous commission when Wagner was still busy with it, because a cornet player who had checked the proofs of an initial set of pieces had found that Wagner had chosen keys that were far too high. Wagner was relieved, and "the sixty vocal scores made their way back to the singular shop in the Rue Richelieu."[32] Minna was less happy about this, however, because she had counted on their getting paid for it. At least Schlesinger gave them half the promised sum, and Richard used the time he gained to complete his large-scale opera *Rienzi*. He now offered it to the Court Opera in Dresden because he knew they had the outstanding singers he wanted, namely the tenor Joseph Tichatschek and the soprano Wilhelmine Schröder-Devrient.

Richard's descriptions of their sheer existential hardship are little short of heartrending. Once, for example, he had to organize the deferral of various bills due for payment, just in order to be able to meet their already meager household expenses. He ran off in the morning to visit Schlesinger about possible jobs, then went to Heinrich Brockhaus (the brother of his

---

31   ML, 187.
32   Ibid.

brother-in-law) to borrow money. Minna knew that raising the money would take a while, and that he would not return home until late in the evening. But Brockhaus sent him away with nothing, and Schlesinger kept him waiting for hours in vain for an appointment, during which time Wagner was compelled to endure Schlesinger's "intentionally protracted and trivial conversations with his visitors."[33] Night had fallen by the time he reached home, and he found Minna looking for him anxiously from their window. She had suspected that his efforts might end in failure, so had as a precaution asked their tenant Brix for an advance. He had provided the money, which meant she could at least give her husband a meal when he got back.

This episode demonstrates why Minna still recalled Paris fondly, despite the hard times they endured there. In these years she was an equal partner to Richard, indispensable for their mutual well-being, and not yet a mere secondary character to be sidelined, as she later felt was the case. Their three closest friends were the bachelors who clustered around her at their evening gatherings, and whom she cared for as best she could; and when they sat and chatted, joked, and argued, she joined them.

Ten years later, Anders recalled their close-knit group and toasted Minna with a glass of wine and the following couplet: "O, herzgeliebte Minna!—Du, die stets meinem Sinn nah'!" (O, beloved Minna of my heart!—You are always close to my thoughts!).[34] Richard also read them the novellas he was writing at this time. He had reworked his own experiences in a story entitled "An End in Paris," and Minna will presumably have listened attentively and offered her opinion on what she heard—whereas a few years later in Zurich, Richard would resort to lecturing her expansively on theories of art that she was barely able to follow. In Paris, Richard was still open about his plans. He was barely known as an artist, so there was little that divided them as yet. After all, the burning issues that dominated their lives involved coping with everyday existence. It was thus Minna's culinary and housekeeping skills, plus her affectionate readiness to help others, that enabled her to play a decisive role in the lives of their bachelor friends and others. Nor should we forget her maternal instincts: it pained her to see others suffer, though this in turn made her better able to cope with her own hardships. Nevertheless, the deprivations to which Minna and Richard were subjected also gnawed away at her and began to undermine her health.

---

33 Ibid., 189.

34 As related by Wagner in a letter to Minna of February 14, 1850, in SB III, 232.

One morning, Schlesinger burst into their apartment and offered Richard 1,100 francs to arrange Donizetti's opera *La favorite*: a "complete arrangement for pianoforte, piano arrangement without words for two hands, ditto for four hands, complete arrangement for quartet, the same for two violins, ditto for *cornet à pistons*."[35] To Minna, this sounded like a bonanza. Even Richard was taken with the commission, despite the tedium involved in the job. When he had got his advance of 500 francs, he piled up the money on their table. Right at this moment, Cäcilie happened to call by, and clearly got the impression that the two of them were doing much better for themselves. They did not dare to enlighten her, and continued to enjoy her invitations to Sunday lunch, which were henceforth issued more frequently than before.

On Richard's birthday, May 22, 1840, Minna gave him a special treat. He had always been careful to maintain a well-groomed appearance, so he was depressed about the current worn-out state of his clothes. Minna knew how much this pained him, so she walked the length of Paris until she could find a German tailor willing to make him a new suit on credit. She succeeded and gave Richard the suit. Wagner later recalled the day in conversation with Ferdinand Praeger, who afterwards committed the incident to paper:

> This delicate and thoughtful attention on the part of Minna deeply touched Wagner, and he related the incident to me in illustration of the loving affection she bore him. He said that during those three years of pinching poverty and bitter disappointments his temperament was variable and trying. It was hard to bear with him.[36]

The various commissions from Schlesinger did little to alleviate either the Wagners' acute money shortage, or the increasing sense of desperation that was eating away at Minna's nerves. Once, a sick German craftsman came knocking at their door, begging for something to eat. Minna bought him some bread—but she did so with the last of their reserves. They simply had no more money. By late June 1840, Richard had 25 francs left, but was due to pay a bill of 140 francs on July 1, and the quarterly rent of 300 francs on July 15. He confided to his diary that he had exhausted all possible sources of income—a fact he had kept from Minna until now, "so as not to further frighten her, as she is already quite shattered by worries [...] Please God, this will be a terrible day if no help comes!" One day later, he wrote in his diary

---

35 ML, 190.
36 Praeger 1892, 88. Wagner, however, does not mention this in his autobiography.

that he had told Minna of the true state of their affairs while out walking with her: "I am sorry for the poor woman from the bottom of my soul! This is a sad chord to be sounded!"[37]

That winter, Richard and Minna had only been able to heat their bedroom, which they had converted into a living room, dining room, and study. It took Richard just two steps from their bed to reach his worktable. He remained at home for three days at a time and only went for a walk every fourth day—a procedure he kept up throughout the winter. He later blamed this sedentary habit for the intestinal problems that would plague him for decades thereafter, and from which he was never quite able to free himself (they ranged from constipation to hemorrhoids; his various efforts to find alleviation using enemas merely upset his stomach all the more).

Richard's lack of recognition embittered him; he felt an outsider. Their cheap apartment also had the disadvantage of thin walls, and the noise that emanated through them was a major annoyance. When a neighbor insisted on practicing Liszt's piano arrangement of Donizetti's opera *Lucia di Lammermoor* repeatedly until Richard could no longer bear it, he called in their lodger Brix to gain his revenge. Brix played the flute, though he had largely given it up in order to spare his landlord. But Wagner now placed him against the wall and had him play his recent arrangement of the Overture to *La favorite* on the piccolo. The shrillness of the instrument had such an impact that the neighbor—a young piano teacher—soon moved out, which made the soft-hearted Richard almost feel sorry for him.

Until now, the wife of the concierge of their building had been responsible for cleaning chez Wagner—including the kitchen, their clothes, and shoes. But now even the small wage they paid her was too expensive for them. Minna had to endure the humiliation of terminating her employment and taking on the woman's tasks. Not only were such activities considered menial, but they were far dirtier and more time-consuming than they are today. Since they did not want their lodger to know about their having sacked the cleaning lady, Minna had to clean his boots herself. Both Richard and Minna now felt ashamed whenever they met the concierge and his wife, though they were relieved when they noticed that they in fact treated them even more politely than before, albeit with a hint of familiarity.

Richard was particularly distressed that he was unable to buy Minna the medicine she needed when she fell ill in the fall of 1840. He wrote to Theodor Apel on September 20, 1840:

---

37 SSD XVI, 5–6.

Figure 2.2. Ernst Benedikt Kietz: *Minna zügelt Wagner in der Kutsche* (Minna harnesses Wagner in the Carriage), drawing, caricature of the Wagners' domestic life when they lived in penury in Paris, 1840–41. Kietz again draws Minna as the dominant partner. Nationalarchiv der Richard-Wagner-Stiftung, Bayreuth.

> Will she survive this misery and will I be able to endure hers? Lord God, help me! I don't know how to help myself anymore!—I have exhausted everything, everything,—all the last sources [of sustenance] for a starving man [...] To have had to turn his wife's last little piece of jewelry, her last essential utensil into bread, and then to have to leave her sick and suffering, without aid, because the proceeds of our wedding rings are insufficient for bread and medicine—what should I call this, when I have in the past already spoken of necessity![38]

Minna too wrote to Theodor Apel, just over a month later, on October 28: "This morning Richard had to leave me and go to a debtors' prison. I am still so terribly agitated that my senses are in a whirl." Wagner's biographer Ernest Newman found her report credible, though the editors of Wagner's complete letters believe that Richard drafted the text for her, and that he only faked

---

38   SB I, 410f. (letter to Theodor Apel of September 20, 1840).

his imprisonment.[39] Schlesinger offered Wagner a commission for a small operetta for a boulevard theater, but Richard had had his fill of menial commissions. According to Praeger, Richard left his publisher and hurried home through the rain and wind: "Excited and wet through, he talked wildly to Minna, the result being that he was put to bed with a severe attack of erysipelas. [...] All his thoughts and feelings upon the future he communicated to his gentle nurse, Minna, who was always a ready listener to his seemingly random talk."[40]

When critics today complain that Minna did not grasp Richard's true greatness, they fail to realize that he did not need her adoration in this phase of his life. He was not yet properly aware of his exceptional talent—things would be different several years later in Zurich—and it sufficed for him simply to have Minna there, participating in his life, listening to him attentively, and creating a comfortable atmosphere at home. According to Natalie, who had joined the Wagners in Paris, that was precisely what Minna did:

She well knew how to make the small household cozily neat and clean, by meticulous order and tidiness. [...] Calmly and quietly she worked like a maid-servant, sweeping, washing, cooking, cleaning his suits and shoes [...]. She always looked rosy, fresh, neat, and exceedingly clean, so that nobody would guess that she did all his menial work. How she enjoyed buying a few cigars or a screw of snuff for her beloved Richard when marketing at a distance, since it was cheaper to buy the needed victuals there, enabling her to save money and so surprise and please him. Richard always welcomed this love offering like a child, and couldn't thank Minna enough with kisses for what she had done.[41]

Their cramped living conditions were nevertheless a strain on Minna's mental state. Once, recalled Natalie, Richard stumbled and knocked a chair against a large wall mirror that almost broke. Minna was startled and rebuked him sharply. He flared up and ran out of the apartment in a rage. He later returned with his friends Kietz, Lehrs, and Anders, who found the incident amusing, and he made his apologies in the form of a doggerel poem put on Minna's bed as a peace offering the next morning.[42] Little tokens of his love such as this will have touched Minna, and no doubt helped her to bear

---

39 Newman 1933, I, 303; Burrell, 88–89, here 88, and SB I, 414, plus
    commentary.
40 Praeger 107–8.
41 Burrell, 91.
42 Ibid., 91–92.

Figure 2.3. Richard Wagner: apologetic poem and drawing for Minna, 1841. Nationalarchiv der Richard-Wagner-Stiftung, Bayreuth.

everything, despite their deprivations. In other words, it was precisely their dire straits that strengthened the bond between them.

The Wagners' close friends kept coming to visit, though they became accustomed to Richard continuing with his arranging work while they entertained each other. New Year's Eve 1840 was a particularly memorable celebration. The friends had arranged everything in secret, and each of them appeared with a different gift. Kietz brought rum, sugar, and lemon, Lehrs brought a large leg of veal, the painter Friedrich Pecht (a friend of Kietz) brought a goose, and Anders had with him two bottles of champagne that an instrument maker had given him for designing a piano advertisement, and which he had been saving up for a special occasion. Wagner immediately dropped his onerous work and plunged enthusiastically into their celebration. We can well imagine how it must have cheered up Minna, for they heated the living room, fetched supplies from the grocer that had hitherto been absent chez Wagner, and helped out in the kitchen. The mood was intoxicating, as Richard later recalled in his memoirs:

> When the punch began to supplement the effect of the champagne, I delivered a fiery speech, which provoked such unbroken hilarity in my friends that it found no end and carried me away to the point that I, who had already mounted a chair in heightened emotion, finally got up on the table itself, and from this vantage point preached to my transported listeners a gospel of the most nonsensical contempt for the world, together with a eulogy of the South American Free States, the whole thing ending only in sobs of laughter, with everyone so overcome that we had to put them up for the night, as they would certainly not have been able to go home.[43]

However, the new year brought a major blow for Richard. It was almost as if the whole world were now conspiring against him. He had given notice on their apartment—on time, as he had thought—only to learn that he had missed the contractual deadline by one day. Now they would have to continue paying the rent for an entire year, and all protests were in vain. Richard and Minna were hopeful of finding new tenants swiftly, so they set out to find cheaper accommodation for the summer in the region around Paris. They found what they wanted in Meudon, a little town just a few miles to the southwest of the capital. But they were unable to find new tenants for their Paris apartment until Easter, which further aggravated their money woes. Richard was at a loss as to how to survive the summer financially since

---

43 ML, 194.

Schlesinger had nothing more to offer him. So he resorted to journalistic work and wrote essays. Some of the newspaper articles that he wrote were simply cobbled together using information from Lehrs and Anders that they themselves had acquired only at secondhand. Richard took a more earnest approach when writing for the monthly magazine *Europa*. It regularly offered musical supplements, so he submitted some songs, and when they were accepted, they became his first-ever compositions whose publication earned him a fee. It was also at this time that Richard's disdain intensified for what he regarded as the triviality of the French opera houses, as did his desire to offer something better himself. To Minna's regret, he sent back tickets they were given for the Théâtre-Français, not least because he was so disappointed by the fruitlessness of his own efforts to gain a foothold in Paris. As a former actor, Minna would have gladly gone. The distraction would have done her good, since she had to spend many hours alone at home.

In May and June 1841, the couple's desperate situation reached its absolute limit. When Cäcilie Avenarius and her husband also decided to spend the summer in the country, they rented an apartment very close to the Wagners. But Minna insisted on keeping quiet about their privations and was adamant about maintaining the outward appearance of a bourgeois livelihood. When they ran out of money completely, Richard had to set out on foot for Paris to raise a few francs. He managed nothing, and after having made the long journey back home, he learnt that a friend named Hermann Pfau had come begging for bread, at which Minna had given him their last piece. Wagner's last hope was Brix, who had moved to Meudon with them. Like Wagner, he had also gone to Paris to find money, and like him, too, he returned exhausted, downhearted, and empty-handed. But now it was Minna's turn to save the day: for the first-ever time, she had managed to get the baker, the butcher, and the wine merchant to hand over their wares without insisting on a cash payment. According to Richard, "she felt it her sacred duty to do battle against the hunger of her menfolk. [...] Minna's eyes beamed when, an hour later, she was able to put before us a superb meal."[44]

As luck would have it, Cäcilie and Eduard Avenarius arrived just as they were sitting down to eat, and were reassured to see that the Wagners appeared to be doing well. The relationship between the two couples had been strained by Richard's repeated attempts to borrow money from Eduard, but they now drew closer. Minna felt accepted and respected by her husband's half-sister and brother-in-law, and she adored their little boy, Max.

---

44   ML, 200–201.

For their part, Cäcilie and Eduard had apparently grasped the difficulties that Minna had endured with her eccentric husband, and gave her credit for it. On September 5, 1841, Minna's 32nd birthday, relations between the two couples were cemented when Richard and Eduard switched to first-name terms and the intimate pronoun "Du." A year later, when he was in Dresden, Richard recalled the moment with delight: "You sat with us at table, and we kissed and rejoiced [...]. Never, never, good Cecilie [*sic*], dearest Eduard, will we forget your fidelity and love, and our thanks shall reach you yet! Long live the sorrows of Paris, for they have borne us wonderful fruit!"[45]

It was in Meudon that Wagner drafted the libretto for his next opera, *Der fliegende Holländer*, inspired by a story by Heinrich Heine. As so often, he here combined aspects of wish fulfillment with experiences drawn from his own life. The awful sea voyage that he and Minna had endured on their way to England provided the sound-world of his opera. He himself identified with the outcast title hero (something we can also observe in his novella "An End in Paris"). Wagner's Parisian circumstances were now reflected in the character of the Dutchman—an operatic incarnation of misery and exclusion. The figure of Senta was influenced by Leonore from Beethoven's opera *Fidelio*, but was also fashioned as Richard would have liked Minna to be. A decade later, he wrote:

> The Dutchman, however, can only win redemption through a woman who sacrifices herself to him for love. It is thus his longing for death that drives him to seek out this woman. But she is no longer the homely, caring Penelope whom Odysseus had courted eons ago: she is woman *per se*, and the as yet inexistent, longed-for, anticipated, infinitely feminine woman—let me say it in one word: the woman of the future.[46]

Richard's emphasis here on Senta's self-sacrifice was a reaction to very real circumstances of his own life. The more Minna suffered under their current situation, the less she was willing to accept all of her husband's demands. At the end of this decade, when Richard lost his position at the Dresden Opera, Minna's pent-up frustrations would burst out in a vehement insistence that they should separate. But she had felt similar sentiments already during their years of deprivation in Paris, and this unsettled Richard. In his opera, Senta

---

45 SB II, 159 (September 11, 1842).

46 Wagner, "A Communication to My Friends" (1851) in SSD IV, 266. Although Wagner wrote these lines several years later, they confirm his convictions at the time that he wrote the opera.

is fixated body and soul on the Dutchman, and the extent to which Richard associated her with Minna is proven by the dedication that he wrote to her at the end of his prose draft of the libretto:

Durch eines Weibes Treu' ward er gerettet,
Befreit aus hundertjährger Leiden Joch;
Wenn noch so schwer sich Trübsal an mich kettet,
Bleib' treu mir nur, so lacht das Glück uns noch!

[He was saved by the fidelity of a woman, freed from the yoke of centuries of suffering; even if similar misery should bind itself to me, stay true to me, and we shall yet see happiness!]

Richard now sold his early French prose sketch for *Der fliegende Holländer*, which brought in 500 francs—enough for him to rent a piano so he could compose his own opera. He drafted the whole work in just seven weeks, leaving only the orchestration to be done. He was delighted that his inspiration had not abandoned him, and this in turn improved his mood and made many things easier, also for Minna. Decades later, he still remembered his euphoric mood of the time.[47] He often accompanied his wife when she went out to hunt for mushrooms—their hunger meant that this occupation was of greater importance than merely sampling the joys of Nature. The same need led them to pick nuts from the trees whose branches hung over the garden walls. (Fruit trees, by contrast, were of little use because Richard had an aversion to fruit.)

In the meantime, the Wagners received news that their tenants had moved out of their Paris apartment. So they now found themselves legally compelled to pay the rent there in addition to that of the apartment in Meudon. This was beyond their means. Then Richard came up with the idea of offering their furniture in Paris to the owner of their apartment in lieu of the rent—despite not having yet paid off the furniture themselves. The solution was brilliant after its own fashion—though as Ulrich Drüner has rightly pointed out, it was simply throwing money away.[48] A cold front now set in. Meudon was ideal for summer quarters and quite inadequate when the weather turned, but their finances made any thought of returning to Paris

---

47 CWT II, 176 (September 15, 1878).
48 Drüner 2016, 123. Wagner's "lament about his poverty being supposedly caused by others continues to be repeated in the relevant literature down to the present day."

quite impossible. Kietz visited them and brought rum along so that they might hope to survive the cold. Richard was expecting to receive money from a former acquaintance, but the man's promises proved worthless. "We now looked forward in total despair to the chilly mists of the oncoming winter."[49] Salvation came from Kietz, who managed to procure 200 francs by roundabout means. This enabled Richard and Minna to move back to Paris and rent a small apartment in the building at the back of No. 14 rue Jacob. Richard worked on the score of his *Holländer* and got Kietz to promise to provide him with the funds he needed. Touchingly, Kietz did just this, in dribs and drabs of 10-franc and 5-franc bills. "During this period," wrote Richard years later, "I often pointed with amused pride to my boots, which became literally only an apparent cover for my feet, as the soles eventually disappeared entirely."[50]

These months of starvation and misery took their toll on Minna. Richard wrote to his friend Ferdinand Heine that he wanted to return to Germany. "What's more, my wife's state of health is not quite what we should like, which makes it my duty to take her to the baths of Teplice this coming summer, as has been recommended to her."[51] Eduard Avenarius and Richard's sister Luise pooled their money to provide him with 500 francs for a new start. He bought a goose, stuck the money in its beak and carried it home to Minna. Richard had meanwhile received promises from the Court Theater in Dresden that it would stage his *Rienzi,* so the idea of returning now appealed to him, too—especially when Friedrich Brockhaus agreed to provide the money they needed for the journey.

All the same, Minna was deeply sad when the time came for them to leave in April 1842 and she had to bid farewell to the friends she had grown to love in Paris. Kietz had generously insisted that they take his final 5-franc piece. Minna sobbed incessantly throughout the journey. When Richard tried to distract her, she would wait a little, then ask: "May I cry again?" The journey itself was extremely grueling. It took five seemingly endless days and nights before they reached Dresden. The reason was the stream of travelers on their way to the Leipzig Easter Trade Fair. This meant that the mail coaches were overcrowded and slowed up everything. A sudden change in the weather brought storms, snow, and rain, and no doubt reminded Minna of their terrible outward journey three years before, as if the gods were always

---

49   ML, 204.

50   Ibid.

51   SB I, 597 (letter of March 16, 1842).

determined to curse her travel plans. She was exhausted and frozen when they finally arrived.

Once in Dresden, they rested for a day before going out in search of an apartment. Minna was still deeply agitated, but Richard remained just one more day to care for her before depositing her with her parents and setting off himself for Leipzig and Berlin. She cried again when he said farewell, and he assumed that this was on account of his departure. But she answered frankly that she was crying because she had no idea how to get back to Paris. She made him promise to return home soon.

Chapter Three

"Home for me is you alone"

Dresden 1842–47

"Oh, my dear children, believe me, I share your feelings," wrote Richard to Cäcilie and Eduard Avenarius on April 21, 1842:

> I am still completely lukewarm in seeing to my affairs because my mind remains too full of Paris and the good, dear people there [...] Minna wants things to go badly for me so that I have to arrange a contract with Schlesinger and go back to Paris:—the poor woman thinks of nothing else other than Paris.[1]

In retrospect, Paris seemed to Minna to have been paradise in its purest form. She had left treasured friends and relatives behind there, and her thoughts were constantly of Cäcilie, her husband Eduard, and "dear, dear Paris." Everything was transfigured in her memory. She had become especially fond of her nephew Max, Cäcilie's son: "I want to kiss my dear little boy Max so much that he will wish his awful aunt eternal life with a thunderclap. I already have a little outfit ready for him that will be just to your taste—oh, God, if only the time were here where I could press you both to my heart!,"[2] she wrote. Her yearnings offer evidence enough to disprove the frequent claims that Minna's sole interests were financial security and a bourgeois environment. Three weeks later, she again wrote to Cäcilie:

> Paris seems to me like heaven, and I can only think back on it in tears. Who would have imagined it, when we arrived in Paris, that it would one day be so

---

1   SB II, 71 (April 21, 1842).

2   SB II, 236–41, here 240–41 (Minna's postscript to Richard's letter to Cäcilie of April 8, 1842).

difficult for me to leave it again! [...] It has never before been so difficult for me to leave somewhere. There is nothing here that appeals to me.[3]

While she was writing, a letter actually arrived from Cäcilie and Eduard that made both Minna and Richard burst into tears. Richard wrote back to them:

> [Minna] told me just now, in floods of tears, that she would do all she could to have my operas flop, because then I'd have no choice but to go back to Paris! [...] I can't give any other reply to your dear, dear letter, Cäcilie, than a general outburst of emotion; Minna finds it impossible to add a single line, she is quite distraught.[4]

Even if we regard these streams of tears on the Wagners' part as a means of emotional release that was acceptable for both sexes according to the mores of the time, their extreme reaction nevertheless demonstrates the continuing intensity of their Parisian experiences. Richard also assured his trio of friends Kietz, Anders, and Lehrs how much he longed to be with them: "Tell me, why did I leave you, what was it that drove me away? Why didn't I stay with you, even if I'd had to starve? Didn't we suffer hardship together and yet we still rejoiced? [...] My wife is in love with you all; I may not mention any of your names, otherwise misery will break out."[5]

But Minna's longings point to another, more serious issue. Her relationship with Richard had been sorely affected by the challenges of the past few years. New ideas could veritably explode out of him, after which he would advocate them forcefully for weeks on end—and then he would come full circle and reject them altogether. Then there was his utter lack of moderation in money matters, coupled with his inability to make any provision for the future. All this put a heavy strain on Minna's attachment to him. In Paris and Meudon, she had been loved and respected by people who were also ready to take her side when necessary. Wagner was possessed of a restless spirit, but if he climbed on the kitchen table and set off on his enthusiastic rhapsodizing, Minna and his trio of bachelor friends were quite prepared to laugh at him together. She was touched by their generosity, by their ability to conjure up money and food, and by their willingness to share both as a matter of course. She did the same in return and was rewarded with their gratitude and

---

3   To Cäcilie Avenarius, April 29–30, 1842, in Geck 2021, 23–25, here 23.

4   SB II, 78f. (May 3, 1842).

5   SB II, 74 (April 21,1842).

affection. They were like a family, and she was at the center of it all as wife and "mother."

Compared to the French capital, everything in Dresden seemed initially small and petty, and Minna avoided her earlier acquaintances. She found distraction by visiting the opera. The General Director of the Dresden Court Theater, August Freiherr von Lüttichau, arranged for the Wagners to be provided with good seats on request. This meant they were able to attend many performances despite their lack of money. Wagner was slowly settling in. By May 12, he was confessing to Kietz that their decision to leave Paris and return to his German homeland had essentially been the right one. He was even able to exclaim: "Damn Paris—I hate you!!!" But Minna was still depressed, in a delicate state, and unable to follow him in this change of heart. "Minna is calling me to table! The poor woman—she is still grieving," he wrote to Kietz.[6] All the same, he also often thought back fondly of the time when he, Minna, and their friends had been as if cocooned, protected from the outside world. "If I were sitting at the last outpost of the world, as long as I had my wife and all of you, I would still be happy and a great artist."[7]

The capital of the kingdom of Saxony nevertheless offered its own delights. The city straddles the Elbe River, lying between two partially forested chains of hills, and its incomparable location made it ideal for all manner of excursions. Upstream from the Elbe there lies Saxon Switzerland, downstream the vineyards of the Meissen region. To the south lie the foothills of the Erzgebirge, to the north the Dresden Heath. Steam ships had been traversing the Elbe since the mid-1830s, and offered numerous possibilities for pleasure trips. The city also boasted a wealth of architectural splendors, monuments and artistic treasures. The Court Church, the Frauenkirche (the Church of Our Lady), the Kreuzkirche (the Church of the Holy Cross), the Baroque Zwinger, the Brühl Terrace and many other buildings made Dresden one of the most beautiful cities in Germany. The art gallery had not yet been built (construction work on it began in the summer of 1847), but Dresden's abundance of historical buildings was already highly impressive.

The spa resort of Teplice lay just a day by carriage to the south of Dresden, and it became one of the Wagners' favorite destinations for vacations and for taking the waters. They traveled there in gloriously sunny weather in June 1842, along with one of Minna's sisters, in order to relax amidst picturesque

---

6   SB II, 202 (May 12, 1842).
7   SB II, 102 (June 12, 1842).

nature and to partake of the warm, healing springs. Minna had been prescribed a cure by her doctor, and so kept to a strict diet and drank plenty
of spring water. She also met Richard's mother there. Richard had to return
to Dresden before her, on July 18, in order to rehearse his opera *Rienzi*, but
he was soon longing to be with her again: "Well, my good, well-behaved,
charming wife, you will come on Thursday, won't you? [...] Farewell, my
dear wife, be good to me and come very soon to your charming Richel."[8] In
the meantime, Minna was having trouble with her mother-in-law, because
the latter liked to be demonstratively generous, only to complain afterwards
about how much money she had spent. Minna preferred sincerity in people,
and when she complained to Richard, he took her side and assured her that
she was right in everything.

But Minna was dealing with far more fundamental problems, for Teplice
also gave her the time and tranquility to reflect on their new situation. She
had sacrificed everything to her husband in Paris: her strength, health, homeland, and belongings, not to mention a career that had provided her with
an income of her own. Richard had banked on making Paris a big success
but had instead remained devoid of good fortune, with all his great promises vanishing into thin air. He had succeeded merely in selling the prose
sketch of his *Holländer* for 500 francs to the director of the Opéra. He and
Minna had been able to endure poverty in Paris because they had no circle
of acquaintances there who might have gloated over it; their friends in Paris
were all suffering similar hardships. But things were different in Dresden.
Here there was a social hierarchy, and they were situated far down it. Minna
did not foresee a secure future for them. Their old, pre-Paris debts had not
gone away, and if they could not find the necessary money, Richard would
be faced with court action against him. His relatives Luise, Ottilie, and
Hermann decided to give him 200 thalers as an advance for the next half
year, but it was merely a drop in the ocean. Richard also began complaining
about the amount of money they had to spend, because people in Dresden
expected him to demonstrate a certain standard of living. No such notions
had ever applied in Paris.

Sometimes Minna and Richard did not even have enough money to eat.
But Minna was thoroughly fed up with saving and starving, and was not
prepared to repeat their Parisian poverty in Dresden. She was particularly
distressed by Richard's habit of asking his immediate family and acquaintances for money, as this only served to alienate them. Such behavior could

8   SB II, 134 (July 25, 1842).

only horrify Minna, who placed great importance on the opinions of those around her and preferred at times to pretend, if this were the only way to create a good impression. She was 32 years old, and thus at a prime age for an actor. Did she perhaps dream of going on stage again, and of once more providing for herself? Although their years in Paris had taken their toll, she apparently still felt capable of returning to her old profession. She wrote to Richard from Teplice, suggesting that they separate for a while. Her letter has not survived, though it was presumably written out of desperation. We do, however, have Richard's reply, which once more reveals his deep attachment to her:

> Dear Minna, we cannot separate for a long time. I now feel this again, deeply and profoundly. An entire city of 70,000 inhabitants cannot replace what you are to me. If I don't have any business to see to, I am all the more sorry to be alone. But if I have toiled away all day, and evening comes and I do not find you at home, then all the domesticity that I otherwise find so benevolent only nauseates me, intensely; and what I find outside our home is truly unable to provide me with adequate compensation for just one minute [in it]. There is one passage in your letter that I have not yet quite understood: You speak of a necessity for us to separate, perhaps for a longer period of time?—What is this necessity? [...] When the storms and dangers were at their greatest, when you saw but a grisly death before you as the reward for everything you had suffered with me, you asked me only to embrace you tightly so that we would not sink into the depths apart from each other! [...] Tell me, what is it that makes you so fainthearted?[9]

He then went into detail about her accusations that he could become a financial burden to his family, and did his best to explain why she was wrong.[10]

Richard was incapable of understanding that it was not faintheartedness that had robbed Minna of all confidence in his assertions that he was the master of his own fate. It was her grasp of reality. He probably did not even believe his own assurances that he would be able to borrow money from their friends in Dresden, because he wrote to Ernst Kietz shortly afterwards that the three shirts he possessed were literally falling off his back, and he had no one left to borrow money from: "I have 14 thalers to live on, for footwear, etc. You can conclude from this how we live with the present inflation, and in what boundless embarrassment I sometimes find myself, given that we are in

---

9   SB II, 138f. (July 28, 1842).
10   Ibid.

a place where there can be no question of borrowing from anyone under any conditions at all."[11] Richard's swiftly shifting moods and the sudden flights of fancy to which he was prone meant he was able to see potential silver linings of hope in every cloud of despair. Unlike Minna, he was able to recover quickly from all setbacks. He now wrote to her to assure her that everything was in good order, and that the rent for the piano and their apartment was already paid up to the following October: "I will no longer be a nuisance to anyone, least of all to my family," he wrote. He went on to include the following verse—a parody of his libretto for *Der fliegende Holländer*:

Mein lieber Südwind, blas' noch mehr!
Nach meiner Minna verlangt mich's sehr!
Grüß herzlich! Ade, mein gutes Weib!

[O dear south wind, blow again! I yearn for my Minna! Greet her kindly! Adieu, my good wife![12]]

Just like the Dutchman himself, Richard too yearned for a partner who would love him unconditionally. His brilliant rhetorical gifts and his assurances of his love enabled him to convince Minna once more to bind herself to him. She abandoned her notions of separation. But on her return to Dresden, it will hardly have pleased her when she found that the apartment on the Waisenhausgasse that Richard had finally chosen for them (the twenty-first apartment he had inspected) was far removed from what she had wanted. It provided her with no room of her own, and she had to share the kitchen with other tenants. "2 decent rooms with 2 windows, and one with 1 window: quite nicely furnished, 2 beds with mattresses etc. […] but the rent is 12 thalers. Nevertheless, everyone has advised me to take it, because they say it would be impossible to find similar lodgings for less money."[13] It cannot have made things easier for Minna when their porcelain plates and other utensils arrived from Paris. She had kept them with her since her days as a young actor, but now they arrived shattered in pieces.[14]

The Wagners had few friends in Dresden in their early days in the city, which also gave Paris a more attractive sheen in retrospect. Their only close friends at this time were four in number: the court theater's choirmaster Wilhelm Fischer,

---

11   SB II, 148 (September 6, 1842).
12   SB II, 140 (July 28, 1842).
13   SB II, 132 (July 25, 1842).
14   To Cäcilie Avenarius, June 14, 1842, in Geck 2021, 25–29.

the theater's costume painter and actor Ferdinand Heine, and their respective wives. The Heines' daughter, Marie Schmole-Heine, later recalled assorted encounters with the Wagners in her parents' house and garden. She described Minna as a pretty woman with a friendly nature. The Wagners would drop in several times a week, and Richard particularly liked the large wine bower in the garden. They ate dinner there as often as the weather permitted. Only later did Heine's daughter understand why Richard could never take his eyes off the food, which was generally simple fare. She learned from Minna that on some days, this evening meal had been their first since breakfast:

> Standing in front of the spread table, he would often say to his wife: "Minel, now we will stock up." His greatest delight before the first course of cold meat was new potatoes in the skin with herrings in a piquant sauce. He called it "Lake" [pickle]. When my mother once jokingly remarked that he consumed too much butter, he handed over to her the next evening a large lump of butter. On those evenings he was harmlessly merry, like a child.[15]

Years later, Richard recalled Minna's birthday on September 5, 1842, as having been the worst he had ever experienced with her, because their entire fortune consisted that day of a single thaler. Nothing seemed to be getting better for them in Dresden. Their sole hope was the forthcoming world premiere of *Rienzi*, which now became the focus of animated discussion among the circle of Dresden friends that the Wagners had built up over the past months. Richard was more than nervous, since his entire career hung on its prospects of success. "I have been pining for ten years to come to the fore as I would like," he wrote to his composer colleague Robert Schumann with remarkable frankness.[16] Minna's mind was more on the potential box office receipts. Just a few days before the first performance, Richard had not even been able to toast Eduard Avenarius on his birthday because there was no wine in the house. The rehearsals had been marked by assorted arguments with the soprano Wilhelmine Schröder-Devrient and the tenor Joseph Tichatschek, but they both nevertheless appreciated Richard's exceptional artistic gifts and ultimately stuck by him. Marie Schmole-Heine later recalled the events surrounding the premiere as follows:

> On the day of the opening (20th October, 1842) the Wagner couple had their dinner with my parents—but they didn't eat much at noon. Frau Minna fre-

---

15   Burrell, 119.
16   SB II, 162 (October 5, 1842).

quently pressed her hands to her heart, anxiously sighing. Richard kept shifting to and fro on his chair, as he always did when uneasy and restless, or he would jump up, run around the room, and every five minutes pull his watch from his pocket.[17]

That evening, Richard and Minna stood together in front of the opera house for some time, and when someone entered, they called out to each other delightedly: "Did you see? He's going to the theater, too!"[18] Minna had initially wanted to stay away from the performance because she was just too nervous. But Ferdinand Heine's wife took her under her wing, and sat with her in her box: "That faithful woman had become so fearful in the company of her Richard that she looked all green and wretched."[19] Before the opera began, Richard hid in a box in the stalls and stayed in the background.

Richard's restlessness continued during the performance itself. Hidden in the corner of his box, he even began scolding himself: "Such an ox—no, what an ass! No, what madness!" And yet, despite its excessive length—the opera did not finish until 11:15 p.m.—this work with its brassy marches, its abundant choruses, and jubilant trumpet fanfares was a resounding success. Wagner himself enjoyed four curtain calls and the audience overflowed with enthusiasm. He laughed and cried at the same time and hugged everyone, with cold beads of sweat trickling down his forehead all the while: the nervous strain of it all had been almost unbearable.

The next day, Richard wrote to Eduard and Cäcilie to tell them about his magnificent success, and Minna added euphorically in the margin: "The opera is going to have several more performances with increased prices: Children, I am too happy, my highest desires have been fulfilled!"[20] At last she seemed to have realized her long-cherished dreams. All those years of toil had had a purpose after all. From here on, surely everything could only get better. The sold-out performances seemed to her to be an act of salvation. In her exuberance, she placed laurel leaves in Richard's bed and asked him the next morning in mock innocence if he had slept well.

There were some who were not of the same opinion, however. Eduard Devrient had found the audience's enthusiasm incomprehensible, because "[while] the music is splendid in places, [it is] enveloped in too much stifling

---

17 Burrell, 119.
18 Kietz 1907a, 426.
19 Kietz 1907b, 12.
20 SB II, 168 (October 21, 1842).

noise at exhausting lengths."[21] But *Rienzi* nevertheless made Wagner famous at a stroke far beyond Dresden. In the next two months he received more letters than during the whole of his stay in Paris. This was a phase in his life such as he had never known before: "Even if I always remain the same, nevertheless everything around me has changed [...]. Before, nobody gave two hoots about me, and now there's no saving me [...] in short, I am fashionable here."[22] As a public figure, he now had to endure not just effusive praise, but also ridicule and envy. For the moment, however, the first of these still outweighed the last two.

When Wilhelmine Schröder-Devrient invited Wagner and Felix Mendelssohn to take part in an evening of recitations in Leipzig on November 26, 1842, Richard conducted excerpts from *Rienzi*. Minna will surely have gone along, for by her own admission she never missed a performance at which Richard was on the podium. It was a benefit performance in honor of Wilhelmine's mother, the celebrated actor Sophie Schröder, who defied problems with her teeth to give a grandiose rendition of Gottfried August Bürger's eerie ballad *Lenore* that was the highlight of the evening.[23]

The opera houses of Berlin and Dresden were soon planning performances of Richard's next opera, *Der fliegende Holländer*, which provided him with yet another remarkable success at its world première in Dresden on January 2, 1843. Minna was just as delighted by it. This time, Wagner conducted the performance run himself. During one of the later performances Wagner found that he was missing a baton. At the time, only a Royal Kapellmeister was allowed to conduct with one, while the lower echelons of conductors had to make do with a violin bow. Marie Schmole-Heine's brother promptly sawed off the handle of a whisk and pasted paper over it, using some flour and water. This gave Richard a conducting baton free of charge.[24]

The Wagners' finances, however, were not progressing as Richard had imagined. His elegant but worn-out kid gloves had already been noticed by Marie Schmole-Heine. His creditors were also now threatening to sue him, but he had to evade them for the moment because his shirts and underwear were in a similarly deplorable condition. He made sure to inform his Parisian friends about this state of affairs, presumably to put them off, because he still had manifold debts in that city. When Minna spent a few days with her sister

---

21   Kabel 1964, I, 264 (May 25, 1845).
22   SB II, 183, 186 (letter to Albert Wagner, December 3, 1842).
23   ML, 237f.
24   Burrell, 121.

Charlotte Tröger in Zwickau in December 1842, Richard sent her a letter with 2 thalers, not without emphasizing that he had spent barely more than a single thaler himself the previous week.

Once Minna had left, Richard fell into a depression. Nothing could give him any pleasure, and he lacked all desire to work. He couldn't bear being at home, and so usually went to the Heines for dinner. He went once to the Tichatscheks, another time to Minna's parents. He even spent an evening with Carl Maria von Weber's widow. He missed his wife and their dog: "No Minel and no Pebs!—Yes, go on and laugh! I want to cry!! [...] Are you coming back soon? Oh, God! Do as you please, but if you want to make me very happy, then you will come quite soon."[25] Since no more letters to her exist at this time, she probably gave in and soon went home.

A close friendship now developed between Minna and the famous singer Wilhelmine Schröder-Devrient. Although Richard was ambivalent in his assessment of her (at times he called her a "damned hussy," at others a "truly noble, magnanimous woman"), his admiration of her as an artist overrode everything. She took Minna to her heart, and at Christmas showered her with luxurious gifts. She also loaned Richard 1,000 thalers, which was more than welcome. He used half of this money to pay off his Magdeburg debts at last, while the other half went to Paris: "I'm not spending a penny of the 1,000 thalers on myself," he wrote to his sister Cäcilie.[26]

These must have been exciting, blissful times for Minna. First there had been the overwhelming success of *Rienzi*, then the rehearsals for *Der fliegende Holländer* with its subsequent successful première. Richard now had the prospect of a prestigious, well-paid position as Royal Kapellmeister in Dresden, and she was the beneficiary of the affectionate friendship of the most famous German soprano of her day. What's more, Schröder-Devrient's generosity had helped them redeem a Paris pawn ticket so that Minna could retrieve the silverware and a watch that she had left behind as collateral. It had been a long time since she had been able to feel any such elation, so she must have enjoyed the moment all the more for it.

One invitation now followed another, and Minna was even able to complain to Cäcilie that there were weeks when they hardly dined twice at home.[27] Richard's growing fame also brought visitors. Clara Schumann

---

25 SB II, 190f. (December 13, 1842). Their dog's name "Pebs" was generally written "Peps" by the Wagners.

26 SB II, 200–207, here 206 (letter to Cäcilie Avenarius, January 5, 1843).

27 Glasenapp 1977, I, 465.

came by, bringing a letter from her husband. She played Robert's Piano Quintet in E-flat major, op. 44, chez Wagner, and when Richard expressed a wish to hear it again, it was granted.[28] Regrettably, no sources record what Clara thought of Minna or vice versa. But family ties were also being strengthened at this time. Wagner's nieces Klara and Ottilie moved to Dresden, and came to visit their uncle and aunt every week. The soprano Johanna Wagner (the adoptive daughter of Richard's elder brother Albert) was given a contract at the Dresden Court Opera in 1844, at which her whole family moved with her into an apartment at Ostra-Allee 23 (namely Albert, his wife Elise, Johanna, and her siblings Franziska and Marie). This resulted in a regular exchange of visits with Richard and Minna. Richard also liked inviting artists to their home, and when Albert's family came along too, Johanna would often help Minna out in the kitchen to provide food for their guests. Minna took a lively interest in her niece's career because Johanna had in fact started out as an actor, and only moved into singing after her uncle Richard provided her with vocal lessons.

When Wagner was offered the position of Royal Kapellmeister at the Dresden Court Opera, he hesitated for a long time. He wrestled over this decision because he felt in his prime and would have preferred to use his time exclusively for composing. But he also knew that he was not yet famous enough to make a living from it. Money in itself was never important to him for as long as he could find enough people from whom to borrow it. And he wanted to achieve recognition in the world through his works, not by holding down some prestigious position, and certainly not by conducting the works of other composers. Minna, however, felt exactly the opposite. She saw the job offer from the Court Opera as a ray of hope on their horizon at last. She knew that Richard's high-flown notions were of no use when it came to the practicalities of existence, and she felt a deep sense of satisfaction and reassurance at the prospect of his being appointed to an important post with a large, fixed, annual income. The money would enable her to engage respectably with other members of the local bourgeoisie, and would also let her provide regular financial support for her impoverished parents. All their friends and relatives urged Richard to accept the job. In particular, Caroline von Weber, Carl Maria's widow, implored him to think of Minna's peace of mind, because if anything untoward should happen to him, then Minna would be provided with a pension for life. Richard still hesitated, because he wanted neither a probationary period nor a position that would

---

28   SB II, 220f. (letter to Robert Schumann, February 25, 1843).

be subordinate to the Court Opera's first conductor, Carl Gottlieb Reissiger. But the authorities proved willing to remove these obstacles without further ado. We can only imagine Minna's trepidation during the negotiations. But when Richard finally signed the contract, "I tumbled into the arms of my poor wife, who was almost delirious with joy."[29]

Minna and Richard now moved from Waisenhausgasse to a two-room, furnished apartment on the Marienstrasse. They had their food brought to them from a nearby diner. Richard had to wear a court uniform on specific occasions, though he took no pleasure in this—not least because he had to pay for it himself. His tasks included conducting at church services and organizing concerts at court. On his 30th birthday on May 22, 1843, he was serenaded by sixty singers drawn from Dresden's choral societies, carrying colorful lanterns. They sang him a song to a melody taken from Weber, the poem for which had been especially written by Anton Pusinelli, a medical doctor who was a family friend of the Wagners. The singers presented Wagner with a ceremonial copy of it, and the honor touched him and Minna deeply.

Not long after, Minna traveled once again to Teplice, where she planned to spend the next three months. She had still not regained her health—the years in Paris had worn her down so much—but she hoped that a strict diet and taking the waters would cure her properly. No sooner had she left than Richard wrote to her:

> When you left and I finally lost sight of you, I had nothing else to do but to think constantly about where you might be: the weather was so changeable! Every gust of wind, every little shower of rain made me think of you, and I was angry that I had let you leave on such a horrid day.[30]

He could not bear to stay at home, so he went out and walked around the city. He ate out for lunch, then went to see his friend Ferdinand Heine. Richard became depressed if he did not get a letter from Minna every day, and when she did not oblige, he joked that she must have struck up a spa romance. In his own letters to her, he chatted about who had come to visit, about his digestive problems, his obligations in Dresden, performances he had attended—and, of course, he expressed his hopes that her health was improving.

---

29 ML, 247 (slightly amended).
30 SB II, 256 (May 29, 1843).

"My weariness has also left me, I feel fresh and sturdy," he wrote. "If only you did too—you know, if you were so properly healthy that you might cope again—well, you know what I mean: with just a very little child!"[31] His desire for a child of his own had not left him. He asked if she had been thinking about Kassel at 6 p.m. the day before, because that was when his *Holländer* was being performed there under the baton of the renowned Louis Spohr—something of which he was especially proud. He drew Minna into his eager anticipation of the audience's reaction, and he copied out for her an enthusiastic letter that Spohr had sent him. He then wrote back to Spohr to say how it pained him to read his letter without Minna alongside him. He had even thought of traveling to her immediately with the letter in his hand, because he knew how much she enjoyed his success, and it mattered to him to have her appreciate him and praise him. He told her jubilantly of his opera's success in Kassel: "You too must rejoice, dance and cry out! Now I'm no longer afraid! Everything is going to work out! Things might go slowly, but I am heading with you towards a glorious future that will be not just a honeymoon, but solid and long-lasting!"[32] Minna shortened her vacation in order to attend the first performance of Richard's *Das Liebesmahl der Apostel* (The Love Feast of the Apostles) for men's chorus in the Frauenkirche in Dresden. It was performed on July 6, 1843, with over a thousand singers from all over Saxony, plus an orchestra of a hundred men. However, two days later Minna was told that her 25-year-old brother, Karl Eduard Planer, had died. She had to go and console her family and help arrange the funeral, all of which naturally set her back after the improvement to her health in Teplice.

As an official Court Kapellmeister, Richard had to live in accommodation befitting his new status. He found such an apartment at Ostra-Allee 6, opposite the Zwinger park, and the Wagners moved there in October 1843. They bought a grand piano made by Breitkopf & Härtel, and Richard embarked on regular book purchases in order to improve himself. The German sagas became a particular focus of his interest, and he studied them intensively. He was proud of his library, and began reading E.T.A. Hoffmann, Ludwig Tieck, and Heinrich Heine for background on the tale of *Tannhäuser*.

It was at this time that the Wagners received a visit from the sculptor Gustav Kietz, the younger brother of their close friend Ernst Benedikt Kietz from Paris. His reminiscences shed a touching light on their hospitality.

---

31 SB II, 262 (June 2, 1843).
32 SB II, 269 (June 9, 1843).

Figure 3.1. Ernst Benedikt Kietz: *Richard Wagner*, 1842; lithograph by Caspar Scheuchzer, 1852. Private collection.

Richard lent him books and took him on walks during which he introduced Gustav to literary worlds hitherto unknown to him. He and Minna also often invited him to dinner parties attended by the tenor Joseph Tichatschek, the painter Franz Hanfstaengl, and others. Richard insisted on inviting Gustav to eat with them regularly on Sundays, because they were always able to put out a nice spread, and they had noticed how thin he was. Richard made sure to give him the biggest portions, and the only discomfort Gustav experienced chez Wagners was that of occasionally over-eating. Natalie often joined them, as did Richard's niece, the singer Johanna, and the latter took to calling Gustav her "Ganymede." Minna herself described him as sympathetic, with a warm, kind heart, and he later recalled his visits fondly:

> I felt infinitely comfortable with him and his dear wife. I had been completely orphaned in early childhood, but their heartfelt, caring manner gave me a small piece of home within their domestic life, which was infinitely beneficial to me. [...] They both displayed the most loving interest in my artistic activity and in my life.[33]

He continued:

> One afternoon, I encountered [Wagner] and his wife in a state of great amusement on account of a dubious pleasure that they enjoyed almost every day at noon when the military band passed by underneath the windows of their apartment. In order to provide me with a graphic impression of the musical delights offered by the passing fusilier regiment, Mrs. Minna stood up and sang in imitation of a clarinet while Wagner accompanied her on the piano, laughing as he did so. She did it splendidly, and her performance was so virtuosic and its effect so comical that we broke out into fits of laughter after she'd finished.[34]

For fun, Richard also sometimes sang duets with Minna, such as "Vergy, Vergy" from André Grétry's opera *Raoul Barbe-bleue*.[35] And there was another visitor to the Wagners at this time: the music critic Eduard Hanslick, who later became an adversary of the composer. Although he was at this time a student of law, he knew the music of *Rienzi* and the *Holländer* well. In his memoirs, Hanslick later recalled his first encounter with Minna:

> His wife [...] a tall, beautiful woman, entered the room for a moment. After she had left us, I could not fail to express my admiration. "Oh, she's barely recognizable now," replied Wagner. "You should have seen her a few years ago! The poor woman has endured a lot of grief and hardship with me. We had a

---

33   Kietz 1907b, 19.
34   Ibid., 21.
35   SB II, 525 (letter to Alwine Frommann, October 9, 1846). The soprano part reaches up to a top b.

wretched time in Paris, and we'd have starved if Meyerbeer hadn't helped us."[36]

In late 1844, Richard arranged for the urn containing Carl Maria von Weber's ashes to be repatriated to Dresden from London, where he had died in 1826. It was a matter that Richard took seriously because he owed much to Weber's operatic aesthetic. He even composed funerary music for the interment in Dresden, and gave a speech at the graveside. The event brought him admiration, but also enmity from certain quarters.

In March 1844, Wagner traveled to Hamburg to rehearse a production of *Rienzi*. On his way, he passed through Magdeburg and was reminded of the time he and Minna had spent there. "Incidentally, it's now ten years since we first came together there: we old lovers!—Did you sleep in my bed? In my thoughts, I spent both nights in yours. If you'd looked, perhaps you'd have found me in it—if Peps weren't in there already!"

Minna always tried to make her husband's everyday life easier, and this in turn helped to keep them close. Thus he wrote from Hamburg:

> I have been incessantly chattering with you, even last night when I woke up and wanted to have a hearty sherbet powder to calm my blood after the journey had shaken it up. There wasn't any light, so I tried to feel the writing on the various packages: but it wasn't necessary because you had prudently made them of different sizes so that I could recognize your care, even in the darkness. In the morning, while still in bed, I immediately began my usual conversation with you and Peps, so that I would still feel as if I were with you.[37]

Richard sent Minna long reports of the rehearsals and the performance in Hamburg—all of which provide yet further proof of just how much she was involved in his work. Richard also brought back a parrot from Hamburg that went by the name of "Papo," and which immediately won Minna's heart. Their relationship was thus still characterized by mutual familiarity, closeness, and sympathy.

In the summer of 1845, the Wagners took a joint five-week vacation in Marienbad, a spa in Bohemia some 90 miles south of Dresden. It did them both good. Minna bathed and drank profuse amounts of the local mineral water, while Richard's head was full of plans for *Lohengrin*. He later wrote of the "inner serenity" he had experienced during this trip. Once, when he was bathing at the spa, he jumped out after just a few minutes in order to hurry

---

36   Hanslick 1894, I, 65–66.
37   SB II, 376 (March 15, 1844).

back to their boarding house and commit to paper the fruits of his latest artistic inspiration. They went hiking in the woods and hills, and Minna will have listened attentively to his descriptions of the plot and structure of the new opera he was planning. For his part, Richard was keen for them to stay at one remove from any of their acquaintances, and just wanted to be alone with Minna. This opera would later be one of her favorite works.

The Wagners returned home to Dresden in mid-August 1845, traveling via Teplice and Aussig, from where they took a steamboat home along the Elbe. In the meantime, however, Richard's finances had taken such a turn for the worse that he had to ask his boss, Baron von Lüttichau, to arrange a loan or an advance for him. This crisis had been triggered by Wilhelmine Schröder-Devrient, who handed over his promissory note to a lawyer after having hoped in vain that Richard might pay back in installments the money she had lent to him. The theater gave him a loan of 5000 thalers at 5 percent interest, but proceeded to retain one third of his salary from now on in order to ensure repayment of what he owed. Richard was upset that most of the money he had borrowed was being channeled into repaying old debts. At times he felt as if he was working for nothing, and this merely increased his burgeoning aversion to his current position.

When Richard was negotiating with Berlin in September 1845 in an effort to promote performances of his works, he kept Minna informed all the while, emphasizing in letters to her that he wanted to discuss everything else with her in person. Her letters to him from this time are no longer extant, but we know that he appreciated them because his replies have survived: "Your delight in writing is so unaccustomed and is proof to me of everything that heartfelt love can bring about [...] Adieu! Dear wife of my heart! Stay healthy and cheerful! Soon your Richard will be with you again in body and soul."[38]

In these years, Richard played an extremely active part in the music life of Dresden. He was conducting operas by Auber, Bellini, Gluck, Lortzing, Mozart, Spontini, Meyerbeer, and Weber, and in the summer of 1845 he organized and conducted a large singing festival in the Frauenkirche through his function as the director of the Dresden men's choir "Liedertafel." He was preparing for the first-ever production of *Tannhäuser* at the same time. He could only smile at Minna's suggestion that he should boost the trumpets and trombones in it because they had been so effective in *Rienzi*. But he took her criticism of the "minstrel contest" seriously and

---

38   SB II, 303 (July 16, 1843).

Figure 3.2. Franz Hanfstaengl: *Wilhelmine Schröder-Devrient*, lithograph.
Nationalarchiv der Richard-Wagner-Stiftung, Bayreuth.

made greater efforts to get his singers "to make the innermost tones of the
soul vibrate."[39] *Tannhäuser* was accordingly given its world première in the
fall of 1845, under Wagner's direction. It seemed as if everything was looking up for them in Dresden—or would have been, had they not still been
suffering from chronic money problems.

---

39   ML, 307.

From mid-May 1846, Richard spent a ten-week vacation with Minna in Graupa, a tiny town some 8 miles from the center of Dresden. It is nestled in an idyllic landscape on the edge of Saxon Switzerland, and offered Richard ample opportunities to go hiking in the woods. The Wagners rented two rooms on a large farmstead that would many years later be converted into the world's very first Wagner museum. Minna invited Gustav Kietz to visit them there, and after some searching, he eventually found their lodgings outside the village. He arrived just as Elise Wagner—the wife of Richard's brother Albert—was playing the Pilgrims' Chorus from *Tannhäuser* on the piano. Kietz was astonished to find the Wagners in a whitewashed, medium-sized room with the simplest of furnishings; their apartment otherwise comprised a bedroom, a little kitchen, and the piano out in the hallway. Wagner was already known for his extravagance and his love of luxury, but nevertheless felt immediately at home in this house, set amidst the Sandstone Highlands of the Elbe Valley. He would often sit in the narrow, picturesque valley that went by the name of "Liebethaler Grund," looking down towards the Wesenitz River and the local mill. He was also making good progress with the composition of *Lohengrin*.

In the spring of 1847, Richard was forced to give up the prestigious apartment they were renting at Ostra-Allee 6 because they could no longer afford it. They now moved into an apartment at Friedrichstrasse 20a in the former Palais Marcolini, in the Dresden suburb of Friedrichstadt. It was situated on the north banks of the Elbe, some two miles from the opera house. The annual rent was 100 thalers instead of the 220 they had been paying on the Ostra-Allee, which was a substantial saving. Once again, Minna had to busy herself with setting up a new home. They had the space to invite the Heines round, and there was a padded stool next to the grand piano on which Peps had to lie whenever Richard wanted to compose. If Peps wasn't there, the household staff were instructed to look for him, and often Minna herself went out to track him down.[40]

The music of *Lohengrin* was keeping Richard busy. In the mornings he worked assiduously on the score, and in the heat of the afternoon he retired to a shady spot in the garden, reading all manner of books: historical works, fairy tales, heroic sagas, and the writings of the Ancient Greeks. Both his overall health and his mood improved. He made daily hikes into the surrounding countryside, usually accompanied only by Peps, where he was able to concentrate on his work. Many friends and acquaintances visited and

---

40   Burrell, 124.

shared a simple evening meal with the Wagners out in their garden. Richard also took delight in climbing the trees like a child, and it would often happen that visitors found him in the branches of a tree or hanging from the neck of the Neptune that formed the centerpiece of a large group of statues on the grounds of the Palais Marcolini.

For Minna, these years in Dresden were among the loveliest of her life. When Wagner wrote to friends "a thousand cordial greetings from my Minna, who is well and contented,"[41] this was no empty phrase but a statement of truth. Four years later, shortly after having lost his post in Dresden, Richard wrote to her: "If I'm employed in the service of an institution, you will only ever have an unbearable man around you who torments you and makes you depressed."[42] But Minna could not agree, because she had seen him happy and carefree during his time as a salaried kapellmeister, despite the occasional tensions that arose.

No sooner had Richard traveled to Berlin in September 1847 to rehearse a production of *Rienzi* there than he was seized, as usual, with a longing for home. He dreamt of Minna during his first two nights in Berlin. He didn't like the food he was served on the journey there, and longed to return to Minna's cuisine. He even wrote of how his love for her was more important to him than his career; while we can hardly take this at face value, it nevertheless sheds light on his attachment to her:

> You can't believe how I long to be able to hug you again and rid myself of the frostiness that ultimately dominates one's whole being when one is so removed from all love in a foreign place! No, I'm not that ambitious—a lovely home for my heart is more important to me than everything!—Well, my good child,—is this the longest we have ever been separated?? Thank God!!! [...] Farewell, my dear, good wife! Love me as unconditionally as I love you, then I shall want for nothing else![43]

When we consider that the Wagners had already been married for eleven years and had known each other for thirteen, the extent of Richard's longing is surely indicative of a marriage that was overall still intact. Minna also still clung to her "hubby" ("Männel") with every fiber of her being.

Richard wrote from Berlin to tell Minna of his artistic impressions of the city, and also mentioned the acoustics of the new opera house. Minna's

---

41   SB II, 465–8, here 468 (to Gottfried Anders in Paris, December 15, 1845).
42   SB III, 61 (May 29, 1849).
43   SB II, 571ff. (October 3, 1847).

extensive experience of attending the opera made her well able to assess the merits of a singer, and Richard treated her as an equal interlocutor when commenting, for example, on the difference in interpretation between Schröder-Devrient and Jenny Lind when they played the role of Donna Anna in Mozart's *Don Giovanni*. Minna loved these letters because they meant she was included in what Richard was doing and thinking—something that she would be denied in later years. But he also kept her informed about his abdominal complaints, asked her to get a tub for his return in which he might perform his cold ablutions, and described countless details of his everyday life such as we might expect after an intimate partnership of many years. His stay in Berlin was scheduled to last over two months, so Minna went to visit him there in the company of Clara Wolfram. On their journey home, the three of them clashed with a traveling salesman who offered a negative opinion of *Rienzi*. Richard was moved to see how his wife argued passionately with the man until he finally had to admit that he had never actually seen the opera himself.[44] It was her favorite, and she wasn't going to let anyone disparage it.

Over time, Richard began to pall of his position as Royal Kapellmeister. It meant negotiating, mediating, and—inevitably—sometimes giving in. That was not for him. In artistic matters, he acknowledged only one valid opinion: his own. The forebodings he had harbored had meanwhile come true. The German theaters were under the rule of the country's princes, which meant that their repertoire could be organized according to the preferences of the court. That in itself was enough to annoy him. His superior, the General Intendant Baron August von Lüttichau, was a former high official in the Saxon forestry department who had little sympathy for Richard's notions. It was common practice at the time in Germany to appoint long-serving, high-ranking officers of the army or court officials to run a theater, even though most of them had no musical qualifications. Richard despised the "repulsive despotism of the Dresden Court Intendant" as he later called it,[45] and grew less and less able to restrain himself in showing it. He made an official request for an increase in salary that he urgently needed, but it was rejected. Creditors from his past had heard of his appointment in Dresden and now reappeared to insist on being repaid. The fact that the salaries of several colleagues far exceeded his own annual income of 1,500 thalers was a source of bitterness. Felix Mendelssohn, for example, was paid 3,000 thalers

---

44　ML, 354.

45　SB III, 115 (August 10, 1849).

by the Berlin court, thus twice as much as Wagner. The singer Wilhelmine Schröder-Devrient had a fixed income of 4,000 thalers in Dresden, which was supplemented by actual performance fees, while even Wagner's colleague Carl Gottlieb Reissiger was being paid 1,800 thalers. Richard's hopes of obtaining additional income by performing his works at other theaters were not being fulfilled. The financial aspect of his job in Dresden thus began to lose importance for him. It had been clear to him for a long time that he wanted to consolidate his fame as a composer, not as a conductor. A clash with the orchestra at this time also made it obvious to him that he would be quite incapable of staying in his current position indefinitely. On the other hand, he knew that his having been appointed Court Kapellmeister for life provided Minna with some compensation for what she had suffered in Paris, and that she derived a sense of joyful satisfaction from their current status. She was never going to acquiesce in his abandoning it.

Richard began dreaming of creating a "German National Theater" in Dresden, and drew up plans for it. It was doomed from the start, not least because it would have made the post of General Intendant that was currently held by his boss Lüttichau superfluous. Wagner might have been right about many things, but his proposal simply stirred up a hornet's nest. He now began refusing to take part in official meetings with Lüttichau, who got his own back by assigning concerts to Reissiger that Wagner had been planning. Wagner was peeved that the high artistic standards he had attained with the orchestra were now, in his eyes, being undone by his colleague's supposedly sloppy work. Things were compounded when Reissiger was given a medal, while Richard went away empty-handed. Given the current impasse, Richard began to believe that a political revolution would be the only means of achieving progress in art. He regularly discussed politics with his friend August Röckel, who had meanwhile been appointed a music director at the Court Theater, and introduced him to the writings of Ludwig Feuerbach, Max Stirner, and Pierre-Joseph Proudhon. Richard also began attending weekly gatherings of artists and intellectuals to discuss the politics of the day. In 1848, the Russian revolutionary Mikhail Bakunin arrived in Dresden from Leipzig, and Wagner soon became one of his friends, often meeting him together with Röckel. "Everything about him was on a colossal scale, and he had a strength suggestive of primitive exuberance," wrote Wagner many years later in his autobiography.[46] But when Richard invited Bakunin to dinner, Minna was appalled at his manners:

---

46   ML, 385.

My wife once set before him for supper some delicate slices of sausage and meat, which he promptly bolted down en gros, without first placing them sparingly on bread, as the Saxon custom is; when I noticed Minna's horror at this, I was actually weak enough to point out to him how we usually served our meat, to which he responded with a smile that he had gone through enough, and should be allowed to consume whatever was put before him in his own way. I was similarly surprised at the manner in which he drank wine from the traditionally small glasses; as a matter of fact he detested wine, on the grounds that it satisfied the needs for alcoholic stimulation only in such paltry and hypocritically prolonged doses, whereas a solid shot of brandy produced much more efficaciously what was after all never any more than a temporary effect.[47]

Richard was fascinated by Bakunin's commingling of low-class philistinism and high-flying idealism; Minna much less so.

In February 1848, King Louis-Philippe of France was deposed, and the Second Republic proclaimed. In Vienna, the reactionary Prince Klemens von Metternich, Chancellor of Austria, was forced to flee by the revolutionary masses, and there were also riots and clashes in Berlin. A general mood of optimism spread across Europe in the wake of these political events, and the liberal forces on the Continent were hopeful for the advent of democracy.

In all the discussions in which he was involved about these new political developments, Wagner always envisaged how his own field of activity might benefit, since he regarded the current regime for music and theater to be outdated and rotten to the core. Nor was he the only artist who thought this way. The architect Gottfried Semper also took part in the meetings held by the would-be revolutionaries in Dresden. But Minna refused to tolerate the notion that Richard might devote himself to his political enthusiasms and thereby neglect his "real" work as a conductor and composer. Given her common sense, she knew that her husband's foray into politics could only end in defeat, and she spoke with him at length to try and make him realize the inevitability of it all. In vain. They had bitter arguments that she still remembered vividly a decade later:

Oh God, I'm glad that Richard has completely put that point of view behind him. What terrible arguments there were between us at that time. These damned politics almost came completely between me and that knucklehead of

---

47   Ibid., 387–88.

Figure 3.3. August Röckel, Wagner's colleague and fellow revolutionary in Dresden. Nationalarchiv der Richard-Wagner-Stiftung, Bayreuth.

Figure 3.4. Gottfried Semper, architect, revolutionary, and Wagner's friend in Dresden and Zurich. ETH-Bibliothek Zürich, Bildarchiv.

a husband of mine. If it hadn't been for that despicable Röckel, Richard would never have got involved in the first place.[48]

These "terrible arguments" did not have much of an impact. Minna could only look on powerlessly as her husband became enamored of the political trends of their time, and she could do nothing to prevent him from joining the rebels. She threatened divorce, but he did not take her seriously. She was also concerned about a recent article he had written, entitled: "How do republican aspirations relate to royalty?," which he read at the "Vaterlandsverein"—the republican-leaning "Association of the Fatherland"—and published in the *Dresdener Anzeiger* on June 14, 1848. It caused a considerable stir. Richard was officially still an employee of the king, but he here gave free rein to his disgust for the status quo, demanding "the downfall of even the last glimmer of aristocracy." He descended to verbal saber-rattling against those of the nobility "who refuse to relinquish the final vestiges of distinction," even threatening that "it could one hot day easily become a shirt of Nessus that burns them down to the bone."[49] The Saxon Court was displeased, its officials demanded Wagner's dismissal, and a delegation from the orchestra joined them in their demands. Richard had no intention of backing down, and in fact took his revenge in the *Dresdener Anzeiger* on June 18, writing: "I wish to inform the scoundrels and rascals that I shall not reply to their anonymous attacks. Richard Wagner."[50] This merely poured oil on the fire, though he had presumably intended nothing less, as he no longer cared about his position at the Dresden Theater.

Quite apart from the satirical poems and the invective that were now directed at her husband, Minna must have been particularly taken aback when *Rienzi* was taken off the program of the theater. She knew full well that Richard had also profited from the support of Dresden's cultural administrators. She vigorously objected to his opinions and accused him of placing his job in danger. He sensed that she was inwardly distancing herself from him but felt unable to pay due consideration to her feelings. According to Gustav Kietz, Richard on one occasion could not contain himself and cried out: "It is terrible; while others only have their opponents outside their house, I have

---

48 January 13, 1858, to Mathilde Schiffner (RWA).

49 SSD XII, 218–227.

50 SB II, 41 (June 18, 1848).

the worst of mine sitting here at my own table." Minna replied: "Oh, you wise men, how foolishly you act!"[51]

Minna never forgot the consequences of this article, and later reminded her husband of it: "Two years ago, you wanted to read me that essay in which you slander whole noble families that had been fundamentally of help to you, and since that time you have resented me and punished me so harshly that you never let me hear any of your works alone."[52] Perhaps Minna was also thinking specifically of Marie von Könneritz and Ida von Lüttichau (the aristocratic wife of his Intendant), who were both great admirers of Richard's work, and with whom she will have been personally acquainted.[53] For his part, Richard sensed that Minna was simply unable to follow him in his boundless abhorrence of the old order, and this put a strain on their relationship because Richard wanted unqualified approval from his wife for whatever he was doing. His relationship with his boss, Lüttichau, became increasingly precarious. Richard had to suffer a bitter blow when preparations were cancelled for the planned première of his last Dresden work, *Lohengrin*, even though the personnel necessary for a production was available in Dresden. He felt increasingly beholden to Lüttichau, who still held the reins of power and was in a position to indulge in reprisals as he wished.

In July 1848, Richard decided to spend a vacation in Vienna, also in order to extricate himself from the commotion that he had caused with his actions in Dresden. He was enchanted by the city and began sketching out his plans for the kind of theater reforms that he was still unable to realize in Dresden. For a time, he seriously considered giving up his current job and moving with Minna to Vienna instead. He wrote to her that the Kärntnerthor Theater—the house that had seen the world première of Beethoven's *Fidelio* in 1814 and Weber's *Euryanthe* nine years later—was willing to hire him as its artistic director.[54] He embellished his report with a description of the magnificence of Vienna. But this merely sufficed to trigger intense anxiety

---

51   Kietz 1907b, 86.

52   Burrell, 291 (heavily amended). Paul Lawrence Rose believes that Minna was referring in this letter of 1850 to Wagner's article "Jewishness in Music," published in 1850 (Rose 1992, 49f.). Perhaps an 1848 version of that essay did indeed exist, though it is unlikely. Minna writes here "Geschlecht," which Rose assumes to mean "race," though this is erroneous, as she clearly means "Adelsgeschlecht", "noble families." Furthermore, there are no sources to suggest that Minna ever protested against Richard's anti-Semitism.

53   SB II, 229 (April 6, 1843).

54   SB II, 613 (July 15, 1848).

on Minna's part—so intense that Richard had to write to the stage director
Eduard Devrient to ask him to visit her and calm her down. Devrient noted
in his diary: "So I'm supposed to put his destiny in order and uplift his wife.
He is a whimsical hothead who always makes things worse and waits until
it's too late before calling for help. What could one possibly do?" It was not
until his second attempt to visit her that he managed to see Minna: "The
woman isn't so much unhappy as annoyed with him, and in the current state
of things seems to be thinking more of herself than of him."[55]

But just what was that "current state of things"? Richard, the artist, wanted
a fundamental reform of the theater and of society in general. Minna, by
contrast, was keen to preserve what they had thus far achieved. A letter survives from Richard to his friend Theodor Uhlig, written just a few months
later, in which we can see clearly how intoxicating he found the revolutionary
enthusiasm of the times (and which was precisely what so horrified Minna):

> My cause is this: to make revolution wherever I come. If I lose, then this
> defeat will be more honorable to me than a triumph achieved on a contrary
> path: even without a personal victory, however, I shall still benefit the cause
> [...] the artwork cannot be created now, but only prepared for, and that by
> revolutionizing, by destroying, and by smashing everything that is worth
> destroying and smashing.[56]

Minna was meanwhile complaining to Cäcilie Avenarius that her "mop-
head husband" was causing her great concern—both politically and financially. It was all making her very sad, "that's why I keep quiet and swallow
what I can."[57]

Serious cracks now arose in the Wagners' marriage that hurt both of them
and could not be repaired. Two years later, Richard reproached her for this
in surprisingly plain terms in a letter intended to get everything off his chest
about what they had endured in Dresden:

> After getting my job in Dresden, your displeasure grew at the same time in
> direct proportion to the degree to which I was increasingly unable, in the
> interests of my art and of my artistic and general independence, to submit
> to the miserable management conditions of that artistic institution (and this
> despite the personal advantages that were provided to me). In this decisive

---

55 Kabel 1964, II, 442–43 (July 25, 1848).
56 SB III, 196f. (December 27, 1849).
57 December 29, 1848 (Staats- und Landesbibliothek Dresden).

period of my life, anyone who observed me closely and tried to understand me would have had to admit that everything I did was an inevitable, logical consequence of my artistic nature.[58]

Everyone would have to acknowledge, he continued, that he had not acted arbitrarily, and that he had truly suffered. And yet Minna had not understood him, despite the fact that "for this you needed no intellectual understanding, but only love!"[59] Nevertheless, he underwent moments of illumination in which he was able to recognize her side of the conflict, such as when he wrote to her as follows in 1855:

> But if I want something that I am not allowed to want, then I promptly go quite mad. You, poor thing, have already experienced this once; if you knew what I suffered for you back then! You would surely not believe it!—Well, now all is well, so let us see how we can end our old days happily and cheerfully.[60]

---

58   SB III, 278 (April 16, 1850).
59   Ibid.
60   SB VII, 107 (April 17, 1855).

Chapter Four

"My knucklehead of a husband"

Revolution and Its Aftermath, 1848–50

There was no stopping Richard Wagner now. The political situation had become especially volatile after the democratic German parliament in St. Paul's Church in Frankfurt passed a new Imperial Constitution for the country in March 1849. The Saxon parliament in Dresden adopted this constitution, but did so against the will of King Frederick Augustus II, who accordingly disbanded it at the end of April. This was the straw that broke the camel's back. The municipal guard reacted by mobilizing. Now the citizens of Dresden armed themselves and rose up against the authorities. Prussian troops joined those from Saxony to fight the insurgents. The sound of cannons echoed everywhere throughout the city, paving stones were upended, and barricades constructed with all manner of furniture, carts, wagons, and much else besides, all piled up high. Fires broke out, and everywhere you could see buildings damaged by cannonballs. General lawlessness reigned. Mutilated corpses were put on display, and people became paralyzed by fear. The rebels received an influx of men from the surrounding regions, while the government forces were reinforced by more Prussian troops. Wagner was convinced that the prevailing conditions of society would only change through revolution, and so he made fiery speeches, wrote revolutionary propaganda, and even showed up at the barricades. His writings from this revolutionary period reflect the contradictions inherent in him. On the one hand, his goal was the "full emancipation of the human race,"[1] but on the other,

---

1   Kühnel 1986, 490.

he was also calling for the "emancipation of kingship,"[2] whatever he might have understood that to mean. This was despite Minna's having implored him never to get actively involved in the issues of the day. Although he later denied it, he placed himself at the forefront of the revolutionary struggle (which is no wonder, given his volatile nature and rhetorical talent). Later, he was indicted for having used his garden to host discussions about arming the people. Even more serious was the testimony of the owner of a brass foundry by the name of Oehme, who claimed that Röckel and Wagner had ordered him to manufacture a large number of hand grenades in May 1849. Wagner denied everything, while Röckel conversely claimed that Wagner was solely responsible. Oehme, however, stood by his statement.[3]

The pianist Clara Schumann was also in Dresden at this time, and her diary entries offer a contemporary eye-witness perspective of the first order. She describes how she and her husband walked into the city and saw fourteen corpses of people who had been killed the day before, and were now lying horribly mangled for all to see. They saw thousands of holes in the façades of houses, the smoking ruins of the burned-out opera house, walls shot through, and they also learned that there were five hundred prisoners in the Frauenkirche. For her husband Robert Schumann, the notion of participating in the riots was beyond the pale. Instead, he fled the city for the countryside. "This is how people have to fight for their smidgeon of freedom! When will the time come when people all have equal rights?" wondered Clara in despair. She continued: "Kapellmeister Wagner is also said to have played a role on the republican side. Giving speeches from the town hall and having barricades built according to his own design, and much else besides!"[4]

There was a brief truce after the king managed to flee the city, and the rebels took this opportunity to elect a provisional government. Richard meanwhile began distributing handbills to soldiers, urging them to join the revolution, and then spent the night atop the tower of the Kreuzkirche, where he watched the government troops move in. He sent word to Minna that he needed provisions, so she sent him a basket of food, wine, and snuff—surely a sign that she was still standing by him, despite all their disagreements. Richard looked on as the old opera house went up in flames, though he was not overly concerned about the loss of his job there. Instead, he saw

---

2   Glasenapp 1977, II, 537.

3   Lippert 1927, 215. Röckel's forthrightness and the consistent thrust of his arguments suggest that he can be believed.

4   Litzmann 1920, II, 185ff.

Figure 4.1. The Court Theater in Dresden, ca. 1840. Eva Rieger Collection.

its destruction as a symbol of a new beginning. Walking around the city, he came upon boarded-up houses, closed shops, and the occasional armed men. When he reached home, he found Minna huddled in their apartment with a group of other agitated women who had fled in fear of the fighting in the city center. Röckel's memoirs tell of women tending the wounded and the dying, despite bullets whistling past them. He also later claimed to have seen several women who took an active part in the fighting on the barricades, some of whom even died for the cause.[5] Minna, however, kept strictly in the background. There is no indication whatsoever that she sympathized with the Dresdener Frauenverein (the Dresden Women's Association) that had aligned itself with the democratic, political goals of the revolutionaries.

---

5   Röckel 1912, 19. The *Frauen-Zeitung* (Women's Newspaper), founded in 1849, also reported that women were actively fighting in Dresden (24/1850); see Gerhard 1983, 202.

Throughout her life, Minna remained convinced that politics was a man's business, though preferably not her own husband's.

Richard's nieces were with Minna at this time, and he later reported how they laughed about the shooting in the city, and of how even Minna was infected by their high spirits. However, their reaction was more likely to have been a result of hysteria, caused by the nervous strain that events had placed on everyone. It is also not impossible that the women in the Wagners' apartment had briefly believed Richard's assurances that victory was certain— so impressed had he been by the sight of the people's militia. However, he subsequently admitted having lied to Minna when he told her that he was about to be appointed the secretary of the provisional government: "I had to describe this to her under the guise of a permanent position, and was also pretending to myself."[6] This deception nevertheless helped him to alleviate her growing sense of trepidation, if only a little.

Prussian troops were now getting closer, so the insurgents considered abandoning Dresden altogether and retreating to the Erzgebirge, where they would have a better chance of organizing their civil war. Richard was determined to join them. It was obvious to him that Minna was never going to approve, as she had already protested repeatedly at his participation in the current revolt. But he did not want to leave her alone in Dresden under any circumstances, and so tried to convince her that the threat posed by the advancing enemy troops made it essential to leave the city immediately. Wagner wanted Minna to take their parrot and dog and go to his sister Clara Wolfram, who lived with her husband Heinrich in Chemnitz, just under 40 miles away. She could wait there until the danger had passed. Minna agreed straightaway to his plan, as she was now desperate with fear. As they departed by carriage, they could hear the distant rumbling of cannon, and when they passed a group of freshly armed revolutionaries, Minna even offered them words of encouragement. Upon arriving in Chemnitz, Wagner deposited his wife with the Wolframs. It was May 8, 1849. He now learned that the retreat to the Erzgebirge had been postponed, and so resolved to return to Dresden in order to see how things stood with the battle. It was his only hope of getting more information.

Minna's world collapsed. Richard was now deliberately putting himself in mortal danger. She felt betrayed—justifiably so—and presumably offered all possible arguments, commands, pleas, tears, and outbursts of despair to persuade him to stay. The Wolframs were on her side. But Richard would not be moved. He wished the rebels to succeed with all his soul. He believed that

---

6   CWT II, 257 (December 13, 1878).

their victory would free him from the yoke of his office and ultimately bring about "the deliverance of art from its shameful fetters."[7]

Once he arrived in Dresden, Wagner went straight to the city hall. He had no more interest in returning to his own apartment. The armed rebels he met there were exhausted, some of them disheartened. Bakunin had proposed a radical plan to blow up the city hall in the event of an imminent victory by the government troops, but his fellow fighters rejected it. The provisional government instructed Wagner to travel immediately to Freiberg—halfway back along the road to Chemnitz—in order to make contact with a reserve platoon stationed there. Wagner did as he was ordered, then returned yet again to Dresden. On his way back, he came across troops who were fleeing the city and also encountered the members of the provisional government who had meanwhile abandoned Dresden, having had to admit that it was lost. Wagner jumped onto their wagon, and now learned from Bakunin that he had had the trees cut down along the Maximilians-Allee in order to prevent a cavalry attack on the flanks (though the residents had complained loudly about the loss of their "scheene Beeme"—their lovely trees).[8] Wagner took part in a discussion among the rebels and the provisional government about the current situation. They were exhausted, but decided to continue on to Chemnitz. Wagner wanted to go ahead of them, but was delayed and so followed after them in a mail coach. He remained alone and did not spend the night in the same guest house. He was lucky: the next morning, his colleagues rode straight into a trap and were all arrested. Some of them were subsequently even sentenced to death—though this was in each case commuted to many years in prison. Wagner avoided their fate through sheer good fortune and arrived at the Wolframs in Chemnitz on May 10.

The revered conductor had now become a wanted criminal. It was decided that he had to leave Chemnitz straight away, as he was under threat of imminent arrest. Heinrich Wolfram offered to take him secretly in his private coach to Altenburg, 23 miles to the northeast, from where he would then take the mail coach to Weimar to meet Franz Liszt and consider his further options. This was no sooner said than done. Richard left Chemnitz that same evening, presumably hidden under a tarpaulin. He arrived in Weimar three days later, on May 13, and went straight to the Hotel "Zum Erbprinzen" where Franz Liszt was staying. A serious conversation ensued, during which

---

7   ML, 246.

8   In ML, 407, Andrew Gray translates this phrase, which mimics a Saxon accent, as "beeyootiful trees."

Figure 4.2. Henri Lehmann: *Franz Liszt*, 1839, Musée Carnavalet, Histoire de Paris.

Liszt appealed to Richard's conscience and urged him to leave politics well alone in future. It was now that the two composers decided to enter into first name and familiar second-person pronoun "du" terms.

Minna was utterly distraught. The moment that Richard left Chemnitz, she set off for Dresden to check on their apartment. To her dismay, a police superintendent appeared at her door, tasked with arresting Wagner and with searching his living quarters for proof of his guilt. He intimated, however, that both the arrest warrant and the flyer announcing Wagner's "wanted" status could be held back for three days. Despite being in shock, Minna realized that he was offering Richard a chance to flee. She immediately wrote to Richard to explain what had happened, and begged him to leave Germany. But she sent it to Liszt's address, and since he was absent when it arrived, her letter never reached her husband. Instead, Minna now received a letter from him, asking to see her one last time before his departure. This can only have scared her all the more, because it now really seemed that his life was in danger.

On May 17, Minna went in desperation to Eduard Devrient to seek his advice and ask what she might yet do for her husband. She assured him that Richard had not really been involved in the Uprising. Devrient realized that this was a white lie:

> I had nothing to say to her except that if he does indeed know how to clean up his reputation, then he must return immediately and demand an investigation. If he cannot, then he must renounce his position. ["]Will he have to do that?,["] asked the woman tearfully, because if that were the case, as she had told him long ago, then that would mean a divorce.[9]

So Richard knew that she would not be following him. Now he too wrote to Devrient, trying to downplay his involvement in the Uprising, and asking him to ensure that his job was kept open for him to return. But he could expect no help from Devrient, who was disgusted at his conduct:

> This way of thinking is fundamentally dishonest. Given his eccentric partisanship, it was only to be expected that he would let himself get carried away by the uprising. But now he should also say "I did it," and not disavow himself. Yet he even addresses his claims for his salary to the king, the very person against whom the revolt is directed in which he is involved.[10]

---

9   Kabel 1964, I, 488 (May 17, 1849).

10   Ibid. (May 18, 1849).

When the fighting in the city was over, Gustav Kietz went to the Wagners' apartment. He found Minna there, utterly distraught. Amidst her sobbing, she assured him that Richard had not spent a single night away from home; it was only during the day that his restlessness had driven him repeatedly into town during the Uprising, despite her warnings.[11] From here on, Minna stubbornly presented a version of events to the outside world that downplayed Richard's actions. To her Swiss friend Eliza Wille, she later insisted that Richard had done nothing culpable; he had merely kept a lookout for the troops from the top of the church tower, she claimed, and had neither stood on the barricades nor taken up arms. This version of events might have convinced Minna's later acquaintances in Switzerland, but the authorities in Dresden remained resolute in believing Richard's guilt.

Emotionally, Minna was at the end of her tether. Richard's loss of his post as kapellmeister was to her a disgrace, and all the more painful because she had foreseen it. A reunion with Richard was arranged for May 22 in Magdala near Weimar, where he was staying under an alias. He had hoped that she would be more accommodating—after all, it was his 36th birthday—but instead she reproached him severely. Nevertheless, she stayed with him for two more days. There was also a second meeting between them, this time at the home of the linguist Oskar Ludwig Bernhard Wolff in Jena, where Richard found her stern and downright unloving:

> I had only one wish: to see my wife once more before I left Germany completely! Nothing else would have mattered to me. I would have let myself be caught—but I did not want to leave without this one consolation. My wife finally decided to give in to my pleas, but not in order to give me that comfort, nor to receive comfort once again from my embrace, but only in order to please a stubborn man so that he might finally leave. But he left to save himself. I can never forget the night in which I was awakened in my place of refuge to meet my wife: she stood before me cold and reproachful, and spoke the words: "Well, I've come as you requested: now you can be satisfied! Travel onwards now. I too shall return home this very night!"[12]

As was so often the case, Wagner's retrospective account of the facts is highly subjective. Minna later confessed to having shed many tears at the time; her supposed coldness towards him was simply her way of hiding how deeply hurt she was, and how desperately afraid that Richard might yet be arrested.

---

11   Kietz 1907b, 100.
12   SB III, 278f. (letter to Minna, April 16, 1850).

Wagner's plan was first to flee to Switzerland, and then to try his luck in France. With Liszt's help he obtained the expired passport of a professor from Saxony. When he reached the border crossing point in Lindau on Lake Constance, however, his passport was taken from him overnight, and he spent sleepless hours imagining how he might be interrogated in the morning. But the next day, his unsuspecting border official came back smiling with three passports in his hand and jokingly asked him to choose which one he wanted. Relieved, Wagner traveled by steamboat across the lake to Rorschach in Switzerland, and from there he continued on to Zurich where he went straight to an old friend, the choral conductor Alexander Müller. Years later, the latter's daughter Henriette Hesselbarth was still able to remember Wagner's dramatic arrival: "He rushed up the stairs, threw his arms around my father and cried out: 'Alexander, you have to put me up, here I'm safe, I've fled from Dresden, leaving behind my wife and all I own.'"[13]

Wagner had barely arrived in Zurich when he penned a letter to Minna that was intended to make Switzerland seem as attractive as possible to her. It was a "heavenly" place, he assured her, where prosperity and freedom reigned, and where Nature was charming and sublime.

> Each time I yielded to my delight I had to exclaim your name as if asking you to share it, but then I remembered your serious look and the dreary cares with which I left you, my poor wife. [...] all I implore from you now is this: shorten your disagreeable job as much as possible; what cannot be solved must be severed, only to escape from that unhappy Dresden as soon as possible and to breathe a different and more wholesome air. [...] Every additional day you spend in Dresden weighs heavily on my conscience.[14]

He now planned on going to Paris, where he would ceaselessly invest all his energies in preparing for a future for them both. He was convinced that he was going to achieve the impossible: an independent, freelance career without any ties whatsoever. Though to be sure, this need for boundless freedom on his part was predicated on a lack of it for Minna:

> You know that, although I love freedom from restraint above all else, I am not in the least inclined merely to roam around the wide world; I must always know a home of my own, and this home for me, my dear wife, is you

---

13   Fehr 1934, 5.
14   Burrell, 238–41, here 239 (May 29 and 30, 1849).

alone. Where my love is, there is my home, and in the last days of our painful parting one thing became convincingly clear to us again—that we really and truly love each other![15]

But how was Minna to believe him, since he was always changing his mind? He had for months been intoxicated by the prospect of revolution but had then been disillusioned at a single stroke. Richard wrote to Liszt that he would never again get involved in politics. He had become an artist again, he claimed.[16] But why then had he not listened to Minna when she was begging him to give up politics back in Dresden? Such thoughts must have tormented her, which is presumably why she decided to remain silent in the face of his entreaties.

Richard obtained a travel pass from the Zurich cantonal secretaries Johann Jakob Sulzer and Franz Hagenbuch, who later became his good friends. With this he left Zurich and traveled via Basel and Strasbourg to Paris. He arrived in the French capital on June 2, 1849, after thirty-six hours on the road. He rented a room with a small bedchamber, but suffered under the extreme heat and noise. Nothing seemed right to him about his current situation. Liszt's secretary Gaetano Belloni was waiting for him with money sent on by his master. Richard now began planning an opera to a text in French and pondered whether to move on to London. But both ideas were soon discarded. Liszt tried to persuade him to organize a performance of *Rienzi*, but in vain. Richard was now inevitably left to his own devices, and he felt all the lonelier for it. Most of all, he was distressed by not receiving any news from Minna. He was utterly blocked and unable to work without her. So his prime concern was now to get her to leave Germany and follow him. His next letter to her is dated June 4: "My courage regained in Switzerland is almost gone, and I have no other longing than to be united again with you, and the familiar remains of our old belongings, in a small quiet place."[17] It weighed heavily on him that he had heard nothing from her, and he implored her to write back. He told her that his friends in Zurich had cordially invited him to move there with her, that no one would demand anything from him, and that he would be able to work there to his heart's content. He was convinced that this was an excellent prospect, but Minna found it dubious since he had no firm commitments from any potential patrons.

---

15 Ibid., 240.

16 SB III, 74 (June 5, 1849).

17 Burrell, 242–44, here 242 (June 4 and 5, 1849).

Richard also mentioned, as if in passing, just how little politics really meant to him now: "I no longer know anything about conditions in Germany. To be frank, I don't much care. All I care about is you and seeing you again *soon*. If only I could get some news from you!!"[18] Several years later, in 1857, Richard even wrote of his "stupid pranks of nine years ago."[19] But such remarks merely concealed the tragedy behind the repeated conflict between him and Minna. His participation in the political events of 1848–49 might have been a "prank," but it had cost him his job and plunged Minna into a deep, personal crisis that had a direct impact on her state of health. Now, suddenly, politics were supposedly irrelevant to him, and his participation in the May Uprising subsequently downgraded to mere youthful high jinks. What was she supposed to make of his claims that he was now only thinking of her? By remaining silent towards him, she could pay him back for the hurt he had visited on her. She could not have realized, however, that her silence only pushed him away in turn, and that this would have fatal consequences for her future.

For the moment, however, Richard was still desperate for her to join him. He went on to explain everything that he wanted to do in Paris to get his works performed and earn money. He described to her his plan to write a long essay about the theater of the future. But time and again he returned to the cause of his sorrow: he was suffering day in, day out from not having heard from her. "For the rest, this frightful city of Paris weighs heavily on me," he wrote to Liszt at this time, "I often bleat like a calf for the cowshed and for the udder of its nourishing mother. How alone I am among these people! My poor wife! I've received no news yet, I feel so deathly limp and flaccid with every recollection." He described himself as "the most miserable wimp," while his fear for Minna was "boundless," and he added that he was hoping to learn more from Avenarius, his brother-in-law, who had meanwhile settled in Leipzig.[20]

Two weeks later, Richard was still waiting impatiently for a sign of life from Minna, as he confessed to Liszt:

My anguish and dejection are great!—I have to find a new home and hearth, otherwise it's all over again with me. My heart is bigger than my reason [...] When I'm there and have got my wife back, I can get back to work, fresh and

---

18 Ibid., 244.
19 SB IX, 58 (October 29, 1857).
20 SB III, 75 (June 5, 1849).

happy [...] I have to start work on something properly, otherwise I will perish: but in order to be able to work right now, I need peace and a home: if my wife is with me—in the friendly city of Zurich—then I shall find both.[21]

Minna was his fixed point around which everything else revolved.

Faced with her silence, Wagner's anguish grew daily. Minna was now living with Richard's sister and brother-in-law, the Avenariuses, in their apartment at Marienstrasse 2 in Leipzig. Richard continued to write to her every few days. He also wrote to Eduard Avenarius in an effort to get Minna to relent: "I am enduring dreadful torture at present and curse every day that passes without news from my wife."[22] He wrote to tell her that he could no longer stay in Paris. Not only did the capital seem noisy and unfriendly to him, but it was becoming increasingly clear to him that Zurich was the only viable place for him to stay. It seemed pointless to travel on to London, and he described to Minna in heartfelt words how pleasant and friendly it was in Zurich, and how he wanted to live with her there in a simple cottage by the lakeside, with a view of the snow-covered Alps:

> Teplice will not help you, but the lake baths at Zurich, the most healthful in the world, will strengthen and refresh you, giving you power and a new zest for life. There in German Switzerland we will feel at home [...]. Everything urges me to create something new; but I must have tranquility of spirit, and that is possible only when I am near you![23]

With his characteristic eloquence, he painted a golden future in an effort to change her mind at last. He was convinced that he would be able to procure a salary from the Grand Duchess of Weimar that would allow them to live independently. In the fall, he assured Minna, the railroad from Paris to Switzerland would be finished (though this would not be the case for several years), and he would at most have to travel to Paris for a week every now and then:

> In any case I would keep writing new works with joy and love, and those works would at last some day come forth and would bring me success in the future; but if success should fail to come, I would still be happy in the process of writing them, having you always at my side.[24]

---

21   SB III, 81f. (June 18, 1849).

22   SB III, 85 (June 19, 1849).

23   Burrell, 245–47, here 246 (June 8, 1849), slightly amended.

24   Ibid.

Minna's deep disappointment with his behavior determined her own. She wanted him to feel just a small fraction of the grief she had been forced to endure. His letters also betray a guilty conscience on his part—but mostly because he had left her alone in Dresden to cope with the demands of his debtors. Richard wrote to Liszt that Minna was "burdened with the dregs of Dresden nastiness"[25] and had to suffer for him. He had made enemies in Dresden and had presumably now heard of the scorn and ridicule to which Minna was being subjected in his absence.

Richard had originally promised to take in Minna's parents, but he now perfunctorily suggested that they would "have to make do at Riedel's for the present, or somewhere else," which will hardly have helped to allay her worries about her aging mother and father who were dependent on her. Richard sent her instructions about how she should store any excess furniture somewhere, bring the rest with her, and then take the train—with Natalie, their parrot and dog in tow—from Leipzig via Nuremberg, Donauwörth, Augsburg and Laufbeuren to Lindau on the shores of Lake Constance. From there, they would have to take the steamship to Rorschach just across the border in Switzerland, where he would meet them and accompany them to Zurich. His letter closed with a cry of despair:

> My good Minna, never before have I implored you so urgently for anything; never has my happiness, my health, my existence so depended on the granting of an entreaty such as I make to you now: say Yes! And come! Come as quickly as possible, Minna, I beg you, for the sake of all you hold dear; say Yes! And come! [...] Oh, be kind to me! Farewell and forgive all the evil deeds of your ever devoted Richard W.[26]

Richard had an opportunity to separate from her and set up a new life for himself in Zurich. But once again, his emotional and physical dependence on Minna came to the fore and he was unable to detach himself. Without her, he could not satisfy his creative needs. His metaphor in his correspondence with Liszt in which he describes himself as a calf, bleating for its mother's udder, speaks for itself. But the result of these weeks was a fracture in their relationship that Minna had felt first, immediately after the debacle in Dresden, and which Richard now also began to sense. They both felt unloved. Minna worked through her pain by taking refuge in illness, and Richard would soon after open up his heart to another woman: the "Laussot

25   SB III, 87 (June 19, 1849).
26   Burrell, 245–47, here 247 (June 8, 1849).

affair," described in the next chapter, was thus pre-programmed. He never again wrote such a helpless, begging letter to Minna.

It would be three long months before Minna was finally willing to move into Swiss exile with her husband. From her point of view, his reckless destruction of his professional and social position weighed all the heavier because they had been ceaselessly confronted with existential financial problems since their marriage back in 1836—in other words, for thirteen whole years. Minna had successfully fended off poverty when living on her own as an actor. But now she had been abruptly cast out of a secure position in Dresden. Nor was she the only one to suffer. Her parents had been delighted to see Richard in steady employment, but were now also at the mercy of events. How could he do this to her? Hadn't she supported him during those miserable years in Paris, providing love and sympathy, turning over every coin and even pawning their belongings just so that they might have something in their stomachs, and always in hopes of future fame and a steady income? Had she not believed his assurances that his operas would soon be successful everywhere? What probably embittered her the most was the fact that Richard had actively joined the fighters on the streets in Dresden, despite her having implored him not to. From her point of view, she had been right all along.

Minna was not alone in this. Franz Liszt was appalled by Richard's participation in the Uprising, and Richard's relatives too could hardly conceal their dismay. Two years after the upheaval in Dresden, the musician Robert Radecke visited the Wagners in Zurich and afterwards wrote: "How sorry one is that such an excellent artist as Wagner (he is the most significant German opera composer of our times) has destroyed his happiness by taking a revolutionary direction in his politics. As a result, he has to live here in Switzerland, far away from real musical life."[27] Many others were of the same opinion.

When Minna finally wrote to Richard in Paris in mid-June, the contents of her letter (which is no longer extant) were so painful to him that it left him utterly depressed. It only now dawned on him what he had done to her: "I finally received a letter from my wife, which awakened many feelings of remorse in me." She steadfastly refused to accept money from him if it was borrowed from others. In doing so, she presumably wanted to express her contempt for a way of life that was reliant on begging. She was not yet ready to promise that she would come, and she asked him not to assail her with

27   Quoted in Fehr 1934, 114.

requests. She was still too sore from having witnessed the destruction of all her hopes and dreams when Wagner gave up his post in Dresden. "My wife is suffering and bitter! [...] My wife is causing me much distress!" he wrote to Liszt.[28]

Minna went silent again, and so Richard in desperation turned to Natalie, who was now 22 and no longer a child. He hoped that she might provide a roundabout means of getting through to Minna. Gradually, criticism of Minna also began to creep into his prose:

> If I write her that I am discontented about my enterprises or affairs, she might be scornful and exclaim: "Don't you see that you brought it on yourself." But if I write about my successes, prospects, and hopes, she would be skeptical and call it a delusion. She might be entirely cautious and prudent in this, but I find no trace of love in it, only lack of affection and stubbornness.[29]

Without her, his creative abilities were failing: "Now while she stays far away, cold and unloving, I don't take an interest in anything and can't go ahead with any enthusiasm."[30]

Richard was quite incapable of imagining that he should have kept his post in Dresden out of love for Minna. He wrote in scorn to Liszt that Dresden was "a mudhole of civic excellence," and he was convinced that he had in fact held out there for far too long. It hurt him to learn how people were treating Minna as a pariah on account of his flight, but he pursued his convictions with what seemed to him to be incontrovertible logic:

> Only love can overcome all that must now be overcome; only love can justify, excuse, understand, and reconcile. But the first admission of this love in our case should be made by the wife, who should go to her husband since he cannot go to her. If Minna is quite incapable of making this decision, then she frankly and clearly proves that she has no love for her husband; that a place, an apartment, tables, chairs and things—about which she is now mourning and complaining—are dearer to her than the living person called her husband; that she prefers listening to slander, narrow-minded judgments, condescensions, et cetera, rather than finding out the truth by joining him.[31]

---

28 SB III, 85, 87f. (June 19, 1849).
29 Burrell, 248–51, here 248 (July 10, 1849).
30 Ibid., 250.
31 Ibid., 248–49 (slightly amended).

This letter was ostensibly addressed to Natalie, but quite obviously intended for Minna. His hopes for royalties from a production of *Tannhäuser* in Frankfurt had just been dashed—hardly the kind of news that was going to move Minna to reconsider her decision. But he nevertheless went on to outline an opportunity in Zurich that seemed to him to be perfectly practicable for the moment: his friend Alexander Müller had invited him and Minna to use two large rooms in his house, in one of which two beds were standing ready for them. Richard thought it appropriate that Minna would help Mrs. Müller in the household as repayment for the hospitality offered, and they would in any case only remain there until his plans had come to fruition. He was busy concocting a scheme by which a wealthy lover of the arts he knew would pay him a fixed salary in advance for all his German operas. It would also be easy for him to find Natalie a job in Zurich, he said—and he could do this straightaway, if Minna didn't need Natalie right now:

> Oh, if only the good spirit, the spirit of love, would soon come to Minna again. If she is not overtaken again by the purest and noblest feeling for me, I am afraid she will *never* again be capable of loving me: then she may well tell me that she will never see me any more, that she can't love me any longer, and then farewell to art and everything essential to my life! Then I am going to take my walking stick and wander out into the wide world where no one will find a trace of me![32]

By linking his prospects in life and work with Minna, Richard was bringing out his biggest guns, for his aim was to make Minna feel guilty if she did not come. He closed his letter with another urgent appeal:

> Nothing will affect Minna from without if she hasn't it inside her heart; if she is moved by love she will come, and come under any circumstances; if she doesn't love me, not even the most pleasant conditions in the world could entice her out of her gloomy, resentful, bad humor.[33]

But Wagner's financial plans came to nothing. The promised benefactor was not forthcoming, nor was there a job for Natalie. His future remained as unpredictable as before. In any case, Minna was not taking his plans seriously. She will hardly have been thrilled at the prospect of helping someone else with domestic tasks. What ultimately mattered to her most was that she

---

32   Ibid., 250.
33   Ibid.

was Richard's wife and that he still loved her. Natalie had passed Richard's desperate letter on to Minna, and on July 18, she relented, albeit with a heavy heart. His humble pleas had indeed touched her. She had replied already in late June to his requests, but her letter had been lost in the mail. So she wrote to him on July 18, repeating that she would come to Zurich.

Richard's reaction was euphoric. He immediately asked Franz Liszt to send her money for the journey, adding that she had bills to pay totaling 62 thalers, but no idea where to find the cash. Her sense of shame had prevented her from asking her husband's family to help her. Wagner justified his renewed begging by insisting to Liszt on how much he loved her:

> O dearest friend! You care about what is the best of me, about my soul: about my art. Make me whole again for my art! You see, I am not attached to any homeland, but I am attached to this poor, good, faithful woman, to whom I have caused almost nothing but grief, who seriously cares for me, without any exaltation, but who nevertheless feels eternally bound to the reckless devil that I am. Return her to me! Then you will be giving me everything that you might ever desire for me, and—look—I would be grateful to you for it! Yes, grateful!—
>
> You shall then see how everything will fly from my hands: my preparations for Paris, the pamphlet, and even two drafts for [operatic] subjects will be finished and on their way next month. Wherever I can't agree with you, I shall win you over: I promise you this, so that we shall go hand in hand and never need to go apart. I shall obey you—but give me back my poor wife, make her come to me soon, cheerfully and with confidence—and quickly—oh! And regrettably, in the language of our dear nineteenth century—that means: send her as much money as you can possibly afford! Yes, this is how I am, I too can beg—I could even steal if it meant I was able to make my wife cheerful now— even if only for a short time![34]

Before she left Dresden, Minna wrote to Richard three more times, and her letters reveal both the inner turmoil that had engulfed her, and just how differently she and her husband approached their current situation:

> What sort of future do I face? What have you to offer me? Almost two years may elapse before you, by a stroke of luck, may count on some income, and depending on the good will of one's friends only is a dreary existence for a wife. When we once lived under the most wretched conditions [i.e. in Paris], we at least had a prospect of better times. But the present restless state of the world leaves art in a very precarious position, since art can thrive only on peace and

---

34   SB III, 98f. (July 19, 1849).

prosperity. I have no wish to dampen your courage; but to venture once again into the unknown, to court worries and misery in a foreign country, for this *my* courage is not enough. I have lost my faith in your beautiful promises, and there is no longer any happiness for me on this earth![35]

Minna wanted to conform to the norms of the world around her, and idle chatter was repugnant to her. Richard had mocked her often enough in Dresden for her readiness to make allowances for petty bourgeois concerns, but he was unable to change her. She found it difficult to get accustomed to new people and new places, and in this they both diverged, as she confirmed in her next letter:

> You are more fortunate than I in this respect—anything new appeals to you more; I believe that is why you are much loved and honored, but it is hardly possible that you will be more worshipped and idolized in Zurich than was the case in Dresden at the beginning. You *know how to be very charming if you want to.*[36]

In his most recent letter, Richard had compared himself with a thoroughbred steed eager to rush onwards, but which was held back by its rider (i.e., Minna). She now took up this simile:

> It is true I once had some courage; but when the rider has been repeatedly thrown by his mettlesome horse, and without quite breaking his neck, but so painfully injured that his courage is gone, he is afraid to mount that unruly horse again and prefers to mount a less highly bred one which will reach its goal a bit later, but with more safety and without neck-breaking danger.[37]

What's more, his accusation that she did not love him had hurt her:

> I really do not understand you; to be sure, I never showed you any unkindness, but what proof of love have *I* had from you? You ought to have set me a good example, but you have not done so; otherwise you would have listened to my entreaties and for once also made a sacrifice for me; now it is over and this shall not be a reproach, but you will admit that you have done me a *great* injustice, and in the end yourself too, by exchanging a carefree life for a highly insecure one. I wish that you may *never* have cause to regret this.[38]

---

35   Burrell, 251–53, here 251 (July 18, 1849).

36   Ibid., 255–59, here 257 (August 3, 1849). Emphasis in original.

37   Ibid.

38   Ibid., 251–53, here 251–52 (July 18, 1849).

Minna's perspective enabled her to see the flaws in Richard's system of thought. To her, he had behaved irresponsibly by giving up the security of his job in Dresden—but now he had the audacity to complain that she was unloving. He still adhered to the notion—common at the time—that a woman had to sacrifice her happiness in life for the sake of her husband, should it ever be necessary. After all, it was what he had variously depicted in his operas with his female operatic characters Senta, Elisabeth, and Elsa, and he was perfectly serious about it applying in real life, too. Later, he confided to Cosima that Minna had been by nature benign, energetic, and helpful to him, but that he had begun to lose his faith in her when she proved unable to follow him. He thus remained unyielding in his convictions in later years, too.

Minna now had the delicate task of satisfying her husband's debtors in Dresden. This led to a dispute with her sister-in-law Elise Wagner, which only made matters even more awkward. One of Richard's admirers in Dresden was a Polish countess by the name of Hélène Kamienska, and she gave Minna money so that she might pay off certain debts—but Elise promptly intervened and took the money in settlement of an old debt that Richard owed her. Whatever the precise reason, Minna for years thereafter refused to see Elise whenever she visited Germany.[39] Minna's second major task was to sort out what to do with their household effects. Wagner had already sold off their most valuable pieces of furniture, and Minna now tried to sell off as much as possible of what was left so that she might have some money to take with her to Zurich. She rightly foresaw that they would not be able to stay for long chez Müller, as it would be awkward for her to have to help out in the household. She told Richard that she was no longer going to play the part of a good-natured boot-cleaner—which was no doubt a reference to their years in Paris when she had been forced to do just that to save money. Minna had meanwhile got used to the status of a "Frau Kapellmeisterin," and she was simply unwilling to return to anything approaching their Parisian poverty. She repeatedly asked Richard to understand her reasons for delaying her journey to Zurich:

> You are wrong in pressing me too much to come to you; don't attribute it again to a lack of affection, for it is natural that my health has suffered a great deal from the terrible excitements and hardships. I am very irritable, even bitter. I tell you this in advance to avoid reproaches in case I should long for my home; alas, I forget that I have no longer a home. In short, I do not yearn for other conditions.[40]

---

39   SB VIII, 340–43, here 342 (June 3, 1857).
40   235 Burrell, 251–53, here 252 (July 18, 1849).

Just how right Minna was to mistrust Richard's financial planning is proven by his assurance to her that Liszt was going to get him an annual pension from the Grand Duchess Maria Pavlovna in Weimar. It never came about. He used this as a means of luring Minna back, but then had to back-pedal again. He casually mentioned to Liszt that "I have not yet informed her that the hoped-for support from Weimar won't be happening now: but she'll easily understand this and submit to it."[41] But to Minna, he couched the Grand Duchess's refusal in a different light, assuring her that Liszt's efforts to get him an annual salary had "been interrupted for the present only, according to my wish, but they have by no means been abandoned."[42] Minna naturally saw through all of Richard's machinations. He appealed to her capacity for love, but at the same time trampled it underfoot by once more subjecting her to unreasonable demands that stretched her emotionally and physically beyond what she could cope with.

All the same: she had agreed to come—though admittedly with several conditions attached. She insisted that Richard tell no one back in Dresden that he was planning to settle in Switzerland: "It has a bad reputation now on account of the insurgents who have fled there by thousands, and people say that the unruly, idle revolutionaries will continue to be a nuisance there."[43] Minna was very worried on account of political events, because all manner of news was rushing in. She asked him if the Swiss were not afraid of being invaded by the Austrians and Germans. If this were indeed the case, then she had no idea where he might turn for asylum, except perhaps to England: "France in particular, as a republican state, is behaving miserably."[44] She also expressed her bitterness at having to furnish a new apartment yet again, and to create a new home with no real prospect of anything lasting. "I am not so eager to establish a little home for me, since it has no permanence; no sooner is it furnished than it is torn away again without mercy, and one must start from the beginning if one has any desire left, which I haven't, for one never prospers that way." Eight days later, she continued:

> The thought of the petty cares which went with the struggle for existence, when I sometimes didn't know what to put into the boiling water because I had nothing: this certainly makes me shudder to contemplate a future when

---

41   SB III, 98f. (July 19, 1849).
42   Burrell, 253–55, here 253–54 (July 23, 1849).
43   Ibid., 255–59, here 257 (August 3, 1849).
44   Ibid., 258.

similar things might happen; I have never concealed from you that I have become discouraged.[45]

Richard's plans to give a series of lectures in Zurich seemed to her to be merely humiliating.

> My greatest pride and pleasure was seeing you as the head of the greatest orchestra in Germany. You may remember that I missed almost no performance which you conducted, I saw only *you* and was happy. I believed that what I was hearing emanated from you only. *Don Giovanni* was your last opera here; it will long remain to me as a sorrowful memory. But the Ninth Symphony will be *forever unforgettable* to me on account of you. You appeared to me like a God governing all the powerful elements and working enchantments upon men. Don't deny that it gave you much joy to be able to integrate such resources, such strength, and to merge them into a great entity. See, dear Richard, you own the power, the glorious gift of creating something great even as a conductor, and you deviate so much from the true course of art that you now want to bring about a concert in Z[urich], but with what forces? How do you feel about it? [...] Farewell now! Please don't take any sudden mountain trip at the time of our arrival. Recommend me to the Müller family. The cholera here is diminishing; you needn't be afraid. Papo calls. Peps barks his greetings to you.[46]

These hardly sound like the worries of a supposedly timid, parochial woman. She knew that Richard was a gifted, brilliant conductor, and she was proud that he was her husband. But it was obvious to her, since their experiences in Paris, that writing essays brought little prestige and even less income. She could not have known that Wagner was processing what had happened in Dresden and turning his failures into a theoretical reflection on the future transformation of opera in Germany. For his part, he needed not just a wife who would see to his physical well-being and recognize his artistic mission (both of which services Minna was able to provide), but also a wife who would trust him blindly and follow him everywhere unconditionally, even if this meant abandoning a secure, permanent position for a life of hardship. This latter path was almost impossible for Minna to accept. In her above letter of August 11, she had exclaimed that "I cannot live over again

---

45   Ibid., 259–60, here 259 (August 11, 1849).
46   Ibid., 260.

what I went through with you before,"[47] which ought to have made him realize that she had reached the limits of what she could endure, emotionally and mentally. In fact, he probably had indeed realized it; but he wanted her back at any price. It pained him deeply to know how much she too had suffered. But for now, he could barely wait to get her back.

Liszt asked his patron, Grand Duke Karl Alexander of Weimar, for travel money for Minna; he granted her 300 thalers. Numerous organizational matters had to be seen to before she could set off for Switzerland, but by late August she was finally able to leave. She was accompanied by 22-year-old Natalie, Peps, and Papo. She also sent on the grand piano, mattresses, beds, mirrors, and various other household objects. Despite everything, her sense of humor had not deserted her: "I think, since I'm not traveling alone for the first time, I'll reach my destination without any detour by Australia."[48] She traveled via Zwickau, taking a hired carriage instead of the mail coach because she did not want to have their dog Peps locked in an animal crate. "This will make some trouble," she wrote, "but I am much too fond of [our animals] to entrust them to strange people."[49]

When Richard was finally able to meet them in Rorschach on Lake Constance, they had four months of separation behind them. Minna realized that many of Richard's physical ailments were actually psychological in origin. "His indisposition was really nothing more than homesickness, a yearning for his other married half," she soon decided.[50] When ironing her clothes on her birthday, September 5, she found gifts that her Dresden friend Mathilde Schiffner had hidden in the pockets. Her only other present was a crocheted collar from Natalie—she could expect nothing from Richard—so this surprise brightened her day a little.[51] She wrote to Mathilde, describing the mountains that rise up beyond the Lake of Zurich, their snowfields merging with the clouds. She had never seen anything so magnificent, she wrote, and was looking forward to climbing the Rigi.

Meanwhile, their old, familiar money worries had returned, which were compounded by a futile struggle against the cold Zurich fall. The money Richard had borrowed was gone by October, and he once again begged Liszt

---

47 Ibid., 259 (slightly amended: Burrell translates "Ich kann [...] nicht" as "I don't want to"; amended here to "I cannot").
48 Ibid.
49 Ibid., 255–59, here 258 (August 3, 1849).
50 Minna to Mathilde Schiffner, September 18, 1859 (RWA).
51 Ibid.

to come to his aid—even though the latter had just helped to have Wagner's grand piano sent to him from Dresden.

> Must I then write in the newspaper, "I have nothing to live on. Can those who love me please give me something?"—I can't do that for my wife's sake, as she would die of shame. Consider it, dear Liszt, and above all, remember to send me soon some—some money. I need firewood and a warm overcoat. My wife didn't bring me my old one because it was so shabby.[52]

Richard and Minna pondered whether or not to redeem a watch he had pawned (after all, she was well used to dealing with pawnbrokers).[53] He felt an urge to return to creative work at last, and wrote as much to his Dresden friend Ferdinand Heine: "The topics of five operas live in my head: I need to bring them to the light of day, one after the other [...] I am an unfortunate man who doesn't know any handicraft that might earn me my daily bread; it has to be given to me—as things stand now—so that I can remain an artist."[54] Wagner recognized his artistic potential, and felt that the world owed him a patron to help him realize it. This, however, was a point of view not shared by Minna.

The Wagners left the Müllers' apartment and moved provisionally into rooms at Ötenbachgasse 7, a house that went by the name of "Acacia." Their quarters were so small that Richard had to work in their living room. In order to get more space, they moved in mid-September to an apartment in the "hintere Escherhäuser" (the rear Escher houses), a relatively new block of houses on Zeltweg in the suburb of Hottingen, just a five-minute walk from Zurich's theater and concert hall. Minna furnished the apartment comfortably, employing a good deal of ingenuity in the process, such as converting a removal crate into a little table. When compared to their former apartment in the Palais Marcolini in Dresden, the simplicity of their new abode even from the outside provided proof enough of their descent in the social pecking order.

It was by no means easy for Minna to get used to the locals. Whenever they moved from one city to another, she suffered from homesickness. Despite establishing initial contact with Swiss women, she longed for her loved ones back home in Dresden. She was relieved that Richard's political

---

52   SB III, 133–39, here 138 (October 14, 1849).
53   Ibid. The watch was sold to Sulzer and is today held by the Wagner Museum in Tribschen.
54   SB III, 149f. (November 19, 1849).

Figure 4.3. The Escherhäuser on the Zeltweg in Zurich. Baugeschichtliches Archiv, Zurich.

activities had ended so abruptly. But she still harbored fears that he might revert to his old ways, and so she was relieved that he was at present not associating with other refugees from Germany. They had a woman to help out in the apartment, but Minna still had to do many chores herself. This placed a considerable burden on her, especially since the November that year brought freezing weather with it. Minna was often very cold in these weeks, and she suffered from being separated from her friends. She wrote to Mathilde Schiffner, imploring her to come and visit:

> At times like these, things are very shabby, and my mood is one of despair. But then I feel revived by the hope of a better future, that is, in the moment; and so I borrow a little good humor in order to be able to stomach the miserable present. We've also been privy to artistic pleasures—but they were truly ridiculous. They were concerts performed by amateurs, I felt as if I were listening to children singing and playing the piano. If that had happened back home, I would have laughed out loud. But we are in a foreign country, so I had to remain serious, and the people found it lovely.[55]

In spite of everything, Minna's gallows humor occasionally also broke through: "Tomorrow, on the 24th of this month, we will have been married for 13 years. It's been a bad year, and it was not without reason that I was apprehensive about it. So I'll close it quite prosaically and go and cook potatoes. It deserves nothing better."

Minna was not wrong in her artistic assessments. A few years later, Clara Schumann toured Zurich, Basel, and Bern, and came to a similar conclusion:

> Musically, it's quite dreadful here. There was singing in the concerts that could hardly be any worse. The musicians don't have much of a life, and my heart ached when I saw the full house and the poor, ragged musicians who were to accompany me. If I didn't have the children, I would have given my fee to them.[56]

The Zurich music society, which Wagner also occasionally conducted, comprised two dozen professional musicians and ten amateurs.[57]

Richard visited Paris during late winter and early spring 1850, during which time Minna engaged on a long hunt for a new apartment—despite

---

55 November 23, 1849, to Mathilde Schiffner (RWA).
56 Litzmann 1920, III, 30 (December 15, 1857).
57 Knust 2007, 166.

having assured him that she would rather separate than ever move again. She finally found one in April 1850 in a house called "Zum Abendstern" (By the evening star), on Sternengasse in the suburb of Enge, on the west bank of the Zurich Lake. She rented it, moved in, furnished it as nicely as possible with their belongings, and was expecting Richard to return any day.[58] They had the use of the upper floor, and now had more space and more sunlight. She had thus endured three moves in seven months—though she had foreseen just this kind of onerous activity before leaving Dresden.

Richard soon had a loyal circle of friends in Zurich, the most prominent being Johann Jakob Sulzer (1821–97), First Secretary of the Canton; Wilhelm Baumgartner (1820–67), a music teacher, choral conductor, and song composer; and Bernhard Spyri (1821–84), a lawyer, newspaper editor, and the husband of Johanna Spyri, the later author of *Heidi*. Wagner nicknamed them his "Trinity," probably in memory of his three "cloverleaf" friends back in Paris. Another close friend of the Wagners was Franz Hagenbuch (1819–88), Sulzer's deputy and then successor as First Secretary of the Canton. The writer Gottfried Keller joined their number when he returned to Zurich from Berlin in 1855.

Wagner was disillusioned with the defeat of the revolution in Germany, but he remained under the influence of Bakunin's writings and was convinced that a social revolution was still on the cards that would "burn down Paris," as he wrote to Theodor Uhlig.[59] His philosophical and theoretical reflections now found expression in a long essay entitled "Art and Revolution," which was followed by "The Artwork of the Future." Richard wrote to his friend Ferdinand Heine in Dresden of his self-appointed obligation to change art:

> This process, however, does not take place while eating oysters and cake, ensconced cozily on a sofa. It's out in the broad marketplace of life that one must first practice grinding stones with your teeth until your eyes becomes as bright as the innermost nature of your eyes will allow.[60]

Minna would not have appreciated comparisons like this (quite apart from the irony that Richard was actually fond of oysters and good food in general). It was difficult for her to comprehend that Richard's essays on the

---

58 Wagner quotes her thus: "Only recently, when you wrote to me: 'if I have to move again at the end of the summer, then I'd rather just leave today.'" SB III, 285 (April 16, 1850).

59 SB III, 460 (October 22, 1850).

60 SB III, 131 (late September 1850).

reform of the theater were founded in a serious aesthetic conviction about how to improve his art—and she would have been surprised to learn that these writings are still highly regarded in our own day. These essays provided him with a theoretical basis for developing his *Ring des Nibelungen*, a project that would occupy him for the next two and a half decades and would ultimately result in the construction of his own festival theater. Minna could not have foreseen any of this. For her, composing was the most important thing, because performances brought in royalties, and these in turn enabled her and Richard to make a living. This is why she was insistent that Richard should follow Liszt's recommendation and go to Paris soon to try his luck with an opera there. In this, she was relying on Liszt himself, who had repeatedly tried to convince Wagner of the advantages to be gained by writing an opera for the French public.

Richard was well aware that his wife was trying her best to make his life easier. He wrote to his sister Clara: "The fact that she gains so much strength through an awareness of how much I need her, despite her inner disgruntlement with me, and that she is willing to bear everything with me: this is what makes her so dear to my heart, and my love for her is the bond that actually still binds me to the world."[61] It is an irony of fate that Minna's mental and emotional turmoil, caused by Richard's participation in the Dresden Uprising, was interpreted by him as proof of a lack of love on her part. This was what soon afterwards would lead him to infidelity. By contrast, Minna had already played out the possibility of separation in her head, but she would soon be the one doing everything she could to save their marriage and get back together.

For Minna, Richard's revolutionary activities in Dresden, compounded by his humiliating flight from the city, were among the most painful experiences of her life. The writer Eliza Wille, who lived in Mariafeld near Zurich from 1852 onwards and often received visits from the Wagners, recorded her own opinion of her as follows: "Frau Minna had experienced a lot with her husband. Her horror at the memory of her last months in Dresden was even worse than what she had endured in earlier days."[62] What's more, Richard now began to believe that Minna would never be able to understand him fully, as he wrote to Ferdinand Heine in November: "At the end of this month, I no longer know what I am supposed to live from. This would not be so fatal for me alone, but it is terrible for me with regard to my wife, to

---

61   SB III, 174 (December 1, 1849).
62   Wille 1982, 30.

whom in some respects I shall fundamentally always remain an incomprehensible enigma."[63] He would be proven right in the course of 1850. For an event now occurred that almost ruined their marriage, and which all their subsequent, mutual efforts at reconciliation were unable to prevent from eating away even more at their relationship.

---

63   SB III, 149 (letter to Ferdinand Heine, November 19, 1849). See also SB III, 188 (letter to Franz Liszt, December 5, 1849).

Chapter Five

"This ridiculous, amorous intrigue"

The Jessie Laussot Affair, 1850–51

In May 1850, Minna wrote to her friend Mathilde Schiffner in Dresden:

> In all haste, just to reassure you. He is currently in Greece—he goes slightly crazy every few years, but this time is the worst. And I, poor creature that I am, have to atone the hardest for it—but as I said, I'll tell you everything in detail next time. You alone shall hear it from me, no other soul. I have no more secrets from you, whom I love so much and who has proven herself so much.[1]

"He goes slightly crazy every few years"—had Richard already strayed before in matters of the heart? To be sure, he found it easy to get along with the opposite sex, and his music did its part to stimulate feminine enthusiasm for him. Or was Minna alluding to Richard's repeated urge to move from one apartment to the next, to travel, to venture into new territory? In fact, he was by no means in Greece. So what had happened?

Richard had gone to Paris at Liszt's urging, albeit unwillingly. His stay there proved unhappy, however, and he found himself at an emotional low point. The year before, he had tried to paint a rosy picture of the future for Minna by assuring her that he had plans for a new opera in the French capital. So she was already expecting him to set off for Paris. But once he got there, he found himself powerless to organize any opera performances. He asked Franz Liszt again for money, telling him that he needed 500 francs to get by. He also needed to go to a tailor's and get new clothes made. The noise

---

1   Minna to Mathilde Schiffner, May 15, 1850 (RWA).

in Paris bothered him too—highly sensitive as he was—and he wrote to Minna to assure her of his homesickness: "Even if I were ill, I would get well again all by myself when I pack my things to return to you, to my friends, and to our dear critters in cozy Zurich."[2]

Just two months later, he would break with his wife and describe their hitherto life together as a failure. So it seems his own words could hardly be trusted. To put it another way: when caught between his well-worn familiarity with Minna and the prospect of a new erotic adventure, he floundered.

In the midst of his ongoing Parisian misery, he received a delightful letter from Bordeaux, sent by one Jessie Laussot, née Taylor, the 20-year-old daughter of a wealthy lawyer. She was married to a wine merchant by the name of Eugène Laussot and lived with him in Bordeaux together with her mother, Ann Taylor. Jessie was musically very gifted, and pretty to boot. She and Hans von Bülow had gone to the same piano teacher in Dresden in their youth, and so knew each other well.[3] Von Bülow admired her, and regarded her as "a very amiable, clever, musically accomplished woman [...] an excellent musician, who reads scores extremely well at sight, has learned a lot, and is tarnished by neither artistic prejudices nor any others."[4] Given that von Bülow—later a fine conductor, pianist, and composer—was always slow to offer a positive opinion of his peers, this was high praise indeed. Four years earlier, when still a teenager, Jessie had seen a production of *Tannhäuser* in Dresden that had remained unforgettable to her, and she had adored Wagner's music ever since. Two years after that performance, she had visited Dresden again and had been introduced to the Master himself. Together with Julie Ritter, a well-off friend of Wagner's in Dresden, Jessie and her mother Ann Taylor decided to offer him financial support. He was to receive 2,500 francs a year from the Taylors, to which Julie would add another 500 francs. Given Jessie's infatuation with Wagner's music, we can probably assume that she had been the driving force behind this act of patronage.

When Jessie learned that Wagner was now in France, she wrote to invite him to visit her, even going so far as to enclose the money he would need to get to Bordeaux. This was an incredible stroke of luck for the composer, who was lonely and out of cash. He set off immediately, and wrote to Theodor Uhlig to express his delight at this turn of events:

---

2   SB III, 222–26, here 225 (February 9, 1850).

3   Walton 2007, 46.

4   Moulin Eckart 1927, 3.

Figure 5.1. Jessie Laussot, at an advanced age. Nationalarchiv der Richard-Wagner-Stiftung, Bayreuth.

My art has always done quite well in attracting women's hearts. This is probably because—despite the prevailing vulgarity—it is still more difficult for a woman's soul to be beaten into submission than has so thoroughly been the case in our rule-abiding world of men. Women are the music of life: they absorb everything more openly and unconditionally in order to beautify it with their compassion [...] so I immediately wrote back as best I could and described the feelings that these signs of love and sympathy evoked in me from someone whom I barely knew at all.[5]

The euphoric tone of his entire letter is adequate proof both that he was interested in Jessie, and that his interest was already erotic in nature. Minna was now relegated to a supporting role, her struggle for their daily bread merely an object of scorn. "My wife should no longer make a disbelieving, worried face when there is stormy weather in our finances; I hope I have managed to convince her that whoever helps me only wants to help my art and the holy cause for which I fight."[6] He clearly feared that Minna might suspect donations from women to be a mere prelude to other enticements—something that would prove to be true in the present case.

On March 14, 1850, Wagner traveled to Bordeaux via Orléans, Tours, and Angoulême. A wave of goodwill met him upon his arrival. He blossomed as he basked in Jessie's admiration, and he read to her from his latest works. Her mother, Ann, was hard of hearing, which meant Richard was able to focus his attention wholly on the daughter. He found Jessie's charms immediately captivating. What's more, she understood him in all musical matters, and he found her utterly devoid of any artistic bias. The restless Dutchman seemed at last to be nearing his goal, and Jessie was unable to resist his charisma. Her marriage was unhappy, she was as emotionally starved as Wagner, and she now fell in love with the famous composer. Her husband's horizons were apparently restricted to his chosen trade as a wine merchant, which placed him in a poor position to satisfy her intellectual and emotional needs.

Richard was ecstatic. At last it seemed he could fulfill his long-held yearnings for a lover and muse who seemed to be the incarnation of an ideal womanhood. He wrote to Julie Ritter that Jessie had "freely, of her own accord, offered me redemption."[7] (His later autobiography phrased things more decorously; there, he claimed that Jessie had asked to place herself under his protection.) An escape plan now matured in Richard. He would utilize the

---

5   SB III, 194–200, here 194–95 (December 27, 1849).

6   Ibid., 199.

7   SB II, 315–31, here 323 (June 26–27, 1850).

Laussots' ample financial resources to flee abroad: first to Greece, then to the Orient. Jessie secretly agreed to run away with him. She would get around her mother by telling her that she was planning to travel to Dresden to visit their friends, the Ritter family.

If we consider that Wagner had just completed several extensive essays on aesthetics that are among the finest he ever wrote, then we cannot but marvel at his sheer mental incapacity, both in assessing his current circumstances in real life, and in acting accordingly. It did not occur to him that Jessie's mother would promptly cancel his promised allowance upon learning the truth. Spurred on by his dream of a woman who could belong to him unconditionally while understanding him completely, he now only had escape in mind. For the moment, he left the Laussots and traveled to Montmorency, a little town on the northern outskirts of Paris, in order to wait for matters to progress. Above all, he felt he had to explain to Minna that their marriage had just come to an abrupt end, and why. On April 16, 1850, he wrote her a long letter in which he listed the differences between them—and did so with a harshness that Minna had never before experienced from him:

> I am completely strange to you; you see only angles and deformities in me; you see in me only that which is inexplicable to you, and nowhere do you find compensation for the suffering I cause you. You cling to the peacefulness and permanence of existing conditions—I must break them to satisfy my inner being; you are capable of sacrificing everything in order to "have a respected position in the community," which I despise and with which I don't want to have anything to do; you cling with all your heart to property, to home, household, hearth—I leave all that so that I can be an individual. You think only of the past, with nostalgia and yearning—I give that up and think only of the future. All your wishes are directed toward conformity with the old, toward giving in and submitting, toward reestablishing—I have broken with everything old and fight it with all my strength. You cling to people, I to causes; you to certain human beings, I to humanity. Thus there is only disagreement between us, irreconcilable disagreement; thus we can only irritate each other without bringing each other any happiness; and perhaps you are the more unhappy—for I understand you well enough, but you don't understand me![8]

Wagner here listed their opposing views of life, rather than providing reasons for the supposed failure of their relationship. At the same time, everything he wrote is open to dispute. It was only partly true that he was indifferent to

---

8   Burrell, 281–85, here 281.

a respected position such as his kapellmeister post in Dresden. After all, he needed possessions in order to create a luxurious environment for himself; Minna, by contrast, needed little to get by. Of course, he also clung to people after his own fashion, as did she. The core issue here is his conviction that Minna thought and lived in petty dimensions, while he had the vast destiny of the world in his head and preferred to ignore the trivialities of everyday life. Such a claim was naturally unfair to her, because as the woman in their relationship it had fallen to her to organize their daily survival—and this was something from which he benefited the most.

Looking back now at the beginning of their marriage, Richard reproached Minna for having stood by him only out of a sense of duty. He accused her repeatedly of having neither loved him properly, nor enough. Weary of her reproaches towards him, he insisted that he needed unconditional solidarity from his partner—and reminded her of how she had broken with him after his flight from Dresden, when she was unable to forgive him for ruining everything that they had so laboriously built up. Her initial refusal to follow him into exile back then was proof of her lack of love, he wrote, and he now saw separation as the only possible solution.

All the same, the thought of henceforth being separated from her and from everything that had constituted his domestic existence was, he assured her, a source of great pain to him:

> While I say this quietly and as a sensible human being, I feel at the same time the tremendous grief that is involved when I take leave of all my old, familiar world! What you have often and violently spoken of, separation, I now confirm after a long and terrible inward struggle: I do not say it thoughtlessly, but in the final and firm conviction *that it must be so* and that it *can no longer be anything else!*[9]

He begged Minna to accept half of the money given to them by Laussot, Taylor, and Ritter, though at the same time he suspected that she would never accept a gift from the husband and mother of the woman who was now his lover:

> I know your great pride, your strong feeling of independence! Oh, don't use it against me! Overcome your resistance just this one more time! Just see! You will drive me crazy and surely hasten my death if you refuse me this last request, if you leave me with the terrible idea that the poor woman who has sacrificed her youth, everything to me—in vain—is destitute or serves strange people![10]

---

9   Ibid., 283.
10   Ibid.

Minna was dumbstruck. It seemed to her, she wrote to Mathilde Schiffner, as if Richard had "trampled her underfoot in the most despicable way, [with] the most pitiful, most unfounded accusations."[11] She was so stunned that she assumed Richard must have written this letter in some feverish delirium. If that was not the case, then she wanted to hear this cruel decision from his own lips. "I remember still as though it were today what Minna suffered after having read these unhappy lines," wrote Natalie in retrospect.[12] Minna was afraid that Richard must have taken ill. She was barely able to go to the post office and collapsed in a faint. And she still did not even know that a woman was behind it all.

Despite all their disagreements and occasional conflicts, Minna had always believed that she and Richard would remain together. A year before, after Richard had fled Germany, he had urgently endeavored to convince her to join him. For weeks on end, he had done all he could to persuade her to move to Zurich, begging money from Liszt to make it possible, painting the loveliest future possible for her, and assuring her that "my dearest thought and wish in all the world is to join my dear wife for good, to set up house with her in one of the most splendid spots on earth!"[13] On page after page he wept, lamented, and pleaded with her in order to convince her how miserable he was without her. Hadn't he repeatedly linked his creative potency to her presence? And even his last letter from Paris in spring 1850 had been affectionate in tone: "Be of good cheer, forget our sufferings and rejoice in the love that we enjoy!" he had written.[14] Was this really to be the end? Had their many years of marriage and all the privations they had suffered together been completely in vain? She no longer understood the world. "Does a man of genius also have the right to be a scoundrel?" she asked Mathilde, utterly perplexed.[15]

Minna felt on the verge of madness, and wrestled with herself for two days and nights until finally deciding that she had to go and hunt for Richard to hear from his own mouth about his intention to separate. This meant traveling to Paris on her own. But she was penniless, and so she took Richard's friends Jakob Sulzer and Wilhelm Baumgartner into her confidence. She showed them Richard's long, accusatory letter—no doubt amidst floods of

---

11   Minna to Mathilde Schiffner, mid-May 1850 (RWA).
12   Burrell, 286.
13   Ibid., 245–47, here 246 (June 8, 1849).
14   SB III, 259 (March 17, 1850).
15   Minna to Mathilde Schiffner, mid-May 1850 (RWA).

tears—along with the letter that he had written to her barely four weeks earlier, in which he had written that

> [I] yearn with all my heart to be back with you in our house! Believe me, I know no other happiness than to be able to live quietly and contently with you in our domesticity: the fact that I can now hope to see your worries placated, and courage and good cheer in your heart—indeed, in your body too—that is what also makes me healthy again, and happy.[16]

Both men had become close enough to the Wagners to witness what had seemed an intact marriage, despite their occasional quarrels. They were as shocked as Minna and assumed that Richard could not be in his right mind. After discussing the situation with her, they gave her the fare to Paris, along with a letter for her to pass on to Richard: They wrote:

> Dear Friend: You can easily imagine what sad hours your last message has caused your wife and us. When you read these lines, you will already know that nothing could have prevented your heroic wife from hearing the confirmation of your fateful decision from your own mouth. Nobody except your wife and we have learned about your intention which—only remember all your proceeding letters—seems to be *without* psychological motivation, and to have been caused by an unfortunate misunderstanding. For this very reason, and only for the sake of you and your own future, we beseech you: examine yourself again without any prejudice, examine the reasons of your recent decision before establishing them irrevocably. A third person, though influenced by the warmest sympathy, could only cause new trouble by interfering in such circumstances. Therefore we will not venture to influence your final decision by arguing with you, much as we are moved to do so. However, you will certainly consider one request of proven friends: you should take the manly resolution not to oppose the arguments of your wife by an unalterable decision, and therefore to listen to her favorably. Of course we were looking forward to your coming to your new home at Zurich which we have already christened "Villa Rienzi" and which certainly would satisfy all your wishes. There, we hoped, you would again grant us many evenings similar to those, which, though spent under less favorable conditions, count among the most beautiful of our lives. However, this hope is not the motive of our request but solely the ardent desire that you yourself may not be at enmity with your own destiny, already laid down in letters of fire, nor obstruct your own well-being. In any case, whatsoever your decision may be, never forget that you have friends in Zurich, the most faithful you could ever find.[17]

---

16   SB III, 255–59, here 257 (March 17, 1850).

17   Burrell, 285–86. Emphasis in original.

This is what Minna took with her to Paris: a letter clearly borne of friendly concern, even fraternal affection, and that ends on a conciliatory note. We cannot overestimate her courage in all this. A woman traveling alone, and to a major foreign city to boot, was almost unheard-of in those times. She was on the road for three days and nights, which must have been a great strain for someone whose health was already weakened. After arriving, she walked the streets in a state of considerable agitation. She spent eleven days in search of her husband, knocking on friends' doors and asking after him. None of her inquiries was successful.

Richard was in Montmorency when he learned that his wife was in Paris looking for him. What should he do? For a while he battled with his conscience, but then decided to hide from her, and so went into Paris to see their old friend Kietz. He implored him to lie to Minna if she showed up at his door, and to tell her that he did not know of Richard's whereabouts. Perhaps he feared that if he met Minna he would relent, and give in to her. Kietz was dismayed at Richard's insistence on separation. He was very fond of Minna, and told Richard that such a deception made him feel "like the axis on which all the world's misery turned."[18]

Minna met Gottfried Anders in Paris, and later wrote to thank him for his kindness and for helping her to cope. She similarly found a sympathetic ear in Leo von Zychlinsky, an acquaintance from their days in Dresden. But no one revealed Richard's whereabouts to her, and so she had to travel home to Zurich without any success. After arriving, she took the trouble to write a comprehensive reply to Richard's letter. She described the shock she had felt and her decision to travel to Paris to hear from Richard his reasons for leaving her. No one had been able to dissuade her from her plan, she said, but nor had anyone been able to tell her where he was:

> Evidently you shrewdly kept your new whereabouts from your friends. [...] you can imagine how I must have felt. I had made the long trip under the most terrible emotional stress and could not reach you. Richard, *now* I am more than ever convinced that there is a Providence; otherwise I would have *this time* lost my mind through this hard blow which you gave me. I implore you, what is happening to you again *this* year? Nothing is holy to you; nothing more remained for you to destroy but our *marital happiness*; that's why you drag in the pettiest, most unjust, most contemptible accusations to guard yourself against reproaches; you talk yourself into things which *never* existed between us; finally you lie to yourself to gloss over the abominable way you are treating me again. [...] First you speak

---

18   ML, 441.

of the complete difference between our temperaments; I confess that I never even heard you say a single word about the fact that we did not suit each other until *now*, after we've already been married *for fourteen years*. You speak of the earliest scenes between us, frequent and ugly; you credit me with a good memory for things like that, and for that very reason I remember those which you repeatedly brought on when driven by a terrible jealousy; after these were overcome, *both* of us got along so well and lived together more happily than is often the case with married people. Only during the last *two years*, ever since you turned to miserable politics, which have destroyed many a happy relationship, have I been unwise enough not to avoid violent scenes with you; I just simply could not understand you *in this matter*, but one thing was clear to my simple mind—that nothing good would come to you from revolutionary activity. For that reason I was also against the association with Bakunin and Röckel, because I saw what a destructive influence they exercised on you, even on your health; for that I can be excused; only for *your sake* did I expose myself to the most violent scenes. But at least we have had no more in Zurich *itself*. Now you unjustly spread these over our entire past. I only wanted to preserve you for your art, which I admire and idolize; I wanted you to let the genius within you have free rein, not to oppose yourself by force; eventually the time would surely have come again when you could see your wishes fulfilled, but you should not have lost your patience right away. I saw with unspeakable anguish how you tore yourself away from the path of art, from Germany for which I so much wanted to preserve you, and I always had the painful feeling that you were also tearing yourself away from *me*. [...] O Richard, you are in a bad state of mind; you are hurting me terribly again!! The reason I did not keep you here was because I was actually not permitted to on the advice of the doctor; you grew more irritable, more violent every day, so that it became clear to me that a change of air, of occupation, would divert you from your moods. The date of the performance of your overture was approaching; Liszt sent the money; you yourself became restless; and now it is my fault that I drove you away for *lack of love*. Just remember how you found me in tears with Sulzer two weeks before your departure; and for so many days before that I swallowed nothing but tears during meals whenever I thought of your going away. I was miserable with longing for you every time; after the departure I was always embittered and angry with the restless Richard Wagner, for it was always *he* who would tear my husband from my side. Oh my God, what else shall I tell you? Whenever I could find a little surprise which made you happy, how happy I was too! [...] I was happy in the knowledge that you were close to me while you created *all* the *beautiful* things, and *that* shows that I understood you *completely*; you always made me so happy, sang and played almost every new scene for me.[19]

---

19 Burrell, 289–92, here 289–91.

It seems strange that Minna should insist on differentiating between her husband, Richard, and the "Richard Wagner" with whom she is angry for snatching away her husband. But it is understandable. Richard might have been suffering from their gradual estrangement for two years now, but Minna had felt it too. All the same, she still had no idea that Richard wanted to leave her because of another woman.

Meanwhile, Richard had traveled from Paris to Villeneuve on Lake Geneva. He had originally planned to leave the port of Marseilles on May 7 and head to Greece on a boat. But a few days after that date had passed, he received a letter from Jessie, who had been faced with no other option but to confess everything to her mother, Ann Taylor. This inevitably meant withdrawing from Richard's plans, as her mother could not allow such a scandal under any circumstances. Richard still imagined that the great love that existed between him and Jessie—or so he thought—would convince her husband, Eugène, to renounce all his marital rights. But he was going to do nothing of the sort, and instead swore to hunt down his rival and shoot him. The absurdity of this well-nigh stage-worthy situation was still insufficient to dissuade Richard from his plans. On the contrary, he wrote to Eugène Laussot to express his incomprehension that a man could use violence to compel his wife to stay with him, despite her having no interest in him whatsoever. Then, summoning up his courage, he fearlessly traveled back to Bordeaux. The fact that he preferred the prospect of meeting his rival to meeting his own wife is proof enough of how difficult he found the latter prospect. Laussot had meanwhile informed the police about Wagner. They checked his visa, and gave him two days to leave the city. Richard was worried about Jessie, and so went to her house in Bordeaux. But her living quarters were empty: she and her family had fled to the countryside. Wagner went into the unlocked house and left a letter for Jessie in her sewing basket. Then he returned to Villeneuve.

Ann Taylor had by now contacted Minna, who sent back copies of Richard's two letters in which he had informed her of his intention to separate. Nowhere in either letter was Jessie mentioned. Nor did he speak of divorce. When confronted with this, Jessie had no choice but to conclude that she was to Richard nothing more than a secret lover on the side—a status from which she understandably recoiled. On June 10, Minna received an anonymous letter from Bordeaux, presumably written by Eugène, from which she learned for the first time that Richard had begun a love affair with a married woman. He had wanted to kidnap her, she read to her horror, and the anonymous writer urged her "to put an end [...] to these nonsensical goings-on." Minna initially refused to believe it, but gradually it became clear to her just why Richard wanted to separate. She was once more overwhelmed by a shockwave of emotion.

In light of Richard's infidelity, Minna found it particularly devious of him to justify their separation by claiming that their marriage was in bad shape. His criticism of her now seemed but a pretext "to gloss over yet another despicable act he has committed against me." What's more, she only had ten guilders left and had no idea how she was going to survive. As a precaution, she wrote to Mathilde Schiffner in Dresden and asked her to use the money to extend a pawnshop note on the silverware she had pawned in Dresden and find her a suitable job in or near the city: "You know what I can do and understand, and how people can rely on my good behavior, so I would not be a disadvantage to anyone recommending me." The idea of taking up a job again was something that had been on her mind for months. She had already pondered returning to Germany back in February. "I shall ask my women friends to get me a job that is appropriate to my sphere of activity, so that I don't have to accept charity, which would be the most dreadful thing for me!" Minna wanted to inform her mother, and asked Mathilde to do so confidentially. "You can be glad, my dear, good Mathilde, that you don't have a husband. You haven't got to know these torments yet, but don't misunderstand me, I'm not jealous, it's just that I have been so rudely insulted. That's what still eats me up." All this again began to affect her health. She lost weight and could hardly sleep. Now that the Laussots had withdrawn the annual pension they had provided, Minna was barely able to assist her parents. She had to sell something to be able to send Mathilde 5 thalers for them: "It is getting so cold and they have nothing but what I can provide. I often cry bloody tears, and this is why I hate R. To let old people go to rack and ruin like this, out of sheer recklessness, it's outrageous!!"[20] Her criticism of Richard intensified in the course of these months, and it would get even worse in the latter stages of their marriage.

Word had meanwhile spread in Dresden that Minna had been abandoned by Richard, and she even received a polite offer of marriage from a gentleman whose name is unknown to us today:

> It has not remained unknown to me that your husband has left you [...] so I feel encouraged as a responsible man to offer you my heart and hand. To be

---

20   These quotations are from Minna's letters to Mathilde Schiffner of mid-May, February 26, and October 26, 1850 (RWA).

sure, I do not possess a great fortune, but what I already have, along with a well-flourishing business, is perfectly sufficient to create such amenities for you that might compensate you for certain hardships you have endured.[21]

He wrote that he desired to lead her back to a permanent home, "where I shall be devoted to you for my whole life, with the most faithful love and devotion." Minna subsequently blacked out the sender's signature, but kept the letter to the end of her days.

Julie Ritter now traveled from Dresden all the way to Villeneuve with her son Karl and her two daughters, Julie and Emilie. Her aim was to clear up the chaos and to have a moderating influence on Richard, who felt deeply wounded but had still not given up his conviction that he might yet snatch Jessie from her husband's clutches. Julie knew Richard and Minna well. She had been a faithful friend to Minna during her last months in Dresden, and was also friends with the Laussot family. It was she who now explained the actual state of things to Wagner. To cap everything, he now also received a letter from Jessie in which she ended their relationship for good. His final illusions now evaporated. He was bitterly disappointed, and exorcised his frustration in a sixteen-page letter to Julie Ritter in which he claimed that: "The one doesn't believe in me because she doesn't understand me, the other because her cowardice means she suddenly doesn't want to understand me anymore!"[22] This would nevertheless have still been an opportunity to leave Minna for good. Instead, he decided to return to her.

Finding some way of maintaining a semblance of bourgeois decency was what mattered now. Julie Ritter did everything she could to soothe his emotional wounds. She gave him enough money for him to go on a hiking holiday with her son Karl. They went along the Rhône Valley to Visp in the canton of Valais, and from there they tramped along the rugged Vispertal and the Mattertal to Zermatt, which took them nine hours. Then they retraced their steps and traveled on to Thun in the Bernese Oberland. Karl went to Zurich at the suggestion of his mother, and with Richard's consent, in order to ascertain the prevailing mood and to reassure Minna. Yes, she was indeed willing to take her "hubby" (Männel) back.[23] And so, after six months away, the penitent returned home.

---

21   Letter to Minna of June 12, 1850 (Pierpont Morgan Library, USA).

22   SB III, 315–31, here 322 (June 26–27, 1850).

23   See Rieger/Schroeder 2009, 37ff.

An apologetic and undated letter from Richard to Minna has survived, to which she added marginal notes. These read today like a tragicomedy, but they also reveal just how hurt she was. Richard wrote as follows:

> She [Jessie] suddenly wrote to me that she was determined to leave her family and place herself under my protection. [Note by Minna: "To roam about the world as an adventuress—very honorable."]
>
> [I] described my situation to her in the most frightening terms, and emphasized the tremendously daring and fatal elements in her decision; she ought to think the matter over. [Minna: "Briefly and to the point—I have already a decent wife."]
>
> It would have been the most insane cruelty on my part to reveal *to you* what had been going on, since I did not even know what the end of it would be. [Minna: "Driven out of Bordeaux by the police—nice end."]
>
> For after such slanders it must have surely seemed as if I had left you for another woman! [Minna: "And so it was, according to proofs I possess."][24]

During the weeks when she had feared that Richard might indeed leave her, Minna had pondered how to go on with life on her own. She could not live on the money Richard might provide: that much was clear to her. A year earlier, the women's newspaper, *Frauen-Zeitung*, founded by Louise Otto, had complained about the restrictive barriers that existed to women's employment: "Given their inability to secure their own existence, thousands of our sex have up to now regarded marriage as an institution of care. [...] Discord, unhappiness and demoralization are the sad consequences of this."[25] Factory work, cottage industries, agriculture and housekeeping were all out of the question for Minna. She planned to apply for a job as an actor. A small theater had just sprung up in the Friedrich-Wilhelm-Stadt district of Berlin (near where the city's main station is situated today), and Minna's friend Alwine Frommann, who was resident in the city, offered to sound out the possibilities of a job for her. "Anything you undertake will be a great mental exertion," wrote Alwine, but "only a desperate exertion will enable you to hold on to life."[26] That did not sound like a viable proposition.

Richard's return made these plans null and void. He and Minna managed to resume their married life together, despite the upsetting events that they had just endured. Minna was aware of her husband's intense inner dependence on her, and the constraints under which they coexisted also

---

24   Burrell 300–307, here 304–305.
25   Gerhard 1983, 208–209.
26   Burrell 299–300, here 299.

contributed to the re-establishment of peace between them. Nevertheless, the shock went deep. Richard wrote as follows to Ernst Benedikt Kietz back in Paris: "To my delight, I have become convinced that my wife's love for me is stronger and more unconditional than was her error about me: and that, consequently, it is not separation, but only a renewed, continued cohabitation that will be able to heal the discord that had spread out between us."[27] He had already written to Julie Ritter some time earlier to say that he still loved Minna:

> What was it that pleased me so much about Jessie, other than her most perfect impartiality in these sickening, bourgeois points of honor? Who understood better than she that I loved my unhappy wife, that I was bound to her by a thousand chains of mutual sufferings in life, and that I could only tear myself away from this poor woman with a bleeding heart, in order to separate her from a fate whose connection was incomprehensible to her, and which could only cause her pain and anguish without her being able to interpret and comprehend it?[28]

A letter that Minna sent to her Dresden friend Mathilde reveals just how much her recent experiences still gnawed away at her. She wrote to say that Richard had returned unexpectedly on July 4. "I, a weak woman who still loves him, have forgiven him, but to be sure, in confidence to you, my dear friend, I can say that I can and will never forget! He cannot make up for the nameless grief that he caused me. May God forgive him as I have done." Minna also received a letter from Jessie herself that was critical of Richard for having behaved so badly toward his wife. Jessie assured her that she was no longer in contact with him. But Minna refused to dignify her letter with an answer. Her resentment was still too deep: "Basically, I am doing wrong to hate that person. In the end, he alone is to blame. A man must be strong— what would have become of me if I had not been stronger than him at all times? But we are called the weaker sex, and how wrong that is!"[29] The allowance that had been promised by the Taylor–Laussots and Julie Ritter would have made her life so much easier, so the loss of it also pained her. But she resigned herself inwardly to her fate.

The Wagners now took it upon themselves to make a new start. This time, Richard really liked the new apartment that Minna had chosen for them. His

---

27   SB III, 348–49, here 349 (July 7, 1850).
28   SB III, 315–31, here 319 (June 26–27, 1850).
29   Minna to Mathilde Schiffner, August 2, 1850 (RWA).

mood changed immediately: "If it were my choice, I should not like to live anywhere else in the whole wide world except here," he wrote to Theodor Uhlig.[30] This was a strange turnaround, in view of his recent plan to emigrate to Greece. He and Minna now lived right by the lake, with a magnificent view of the mountains and a garden of their own. Richard could walk down to the water in his bathrobe and take a dip. There was even a boat at their disposal. On July 7, shortly after his arrival, Sulzer, Baumgartner, and Spyri came for a get-together with the Wagners in what they called the "Villa Rienzi." They were keen to demonstrate high spirits, but the shock of what had happened must have sat deep in all of them.

What would have become of Wagner if he had indeed traveled to the Orient with Jessie Laussot as originally planned? It would have been impossible for him to get his work known in Europe if he was situated on another continent. He would have been unable to organize performances, and would have been so far away from the publishing scene that he would have been quite divorced from the contemporary discourse on music. He would also have been without the books that he needed as a source of repeated inspiration in his work. Minna had made a decisive contribution to thwarting his plans and had taken back her emotionally wounded husband. His verbose explanations for their separation had hurt her deeply, and she made sure that he knew it. But she could live with the hurt because his excuses had been so far removed from what she knew to be the truth. All this meant that they were now able to embark on a new beginning in their relationship.

There was a longstanding agreement between Richard and Minna that they would not talk about the past. They had kept to it after Minna's failed attempt to flee their marriage back in 1837, when she had returned to Richard, full of remorse. This time, too, they practiced silence about what had happened. But Minna could not forget. As so often in her life, her emotional suffering manifested in physical illness. She could cope with Richard's infidelity, though it was painful to her. But she could not cope with allegations from him that were injurious to their marriage and all it meant. As regards his infidelity she was able to regard herself as blameless, which meant it was up to her to extend a hand of forgiveness to her husband. But his allegations portrayed her as a failed wife who had essentially compelled her husband to commit his infidelity. That was something she could not and would not accept. Even though Richard had now returned full of contrition, his accusations had deeply wounded her. Perhaps there was even some

---

30   SB III, 360–71, here 369 (July 27, 1850).

unconscious mechanism of revenge at work on his part, since Minna had hurt him deeply by remaining silent for weeks on end in the late spring of 1849, when she had hesitated to follow him to Zurich.

Richard was touched by Minna's loyalty and her attachment to him, and in his autobiography he later wrote of how "our domestic life was soon marked by a tolerable happiness."[31] Minna also made an effort, because he was still the center of her life, despite the recent catastrophic events. Her spontaneous trip to Paris to find him—which was far from a trifling matter for her—will have impressed him accordingly. However, he still had not satisfied his longings for a muse who might understand him, who would steadfastly love him and be devoted to him. He had to come to terms with his bitter disappointment at Jessie. He had to occupy himself with other things. "I was really beside myself, and am now back to myself," he wrote. He also insisted in a letter to Uhlig that Minna was well, and "completely Helveticized."[32] Not only did he like the new apartment, but he also liked the furnishings. Minna had procured a large, broad divan and a carpet and had made various other improvements. Richard had asked for a green cloth rug over the desk and light green, silk curtains for his study. To make him feel comfortable in his new surroundings, Minna sewed him a comfortable dressing gown.

Richard now channeled his energies into conducting and writing. He conducted in the Zurich City Theater and the local concert hall, and read the complete manuscript of his aesthetic tract "Opera and Drama" to an interested circle of friends (he did so in a room in a restaurant, so that Minna would not have to provide food and drink for his guests). He completed this book in February 1851, but it took until November for it to be published, and even longer before he earned any money from it.

In the summer of 1850, Richard took Minna on an excursion to the Rigi, from where they enjoyed magnificent views of Lake Lucerne. In the fall, Hans von Bülow came to visit Wagner. He was still pondering his career options, and Richard took him under his wing. Hans also awakened Minna's maternal instincts. "At noon we eat at Wagner's, where the cooking is very good, as his wife has a thorough understanding of it," wrote Hans to his sister. Minna's friendly, obliging nature impressed him, as did her solicitude— such as when she once repaired his torn umbrella without saying a word about it.[33] But Richard's darker side now also came to the fore. It was at this

---

31   ML, 451.

32   SB III, 497–500, here 499 (November 9, 1850).

33   Glasenapp 1977, II, 449.

time that he wrote his fateful tract "Jewishness in Music," which positively oozes aggression, and in which he made a dreadful attempt to assign negative character traits to a whole religious group. "My resentment against the Jews is as necessary to my nature as gall is to blood," he wrote to Liszt.[34] Did he feel isolated because of being compelled to leave Germany? Had the emotional wounds left by the Jessie Laussot affair pushed him into seeking some belligerent means of venting his frustration? Did he hope to turn defeat into some strange victory in order to regain his inner equilibrium? Conveniently ignoring the fact that Jews had been officially excluded from participating in art until the 19th century, he now claimed that Jews were somehow inherently incapable of true creativity. For her part, Minna knew that Meyerbeer had recommended both *Rienzi* for performance in Dresden, and *Der fliegende Holländer* to the Berlin Court Theater. To be sure, she too cursed Meyerbeer on occasion, nor was she beyond inventing offensive expressions such as "Wasserjude" (literally: water Jew) for the director of the spa in Albisbrunn just outside Zurich (a term that greatly amused Richard). But overt anti-Semitism was not for her. In any case, she had a low opinion of Richard's essays. Once, when he read from his essays at what he termed his "rustic evening gatherings," the journalist Adolph Kolatschek fell asleep, and Georg Herwegh focused his attention instead on the punch. Minna keenly observed all this, and made sure to tell Richard about it.[35] Given the complex intellectual twists and turns of his writings, we can probably assume that her response will have been not dissimilar when Richard read them to her.

A lack of money continued to dog them. Minna's bitterness at Richard's careless manner with money was compounded by his refusal to accept a conducting engagement at the Zurich Opera, whose director had offered him 200 francs to do so. She wrote to Mathilde Schiffner about it:

> He finds it beneath his dignity to earn money, preferring to live on handouts or borrowed sums. [...] I sometimes almost cry my eyes out and am truly completely consumed by the grief that this man causes me. If only I knew a way out, I think I could overcome everything now, not least for the sake of my old parents, about whom I worry with no means of doing anything about it. To know that they have no support from me is something that gives me countless sleepless nights.[36]

---

34   SB III, 544 (April 8, 1851).

35   ML, 462.

36   Minna to Mathilde Schiffner, November 16, 1850 (RWA).

Minna now concocted a plan: Mathilde was to send her a letter pretending that Minna's father was very ill, and that her parents were begging Richard for help. "I have no scruples about it because it's nothing evil, and I hope that I'm not asking you in vain. You can insert an extra little letter in which you can tell me private secrets." She continued, as if crying out in pain: "Oh, Mathilde! If only things could work out, if only my wishes could be fulfilled and I were happy once again, how many more would be happy with me!"[37]

It was typical of Richard that he could discriminate against whole groups of people with a mean stroke of his pen, but would weep bitter tears if any harm came to one of his pets. However, the Wagners' animals were a substitute for the children they never had, and as such were much loved by both of them. When their adored parrot Papo became sick, Richard wanted to take it to a veterinarian, but postponed it because of work that tied him to his desk. The next morning the bird was dead. Even weeks later, he would still dream of Papo and wake up, weeping loudly.[38] Minna and Richard were already estranged in many ways, but their love for their pets still united them, and the tears they shed together when one of them died served to unite them in their grief.

In March 1851, Richard had to beg Liszt for money again:

If I am to undertake a larger creative task now, I have to have some security for my immediate future [...] otherwise I shall not be able to find the necessary degree of serenity nor be able to compose myself—if only because of my wife. In spite of all the excellent qualities that she possesses, she regrettably does not understand my innermost essence at all: in what I am and accomplish, this poor woman is unable to rise above those things that have to be endured for the sake of that which is higher. She only feels the bleakness of our situation, and is utterly unable to console herself for it by anything that I achieve. I am inwardly alien to her.[39]

He thus implied that Minna would feel their financial hardship less, if only she could recognize his artistic greatness. His later lovers Mathilde Wesendonck and Cosima von Bülow were wealthy enough to be able to concentrate entirely on the spiritual dimension of his work. As the person responsible for running their home, however, Minna inevitably had to insist on money to keep the household in decent shape. Their estrangement

---

37   Ibid.
38   SB IV, 168 (November 9, 1851).
39   SB III, 517–21, here 519 (March 9, 1851).

gnawed away at their relationship, for she will not have understood why her husband was planning an entire tetralogy that would take years to complete. She understandably preferred individual operas as sources of money.

Richard read the writings of Ludwig Feuerbach, and continued to write his essays. But he also made the first prose draft for *Der junge Siegfried* (Young Siegfried) and started noting down the initial musical motifs for the *Ring*. However, his compositional powers faltered, which was a source of distress to him. It was only when Liszt published an article about *Lohengrin* in the *Illustrierte Zeitung* in 1851 that Richard's creative block lifted. Liszt had conducted several performances of that opera in Weimar a year before, acknowledged its outstanding musical qualities, and now accordingly penned a hymn of praise about it. Wagner promptly wrote to thank his friend, telling him that he was "moved, delighted, gratified, and thrilled, to a point where I was swimming in tears. Suddenly, once again I knew no higher desire than to be an artist and to create works." He intended to get down to work on *Siegfrieds Tod* (which later became *Götterdämmerung*, the final opera in the *Ring* tetralogy) straightaway. In his elation, he also sketched out a plan for how Liszt might support him financially in the future. "Here and there, now and then, you will put aside a few pennies for me, and when I'm at my greatest need, you can help me out with just as much as you have at your disposal for your poor friend."[40]

In order to ease things for Richard, Minna had for quite some time been borrowing from her friend Mathilde back in Dresden. On one occasion in January 1850, Minna had to apologize for being behind with a repayment of 5 thalers. "I can't do without to the extent that my husband would have to suffer. So don't be angry, you will in any case receive the 5 thalers from me this year, if not sooner."[41] But she still owed this sum almost two years later, as she was sending all her spare money to her parents: "God, it almost breaks my heart, but they are poor, bashful people who are truly to be pitied."[42]

In May 1851, the Wagners finally received several pieces of good news at once. The vocal score of *Lohengrin* was going to be published soon, and this meant that they could pay off an outstanding debt on the grand piano that Minna had brought from Dresden. Richard was also promised a fee of 500 thalers for completing *Siegfrieds Tod*. All this helped to lift his spirits and renewed his desire to compose, especially since the worst of his money

---

40   SB III, 542–47, here 543–44 (April 18, 1851).
41   Minna to Mathilde Schiffner, January 26, 1850 (RWA).
42   Minna to Mathilde Schiffner, September 8, 1851 (RWA).

problems were now alleviated by an annual allowance of 800 thalers that was granted to him by Julie Ritter.

In July 1851, Richard walked from Zurich to St. Gallen via Rapperswil, Uznach, the Rickenpass, Wattwil, Lichtensteig, and Teufen in order to visit Karl Ritter, the son of Julie, and thence to Rorschach to meet his faithful friend Theodor Uhlig, who was visiting from Dresden. On the way home, the three men climbed the Säntis mountain (8,200 feet) and spent a night in an alpine hut. Their ascent of the highest mountain in Canton Appenzell afforded them magnificent views of the surrounding country. They took a mountain guide with them since there were no hiking trails in a modern sense that they could have followed. Minna did not join them. To be sure, she had climbed the Rigi with her husband just the previous summer, and, as she told Mathilde, she had endured a hard climb for four hours at a stretch. But her constitution would not have coped with Richard's forced marches, let alone an ascent that was scheduled to take two days. Her heart had deteriorated to such an extent that she soon would be unable to manage even the one-hour hike up the Uetliberg, the hill behind the city of Zurich. Richard would also have been unable to help her, because Uhlig was wearing inadequate footwear and kept slipping, while Ritter suffered from a fear of heights and had to be accompanied down by their mountain guide. Wagner and Uhlig descended alone without a guide on the Toggenburg side, which was not without its own risks.[43]

In the fall of 1851, Wagner began imagining a festival at which *Siegfrieds Tod* could be performed. He envisioned the third performance ending with the theater being torn down and its score burned. What might Minna have said when she heard this? Was she taking care of him, cooking for him, and serving him, only for him to invest his energies in creating a work that would be destroyed after three performances? By contrast, it was the repeated productions of *Rienzi, Holländer,* and *Tannhäuser* in assorted opera houses that were bringing the income they needed to survive. She will surely have expressed her disapproval of such self-defeating plans. For his part, Wagner knew that she adored his music, but was also less and less able to follow him on the artistic and intellectual paths that he had chosen for himself. Probably to reassure her, he gave her a new dress and hat for her birthday, taking the money for them from the royalties that Breitkopf & Härtel had paid him for the recent publication of his libretti for *Holländer, Tannhäuser,* and *Lohengrin.*

---

43   Rieger/Schroeder 2009, 52ff. See also Uhlig, 1913.

Richard's intense concentration on his work began to take its toll. Sitting at his desk for hours on end had again proved detrimental to his bowels, which now rebelled. It was at this time that he read a book that Uhlig had given him, namely *Wasser tuts freilich* (Water will do it, of course) by one J. H. Rausse. He was instantly enthusiastic and now became a fanatical adherent of Rausse's so-called hydrotherapy. It is only surprising that Wagner did not experience any lasting, negative consequences of the physical mortification that his subsequent strict water diets entailed. He gave up wine, beer, and coffee, and drank only water or cold milk. In the morning he drank a few glasses of water, then had Minna wash his whole body with cold water. Even when the winter was at its coldest, she had to light his way down to the lakefront with a lantern in the early morning so that he could submerge himself in the icy waters.[44] At lunchtime, he also either went down to swim in the lake or took a hip bath.

Richard now decided that a more intensive therapy was needed. In September 1851, to Minna's great concern, he began a ten-week course of treatment at the water cure institute at Albisbrunn on the edge of the Sihl Forest, some ten miles to the south of Zurich. "I have a stubborn enemy of water in my wife," he later wrote to Ernst Kietz in Paris, "who thinks that a water cure—like almost everything I take up—is exaggerated and stupid: I can't achieve anything with her through reason."[45] This time, however, reason was clearly on Minna's side, because Richard very nearly felt compelled to return home on his very first day at Albisbrunn. He was bored, and whiled away his time playing whist, dominoes, and billiards. The program of the institute sounds at best like an attempt to turn halfway healthy people into wholly sick ones. They were given a wet wrap at 5:30 a.m., were put in a cold tub at 7 a.m., and then taken for a walk. Breakfast was at 8 a.m. and consisted of dry bread and milk or water. After a short walk, they were given a cold compress. At 12 noon they were given a wet rubdown, took another short walk, and were given yet another cold compress. After lunch, the patients had to rest for an hour before being sent out to walk on their own for two hours. At 5 p.m. they were given another rubdown, and took another brief walk in the fresh air. This was followed by a hip bath at 6 p.m., a walk to warm up, and another compress. Dinner was at 7 p.m. and again comprised dry bread and water. The patients then indulged in a round of whist. After a fourth and final compress for the day, they went to bed at 10

---

44   ML, 476.
45   SB IV, 372–73, here 373 (May 1852).

Figure 5.2. Franz Hegi / Salomon Brunner: *The Albisbrunn Water Institute*, ca. 1845. Zentralbibliothek Zürich, Graphic Collection.

p.m. Richard's bowels began to function better in the wake of all this internal and external hydration plus his daily physical exercise. After six days, Richard even began to fantasize that he might indeed be able to "detoxify" his body—a notion that continues to have its adherents in our own day—and he was delighted at the notion of having "sweated out" poisons that had lurked within him: "and then the bad blood substances came out that the sulphur had only forced back into me. I then truly knew that something evil was in my body," he wrote to Minna from Albisbrunn.[46]

At the beginning of his cure, Richard was unhappy that Minna delayed visiting him on account of inclement weather—he had been "incredibly looking forward" to seeing her. She had planned to visit him together with friends from Zurich, but he was annoyed at this as he wanted to see her alone. He wrote to her that she ought to just get in the mail coach, spend the night with him and experience "how you can enjoy yourself with me."[47] It pained him that all the

---

46   SB IV, 167–69, here 167 (November 9, 1851).
47   SB IV, 122–23, here 123 (October 5, 1851).

other guests had already received visitors. But he was conveniently overlooking the fact that Minna was fully occupied with moving yet again, this time to Zeltweg 11. Her task was complicated by Richard's desire to have some new furnishings too. Their previous apartment had been too far out of town, and since there was no convenient means of transportation to the city center, it had proven too troublesome for friends to come and visit. Continuing money worries made Minna consider giving away her formal satin dress, because it needed altering but she did not have the necessary money. Richard was at least able to have 3 louis d'or sent to her by the Zurich music shop Hug, but he asked her not to trouble him with any bills: "You know that I cannot do sums at all."[48]

When Minna realized that Richard was suffering from her continued absence, she went straight to him. She was laden with many gifts including cigars, nuts, stockings, a brush, and a knife, and she succeeded in dispelling his depression in one fell swoop. She indeed paid regular visits to him from now on, and on one occasion even stayed for four days. The games played at Albisbrunn were for money, and Minna lost some while she was there—but Richard wrote of how he aimed to win it back after her departure. His lines display familiarity and affection. He runs through a gamut of pet names; she is his "dear Mietz," "Muzius," "dear Mienel," his "good dear wife," "my good, dear—bad, naughty—wife!" Another time he writes: "Oh, you good woman, you've written me such a beautiful letter! What a pity it is that I have to answer it like this, and that I cannot thank you for it in person today, as you had imagined!"[49] They sent each other doggerel for their mutual amusement, such as the following:

Minna, schicke mir bald Strümpfe!
Hier giebt es nichts wie lauter Sümpfe!
Davon bekomm ich nasse Klümpfe!
Im Whist fehlen mir auch die Trümpfe!
Drum bringe Du mich wieder auf die Strümpfe!
Schick' mir nur ein Paarer Fümpfe!

[Minna, send me stockings soon! There's nothing here but marshes! They're giving me wet clods! In whist I also lack trumps! So help me take to my heels! Send me a pair of fives![50]]

48   SB IV, 159–60, here 159 (November 2, 1851).
49   SB IV, 119–121, here 119 (September 28, 1851).
50   SB IV, 163 (November 3, 1851). Wagner's wordplay, with its twisted end rhymes on "-ümpfe", does not allow for precise translation.

As for Minna's fears of being confronted with new, unpleasant facts or eccentric ideas like his water cures, Richard also resorted to humor to assuage her:

> So you think I've undertaken something weird and wonderful every few years, and are only worried about what I'll fall for next year? I can tell you immediately: I hope that next year we will make a really lovely trip to Italy *together*. Would that be such a great misfortune? [...] I am already counting the days, and I tell myself every day: tomorrow it will only be so many days to go. You can see from this just how much I'm looking forward to home and to you again.[51]

Richard asked her to set up a bathtub somewhere, despite their apartment being cramped already. He would only need to immerse himself briefly, so it would be fine if the tub were high instead of long. He wanted it placed in Natalie's room—though for once he was realistic, and admitted that she would no doubt curse him for it. But all in all, his letters reveal no vestiges of his earlier desire to separate from Minna. His brief affair with Jessie was apparently well behind him, and Richard even made a salacious allusion to Minna when explaining how he planned to continue his water therapy at home: "If necessary, you can or must give me my wraps, though I can't have these wraps regularly—for therapeutic purposes—at home with you, because certain—hm! hm!—things are quite incompatible with it." He closed by joking: "Don't flirt too much, it could harm you!"[52]

Richard nevertheless still felt an inner emptiness that would only be filled the next year when he encountered the rapturous Mathilde Wesendonck. For the time being, both he and Minna believed that they had ushered in a new beginning that was destined to lead to success. He cautiously tried to convince Minna once again of his artistic mission, for the sake of which he ought to be allowed all necessary liberties:

> Take me as I am, and let me do what I want and enjoy: don't submit me to little torments to force me to do something that I don't want to do and can't do. But on the other hand, be assured that I will always do something that somehow gives pleasure to others and satisfies my inner self.—In this manner, if we do not torment each other, we can still lead the loveliest life that circumstances can possibly allow us.[53]

---

51   SB IV, 167–69, here 168 (November 9, 1851); emphasis in original.
52   SB IV, 164–65, here 164 (November 7, 1851).
53   SB IV, 167–69, here 168–69 (November 9, 1851).

Richard returned from his cure on November 23, 1851, just in time for their fifteenth wedding anniversary. Afterwards, as was his wont, he began to proselytize for the blessings of hydrotherapy among all his friends and acquaintances in an effort to recruit them too. So great was his enthusiasm that he exclaimed in a letter to Liszt: "Truly, all these parasitic growths in our life today emerge from only one source—our ruined digestion!"[54] Liszt—secure, urbane, and a lover of good food—will have simply ignored this, but what was Minna to do when Richard spouted forth such claims? Her digestion was still functioning perfectly well; it was her heart that was causing her problems. She will have complained about all the work that Richard's return placed upon her shoulders, because she had to wrap him up in a wet towel in the morning, then unwrap him again and rub him dry after his bath. Another rubdown followed at noon, then a hip bath on the evening that was not allowed to exceed 10 degrees Celsius. Richard advised her to hire someone robust enough to fetch all the water he needed, and who could also deal with scouring out the bathtub afterwards. Minna found this water therapy abominable: "Once Richard becomes enthusiastic about something, he has to spoon it out to the very bottom, even if means the end of him," she wrote to Johanna Wagner.[55] Minna detested anything fanatical. Richard, on the other hand, delighted in instructing his friends, and promptly got into a bitter dispute with Sulzer. The latter was sober by nature, given to critical questioning, and tried to make it clear to Richard that there was no scientific basis for all the supposed watery wisdom that he had acquired, which meant it should be regarded as merely subjective. Richard, however, could not let this be, and felt insulted. He became increasingly heated in his reasoning. At a lunch invitation chez Wagner, Sulzer became embroiled in such a harsh argument that he simply walked out. Richard was only able to calm the waters by means of a conciliatory letter in which he admitted to having "acted in the most aggravating fashion, as can happen on account of my passionate nature." He vowed to mend his ways.[56] All the same, he could not refrain from advising his friend to read specific chapters in Rausse's book, including his "Treatise on absorbing and depositing toxins." Minna had become fond of Sulzer since he had stood by her during the Laussot affair, and she must have been infuriated by Richard's dispute with him.

---

54   SB IV, 183–93, here 192 (November 20, 1851).
55   November 1, 1852 (RWA).
56   SB IV, 223–25, here 223 (December 15, 1851).

But Richard continued to adhere to his ascetic way of life, so she had to keep serving him his dry bread with milk in the morning. He also now instructed her to procure a spit on which they might roast meat—he had presumably read somewhere that this was the best way of cooking it. When guests arrived to congratulate them on their wedding anniversary, they naturally drank wine to toast them. Afterwards, Richard complained bitterly to Theodor Uhlig: "They boozed as usual, and my disgust at this wine-guzzling, without which these unhappy people are completely unable to get into the mood, has fully convinced me that I am truly cured."[57] We do not know whether or not he allowed Minna to imbibe with them (after all, she was rather fond of champagne). However, Wagner finally abandoned his abstinence by 1854 at the latest. We can be sure of this because he wrote to Minna on July 5 of that year that he was having a game of whist with his male friends, but that he would be taking care not to get a hangover afterwards.

Minna wrote to tell Mathilde Schiffner that Richard had now been made an honorary member of the Swiss Music Society. She was also happy with things at the City Theater in Zurich. They were sometimes given free tickets, though they were leaving them unused for the moment because Minna had to mend their clothes. She fervently wished that Richard would return to composing, because this seemed to her to offer the possibility of building on his previous successes (quite unlike his current activity of writing essays). What's more, she loved his music. Minna closed her letter by thanking Mathilde for providing Dresden gossip, which she undoubtedly will have passed on to Richard without hesitation: "The story about Reissiger really amused me, as did the one about Devrient. Thank you for that."[58]

Although Richard almost never mentioned Jessie again, she remained vivid in his memory for many years. Seven years later, long after he had fallen for the charms of Mathilde Wesendonck, he wrote to Emilie Ritter as follows:

But could you believe that I could forget J., and that I could become indifferent to her? What I have heard about her was only ever news about her outer life: can't you tell me anything about her inner life? What I have learned about her in recent years is sufficient to make me feel the highest degree of sympathy for her. While I once believed that she had hurt me in a hateful, inconsolable way, I have now ultimately understood that she had only temporarily succumbed to an extraordinarily arduous ordeal.[59]

---

57 SB IV, 201–204, here 202 (November 29, 1851).
58 Minna to Mathilde Schiffner, November 20, 1851 (RWA).
59 SB IX, 83–85, here 84 (December 25, 1857).

And what about Minna? Perhaps, in her quiet moments, she took to heart one of the numerous letters in which Richard had so eloquently assured her of his love for her, two years earlier: "So I shall spare no effort, no step, no matter how repugnant it may be to me, as long as it brings me up to where I can choose freely, and what I choose—and this I know—will always be to be with you!"[60]

---

60   SB III, 65–71, here 66 (June 4, 1849).

Chapter Six

"That good, foolish man ..."

Exile in Zurich, 1852–54

When New Year 1852 arrived, Minna had no real conviction that it might bode well. She simply hoped that the events of the previous year would not be repeated. The winter was bleak, but things did seem to look up as it drew to a close. In March and April 1852, Richard was able to report to his niece Franziska that Minna was enjoying herself more than she ever had in Dresden. She had "girlfriends and entertainment," he wrote.[1] She had made friends among the women in Zurich and appreciated the entertainments that the city offered. He, by contrast, was inwardly unhappy, even despite having indulged in "wanton luxury" that same spring, buying the finest fabrics and furniture in order to recreate "the fantasies of 1001 Nights" in his study, as he wrote to Julie Ritter.[2] There were several reasons for his general dissatisfaction. He felt he lacked appreciation and encouragement for his work, and he suffered from hypersensitive nerves. Most of all, he longed for a woman in his life who might provide him with unqualified understanding. In January 1852, he wrote to Uhlig: "I would give *all my art* to regain my youth, health, nature, an unreservedly loving wife and able children! Go on, take my art! And give me the others!"[3] He had often enough emphasized that his artistic work was the most important thing in his life, but what mattered to him now was woman (though the two were in any case intertwined for him).

The Wagners were nevertheless managing to settle into their new life in Switzerland. The brief Swiss civil war of 1847 (the "Sonderbund" war) was now a few years past, having ended with a victory for the (largely Protestant)

---

1   SB IV, 322–24, here 324 (March 21, 1852).
2   SB IV, 331–36, here 336 (April 4, 1852).
3   SB IV, 245–49, here 249 (January 12, 1852).

liberals over the (mostly Catholic) conservatives. The modern federal state of Switzerland was founded in its wake in 1848. Zurich, originally a tiny town, would soon become the largest city in the country. There was a sense of a new beginning, and these years were characterized by expansion and building work. The city walls from the 13th century had already been demolished in 1811, and by 1829 almost all the old towers and gates of the city had disappeared. The last remnants of the fortifications were removed in around 1860. The cityscape had thus expanded rapidly in just half a century. Industry and commerce were established, many imposing buildings had already been erected by 1840, and the volume of trade increased. Wagner benefited personally in many ways from this modernizing surge. The importance of trade meant that transport routes expanded. The first railway in Switzerland was established in 1847 between Zurich and nearby Baden, and the network thereafter grew continuously. The stagecoach connections between Zurich and other cities were also soon supplemented by steamboats on Lake Zurich. Private citizens were thus getting more mobile—and they included Wagner, who utilized the improved transport infrastructure to help him explore the wider country.

This economic boom brought with it a corresponding increase in culture, and Zurich began to attract more and more intellectuals and talented people of all kinds. The Wagners also kept up a lively social life. Richard and Minna attended various opera performances such as Mozart's *Die Zauberflöte* and Marschner's *Der Vampyr* (The Vampire). As the wife of an increasingly famous conductor, composer, and writer, Minna will have been an object of interest to the ladies of the Zurich upper classes, and she accordingly found acceptance in Zurich society. The local landscape thrilled her, and she described it to Mathilde Schiffner in an effort to persuade her to come and visit:

> You only need a day from here to go up the Rigi. It's just a four-hour strenuous walk from the foot of the Rigi, and then you see the sunset, if it isn't overcast, and the sunrise the next morning. When the weather is fine you can see the whole of the Bernese Oberland, which is probably the most magnificent thing of its kind that one can see: all around the majestic snow-covered mountains, everywhere such wonders. You can hardly believe your eyes.[4]

---

4   Minna to Mathilde Schiffner, March 22, 1852 (RWA, also Zentralbibliothek Zürich, Mus. Ms. L 367).

As a former actor, Minna also had a particularly keen eye and ear for the artistic offerings in Zurich. Richard discussed these performances with her, and since the quality of them had by now improved, she often went out. But we also know that she had opportunities to go dancing, because Richard mentions in February 1852 that she had gone to a ball while he stayed at home. Nevertheless, Minna was a down-to earth woman who still felt attached to their former life in Dresden, just as she had found it so difficult to leave Paris before that.

Richard was busy with preparations for a production of his *Tannhäuser* in Berlin, and drew his niece, Johanna Wagner—now a famous singer—into the negotiations. She had a ten-year contract with the Berlin Court Opera, and her father Albert had been commissioned by the theater management to negotiate with Richard about having his work performed there. All this kept Minna busy, too. She thanked Johanna for the gift of a dress, and wrote a warm letter to her in November to assure her, both that she was following her artistic successes with much interest, and that she was always pleased when she saw her praised in the press:

> Regrettably, my dearest wish—to be able to admire you [in person] in your artistic work—will remain denied to me for a long time, although my husband is very much encouraging me to accept Frommann's invitation to visit her [in Berlin] and live with her in her "nutshell" [...]. This is compounded by my boundless fear of how *Tannhäuser* will be received; if only I could hide myself in a mousehole to be able to hear and see you [...] then my greatest wish would be fulfilled.[5]

With regard to the discussions about the planned production of *Tannhäuser*, she asked Johanna to show a degree of understanding for her husband. He was suffering from his banishment, she said, because he could not go to Berlin in person to direct the rehearsals and the performances. "You must have patience and forbearance with him, as I also ask your dear, good father, to whom I send my warmest regards, to show tolerance and patience towards his restless brother!"[6]

In 1852, Richard met Otto and Mathilde Wesendonck. This was an encounter that would prove fateful for his future work. Mathilde (1828–1902) was the daughter of the entrepreneur and Royal Commercial Advisor Karl Luckemeyer and his wife Johanna, née Stein (who in turn was the

---

5   November 1, 1852 (RWA).

6   Ibid.

daughter of a banker). Mathilde thus came from the upper classes. She had married Otto Wesendonck (1815–96) in 1848. He had traveled to New York for business purposes and on his return had been appointed the European representative of his US silk import business. It became one of the most powerful in New York, and made him a wealthy man. Mathilde's real first name was Agnes, though she had abandoned it for Otto's sake, since his first wife—also called Mathilde—had died suddenly on their honeymoon, and he had asked his second fiancée to take her name.[7] The fact that Agnes acquiesced in this strange request suggests that both she and her future husband had a poorly developed sense of self-esteem. In 1849, she bore a son, Paul, though he died just a few months later. Her only daughter, Myrrha, was born in 1852, then Guido followed in 1855 (he died three years later), Karl in 1857, and their last child Hans in 1862. Maternal duties were thus a significant reason for Mathilde's steadfastness in her marriage.

In the absence of an apartment befitting their station, the Wesendoncks resided for the time being in the elegant Hotel Baur au Lac in Zurich. On January 20, 1852, they attended a concert in the Zurich concert hall (the Casino), at which Wagner conducted Beethoven's *Egmont Overture* and 8th Symphony. Mathilde was a gifted young woman with an interest in literature and the arts, and she was immediately attracted by Richard's conducting. The second movement of the 8th Symphony henceforth became her favorite piece. Six years later it was included in a private concert in the Wesendoncks' new villa—and for Mathilde and Richard it was quite possibly a work that reminded them both of their first encounter.

After a second concert, in February 1852, in which Wagner again conducted works by Beethoven, Mathilde felt she needed to tell the conductor in person of her enthusiasm. This ignited a spark that would later become a conflagration. She was a young, attractive, receptive, artistically ambitious woman; he was a man who felt emotionally and sexually deprived, was plagued by illness, and highly sensitive to feminine charms. He was fifteen years older than she, had an air of importance about him, and knew how to dress well. His eloquence and erudition also set him apart from the rest of Zurich society. Mathilde found this aspect of him exhilarating, as she too was possessed of literary ambitions. She asked to be allowed to attend the rehearsals for his next concert on March 16, which Richard was only too happy to grant. "I will never forget the impression that the first rehearsal of the *Tannhäuser* Overture made on me under his direction," she later wrote,

---

7   Walton, in Langer/Walton 2002, 94.

Figure 6.1. Clementine Stockar-Escher: *Minna Wagner with Peps the dog*, watercolor, Zurich 1853. Nationalarchiv der Richard-Wagner-Stiftung, Bayreuth.

"in the dark hall of the old *Kaufhaus* in Zurich. It was a frenzy of happiness, a revelation; both listeners and musicians were electrified."[8] She felt a rapturous enthusiasm that moved her to violent tears (the "frenzy" was thus her own). Mathilde's recollections reveal an erotic undertone that had been intensified when she had discussed the overture afterwards with Richard himself. Mathilde interpreted Tannhäuser's fate as a rallying cry against hypocrisy. Could anything better have happened to Richard? A woman who rejected hypocrisy in matters of the heart was the very opposite of what he saw in Minna—who, despite her life as an actor and her own past transgressions, still adhered to bourgeois notions about infidelity. Minna had no idea of any of this. She was delighted with the immense success of the overture in the concert, noting that the musicians were qualitatively beneath their peers in Dresden, but made up for it with such hard work and goodwill that Richard had enjoyed rehearsing it with them.

> The public was quite astonished to hear something so entirely new, Richard was once again summoned to his conductor's rostrum by a storm of applause, and there were incessant shouts of "encore," though this was impossible because the musicians had already played a great deal and still had to play a symphony by Bethhofen [*sic*] under Richard's direction.[9]

Richard found once more in Mathilde what he had experienced two years before with Jessie Laussot, if only briefly back then: a woman who was seized by enthusiasm for him and who was moreover educated in artistic and aesthetic matters; someone who understood him deeply, who listened to him, and admired him unconditionally. A particular stroke of luck for Wagner was the fact that Mathilde also had a wealthy husband who found his wife's enthusiasm infectious.

All this obviously did Richard good. A few days after the rehearsal that had so enthused Mathilde, he wrote to Uhlig: "It is always the 'eternal feminine' that fills me with sweet delusions and warm shivers of lust for life. A moist, shining eye of a woman often infuses me again with new hope."[10] Mathilde's convulsive tears made him deeply happy. He wrote in similar terms to Julie Ritter, claiming that the impact of his music had "suddenly, as if in a tempest, opened up hearts to me whose dull beating must until then

---

8   Schwabe 1988, 237.
9   Minna to Mathilde Schiffner, March 22, 1852 (Zentralbibliothek Zürich Mus. Ms. L 367).
10   SB IV, 297–302, here 301 (February 26, 1852).

have been completely indifferent towards me. That I am speaking of women goes without saying."[11] Finally, Liszt also had to be kept informed that there was a very lovely woman among Richard's Zurich friends. Richard initially described his feelings in cautious terms, but a year later, in 1853, they had fully blossomed: "Oh, I'm in *love*! and am animated by such a divine *faith* that I do not even need *hope*!"[12] As a man and an artist, he delighted in Mathilde's adoration, and even began to initiate her into his composing plans. In her later memoir of him, she wrote: "Thus I came to Zurich quite uninstructed. Wagner himself called me a white sheet of paper, and took it upon himself to write on it."[13]

Since Mathilde loved Beethoven, Richard played her the sonatas and explained them to her. Whenever she wanted to attend a concert where he would be conducting music by Beethoven, he would play her the symphony in question on the piano in advance, over and again until she knew everything well. He taught her the rudiments of counterpoint and was delighted when she was able to follow him, being inspired by his own enthusiasm. It was from him that she learned much about Buddhism, and he shared his thoughts with her when he visited her in her hotel for tea. Years later, she revisited all this in poems and stories that she wrote herself. The hierarchy between them was naturally a given—after all, she was the "white sheet of paper" on which he wrote—but all the same, this exhilaration of experiencing a kindred spirit was what ultimately enabled him to return to composition. Whenever he read the libretti for his *Ring* to an interested audience and introduced them to his prose writings, Mathilde was always there.

But Mathilde was not merely a passive, gushing woman: she possessed immense drive herself. She wanted to do something for the composer she idolized, and so played a part in making possible a production of *Der fliegende Holländer* in Zurich. Her gentleness belied a dogged persistence, and her status as the wife of a wealthy industrialist opened doors for her. Richard took on the task of conducting his opera, which caused a local sensation when it was given to full houses in April 1852. Mathilde saw the work four times in a row and was surely deeply moved—after all, it tells the story of a lonely man redeemed through the unconditional fidelity of a young, pure woman. But Minna will also have attended all the performances with a sense of great satisfaction. The response in the press was

---

11   SB IV, 331–36, here 332 (April 4, 1852).
12   SB V, 463–64, here 463 (November 14, 1853).
13   Heintz 1896, 92.

tremendous. To be sure, Wagner had his detractors, but they were this time heavily outnumbered by his admirers.

For Richard, this event signaled a realization that he was in love—and it was a love that would hold him spellbound for years to come. Six years later, he wrote of it to his sister Clara:

> What has sustained me [...] comforted me and also bolstered me to endure life with Minna—despite the enormous differences in our character and nature—has been the love of that young woman who initially, and for a long time, drew tentatively towards me, doubting, hesitant and shy, but then ever more assertively and confidently. Because there could never be any talk of a union between us, our deep affection took on that sad, wistful character that keeps at bay everything that is base and ignoble, and only recognizes the source of joy as existing in the well-being of one another.[14]

It remains unclear what Wagner here means by "base and ignoble," given that he was actually an advocate of the natural ecstasy of physical love, as we can see in his depictions of Tristan and Isolde, Brünnhilde and Siegfried, and Siegmund and Sieglinde. He was presumably thinking of desires that were limited purely to the sexual. In the years that followed his encounter with Mathilde in 1852, he enjoyed the happiness of being truly loved and of having a muse to inspire him, but also frustration and sadness because he was unable to suppress forever his desire for physical union with her. Mathilde probably also awakened wistful memories in him of Jessie Laussot, for he wrote to Julie Ritter of how it had become clear to him that there could be no more happiness for him on earth: "Yes—dear friend, until that event in my life of which you know so well, I was still young: then at a stroke, I grew old [...] I sank back into the world of fantasy and imagination."[15] Since Mathilde Wesendonck was recently married and had a family, he realized—realistically, for once—that he had no hope of supplanting her husband.

Minna had her suspicions, but at first simply accepted things as they were. In 1858, she confided to Mathilde Schiffner that "when it comes to indulging men, I am just as enlightened as other women, and have already often looked away, not wanting to notice things, after all, I have been blindly tripping alongside [him] for six whole years."[16] It thus did not take long for her

---

14   SB X, 27–32, here 27 (August 20, 1858).
15   SB IV, 431–33, here 432 (August 7, 1852).
16   Minna to Mathilde Schiffner, August 2, 1858 (RWA).

to grasp what was happening between Richard and Mathilde, even if she had not yet comprehended the intensity of their relationship.

Everyone involved endeavored to retain a semblance of normality throughout. For her part, Mathilde Wesendonck corresponded with Minna in a friendly manner—such as in a letter of July 4, 1853, when she reported on a family holiday she had just enjoyed with Otto and the children in Bad Ems. But there were also passages in this letter that might have alarmed Minna, such as when Mathilde thanked her for sending her a piano sonata that Richard had composed:

> For the last few days, I have once more been the owner of a piano and am playing with increasing delight this magnificent work that has so undeservedly been shared with me. I well feel that I am only able to reproduce the merest shadow of it, but even this gives me infinite joy. Will I be able to fully fathom "Do you know what will come"? I do not know—probably not until the Master himself reveals its meaning to me through his playing. Only then will the work receive its true consecration. Until then, I shall delve into it to see if I can grasp it.[17]

Minna will not have taken kindly to such a reverential tone, with Mathilde voluntarily relegating herself to the status of a child while exalting the "Master." It was clear that these words were really meant for Richard, who could look forward to spending time at the piano with the woman he adored.

Richard now had to find a vacation apartment for friends. He located something suitable in the "Rinderknecht" guesthouse in the village of Fluntern on the Zürichberg (today a suburb of Zurich). Fluntern affords a wonderful view of the Limmat valley, the Zurich lake and the distant Glarus Alps, and Richard so liked the landscape there that he spontaneously decided to rent an apartment there himself from May to July 1852. He had meanwhile ceased seeking physical salvation exclusively in cold ablutions and compresses and sought it now instead in sun and fresh air. This summer move was made somewhat easier because the Wagners did not have to take all their furniture with them. But Minna was still dissatisfied, as she preferred staying put. They had to endure the blazing sun with no shade nearby, and there was no opportunity to take a pleasant walk unless you climbed uphill. This was

---

17   Translation of the original as given in the German edition of Burrell, 481; the English edition of Burrell gives a translation of this letter on 362–63. "Do you know what will come?" was the motto that Richard had placed at the head of the sonata, a quotation from the Norns' Scene in the *Ring*.

their fifth move in the space of almost three years, and they had exhausted Minna. She wrote to Mathilde Schiffner that she had endured enough hardship and envied those who had a permanent home. She was looking forward to her friend's visit, and begged her not to reverse her decision to come:

> Obviously, you must stay with me—many patient sheep can fit in a shed, as they say […] right after receiving this little letter, you can pack your things together and come straightaway, if your time permits. We can be free and easy since Richard isn't here. You can sleep in his bed, and you can be here in three days.[18]

At the same time, Minna was doing her best to make things nice for her "hubby." On his birthday, May 22, 1852, she invited Bernhard Spyri, Johann Jakob Sulzer, and Wilhelm Baumgartner to dinner at their holiday apartment. The Wesendoncks came too. Minna roasted veal on a spit, and Mathilde was impressed by her culinary skills.[19] They returned to the Zeltweg in July, which once again meant work and upheaval for Minna.

1852 also brought a welcome addition to the Wagners' circle of friends in the shape of Eliza Wille and her husband François. They lived in a stately country house in neighboring Mariafeld above Lake Zurich, sheltered picturesquely among walnut, linden, and maple trees. Dr. François Wille had worked as a journalist in Hamburg and had represented Schleswig-Holstein in the democratic German parliament in St. Paul's Church in Frankfurt back in 1848. The Willes enjoyed a dignified lifestyle and had a well-stocked wine cellar whose contents often helped to fuel fiery discussions among their guests. After he had abandoned his period of water-cure-induced abstinence, Richard liked to drink an obligatory half-bottle of champagne "to refresh his nerves," as he put it. He sometimes even invited himself to stay overnight, since it was a two-hour walk each way from Zurich to Mariafeld and back. Minna often joined him, and their other guests also included Georg Herwegh, a popular poet of the time who had taken part in the failed 1848 revolution in Germany, and whose subsequent exile brought him to Zurich in 1851.

Eliza Wille was a highly educated woman and an author in her own right. Nevertheless, as she later wrote:

> The customs of the time, to which I owed my upbringing and education, considered it presumptuous for a woman to talk about things that she knew super-

---

18　Minna to Mathilde Schiffner July 12, 1852 (RWA).
19　Cabaud 2017, 53.

ficially, without ever having delved to the bottom of them.—From my earliest youth I had read much, infinitely much [...] but neither my father nor the other men whom I revered would have reacted welcomingly, had I revealed my knowledge [...]. A know-it-all, a bluestocking! The male nature dreads this; all graces flee from it.[20]

While the men chatted about literary and philosophical topics, she was required to keep quiet and was not to interfere in what they knew. Educated women were to be kept in check, and all power to make decisions lay solely with men. However, Eliza many years later did not miss the opportunity to commit to paper her reminiscences of Wagner.

Richard enjoyed the intellectually stimulating atmosphere chez Wille, for he was always enthusiastic about new ideas, often advocating them with a passion until the next idea seized his imagination. One example was his conviction of the benefits of "water cures," which he urged on his friends so vigorously that it ended in intense arguments. In her memoir of Wagner, Eliza recalled with irony the conversations that ensued after he had discovered Schopenhauer, whose ideas also left their mark on his operas:

> Wagner possessed incredibly quick powers of comprehension and had soon flown through Schopenhauer's works. He and Herwegh marveled at how the riddles of the world had here been solved by renouncing it, and by means of asceticism—that had to be the goal of mankind! But renunciation of the world and the virtues of the saints could only be empty noise for men who actually needed the world for their works and for their continued existence, and who were unwilling to spurn or scorn the enjoyments that life offered.[21]

Richard was especially prone to be overwhelmed by new ideas when they coincided with experiences in his own life. It was under the guise of abstract philosophy that he now sought to legitimize his love for Mathilde Wesendonck. Eliza was friends with Mathilde, and remembered it well:

> It was in general a time of unclear ideas and confused opinions about relations in the family and the duties of life. The honor of man, whose fidelity was rooted in his acceptance of duty, and the humility of woman, subordinating herself to man in the deep strength of her love, were all supposed to stand back before the divine rights of passion![22]

---

20   Wille 1982, 32–33.

21   Ibid., 33.

22   Ibid., 34.

Eliza clearly had Mathilde in mind here, even though she refrained from mentioning her name. Since Richard himself was bound in marriage, and since the woman he loved was both a wife and a mother, his insistence on the rights of passion was thus doubly disreputable according to the ideas of the time.

Richard felt burned out after his recent work, and so for the summer of 1852 he planned to relax on a trip through the Swiss Alps to Italy—a country he had long wished to get to know. Although tourist travel was in vogue in the mid-19th century and there was an extensive mail coach network (soon to be replaced by the railroad), he decided to do most of his traveling on foot. After a five-day walk through Lucerne and the Bernese Oberland, he hiked over the Griespass (8,000 feet above sea level) into Italy. He went via Domodossola to the Lago Maggiore, where he took a boat to Locarno via the Borromean Islands and Pallanza. He then swung south again to Lugano. On a whim, he wrote to Minna and asked her to join him. She promptly agreed, and he asked her to "pack your 3 sets of stockings and 2 vests, get Peps and take him with you in a mail coach."[23] He was very much looking forward to seeing her again. Georg Herwegh and François Wille also joined him the next day, but they stayed only for three days, and together they all visited the area around Lugano, the Lago Maggiore and the Borromean Islands.

After Wille and Herwegh had left, Minna and Richard went on to Domodossola with Peps. Then they took the Simplon Pass back into Switzerland and traveled on through the Rhône valley to Martigny in Canton Valais. All the guest houses were full, however, as Wagner later recalled in his memoirs: "We could find no accommodations in the overcrowded hotels and were obliged to exploit a love affair between a postilion and a maid-servant to obtain clandestine shelter in a private house, whose owners were temporarily away."[24] From Martigny, they proceeded south, spending the night in the Hotel de la Tête Noire in the village of Trient (not to be confused with the city in Italy), and then crossed the border into France. At Chamonix they visited the so-called Sea of Ice and La Flégère, from where they could see Mont Blanc. Minna slipped there and injured her leg, which meant she could only limp along for several days. They continued through the Arve valley up to Geneva, and from there traveled back to Zurich via Lausanne and Bern. Since Minna already had a heart condition, this long journey must have been extremely strenuous for her, though Richard will presumably have

---

23   SB IV, 413–16, here 414 (July 21, 1852).
24   ML, 487.

tried to spare her too much exertion by covering much of the journey by coach. He, too, was exhausted at the end of their mighty tour.

Minna proved a charming hostess who knew how to entertain the visitors who came to see them on the Zeltweg. Richard was also sociable, and their circle of friends gladly accepted invitations to their home. After a day's work, it lifted his spirits to be able to come together with people who were clever and understanding. However, his everyday life was burdened by his neuroveg-etative diseases (skin rashes and constipation) and by his tendency to depres-sion and irritability. Herwegh had admonished Minna to compel Richard to drink alcohol again, and he gradually reaccustomed himself to drinking wine, coffee and tea. Minna dearly wished his operas to be performed. For all his protestations that he wanted nothing to do with the outside world, she knew from experience just how important it was to him to enjoy successful performances and good reviews. Mathilde Schiffner attended a performance of *Tannhäuser* in Dresden on October 26, 1852, and reported back to Minna about it. Minna's reply reveals that she was well informed about the state of performances in Germany. "Oddly enough," she wrote,

> we remained for several days without any news of *Tannhäuser*'s reception except for your report. Our only friends, Fischer, Heine, Uhlig had relied on each other [to report back to us], until at last poor, sick Uhlig wrote to us. So you, my dear Mathilde, have won the victory of being the first to break the anxious silence in such a lovely way. Thank you, thank you again for that!
>
> Those dear hicks writing in the *Dresdener Anzeiger* still can't cope with the fact that the Court Opera has once more performed an opera by their head scoundrel, and it's precisely this opposition that ought to move Lüttichau to bring *Lohengrin* too this winter. Scores of *Tannhäuser* have already been obtained for performance this winter at the following theaters: Prague, Rostock, Riga, Frankfurt, Cologne, Düsseldorf, Berlin. It has already been given with the greatest of applause in Wiesbaden and Breslau—in the latter it was even given 12 times in 4 weeks to packed houses. It seems as if Wagner's music is finally having its breakthrough. May God grant that these pleasing successes have an invigorating effect on his spirit and his health, so that I, his nearest, don't have to suffer so terribly from his restlessness and his moods. To be sure, my dear friend, I often have to summon up all my reason and strength so that I don't lose my patience. But I do believe that I also suffer from my nerves; sometimes I am overcome by weeping, against which I can do nothing at all until the well of tears closes again of its own accord—and this only hap-pens as a result of his eternal goading and agitation.
>
> In February, Richard wants to go with me to Paris to take a cure under the supervision of a doctor he knows, and I dread it! We will return here in the spring: in general, Zurich ought to become a home for us in every aspect of

life, even if anarchy should ever overtake it, which I doubt for my part [...] Natalie is barely a help to me, and looking after my husband is like having 4 little children to care for. Even the two baths he takes each day in the apartment need to be warmed up and require a lot of effort.[25]

Minna went on to list some of the daily chores she struggled with. Early in the morning she had to rub Richard down, then prepare a shower bath for him a few hours later, at 18 degrees Celsius, and rub him down again. In the evening she washed him and rubbed him with oil. Cooking took a lot of time, as he was currently eating only game. She had to prepare two different meals, as she only cooked inexpensive fare for the servants, Natalie, and herself. Meanwhile, visitors might arrive, and looking after them was again her task, especially when Richard was working. There was also plenty to sew and embroider.

In early November 1852, Richard finished the libretto for his *Rheingold* and undertook a long-planned trip to the Alps with François Wille and Georg Herwegh. By mid-December, the entire libretti for his new tetralogy had been completed—a remarkable achievement. "While Richard also has his moods, under which I suffer terribly, it is always on account of his illness, and then a moment comes again when you can forgive him. Then he works in his study and we only see him from noon onwards. Until then, we can be with each other and can feast on wonderful nature,"[26] wrote Minna to Mathilde Schiffner at this time, in an effort to get her to visit Zurich again. Minna also continued to worry about her parents. Richard was already well-acquainted with her problems, but often could not help her. Once again, she had to ask her best friend for money to send to her mother.

Minna was regularly invited to balls, but was rarely in the mood, since Richard was frequently grumpy:

I should often like to have a good cry, and I when do, I feel better. Lately I didn't feel well at all. I dared to say it, but that didn't go down well. Richard shouted at me and said: well, we can go straight to the hospital, if you also want to start getting sick [...]. May God grant that I remain healthy, otherwise they will throw me out on the dung heap like the Jews. Richard's operas are now being performed frequently in Germany, but since he cannot be present, he feels his banishment twice over. I saw this coming, and nothing more can be done about it now.[27]

---

25   Minna to Mathilde Schiffner, November 19, 1852 (RWA).
26   Minna to Mathilde Schiffner, February 9, 1853 (RWA).
27   Ibid.

Mathilde Schiffner was an emotional anchor for Minna, who clung to her. She needed a confidante to whom she might express what she was feeling, and she received encouragement and comfort in return. Minna offered another warm invitation for her to visit Zurich in the summer. In July, Richard was going to go to St. Moritz for four weeks to strengthen his nerves. Then Minna would be alone: "During this time, I shall be as free as a bird in the air, how pleasant it would be if you were here […] I know all the beautiful spots hereabouts, I shall always accompany you, and we shall pass the time here as pleasantly as possible."[28]

In February 1853, Richard conducted a concert of the local orchestra and read the libretti for his *Ring* tetralogy in public at the Hotel Baur au Lac. He had already read it to François and Eliza Wille at their house in Mariafeld shortly before Christmas; Minna was presumably in attendance at all these events. While Richard was reading chez Wille, Eliza had to leave the room because of a sick child. Richard reacted angrily, calling her "Fricka" after Wotan's nagging wife.[29] But Minna will have suspected that Fricka was actually modeled on her—she had all-too-often incurred Richard's displeasure by criticizing his utopian flights of fancy. Nor will she have been pleased by the final words of the *Ring* in the version of late 1852: "Nicht trüber Verträge trügender Bund, noch heuchelnder Sitte hartes Gesetz: selig in Lust und Leid lässt—die Liebe nur sein!" (not the deceptive covenant of murky contracts nor the harsh law of hypocritical customs: rapture in joy and sorrow is provided by—love alone!). She was still smarting from the Laussot scandal, and far from ready to give such a free pass for amorous adventures. The *Ring* was simply never going to enthuse her as had the operas that Richard had written before.

Richard now decided to organize some concert performances of his music. Giuseppe Verdi's opera *Nabucco* had recently been reviewed euphorically in the press, and Richard felt he had to promote himself more aggressively if he was not to fall behind the competition. He had not yet been able to hear his *Lohengrin* at all, and had long wished to do so. So the Zurich Music Society agreed to put on a festival featuring a concert of his music, to be given three times over the space of a few days. They intended to cover the costs through increased ticket prices and subscriptions, but when the finances did not proceed as smoothly as planned, Otto Wesendonck stepped in, together with a wealthy colleague. In this, too, Mathilde had probably pulled the strings in the background.

---

28 Minna to Mathilde Schiffner, April 25, 1853 (RWA).
29 Wille 1982, 42.

During the planning and preparations for the concert, Richard decided that he and Minna should move from their upper-floor apartment at Zeltweg 11 to a brighter, more spacious apartment next door, at Zeltweg 13. Their landlady was the talented watercolorist Clementine Stockar-Escher, who also painted portraits of the Wagners. To finance the move, he again took an advance on fees he expected to receive from an increase in performances of his works. Minna was completely occupied by the logistics of the move. Two guest beds had to be installed, and various workmen were commissioned to supply the materials and set up everything according to the Wagners' wishes. The piano room now also featured an ensemble of plush furniture, and Richard had the connecting doors to the front rooms taken off their hinges and replaced by curtains. Liszt visited the Wagners in their new apartment in July 1853 and spoke admiringly of its "little elegance." The lavish expense involved was what Richard needed for his creative well-being, and he modeled his aesthetic on that of the upper classes. But Minna regarded such costly purchases as quite superfluous. Richard once again found himself in severe financial straits but was keen for Minna to remain unaware of it if possible. He simply had to have such luxurious surroundings if he were going to start writing the music for his *Ring des Nibelungen* later this year. The encouragement that he received after his public recitation of his libretti in early 1853 provided him with the extra encouragement he needed to begin the strenuous work that such a vast intellectual and artistic project would entail.

The Zurich concerts of May 1853 were a highpoint in the relationship between the city and the composer. Never before had Wagner been so persistently and warmly applauded. The lists of visitors in the city's hotels recorded a third more guests than usual, and even foreign newspapers reported on the event in advance. The program featured excerpts from *Rienzi, Holländer, Tannhäuser,* and *Lohengrin,* for some of which Wagner composed new concert endings. This was the very first time that he had heard any of his music for *Lohengrin.* The audience was enchanted. The concerts brought together 70 excellent musicians and a chorus of 110 voices, and the local *Eidgenössische Zeitung* wrote:

> In front of this orchestra, on a small podium, stood the splendid man whose mighty spirit has united everyone here for the most beautiful, collaborative task, and whose magical staff they all willingly and joyfully obeyed [...]. We have seldom seen such jubilation in our theater; every number was greeted with rapturous applause, and at the end, the Master was called back to the podium by stormy applause and showered with garlands, bouquets and expressions of joy by the audience, musicians, and singers alike.[30]

---

30   *Eidgenössische Zeitung* of May 19, 1853, as quoted in Fehr 1934, 225f.

Figure 6.2. The Zurich City Theater, ca. 1840. Baugeschichtliches Archiv, Zurich, BAZ.

Both Minna and Mathilde were there, a few seats away from each other. What must they have felt as they witnessed this jubilant success? After the exhausting concert, Richard invited all the performers and the members of the Music Society to a convivial gathering in a café—a generous gesture, given his current lack of money. Minna and Mathilde will again have joined in the celebrations without an inkling of the psychological drama in which they would later participate. Richard was the undisputed center of attention during these carefree days, and enjoyed to the full the recognition he was afforded.

At the second concert on May 20, the house was again sold out. The orchestra welcomed him onto the podium with a threefold fanfare, and the press continued its euphoria:

> Once again, these musical marvels that Wagner's artistic life and development have brought forth were presented to our rapt hearts in musical perfection. The jubilation increased after every piece, until it broke out in unprecedented enthusiasm in *Lohengrin*, which is surely the crown of Wagner's creations. The

audience, musicians, and singers vied with each other in offering their gratitude, adoration, and admiration to the master.[31]

The celebrations continued the next day, this time with a boat trip on
the lake in honor of the participants. Accompanied by music, they sailed
to Rapperswil at the far end of Lake Zurich, and returned after four hours.
Wagner invited everyone to dinner. Fortunately for him, the costs were borne
by the Music Society. Its president, Hans Conrad Ott-Usteri, gave a speech
to which Wagner spontaneously responded. He did not want to acquire fame
or riches through his work, he said, nor any superficially brilliant position;
instead, he wanted to provide people's hearts with everything that was noble,
pure, and divine so that they may be blessed in love. Mathilde and Minna
no doubt each had a very different perspective on this innermost conviction
of Wagner's. For Mathilde, they were noble words, and his reference to love
as the highest value of all existence was something she will have found especially moving. For Minna, in contrast, they were lofty-sounding words that
had already proved to be of little use in the practical circumstances of life.

But the celebrations were not yet over. The third concert took place on
May 22, 1853, Wagner's 40th birthday, and Mathilde had organized something special for it. Her servant went from box to box, handing out bouquets
of flowers to be thrown onto the stage during the final applause. And just as
planned, the garlands and bouquets flew from everywhere onto the podium.
Everyone cheered, and the orchestra intoned a fanfare. The *Eidgenössische
Zeitung* reported that a singer had then recited a poem praising Wagner's
work, and the composer received a laurel wreath from a beautiful lady. A second woman then presented him with a silver goblet on behalf of the female
chorus members. "Delighted and moved, everyone then left," wrote the local
paper. "The days of this festival will remain unforgotten and unforgettable.
This is the impact of art and of the noblest human spirit."[32] According to
Fehr, the author of the poem was Mathilde Wesendonck, though Wagner
scholars now attribute it to Johanna Spyri. In style and content it is reminiscent of Mathilde's work, but Johanna Spyri had also mastered the panegyric
tone. In any case, its author preferred to remain anonymous.

In a letter to Liszt, Wagner revealed that "I laid the whole festival at the
feet of a beautiful woman," thus hinting already at the existence of secret
communications between him and Mathilde. The festival closed on May 23

---

31 Quoted ibid., 228.
32 Quoted ibid., 231.

with a walk to the Waid, a vantage point to the northwest with a view of the city center. Richard arrived there with Minna a little later than the others. He was in gregarious mood, and delighted with the honors bestowed on him. The following day, the Wagners received their closest friends on the Zeltweg in order to christen the silver goblet that the singers had donated to the Master.

Such celebrations delighted Minna because they put Richard in a good mood. He was positively blissful, and this served to improve the general atmosphere at home. However, her satisfaction cannot hide the fact that she had begun to view her husband much more critically than before. It seems as if she was shifting her affections more and more to her friend Mathilde Schiffner in order to compensate for the problems of everyday life with her highly sensitive, often irritable husband. Minna became positively exuberant in a letter written after Mathilde visited:

> That you found such rich bouquets on your arrival is natural; if I had known the day of your arrival here, I would have built a gate of honor from here to the town hall, and placed Sulzer on top of it as our guardian spirit. He often eats with us, and sends you his very best regards [...] Baumgartner also comes often, and we spend the long evenings here quite cozily.[33]

Their loyal circle of friends in Zurich was gradually compensating her for the friendships she had lost after leaving Dresden.

Health-wise, however, Minna was ailing, and tormented variously by pains in her chest, shortness of breath, and aching feet. Richard decided to take a cure in Brunnen to help him recover from his own exertions at the recent festivities, and he was determined to take Minna along too. Julie Ritter's daughters were at this time also on vacation in Interlaken in the Bernese Oberland, and Richard and Minna decided to visit them there. But the weather proved so bad that Wagner withdrew to concentrate on his work, and Minna had to spend the rainy days alone with the two women.

At the beginning of July 1853, Franz Liszt finally came to visit—something that Wagner had long been looking forward to. Minna now had to be on top form, as her cooking and organizational skills were in demand. Up to twelve people at a time squeezed into their apartment, including Sulzer, Baumgartner, Herwegh, the Willes, Alexander Müller, Johann Carl Eschmann, and Theodor Kirchner. Liszt's servant Hermann helped Minna out, and was delighted to find both the cellar and the kitchen filled amply

---

33   Minna to Mathilde Schiffner, October 3, 1853 (RWA).

with food. Wagner had spared no expense in welcoming his friend with a daily *table ouverte*. Minna performed her duties to the greatest satisfaction, and Liszt wrote to her after his return, thanking her for all the kindness and love that she had shown him. In return, she sent Liszt honey. She found him sympathetic because his artistry and fame had not obscured his down-to-earth nature. Nor did she ever forget that he had censured Richard for his political activity back in Dresden, thereby providing her with welcome support at the time.

Liszt's visit concluded with a two-day excursion to central Switzerland with Wagner and Herwegh. Two days after Liszt's departure, Wagner was the recipient of a further act of homage when the Zurich singing associations honored him with a torchlight procession, a ceremonial speech, an honorary diploma, and appropriate musical offerings, the finale of which was the sailors' chorus from *Der fliegende Holländer*. Minna was as delighted as Richard with the veneration he was shown.

Afterwards, Richard went to St. Moritz with Georg Herwegh to take the waters. He was so enamored of the many honors he had experienced that he jokingly referred to himself as the "torchlight-processed, famous composer, poet and stargazer R." He and Herwegh spent their first night in Chur and continued on to St. Moritz by mail coach the next morning. But when they arrived, Richard's mood changed rapidly because their "cure" was more torture than relaxation. Many aspects were less than comfortable: their room was extremely simple, and Richard also became bored. In order to distract himself, he went on strenuous mountain hikes. For example, he persuaded Georg Herwegh to hike across the Rosegg glacier, where they had to jump over ice crevasses. "Herwegh often declared that he could not cross here or there; I constantly had to turn back and show him the way again. (Don't tell his wife that, by the way!)" Richard wrote to Minna. "It was indeed very strenuous, entailing eleven hours of constant climbing and scrambling; but I have never experienced anything so magnificent, I have never been in such a sublime icy mountain world!"[34] Eleven hours of mountain hiking is a supreme achievement for anyone without appropriate training. Wagner is known to have possessed great physical agility until the very end of his life—but we must also admire his courage, and Herwegh will surely never have forgotten their dangerous adventure.

In St. Moritz, a hunt was underway for a bear that had killed six sheep, and this was immediately reported back to Minna. Otherwise, Richard often

---

34   SB V, 372–74, here 374 (July 26, 1853).

had to clarify misunderstandings and fears on her part. She was worried that he had given her the names of two hotels, she doubted his word when he told her that he was expecting money to arrive, and she asked why he criticized her writing style. He clarified everything, however—he called her his "eternally mistrustful wife"—and rightly concluded that she still had little confidence in him. "You foolish women! Don't you understand that your greatest pride should lie in the fact that your husband is ready to turn away from the fullest freedom and ultimately always turns back to you? If only you knew what real fidelity in love is, i.e., real durability!"[35] Although he afterwards struck up a conciliatory tone, this minor dispute nevertheless had a more serious undertone, and was typical of the manner in which communications between them developed in the years that followed. Richard did not understand that it was he who had deprived Minna of a sense of security, and instead accused her of a lack of love and of mistrusting him. Minna, for her part, was well acquainted with the eloquence with which he sometimes maneuvered himself onto the cusp of untruth, and so she frequently gave little credence to what he said.

When Minna wrote to him about her uncertain state of health, Richard replied by painting a utopian future—though it was doomed to remain a fantasy because of their lack of money. From now on, he wrote, she should "lead a comfortable, quiet life of idleness. It shall entertain you to dress slowly on a morning, prettily and as you please; you shall presently receive from me a very comfortable, beautiful negligee: Your occupation shall comprise a little embroidery, some pleasant reading, receiving visitors, dressing yourself serenely to go out and pay visits to others, and so on." It is as if he were comparing her to Mathilde Wesendonck, who belonged to the upper classes and indeed led the life of a distinguished lady. "You should and must become a distinguished woman; you may only wear velvet, silk and satin: and yet all very comfortable [...] (And we will also make ourselves a little room of Venus: that goes without saying!)." Minna had known about Richard's habit of wishful thinking since she had first lived with him, and she will have simply ignored all this. But he liked the image of the little "room of Venus,"[36] and later returned to it: "Farewell, old Mietzel! Receive me well: make sure about the bed of Venus; it shouldn't be lacking when I visit. Adieu! Shake Peps's paws!"[37]

---

35   Ibid., 373.
36   SB V, 381–84, here 383 (July 28, 1853).
37   SB IV, 390–91 (August 5, 1853).

Richard afterwards traveled on to Italy. On Minna's birthday, he had Baumgartner deliver her a gold bracelet, a bonnet, and gloves. He loved giving generous gifts, regardless of his financial circumstances. He had even thought of giving her silk bracelets to cover the sunburn that she had suffered during a one-hour hike up the Uetliberg on the outskirts of Zurich. Minna wrote with pride and a certain degree of surprise to Mathilde Schiffner about Richard's homesickness: "On my birthday, I received a letter from him in which he expressed such painful homesickness that I barely thought he was serious. For example, that he would like to cry out loud in pain and sorrow because he cannot be with me on this day, and that he would give all of Italy for it."[38] Richard's letter is no longer extant. On September 3, however, he was already writing from Genoa: "Today I almost burst with homesickness—oh God! Yes, yes!—I shall certainly be back soon, however heavenly beautiful it is here! Adieu! dear good Mienel! Many, many kisses from your husband."[39] He interrupted his excursion to Genoa because he could not bear to stay any longer. As a holiday gift for Minna, he used the money he had left to buy two dresses: one black and one colored, of which Minna enclosed a fabric sample for her friend, who was a seamstress by trade. Minna had her dress garnished with black lace. She was still considered an attractive woman, and knew how to make the most of her wardrobe.

After Richard's return, Minna went to Baden in the canton of Aargau for a cure. To console her, Richard bought her a parrot named Jacquot, to which they gave the pet name "Knackerchen," and which became the family favorite. Minna taught him the words "Richard Wagner is a bad man!," which he called out to everyone.

In October, Richard traveled to Basel to meet Liszt and Princess Carolyne zu Sayn-Wittgenstein. His relationship with the intellectually gifted princess was complicated, and his reminiscences of this meeting have an ironic undertone: "She was vitally interested in the loftiest questions engaging our interest as in the most trivial details of our personal dealings in the world, and this interest flattered everyone to such an extent that he was transported into a state where he felt impelled to give of his very best at all times."[40] Richard was also delighted to meet the musicians Peter Cornelius, Joseph Joachim, and Hans von Bülow in Basel, who had accompanied Liszt there. They all intoned the trombone passage from *Lohengrin* as they entered the

38 Minna to Mathilde Schiffner, October 3, 1853 (RWA).
39 SB V, 416–19, here 419 (September 3, 1853).
40 ML, 501.

guest house, he wrote to Minna, knowing that she preferred comedy to anything venerable (he was referring here to the opening of the Prelude to Act 3). Princess Carolyne had brought along her beautiful, 16-year-old daughter Marie, whom Emma Herwegh christened "Raphael" because of her angelic appearance, and Richard developed a soft spot for "the child" as he called her. Liszt subsequently invited Richard to Paris, and the princess, who had only just made a toast to Minna's health at lunch, spontaneously decided to join them. While he was in the French capital, Richard met Liszt's own children for the first time, among them the shy, 16-year-old Cosima, who almost two decades later would become his second wife.

Despite having many fellow musicians around him, Richard wrote to ask Minna to join him: "Naturally, I couldn't get you out of my head, and I was very much looking forward to strolling around here with you soon."[41] He did not have to pay their travel costs, but he knew from experience how expensive Paris was, so he asked Sulzer for an advance, which was granted. Minna stayed overnight in Basel before traveling on directly to Paris by train the next morning. The trip lasted seventeen hours, but Richard had assured her that it was quite pleasant and not at all exhausting. He wrote to her that the Wesendoncks were also in Paris, although he tried hard to nip in the bud any possible suspicions that Minna might harbor: "Mrs. Wesendonck was very pleased when she learned that you were also coming; they want to stay here for 14 days in total; it will be very pleasant for us, only I don't think we will stay that long, if only for poor, poor Peps's sake."[42] Richard's desire to have Minna with him shows that the old ties between them were still strong. His Parisian friends Kietz and Anders also only came regularly to dinner after Minna arrived,[43] and they will have relived many happy memories together.

But Minna's memories of Paris were not all happy; she was still haunted by her futile search for Richard three years before, when he was planning to elope with Jessie Laussot. He was accordingly anxious now to offer some compensation by giving her gifts—a silk robe, two hats and a coat. But the biggest surprise came on her return to Zurich, when she found that her furniture had been put away and replaced with furniture trimmed with silk and velvet, and red curtains with embroidered net lace. She was horrified, and confessed to Mathilde Schiffner that it pained her more than it pleased her.

---

41 SB V, 446–48, here 447 (October 11, 1853).

42 SB V, 451–52 (October 16, 1853).

43 ML, 504.

It was as if I had entered a room that was foreign to me, it was no longer the homely room with which I was perfectly content. I first had to have a good cry. That good, foolish man—my happiness does not lie in such external frippery.

Richard is composing diligently and now needs the external, welcoming impressions that he failed to find in Italy, so I won't say a word about this luxury. But I cannot take any pleasure in it.

Richard's needs remained her prime consideration. But life otherwise continued on its quiet course. Sulzer, Baumgartner, Hagenbuch, and the Wesendoncks visited them often. Sulzer brought her winnings of 40 francs from the Frankfurt lottery: "he always includes me with a share, without my contributing anything. I'm sending these two gold Napoléons along with this letter to my mother. I have nothing else in cash,"[44] she told Mathilde Schiffner. Richard had thus ordered luxury furnishings for their apartment behind her back before leaving for Paris, while Minna had to rely on modest lottery winnings to be able to send money to her needy parents. She remained frugal in her housekeeping, while Richard was dependent on lavish surroundings.

After a long break, Richard was now back at work on his *Ring des Nibelungen*. He wrote his libretti while seated at his desk, but he composed at a standing desk. When composing, he would also walk up and down the room, and occasionally step into the next room to try out chords at the piano before returning to continue writing his music at his standing desk. Minna had to keep any and all visitors away from him in the mornings. She did that gladly, because he was in a good mood when his work had gone well. But when he invited friends round, she had to act quickly. He would write notes to Sulzer and others along the lines of "Stay for lunch tomorrow. There'll be a hare on the spit."[45] Even while he was still in Paris, he began sending lunch invitations to his Zurich friends for the time after his return. On their way back from Paris, they passed through Strasbourg where a market was being held on the square beneath the cathedral tower, and Minna took the opportunity to purchase cauliflowers, lobster, and oysters.

Minna had become noticeably emaciated, and Richard was worried about her. So he wrote to Natalie in Leipzig to ask her to return to Zurich, offering her 200 francs a year if she would take over assorted tasks from Minna. Natalie accepted the offer, though it must remain doubtful as to whether she ever saw the money.

---

44   Minna to Mathilde Schiffner, November 14, 1853 (RWA).
45   SB IV, 366–67, here 367 (May 18, 1852).

The Wesendoncks' frequent visits to the Wagners meant that Richard could see Mathilde on a regular basis, and their encounters were in these years balsam to his heart, mind, and soul. Mathilde's archives hold copies of many brief notes that Richard sent either to her, or jointly to her and her husband. They are mostly undated: "We herewith kindly invite Mr. and Madame Wesendonk to lunch on Sunday. RSVP the Wagner family." Or: "Dear Madam! Please allow me to inquire today whether you might like to join us for a little while this evening. If yes, then I suggest that you spend a few quiet hours with us until 10 p.m. I shall invite no one else, so as not to let anything spoil this holy evening."[46] By "holy," Richard meant the delight that the presence of his beloved would bring him. But there were also return invitations. They continued to visit François Wille and his wife Eliza on a regular basis, while their friendship with Emma Herwegh—who after several years of separation had reunited with her husband Georg—became an especially important source of stability for Minna.

It was at this time that Richard became particularly aware of the inadequacy of his relationship with Minna. He began to imagine how heavenly his life could be with Mathilde Wesendonck by his side instead. On January 15, 1854, he wrote a long letter to Liszt, explaining in detail how love was the most important thing in his life, and that he was only composing in order to bear the sufferings of his life. As always in such situations, he painted everything in the deepest black. Nevertheless, this letter reveals in an almost tragic fashion just how much he lacked female, erotic support, and how wrong it would be to attribute his creative work solely to aesthetic, political or philosophical concerns.

> Due to a hasty marriage in my 23rd year with a woman who is respectable but does not belong with me at all, I became an outcast for life. For a long time, the common pressures of my situation in life were able to obscure the real wastelands of my heart—with my ambitious plans and desires to escape these pressures by becoming famous and wealthy. Truly, I lived until my 36th year before I became completely aware of that terrible desolateness [i.e., in 1849, when Minna initially refused to move from Dresden to Zurich]. Until that moment, my being was maintained by a balance of two desires that fought within me; the first I endeavored to satisfy through my art, while I periodically gave vent to the other through sexual ["brünstig", literally "rutting"], fantastic, sensual debaucheries. (You know my *Tannhäuser*, with its idealization of this behavior that is in reality often so trivial!) But then—perhaps in *Lohengrin*—I

---

46   The M. Wesendonck archives in Stadtarchiv Zürich, shelfmark 84 VII.

gained a feeling, a knowledge of the unity of those two currents in true love, the love that I had only known in longing, never in experience. God, how gladly would I have fled naked into the world, to be nothing, nothing more than a happy, loving, and beloved person! Now—this one thing—I shall no longer be able to be: I shall no longer be able to love happily, but only unhappily—an "outcast—an impossible man"!

My dear, since then, art has really only been of secondary importance to me, a mere stopgap—nothing else! But it ultimately, again and again, becomes a true makeshift remedy: necessity compels me to aid myself through it, just to be able to continue to live. But it is really only in a state of true despair that I take up art time and again: when this happens, if I have to renounce reality again—if I have to cast myself once again into the waves of artistic imagination in order to satisfy myself in an imaginary world, then at least I have to help my imagination, my powers of inspiration. Then I cannot live like a dog, I cannot lie down on a bed of straw and refresh myself with alcohol: my sensuality, which is highly irascible, discriminating, incredibly desirous, but also uncommonly delicate and tender, has to feel flattered somehow if my spirit is to succeed in the onerous, bloody work of creating a hitherto inexistent world.[47]

Art was by no means a "stopgap" for Richard, and only seemed thus now, in the midst of his infatuation. Although he had passionately courted Minna and written her fervent letters in his youth, he was now convinced that he had actually found the ideal woman of his life in Mathilde. Perhaps the lavish furniture and fabrics he had ordered for their apartment were also intended to serve as some form of compensation for his hopeless love. No wonder Minna had criticized them for being mere "frippery" and "silly furnishings." If we interpret this letter to Liszt not merely as a snapshot of Wagner's feelings but as a serious confession, then it is proof of how the strength of Wagner's love for Mathilde overshadowed everything else. Even ten years later, these years were so fresh in his memory that it was as if but a day had passed. He reminisced about this period in a letter to Eliza Wille of June 5, 1863:

It was the highpoint of my life: those fretful, beautifully anxious years that I spent in the growing enchantment of her nearness and her affection, contain all the sweetness of my life. I only need the slightest inducement, and I am back in the midst of it, completely full of the wonderfully tender mood that even now takes my breath away as it did then, and only allows me a sigh.[48]

---

47   SB V, 494–98, here 494–95 (January 15, 1854).
48   SB XV, 186 (June 5, 1863).

Even if we are careful to avoid erecting any banal equivalency between a composer's life and works, we still cannot deny the fact that the latter are suffused with examples of this topos of female devotion. It was clearly of existential importance to him. He himself mentions *Tannhäuser*, in which sensual and spiritual love are divided between two different female characters. The Dutchman needs a woman who is willing to follow him unto death, while Lohengrin requires his female partner to trust him unconditionally. In the *Ring*, it is Brünnhilde who is held up as an example of a self-sacrificing lover, and Wagner leaves us in no doubt that the idealization of the female power of love (here dressed up as the more general concept of "redemption") is the very essence of his tetralogy.[49]

Minna suspected something but she was not yet seriously alarmed, as we can see from a letter she wrote to Mathilde Schiffner on March 13, 1854:

> Our dealings with the Wesendonck family are very pleasant, especially since the Zurichers themselves always remain dry old sticks, with only a few exceptions. I didn't get to a ball, everything of that sort was roundly dismissed because I am no longer in the mood for dancing. Sulzer and Baumgartner are our usual Sunday dinner guests, with Müller coming more often too. Our dear little chatterbox the parrot is quick and eager to learn, and while I'm writing to you he is calling out "Jakob Sulzer"![50]

Sulzer often gave Minna a gift of port, and for her part she told him she wished with all her heart that he might find a pretty, rich, clever wife. It perturbed her that Richard often quarreled with him. On one occasion, when things culminated in a heated argument, she intervened in an effort at conciliation, but Sulzer nevertheless grabbed his hat and walked out without saying goodbye. She wrote to Mathilde Schiffner that Richard was a "hothead" who had simply attacked his "fundamentally decent friend."[51] Otherwise, their gatherings were cozy. The poet Gottfried Keller took up residence again in his native city of Zurich in late 1855, and on January 13, 1856, he wrote back to his publisher's wife Lina Duncker in Berlin about the circle of friends around Wagner:

> Here in Zurich I've been doing well so far, I have the best of company and see all kinds of people such as don't come together so easily in Berlin. There is also

---

49   See Rieger 2011; also Rieger 2018.
50   Minna to Mathilde Schiffner, March 13, 1854 (RWA).
51   Minna to Mathilde Schiffner, February 16, 1856 (RWA).

a Rhineland family here, the Wesendoncks, originally from Düsseldorf, but who were in New York for a while. She is a very pretty woman, by the name of Mathilde Luckemeier, and these people make elegant company, they are building a magnificent villa near the city; they have received me kindly. Then there are fine dinners chez an elegant member of the government council [presumably Jakob Sulzer], where Richard Wagner, [Gottfried] Semper, who built the Dresden theater and museum, [Friedrich Theodor] Vischer from Tübingen, and several Zurichers come together, and where after modest indulgence you get a cup of hot tea and a Havanna cigar at two in the morning. Wagner himself offers a decent lunch where we carouse valiantly, so that while I had believed myself to have emerged from Berlin's materialism, I have jumped out of the frying pan into the fire.[52]

In July 1854, Minna took a "goat whey cure" in the health resort of Seelisberg that lies above the Rütli meadow on the opposite bank of Lake Lucerne from Brunnen. It offers a magnificent view of the surrounding countryside. She had actually planned her cure for the previous November, when she had learned via Mathilde Schiffner of the death of her sister Henriette Wilhelmine (Jette). The news had triggered physical ailments, her earlier agitation had set in again, the pain in her heels was more severe, and she had lost weight.[53] Minna was initially quite unhappy during her cure, as she was almost the only one there and it was pouring with rain. Richard told her to return home if she could not bear it. But she persevered, and the weather cleared. Despite their growing differences, Richard still missed his wife. He suffered from both her mistrust of him and from the skepticism that she demonstrated towards his new works, but he did not want to do without the care she provided. He sent her the satirical magazine *Kladderadatsch*, which they both enjoyed reading, and reported on assorted performances of his operas. And he sent her his shoes, which also fit her, because his short stature meant they had the same shoe size. He delighted in receiving mail from her and encouraged her to write more often: "What you write to me, be assured, always gives me great pleasure, especially when you let loose your wit, which suits you very well!"[54]

Despite the bad weather, Minna was glad to have escaped her household and all its worries and to be able to recuperate in peace and quiet. She loved wandering through the woods and will certainly have visited the little chapel

---

52   Keller 1951, II, 145–48, here 146–47.
53   Minna to Mathilde Schiffner, November 14, 1853 (RWA).
54   SB VI, 182–84, here 184 (July 13, 1854).

dedicated to the Virgin Mary that had made Seelisberg a place of pilgrimage since the 16th century (and which still stands today). Minna sent Mathilde Schiffner a picture of the area, and described Seelisberg as being surrounded by

> the most magnificent, most splendid nature. The snow-covered mountains—namely the magnificent, proud Uri Rotstock, which lies on this side, are of course missing from the picture. You already know Lake Lucerne, and from my window I can look out on it, 2,000 feet below me, opposite Tell's Chapel, and also the Rütlihaus where the three springs emerged after the three original cantons took their oath. In short: I am quite surrounded by classical landmarks, and they alone ought to restore my health.[55]

She drank goat's milk whey, and felt so good that she already began dreading the journey home:

> No silk furniture oppresses me here, why this mere frippery, my life was already colorful enough that it no longer matches my mood. I am expecting Richard in the next few days, God grant that he may like it for a few days at least; but I'm already worried about this restlessness, his eternal rationalizing and finding everything bad.

She knew of Richard's high degree of sensitivity, but was unable to understand that his nervous, heightened state could be a consequence of the creative tension that composing demanded of him, let alone a result of his suffering from the impossibility of his love for Mathilde Wesendonck.

Minna was looking forward to the fee that Richard was due to receive for conducting Beethoven's 7th Symphony and the overture to *Tannhäuser* at the Swiss Music Festival in Sion in Canton Valais in July 1854. But Richard deemed the quality of the musicians in the orchestra to be inadequate, left in a huff, and waived his fee. He expected Minna to be displeased at the loss of income, and wrote to her apologetically: "I would certainly have become seriously ill from pent-up anger and shame over the debasement of my task [...]. So do be sensible too, dear Muzius, and don't chide me about it!!!"[56]

---

55   Minna to Mathilde Schiffner, July 18, 1854 (RWA). The institute no longer exists, but one can still admire the view from its former viewing platform. Today, one can reach Seelisberg by a cog railway from Treib by the lake's edge; back then, the road from Treib to Seelisberg had to be traversed on donkeys or in sedan chairs.

56   SB VI, 182–84, here 183 (July 13, 1854).

Figure 6.3. Theodor Uhlig, relief. Nationalarchiv der Richard-Wagner-Stiftung, Bayreuth.

Richard then traveled to her at Seelisberg, and they returned to Zurich together on July 28, not without first stopping off at the Golden Eagle hotel in Brunnen. Richard promised his host that he would send him marches from *Rienzi*, arranged for wind band, so that the local band in Brunnen might play them. Wagner had no compunction about allowing popular arrangements of his music.

In his composition sketch for the first act of *Die Walküre*, which he completed on September 1, 1854, Wagner included a total of sixteen exclamations of yearning for Mathilde that are easy to decipher, such as "L.d.m.M.?" ("Liebst Du mich Mathilde?" / Do you love me Mathilde?), or "W.d.n.w.G.!!!" ("Wenn du nicht wärst, Geliebte!!!" / If you weren't here, beloved!!!).[57] Mathilde herself deciphered one of these abbreviations in her autobiographical account of the Wagner years: "G.s.M." = Gesegnet sei Mathilde / Blessed be Mathilde.[58] In *Die Walküre*, Sieglinde dares to do what society forbids and gives herself physically to Siegmund, the man she loves. In Richard's imagination, she was associated with Mathilde, while Wotan's nagging wife Fricka bore similarities to Minna. A few days after Wagner had begun composing this opera, he wrote to Liszt to say: "How curious are these contrasts between the first love scene in the *Walküre* and that in *Rheingold*."[59] It is striking that no less than seven of the above annotations in the composition sketch concern glances exchanged between Siegmund and Sieglinde. This makes sense, given the situation in which Mathilde and Richard found themselves: they had to put on an act and could communicate in public only by looking at each other. Wagner had written to Theodor Uhlig in March 1852: "A moist, glistening woman's eye often pierces me with renewed hope."[60] Now he had Siegmund exclaim: "The rays of her eye touched me there: I won warmth and the light of day!"

After the Wagners had returned home, one August Lesimple from Weimar arrived at their apartment with a letter of recommendation. Minna received him in Richard's stead and told him he was welcome to call in the afternoon. Lesimple later recalled: "I have retained an impression of her as possessing a benevolent, engaging nature. But her vaunted beauty could no longer be read in her features; sorrow and grief had left their mark on that face."[61]

---

57 See Westernhagen 1973, 88ff.
58 Heintz 1896, 93.
59 SB VI, 175 (July 3, 1854).
60 SB IV, 318–21, here 321 (March 20, 1852).
61 Lesimple 1884, 9ff.

Chapter Seven

"I'm a poor, stupid woman to have let you go …"

Zurich and London, 1854–56

Despite her goat whey cure, Minna's state of health continued to worsen. In order to undergo a thorough medical examination and get appropriate treatment, she began planning a visit to her brother-in-law Adam Tröger in Zwickau, who was a doctor. Her parents were also ailing, and for that reason alone she was keen to see them again, along with her other relatives back home in Saxony. The memories of her enforced departure from Dresden were still painful to her, so she initially planned to leave the city off her itinerary, and arranged for her parents to visit her in Zwickau instead. But what had initially been planned as a family reunion—with a brief extra trip to see Alwine Frommann in Berlin—was soon expanded into a tour of no less than nine cities in nine weeks. This was an extraordinary undertaking for an unaccompanied woman at that time. But Minna had already been accustomed to traveling alone when she was a young, unattached actor, and that experience now stood her in good stead.

Minna left Zurich on September 2, 1854, and arrived in Zwickau after a long, exhausting journey. She was met by her sister Charlotte, her brother-in-law Adam, and her parents. After Adam had treated her, she set off on the round trip she had planned. Chemnitz was her first stop, to visit Clara and Heinrich Wolfram. As chance would have it, an old boyfriend of Minna's now happened to call on Richard in Zurich. He left his best wishes for Minna, along with the mysterious message that she should be sure to remember the "Concordia." Richard wrote to her, groaning: "That's a nice story! and I, poor thing, have to pass it on!!"[1] And in his next letter, he joked: "Natalie said that the people at the post office are going to start making comments about all the gentlemen my wife is hanging out with—one day it's a Dr. Tröger, then a Mr. Wolfram."[2]

Richard was at this time tormented yet again by worries about money, but refrained from telling Minna. He had purchased the luxurious furnishings for their apartment on the Zeltweg a year earlier without regard for the financial consequences, and now the income he was anticipating from the smaller German theaters for the fall of 1854 turned out less than he had hoped. In his desperation, he confided his problems to his friend Sulzer, who in turn asked for advice from Otto Wesendonck. Presumably at Mathilde's instigation, Otto now decided it was time to pay off Richard's debts and put in motion a complete reorganization of his finances. He gave him 7,500 francs, but appointed Sulzer as Wagner's financial administrator, with instructions that no money at all was to be placed in Wagner's own hands. "From the very start, I had intended to give these funds to Madame Wagner, but then I realized it could be humiliating and perhaps a source of discord between the two of them," said Otto. "So I gave up the idea."[3] Giving the money to the thrifty Minna would indeed have been problematic, since she would probably have handed cash to Richard only under protest if he wanted things that she considered superfluous. A year later, Richard was still complaining about "the most peevish, fractious scenes" with Minna that were a result of money disputes.[4]

Five days after Minna's departure, Richard was already in turmoil, for he had not yet received any mail from her. He wrote to her to describe in meticulous detail how eagerly he had been waiting for word to arrive from her, and how he had resolved to drink a "half" (presumably a half-liter of beer, or perhaps a half bottle of champagne) when a letter from her finally arrived. "But there was no letter, which upset me so much for the whole day that I worked furiously, but did not think of my 'half': I really became quite anxious about you, and tortured myself with the most dreadful imaginings that I

---

1   SB VI, 209–11, here 211 (September 7, 1854).

2   SB VI, 228–30, here 230 (September 23, 1854).

3   Quoted in Fehr 1934, 298.

4   It is all the more perplexing that Wagner decided to hand over the management of his earnings to Minna three years later. He wrote this to Liszt; perhaps it was merely a white lie: SB VIII, 256–58, here 257–58 (February 8, 1857).

slept miserably in the night. I was up for 2 hours and longed for the day that I hoped would bring me news."[5]

But Minna then sent him three partridges, which delighted him, as did her news that she was recovering well, sleeping well, and had developed an appetite. After learning of Minna's recovery, Richard too felt better straightaway:

> I immediately gave the order: all three [partridges] had to be roasted, and at noon Friederike was called in, who twice had to drink a glass with me and Nette [Natalie] to your health, though it no longer tasted like schnapps to her. Then my headache also went away; now I'm smoking my cigar while having a cup of coffee and am writing to you quite cozily in order to tell you how happy I am about your condition.[6]

He let her know that the partridges had become "somewhat *piquant*," but that they had tasted very good, and perhaps for that very reason had occasioned "very pleasant digestive functions."[7] This relief from his regular constipation is presumably the kind of news he would have refrained from communicating to Mathilde Wesendonck. These intimations of a close connection between the spouses—one that reached into the very fibers of his bowels—also stand in contrast to Richard's letters to Franz Liszt, in which he reveals a different side of his nature: "I am now enjoying living for my wife: if love is measured by its sacrifices, then surely no one has been so loved, for no one has been brought such conscious sacrifices."[8] He presumably means the role of good, faithful husband that he was playing for Minna. He felt bound to her, but claimed he would have preferred to travel the world, ignoring all financial cares: "With the insights that I have gained this summer, I would gladly repent, sell all my furnishings etc. and go out naked into the world again, where this time, I swear to you, no more illusions would seize me!— But—my wife would not bear such a drastic step again, I know, it would be the death of her. Well then, for love of her I have decided to endure things."[9] Hans von Bülow also received a similar letter. Richard clearly feared that Minna would not survive another move of apartment (though in fact she would survive several more). He thereby implied that he was staying with Minna only out of loyalty, and was suppressing his own feelings. There was

---

5   SB VI, 209–11, here 210 (September 7, 1854).
6   SB VI, 216–18, here 216–17 (September 13, 1854).
7   SB VI, 228–30, here 230 (September 23, 1854).
8   SB VI, 233–34, here 234 (September 29, 1854).
9   SB VI, 248 (October 7, 1854).

a bond between them that held them together, though it was one founded variously in habit, friendly loyalty, genuine affection, and compassion.

Richard's light-hearted correspondence with Minna continued. When she complained that she was receiving too few letters from him, he reacted with a mixture of good humor and irritation: "Oh, you overly hasty, unjust, mistrustful, in short—bad woman!". It was only right, he continued, that she should be writing to him, because she had so much to report of her travels. His life, by contrast, was at present utterly uneventful, he said, and so he had decided to get back to the second act of his *Walküre*. "When I received your somewhat mistrustful letter yesterday, I was just about to compose the entrance of Fricka; that fitted together pretty well."[10] The composition draft for the first act of the opera was finished by the beginning of September; work was proceeding smoothly. While his beloved Mathilde delighted in learning of the progress of the opera, Minna—being more realistically minded—reckoned that it had no future chance of success whatsoever. "You think that I am only writing this for myself alone," wrote Richard. "If so, that's fine—I would not like to live any more if I cannot work on something like this. So you have to allow me this kind of work: I can't compose anything for the Leipzig Trade Fair and its like anymore. Others can take care of that."[11] He saw with increasing clarity his artistic mission in life—to complete his *Ring* tetralogy—and understood the path that he must take. Minna harbored justified doubts about the viability of Richard's plans, given that he had failed to secure a regular income since leaving Dresden, and in light of the extended timeframe within which he was now working. She could not have suspected that Richard was simply doing his best to suppress all thought of their vexed money problems and was processing his current psychological distress through the characters he had invented in Act 1 of his *Walküre*. The core problem was the same that would soon after occupy him to an even greater extent in *Tristan und Isolde*: the obsessive love that brings together Sieglinde and Siegmund, and from which they cannot escape because love for them is stronger than any rational will. Richard presumably hoped to convince Mathilde that their love, too, was fated to come about, and this probably also helped him to assuage his feelings of guilt toward Minna.

From Chemnitz, Minna traveled on to Leipzig, where she met Richard's brother Carl Julius, his sisters Ottilie and Luise (who was married to Friedrich Brockhaus), and his half-sister Cäcilie Avenarius. Wagner jokingly called his

---

10 SB VI, 236–38, here 236 (September 30, 1854).
11 SB VI, 236–38, here 236 (September 30, 1854).

relatives "the Leipzig brood."[12] Minna stayed there with Cäcilie and Eduard. She was even privileged to hear a private performance of excerpts from *Lohengrin*, which moved her greatly. In late September, she spontaneously decided to visit the conductor August Röckel, who was in jail in the little town of Waldheim, roughly halfway between Leipzig and Dresden. Richard was delighted to hear this, since Minna had hitherto regarded Röckel as her "supposed mortal enemy."[13] She was convinced that he was the real agitator behind Richard's politically motivated misdeeds back in Dresden in 1849. Now, five years later, her anger was no more. She felt pity for Röckel instead—a change of heart that Richard found worthy of praise (though he managed to express this to her in an arrogant, condescending manner):

> Your heart is broader and more encompassing than is your insight into the essence of people who nevertheless must seem strange and repugnant to you, because we cannot expect you women to comprehend the ways of the world with such a far-reaching perspective, nor be able to reconcile the strangest connecting views, because this is reserved for man—for the poet.[14]

What Richard had not realized, however, was that Minna went to Waldheim primarily out of pity for Röckel's wife, who lived in Weimar. But her visit was not particularly successful, because she was shocked to hear Röckel speak coldly about his family. So he remained a "villain" to her, and she continued to blame him for Richard's involvement in the Dresden Uprising. Nor was she alone in her conviction; Richard's brother Albert was also of the opinion that Röckel had exerted a baleful influence on him.[15]

From Leipzig, Minna traveled on to Berlin, where she stayed with Alwine Frommann, a die-hard devotee of Wagner's who worked at the Prussian Court as a reader to Queen Augusta. Richard wrote jokingly to Minna about her: "She's on the most intimate footing with all the princesses of the world—so I'm sure she'll get you acquainted with a few of them, and once you're at court, you'll soon forget Switzerland and the Zeltweg."[16] Minna's stay in Berlin was marred by an eye injury she sustained at the Anhalter Bahnhof when she slipped on the tracks, searching for a purse she had lost. Alwine accordingly had to take dictation for Minna's next letter to Richard. Minna

---

12 SB VI, 242–43, here 243 (October 5, 1854).
13 SB VI, 243–46, here 245 (October 6, 1854).
14 Ibid.
15 Burrell, 623.
16 SB VI, 236–38, here 237 (September 30, 1854).

later wrote to Mathilde Schiffner that the incident had made her famous, since almost all the newspapers mentioned it, "naturally embellished with all manner of lies."[17] She initially did not dare to tell Richard about the loss of her purse, but then wrote to tell him anyway, and he hurriedly transferred her 50 thalers: "O you poor, unfortunate woman! If only you'd have some proper good luck for once! You truly deserve it."[18] He had entrusted her with the important task of investigating a proposed production of *Tannhäuser* in Berlin. Wagner had originally insisted on Liszt being appointed to conduct it, but then became embroiled in a long correspondence about it with the Berlin Intendant, Botho von Hülsen. Wagner's insistence on Liszt's participation held things up, and he became nervous about the knock-on effect that this was having on other opera houses that were waiting to see how the work fared in Berlin before performing it too. To expedite matters, Wagner decided to forgo Liszt's cooperation—but since Liszt would lose face if he were to resign of his own accord, Richard asked Minna to resolve the conflict in person in Berlin. It thus became her responsibility. But she was unable to achieve anything, and so Richard finally released the opera for performance without any conditions.

Richard also suggested that Minna should go and pay her respects to the Grand Duke or Grand Duchess in Weimar, in order to talk to them about a possible amnesty. He urged her twice to go there, writing that Liszt was already asking about her in his letters. But in a longer, undated letter, Richard dropped the usual, light-hearted style of his letters to her, in which he usually restricted himself to everyday problems. Instead—surprisingly— he assigned to her alone all decisions about their future. If the Grand Duke could procure an amnesty for him from the King of Saxony, wrote Richard, then he was prepared to move to the Grand Duke's realm of Thuringia, never to leave it unless the Grand Duke allowed it. For his part, he liked the idea of being near Weimar. If, like him, Minna found the prospect of Thuringia attractive, then she should go and make the necessary enquiries: "I ask you to act as my proxy, and in any case, you should go to the Grand Duchess yourself.—I can assure you that I completely trust your good sense and your discretion in this matter!"[19] But if she preferred to stay in Zurich, then he would acquiesce and make it their permanent home. He had not yet begun

---

17   Minna to Mathilde Schiffner, November 7, 1854, written from Zurich
      (RWA).

18   SB VI, 243–46, here 244 (October 6, 1854).

19   SB VI, 265–68, here 267 (second half of October 1854).

to dream of a possible life together with Mathilde Wesendonck; the impossibility of such a future was so obvious to him that he was still toying with the possibility of leaving Zurich.

It was presumably this letter that prompted Minna to travel to Dresden, contrary to her original plan, and to present the authorities with a personal petition to the king of Saxony.[20] She will also have remembered the discussion that had taken place the previous spring between Liszt and Richard, when the latter had asked his friend what he thought of his chances of success with another petition to the king. Liszt had been unable to conceal his skepticism, at which Wagner had dropped the matter. But Minna knew that the possibility of a return to Germany was always on Richard's mind, and that her letters from Germany had merely intensified his desire to hear good performances of his music once again, as he confirmed in his letter to her of late October 1854:

> For a year, however, since I have returned to composition, this complete lack of stimulation has ultimately had a completely depressing effect on me. I can feel it clearly in my present work,—I notice that it is becoming more and more difficult for me to want to work, and if it should continue like this for a long time, I fear that I will give up music again. It is too bad for me![21]

Such words will have alarmed Minna. It was his operas that were bringing the income that they desperately needed, and she was also aware that composing was simply his true purpose in life. She could have reacted by gloating about how her own warnings had come true after the loss of his job in Dresden: not only was he penniless, but he now also lacked artistic inspiration. But the bitter lament on Richard's part seems to have convinced her that it would be more appropriate for her, as his wife, to present a personal petition to the king and thus do everything that she could to rectify things.

The courtly tone of the petition for Wagner's amnesty is laid on thick. Minna wrote it herself, and a draft of it in her hand has survived:

---

20   The editors of Wagner's collected letters place Minna's visit to Dresden before her trip to Weimar (see SB VI, 238), but this seems doubtful. Richard's undated letter, SB VI, 265–68, was sent to Weimar and was presumably what triggered Minna's decision to travel to Dresden to petition for an amnesty.

21   SB VI, 265–68, here 267–68 (second half of October 1854). It is typical of Wagner's contradictory nature, however, that he had only recently written to Wilhelm Fischer to tell him that he did not feel drawn back to Germany. See SB VI, 197–99, here 199 (August 8, 1854).

The wife of Richard Wagner, who is banished, dares to prostrate herself before His Majesty to ask that He, being a protector of art and science, may deign to grant mercy to an errant artist who is weighed down heavily by being inhibited in his strivings though the impossibility of hearing his new compositions. May Your Majesty grant mercy and forgiveness to my husband who was so ensnared, Richard Wagner, and grant him the opportunity to attend performances of his works in person, and to advance his further work through the grace and magnanimity of Your Majesty.

It only remains for me to beg humbly for Your Majesty's forgiveness, that a sorely afflicted woman should dare to implore Your Majesty's magnanimity on behalf of a guilty, errant man who is in a state of severe atonement through being inhibited in his art.

Your Majesty's most humble, deeply bowed servant hereby addresses her most gracious, magnanimous King in faith, and in trust, Minna Wagner.[22]

Richard himself had never felt "guilty" or "errant"—the whole letter reeks of hypocrisy. Nor did Richard mention this initiative of Minna's in his autobiography. But Minna seems to have been proud of her efforts, to judge from a letter to her confidante Mathilde Schiffner: "Now I am only eager to see if the seed that I have sown in Dresden will one day bear fruit, is there no talk of my having been there and of my kowtowing?"[23] She probably submitted her petition to the cabinet office, from where it will have proceeded from the king to the justice minister. In order to give the necessary emphasis to her request, she paid a personal visit to the General Director of the Dresden Court Theater, August von Lüttichau, who promised her that he would intercede for her with the king. This conversation will have required no little skill on her part, but she was buoyed by Wagner's assurance that he trusted her "good sense" and "discretion" in these matters. After a wait of several months, she asked a Dresden friend to inquire of the outcome from Lüttichau himself. Her request, however, had been denied.

Before leaving for Weimar—the last stop on her round trip through Germany—Minna made another detour to Leipzig. Her niece Rosalie Wolfram had become an actor, and Minna wanted to see her in a performance. But she was only able to attend a rehearsal. As a former professional actor herself, she was confident in her judgment—and was not very impressed. Nevertheless, she refrained from mentioning this to Rosalie's mother. Then Minna moved on to Weimar, where she stayed with Liszt and

---

22   Lippert 1927, 48–49, Herzfeld 1938, 229. Copy of the draft in RWA.

23   Minna to Mathilde Schiffner, November 7, 1854 (RWA).

the Princess Carolyne zu Sayn-Wittgenstein. She attended a performance of *Der fliegende Holländer* on October 15, and *Lohengrin* a week later, on October 22. Richard had managed to wangle these particular performances. The *Neue Zeitschrift für Musik* of November 17, 1854, even mentions that they were given at Minna's special request. Minna's report made Richard melancholy, as he would have gladly been there in person. Liszt celebrated his birthday on the same day as the performance of *Lohengrin*, and he was greeted in the sold-out theater with stormy applause, flowers, and garlands. Minna will most likely have been sitting with Liszt's partner, the princess, and her daughter Marie, and will no doubt have had to answer questions about her husband and shake hands with many visitors from Jena, Erfurt, Berlin, Leipzig, and elsewhere. And Liszt will have ensured that she had a place of honor at his birthday party afterwards.

Just three days later, on October 25, Minna attended a performance of *Tannhäuser* in Frankfurt am Main. She had written to the theater's music director Gustav Schmidt and asked him to organize it. She once more wrote a report to her husband and added her own assessments of the singers. This especially interested him: "Your news about *Der fliegende Holländer* and [Rosa von] Milde the singer has pleased me very much, though you intensified my longing to make music again in my own way!"[24]

After Minna returned at the end of October, she wrote to Mathilde Schiffner about her experiences in Leipzig, Weimar, and Frankfurt. She judged the singer in the role of *Lohengrin* to have been:

> a boor without a voice. On the other hand, the music enraptured me in a wonderfully powerful way. It was only a pity that everything rushed past me too quickly, I almost wanted to hold it fast to be able to absorb everything properly. As you know, I lived with the Princess and naturally enjoyed the greatest luxury there. And yet I longed for simpler things, for an hour of peace to be alone, which was unfortunately impossible. In Frankfurt, I heard an excellent *Tannhäuser*, with Tichatschek and Mitterwurzer being minor exceptions. Otherwise, the others were all better, fresh, beautiful young voices. The sets were just as good as in Dresden, and the orchestra and conductor were unsurpassable! In short, I was completely spellbound with joy and delight. I wept incessantly, so much so that the newspapers wrote about my visible emotion the day after.[25]

---

24   403 SB VI, 265 (second half of October, 1854).
25   Minna to Mathilde Schiffner November 7, 1854 (RWA).

These undertakings show that Minna was quite capable of assuming responsibility for matters on Richard's behalf. The long journey was no small matter for her, and she was otherwise accustomed to listening quietly at Richard's side and letting him do all the talking. But she carried out all her allotted tasks faithfully, and was independent enough to decide when to embark on activities of her own. She experienced an audience with a Grand Duke, visited a prisoner in jail, was presumably introduced to members of the Berlin Royal Court by Alwine Frommann, and in Weimar she was the guest of one the most famous composers of the time and had to fit in with the courtly, aristocratic lifestyle that he enjoyed. None of this was in any way familiar to her as a woman of the bourgeoisie who was generally expected to follow her husband and stand passively by his side.

During Minna's absence, Richard went on an excursion of several days with the Wesendoncks that took them on a circuitous route via Glarus, Stachelberg, Klöntal, the Pragelpass, and Schwyz to his beloved Brunnen on the banks of Lake Lucerne. He wanted to show them the most beautiful places that he knew in Switzerland. They crossed the lake to Seelisberg, where Minna had been on her cure some months before. He wrote to her that he had been "dragged here," and consoled her immediately afterwards by adding: "Here, my good old Minna, everyone on all sides reminds me of you with such love that I cannot refrain from sending you a heartfelt greeting from here. Everyone is still gushing about you—the guests of that time are all gone now, but the locals of Se[e]lisberg are singing your praises." Was this gesture intended to counter her possible distrust of Mathilde? The apparent insincerity of his tone seems to suggest it: "I, however—am truly devoted to you with ever faithful love and affection! Adieu! Send good news again soon to your really bad hubby."[26] Minna repeatedly succumbed to fears that Richard might fall in love again, for she saw that there was a suitable candidate on his horizon. For her part, Mathilde clearly enjoyed her outing with the two men. She later recalled how Richard had played excerpts from Beethoven's *Eroica* and his C minor Symphony "on the old piano in the dining room" of their hotel in Brunnen as darkness fell outside. And in the early morning, he greeted her with excerpts from *Lohengrin*.

On December 23, 1854, Sulzer invited the Hagenbuchs, Wesendoncks, and Wagners to a Christmas party. Minna wrote a report of the occasion to Mathilde Schiffner in the new year, though there is one aspect of it that remains puzzling:

---

26   SB VI, 212–13 (September 12, 1854).

The distribution of the gifts was as meaningful as the whole man himself. Like the others, I was given a suitable book, along with a little guest book and a poem that I include here. I can hardly believe that there is anyone in the world who understands me and my circumstances better than Sulzer, which is why, of all the poems that I have received in the past, this is the only one that I shall keep.[27]

Did Sulzer's lines perhaps allude to their constant lack of money? That would hardly have been in the best of taste. Had Sulzer realized that Richard was busy cultivating an ideal love besides his wife? Did he know that Minna suspected something, and wanted to offer some kind of moral support? Whatever it was, Sulzer did his best to cheer up his guests with his gifts, for Richard was given a depiction of Seelisberg in winter with himself on it, freezing, and playing a flute while wearing mittens. The picture also featured the donkey that carried him up the mountain, listening to him intently alongside a bear and a marmot.

The Wesendoncks held their own Christmas gift-giving on Christmas Day itself. Minna received a tea caddy, Natalie a lace collar, and Richard a piano score of Mozart's *Don Giovanni*, though he had long owned a copy of it already, as Minna immediately noted. "We had a lot to do," she wrote to Mathilde Schiffner, "we were given presents and, of course, we had to give presents in return, which, as you can imagine, could only consist of works of our own."[28] Minna then changed the subject and gave free rein to her mockery—for when it came to the quality of theatrical performances in Zurich, she had little good to say: "During my absence, Richard sold the score of *Tannhäuser* to the local [theater] director for a pitiful sum. I thus have the prospect of seeing this opera performed here soon, but in the ghastliest manner. The whole personnel is atrocious!"[29] When the opera was actually given in the spring under Richard's direction, Minna had to revise her opinion because he succeeded in getting the very best out of the artists at his disposal—performing "true miracles" with the singers, who had previously looked more like "lumps" on stage than artists, she wrote proudly. It was given six performances to full houses and to great applause. Richard himself wrote to Hans von Bülow: "For the sake of Frau Wesendonck, I even offered to conduct *Tannhäuser* myself in our divine local theater."[30] Minna

27 Minna to Mathilde Schiffner, January 14, 1855 (RWA).
28 Ibid.
29 Ibid.
30 SB VII, 37–39, here 38 (March 3, 1855).

was not allowed to have any inkling of Richard's real motives for organizing the production. While she was wishing for Mathilde Schiffner to come and visit, Richard could only think of a different Mathilde.

At the end of 1854, Wagner wrote to Liszt about his plans for an opera on the story of Tristan and Isolde: "Since I have never enjoyed the true happiness of love in my life, I want to erect a monument to this most beautiful of all dreams, one in which this love should be satiated from beginning to end."[31] He here disavows the passion of his early years of marriage to Minna in order to magnify the radiance of his love for Mathilde Wesendonck and transform it into an artistic artefact. This opera enabled him to work through the desire he felt for Mathilde, and which over the course of his encounters with her in the ensuing years intensified to a point at which it became almost unbearable and threatened to consume them both.

The turn of the year 1854–55 was spent at the Hotel Baur au Lac with the Wesendoncks (who were still resident there), Sulzer, and Baumgartner. Richard gave Minna a gift of lace, and at midnight the champagne corks popped and those present made a toast to wish happiness and health to everyone in the new year.

Richard had allowed his friends to persuade him that a conducting engagement in London could prove financially advantageous. From the outset he was unenthusiastic about it, but Minna had a further reason for him to go: "Germany will probably remain closed to him for a long time or even forever, [and there will be no] good German opera company able to perform his *Lohengrin*."[32] She also wrote to Mathilde Schiffner about this upcoming trip. Richard expected to make a profit of 5,000 francs from it, she wrote, adding skeptically: "Who'll believe that?" And he indeed returned with only 1,000 francs. When Richard said goodbye to her, she cried, which he found touching: "How difficult it was for you to say goodbye again this time; I was very moved."[33] The subsequent, long weeks of separation, from March to the end of June, were difficult for both of them, and Minna remained throughout his most important addressee. She received thirty-two letters with numerous details about the state of musical life in England, the food (he usually ate a dozen oysters as an appetizer, followed by roast beef), his expenditure, and his state of health (including matters pertaining to his digestion). Richard described the state of the orchestra, his concert programs, the progress of

---

31   SB VI, 298–99, here 299 (December 16, 1854).

32   Minna to a friend, March 14, 1855 (RWA).

33   SB VII, 41–45, here 44 (March 6, 1855).

his rehearsals, and offered his assessments of the local singers. He discussed in detail the high prices in London—probably to cover himself from later reproaches about bringing too little money back. He and Minna wrote their letters to each other on differently colored paper: pink meant that the letter writer was in good spirits, while yellow was a warning sign. And time and again, the old attachment between them revealed itself: "you'd surely have quite a bit of room in my big bed," he wrote.[34] As is often the case with long-married couples, everyday life took up a lot of space in their correspondence. They discussed whether Minna should discard the cover over the piano chair, and Richard drew a sketch of a camp stool that Minna was to have made for him. Because of the cold, he was wearing two pairs of underpants, he told her, while she enclosed a feather from the parrot, about which he was delighted. He also expressed astonishment that she had been able to celebrate her birthday with champagne, despite the illness she had just overcome.

Minna reported to Mathilde Schiffner that Richard did not like London, as he could not cope well with the foggy climate and was constantly unwell. In one of his letters, he made fun of the English ladies he encountered, which Minna promptly communicated to Mathilde: "He tells me, if I could get a glimpse of his audience I would laugh out loud at the heaps of ladies I'd see. All of them wearing crimson mantillas, none of them able to close their mouths, and all you can see is two big naked teeth. They have lots of curls and roses in their hair, but with glasses on their noses. I can imagine how all of Richard's illusions are disappearing."[35] While she delighted in such stories from him, she was still troubled by nagging doubts:

> Believe me, my dear Mathilde, that I am in general not at all jealous where my husband is concerned, which is why I see things blacker than is necessary. And I entrust these things only to you, not to any other soul. But it is certain that London does not please him because it harbors fewer effusive ladies who know the works of R.W. and who court him because of it. After all, it's not because of him personally that people go into raptures, though a weak man such as him cannot believe it.[36]

---

34   SB VII, 83–86, here 84 (April 5, 1855).

35   Minna to Mathilde Schiffner, May 7, 1855 (RWA). She is here referring to Richard's letter of April 7, 1855, in which he makes fun of his female audience. See SB VII, 95–97, here 97.

36   Minna to Mathilde Schiffner, May 7, 1855 (RWA).

Richard tried to dispel any possible suspicions on Minna's part towards Mathilde Wesendonck by referring to her in mildly derogatory fashion as "aunt," "Auntie Wesendonck," "the woman" or just "die Wesendonck" (i.e., using her husband's surname but with the feminine definite article). Minna, however, was unable to dispel her fears that he might be making eyes at the women in London: "To stay away from home for 4 months is really a long chunk of one's life, and I would never allow it again, since in certain matters I cannot remain calm at all where my dear consort is concerned."[37] But she missed him a lot, and her letters to him were so affectionate that he responded in a similarly affectionate, grateful tone. He learnt from her that Otto Wesendonck was afraid he might be squandering his money in London, so he meticulously listed his living costs for her. He disliked the idea that the husband of his beloved Mathilde might think ill of him, and so he took advantage of Minna's report to write a long letter to Otto straightaway in which he made it clear to him that he was never going to be much good at earning money.

When his concerts went well, this put Richard in a good mood—though it was precisely at times like this that he missed home the most, and he told Minna so. After one concert, he was accompanied home by the pianist Karl Klindworth, a former student of Liszt. They ate oysters and cold cutlets and chatted until 2 in the morning. "Was I thinking of home?? Dear child—it remains my only hope that things will come to an end here, so I can finally return to my cozy homeland. For that's what Zurich is to me now, my house, my friends, my animals—and—I have to tell you, my old, good, naughty, good-as-gold—I mean—my dear wife—more than ever!"[38]

Money remained an important topic, for he had not forgotten the tortuous financial problems from which Otto had delivered him, and he had only accepted the invitation to London because of the prospect of making money there. During Richard's absence, Minna dismissed their maid so that she could save money to send to her parents. At that time, a maid cost 284 francs a year, a male servant 364 francs—plus one had to provide them with food.[39] (When Richard had begun to employ Natalie in 1853, he had done so for just 200 francs a year—which was a very good deal on his side). In late January 1855, Minna sent 100 francs to her parents, then the same sum

37 Minna to Mathilde Schiffner, April 6, 1855 (RWA).

38 SB VII, 70–73, here 73 (March 27, 1855).

39 Gartmann 1985, appendix: "Zu den Lebenshaltungskosten um 1850 in der Schweiz," 286.

once more, a little later. She could do no more for them, and was glad that Richard was not monitoring her expenditure.

Minna was living as simply as possible with Natalie back in Zurich. She never invited any guests, but they came anyway. She was somewhat annoyed that Richard was able to spend 50 francs a day in London, whereas she had to cope with a total of 150 francs from the money Sulzer paid her from the Wesendonck allowance. This had to cover the cost of food, wood for heating purposes, and also expenses such as repairing her hats, which all left little to spend on anything else.

Nor was Minna idle in her continued efforts to wangle an amnesty for Richard. She wrote about it to one Wilhelm Fischarch in Dresden, who replied that only a comprehensive, group amnesty would be possible. "Don't give up hope," he wrote, "as strict as our king is when acting in accordance with the law, he is also just and lenient."[40] But this was little consolation.

Although Wagner took pleasure in demonstrating to London audiences how he felt Haydn, Mozart, and Beethoven should be conducted, he detested the whole enterprise overall. Several remarks in his correspondence with Minna reveal that he still regarded her as a sounding board in artistic matters. He criticized the singer Elisa Rachel, for example, adding that he would tell Minna more in person when he got home. And his descriptions of the hardships he endured read most of all as if he is simply chatting with her: "I am very scared of the concerts themselves. It's a very good orchestra, but it is said to be incapable of playing piano, always only forte, without any nuances. You only have one rehearsal, yet you've got to get through two symphonies, two overtures and the other concert pieces. How am I supposed to manage?"[41] He was grateful for everything Minna did to try and cheer him up. She asked him if there was anything in the way of clothes she might make for him. He replied that he would be leaving his old dressing gown behind in London because it was worn out: "You know what luxurious appetites I have in this regard. But in any case, you shall remain my dressing-gown supplier."[42] He did not need to tell her twice. She had already sewn him a dressing gown for the winter, and would now provide one for the summer, too. He asked for a soft, loose-fitting jacket of velvet or silk, not padded, plus a pair of pants lined with silk taffeta. It took some convincing before Minna agreed to follow his wishes for

40   April 20, 1855 (Pierpont Morgan Library, USA).
41   SB VII, 41–45, here 43 (March 6, 1855).
42   SB VII, 98–101, here 100 (April 12, 1855).

its luxurious design. But she ultimately submitted to his "demons of volup-tuousness" as he once called his expensive appetites.

Wagner was unhappy that his conducting duties in London prevented him from composing, and he began venting his displeasure in various direc-tions. His letters to Liszt do not hold back in their criticism of the "swamp of convenience and habit" with which he felt confronted in London. Nor could the orchestra in London do anything to console him. English musicians seemed to him like skillful machines that could never get into the proper gear. The audiences were taken by him, but were difficult to impress (or at least this is how it seemed to him). He also found London musical life too commercialized: "Then there is this ridiculous Mendelssohnian culture, and the complete, insolent hypocrisy of this absurd people."[43] The harsh injustice of these judgments simply reveals his own sense of grievance: he was well aware of his own exceptional stature as an artist, and detested anything that distracted him from his creative work. But he lacked the courage to abandon his engagement in London, as his fear was too great of the inevitable domes-tic turbulence that would result. It was primarily out of consideration for Minna that he was determined to hold out until his last concert. We find a similar attitude expressed in general terms a year later, in a letter to Liszt: "If I did not have my wife, you should now experience odd things from me, as I would be proud to go about as a beggar. But this eternally inadequate, stingy existence of ours is increasingly arduous to my poor wife, whose peace of mind I can preserve only by also ensuring a modicum of economic peace."[44] There was naturally no willingness at all on his part to embark on the exis-tence of a beggar. Richard did not merely like artificial stimulants around him when he was composing—such as luxuriant fabrics and perfumes—for they were a physical necessity to him. But he was right about his constant lack of money becoming increasingly injurious to Minna's emotional and nervous state.

When Richard told Minna that he would give all of London for a cozy evening back home with her, she decided to pour out her feelings in return:

My dear Englishman! Two months ago today was a hard day for me, the poor wife you left behind, fainthearted, beyond the seas. For a wife to sit alone at home, far away and separated from her husband, that in itself is inexpressibly hard (says Clytemnestra). Only there is this difference, that she was feigning, whereas what I am writing here comes from the most profound depths of my

43   SB VII, 161–63, here 161 (May 16, 1855).
44   SB VII, 347–50, here 348 (January 18, 1856).

heart. I could not spend this day more worthily than by talking a bit with you, though I have nothing to tell you. From next Monday onwards, you will have only four more concerts to conduct, then only three, etc. Then your duties will drop off with gigantic strides, then I shall see you soon, then I shall feel quite well again, and then at last we shall go up to the divine Seelisberg, and we shall be happy to have each other again; we shall enjoy the heavenly air, and admire nature. [...] You poor little child, now I hope that you will be all right again very soon, and not cross.[45]

And not long after, she wrote:

My poor, poor hubby! What you wrote me is really heartrending and horrible! You are certainly right in what you say about the last and the next concert programs (excepting the *Tannhäuser* Overture). For that you need not have parted from your very good wife for four eternally long months, just to stroll about London like a lost sheep for such a long time—terribly bored and conducting the worst music, and not confining yourself to classical and good, significant music, as it had been previously stated. I quite realize that the directors of the Philharmonic had to take their obscure local composers into consideration, and finally they had to have such trash performed in winter and at the fifth concert, only they should not have brought you over there for it—for that, Hiller and his sort would have been suitable.[46]

Richard's happy anticipation of a return home to Minna comes across as genuine. He wrote to her that he could hardly wait to move into a house where he would be with his animals and with a woman who would pamper him and care for him so that he might recover after the exertions of London. But his love for Mathilde Wesendonck remained the essential aspect of his life. When Liszt was planning to visit Wagner in the summer of 1855, the latter asked for a postponement until the following November because Mathilde was about to give birth. "She is—all in all—my only resource here. She also has the greatest of interest in you, and for a long time has cherished a wish to be able to participate to her heart's content when we come together [...]. This will be a rare instance of happiness; let us intensify it as best we can, and enjoy it: I think that having the company of our lady friend will achieve this."[47] Franz complied with Richard's request, and Mathilde sent her thanks for it.

---

45   Burrell, 352–55 (slightly amended).
46   Ibid., 355 (slightly amended).
47   SB VII, 250–51 (July 22, 1855).

When the time for Richard's departure from London approached, it felt like an act of salvation. He went to the finest stores on Regent and Bond Streets and bought silken underwear for himself, and expensive Irish lace for Minna. She also received socks, a needle case, and a thimble from the wife of the musician Ferdinand Praeger, who had been Wagner's first host in London.[48] After his final concert, Richard celebrated at his Portland Terrace apartment together with a group of devoted friends: Karl Klindworth, Praeger, the violinist and composer Prosper Sainton, the latter's friend Charles Lüders (who had organized Richard Wagner's invitation to London in the first place), and Hector Berlioz and his wife. Wagner arrived back in Switzerland on June 30, 1855.

As promised, Minna had sewn him a new dressing gown and silk summer house pants. He lazed around, wallowing on one sofa then another (as he himself put it). In early July, Richard, Minna, and their parrot went to Seelisberg in order to spend three weeks recuperating. Their dog had died shortly before, and they were both distraught about it. They spent their vacation at the spa there until the beginning of August, and Minna took a whey cure in order to try and improve her state of health. The mountain air and the magnificent view did them good; these were restful weeks for both of them. Minna presumably bore in mind how much she had missed Richard during his trip to England, and will have avoided criticizing him. But physical indisposition compelled her to end her cure prematurely. Richard also struggled with illness after his return, for he was now troubled with a recurrence of the erysipelas that had plagued him time and again.

The Wagners spent New Year's Eve 1855–56 with the Wesendoncks once more. They were picked up in a horse-drawn carriage and greeted with champagne. Then they gave each other end-of-year gifts. Minna was given an expensive muff that delighted her because her old one had served her for twelve years and now looked "very rough." Richard was presented with a black marble writing set, while Natalie got a pretty, gray scarf. Richard and Minna hardly gave each other any presents: "My capricious husband got an embroidered velvet cap, and I made him fresh covers for a couple of satin cushions. I got nothing."[49] Minna wavered in her suspicions about Mathilde, but for the moment she felt reassured, probably also because Mathilde was making an effort to engage with her. "Mrs. Wesendonck has very solid principles such as are surely possessed by few women, and this does

---

48   Praeger 1892, 270.
49   Minna to Mathilde Schiffner, February 16, 1856 (RWA).

not suit everyone.—What's more, I believe that this woman really loves and respects me, which helps to ensure that those good principles are not so easily rattled. In short, I am completely calm about this matter." She continued:

> Richard, thank God, is now also pretty healthy again, though he still has to keep himself in check so as not to trigger a relapse of his dreadful facial erysipelas. He had to spend more than 9 weeks in bed, most of the time. Given Richard's skittishness, but especially his distressful mental agitation, it was very difficult and I had to endure a lot of nasty moods that were not exactly congenial to me, but none of it was my fault.[50]

She had also lost weight, she said, and she wrote that she could no longer climb the Uetliberg but could only ascend it on the back of a donkey or a horse.[51] The fact that she could no longer manage this mild, one-hour hike, shows just how much her heart was already damaged.

In December, Minna's sick father died. Although it was not unexpected, she was still shaken. Richard declared that he was willing to take in Minna's widowed mother in their Zurich apartment. Since Mathilde Schiffner lived in the same house as Minna's mother, Minna asked her to find out if she would be physically capable of such a journey. But none of this came about, because Minna's mother also died, just three months later; she had neglected her own health in taking care of her husband. This second blow also hit Minna hard. "My father's death 3 months ago touched me deeply, despite everything, but the loss of my kind-hearted mother has affected me terribly."[52]

In 1856, Ferdinand Praeger, Wagner's friend from London, came to visit Richard and Minna in their Zurich apartment. His description of Minna is somewhat idealized, and his reminiscences must overall be read with caution. Nevertheless, something of the Wagners' situation at the time shimmers through his account.

> In Minna I recognized a pattern of devotion; her place in their chalet was characteristic of the whole relationship between her and her husband. She was devoted to him, saw from his eyes what he desired, did everything that could give him pleasure, and did not make the slightest demands; his satisfaction was her reward. One could almost speak of a relationship such as that of a mother

50　Ibid.
51　Ibid.
52　Minna to Mathilde Schiffner, December 19, 1855 and March 29, 1856 (RWA).

with her favorite child; she watched over his condition and sensed in advance if he was about to have any attack of illness, and thereby endured all the commotion of a man who was passionate in his lamenting.[53]

In the summer of 1856, Richard took a cure of several weeks in Mornex at the foot of Mont Salève, just across the French border from Geneva, in an effort to rid himself of the erysipelas from which he had been suffering for months. Minna had in this time been fully occupied with caring for him, and the therapy in Mornex seemed to be his last possible hope. Since Richard's doctors forbade him from working on medical grounds, he did not compose in Mornex, but wrote all the more letters instead. The matter of his amnesty continued to preoccupy him, and he asked Liszt to take action on his behalf. He also sent a petition for clemency to King Johann of Saxony. But none of it worked. He was also in love, and correspondingly irritable. He had no prospect of freeing himself from the vexatious business of needing money, nor had he any prospect of erotic fulfillment with Mathilde. Was his attempt to move back to Germany simply an effort to escape the complications in his life? Back home, the Wagners were also having problems with Natalie, who frequently quarreled with Minna and had become a disturbance to their domestic peace. Richard had tired of her and wanted her to leave their household. He was also in the midst of problematic negotiations with the publisher Breitkopf & Härtel, to whom he had wanted to sell the complete score of *Der Ring des Nibelungen*. He had formulated his preferred contract in rigid terms, and was demanding a lump sum of 10,000 thalers. But Breitkopf initially offered him only half of this fee, and Wagner was trying to alter their agreement in his favor. He wanted the second half of the fee to be converted into a kind of life annuity with a term of twenty years. This was unacceptable to his publisher, however, who accordingly refused to take on the work.

The biggest problem for Richard at the moment was finding a more suitable apartment. He was constantly being disturbed by the noise of various pianos and flutes in the same building. While he was still at his cure in Mornex he wrote to both Minna and Mathilde Wesendonck to ask them each to try and find something—to check out more appropriate apartments and speak to potential landlords or even people willing to sell him a place.

---

53   Praeger 1892 (German edition), 306. This passage is not included in the supposedly "original" English edition of Praeger's book, which he himself translated into German.

Minna had already taken a cure herself the previous summer—she needed help with her nerves, breathlessness, and insomnia. Richard now sent her a pressed flower—perhaps symbolizing his dream of procuring enough money to purchase a house on a small piece of land with a garden in the countryside: one that might satisfy his need for peace and seclusion. Minna, as always, was more realistic. It seemed more economical to her for them to rent a house with a garden along the Zurich Lake, rather than buying or building one. She was well acquainted with Wagner's restlessness and knew full well that even a house of his own might not tie him down for long.

Richard's imagination now ran riot with all manner of plans. To Minna he spoke of the home he wanted to build as if it were already real, and he told her they would begin construction in early September. He had envisioned earning 20,000 francs (though it never materialized), decided he would purchase a horse-drawn carriage, and even made a U-turn on his decision to send Natalie away. Suddenly, he was fine with her staying. Minna had lived for years with Richard's inability to acknowledge reality, and regarded this as a sign of weakness. She could simply never rely on him in practical matters. But in his correspondence with Mathilde Wesendonck, by contrast, Richard's senses were perfectly acute, and he weighed up every sentence. Richard's letters to Otto Wesendonck—who at this time was in Paris—show him at pains to come across as innocent, just as he also downplayed everything about Mathilde in his letters to Minna. From his cure in Mornex he wrote to Otto, alluding to the latter's plans for his family to spend the next Christmas away from Zurich: "Do I really have to find out again how it is to spend a winter in Zurich without the Wesendoncks? [...] You vagabonds: you build a house, but then run away."[54] He could only hope that Mathilde would read between the lines of his letter, and persuade her husband to spend the winter in Zurich after all.

But Richard's thoughts also often returned to Minna. He had two dreams that he faithfully committed to paper for her, and which testify to fears of loss on his part. In the one she had left him, and when he searched for her, he found her living in poverty with her parents. She refused to leave them until he shouted to her that her parents had died, then he finally cried out her name and woke up. In the other, he was searching for her and found their apartment, but there was no one in their parlor and the apartment was

---

54　SB VIII, 129–31, here 131 (July 29, 1856).

abandoned. When he went in, a sharp draft swept toward him. But no matter how many times he tried, he was unable to close the window.[55]

Meanwhile, Richard's request for amnesty had again been rejected. So not only did he have no amnesty: he had no new apartment, no money, no contract for the *Ring*, no horse-drawn carriage, and the woman he loved was still unattainable. He began to wonder how his life should proceed at all. "God knows, if someone doesn't make me really enjoy my work, I'll leave it," he wrote to Liszt from his cure. "Why should a poor devil like me toil away and torment myself with such a terrible burden, when the present cannot even grant me a proper place to work? I have told Härtel: if they can't help me find a quiet, free house to live in like I need, then I'll put all this nonsense aside."[56] Despite his repeated setbacks, Richard's self-confidence remained undimmed, and he continued to claim special status for himself. In light of what he had already achieved artistically and in the context of operatic history, his desire for privilege was thoroughly appropriate. But hardly anyone bothered to notice.

Minna, on the other hand, was very much looking forward to a visit from Mathilde Schiffner and Clara Wolfram, who had written to tell her of their impending arrival. Minna's health had improved, and she was keen to go on excursions with the two women.

> In the worst case, I'll ride and let you young people walk beside me [...] I hardly dare burden you with things to bring along. You can find both porcino and morel mushrooms here, though they are barely affordable—it's really an old, expensive hole here. Then two pairs of boots [...] if they don't fit me, I will still be able to sell them here. If I think of anything else, I will write to you. In any case, I have to go to Seelisberg, even if just for 2 weeks, in order to undergo a little goat's whey cure. My financial resources won't allow me to stay any longer, it's 5 francs per day in such a spa, and there's no other way to do it.[57]

Minna also asked Mathilde to bring a small smoothing iron that allowed one to fold ruffs and other finery into a cone or a roll. She did not want to invite her friends to any concerts. Despite her occasional praise of the local offerings, she still thought the quality of them too poor.[58]

---

55   SB VIII, 95–98, here 96 (June 25, 1856).
56   SB VIII, 119–22, here 122 (July 20, 1856).
57   Minna to Mathilde Schiffner, June 15, 1856 (RWA).
58   Minna to Mathilde Schiffner, July 19 and 30, 1856 (RWA).

Richard's cure in Mornex was a success: his erysipelas disappeared. On his way home he met Otto and Mathilde in Bern, and two days later he was back in Zurich. Clara Wolfram and Mathilde Schiffner had arrived in the meantime. On Minna's birthday, Richard's gift to her was to take all three women on an excursion to his beloved Brunnen. They experienced a glorious sunset, heard yodeling, and watched cows being milked.[59] At nightfall, they were treated to a musical homage to Richard. Their hotelier Auf der Maur, to whom Richard had already sent wind-band arrangements from his operas, now got the local band to perform pieces by him on two colorfully lit barges. "This was followed by a little speech in my honor and an equally hearty reply on my part, after which I shook a large number of calloused hands while we drank a few bottles of wine at the lakeside."[60] This was a special experience for the three women, who were as delighted with the appreciation shown to Richard as they were about the magnificent landscapes around them.

In October 1856, Franz Liszt arrived in Zurich for an extended visit, along with the Princess Carolyne zu Sayn-Wittgenstein and her daughter Marie. They stayed at the Hotel Baur au Lac, and immediately triggered a flurry of activity. Waiters and waitresses buzzed back and forth, there were alternate dinners and "suppers," and the coaches of the local bigwigs came and went. Liszt and his partner enjoyed numerous meetings with illustrious guests, and Emma and Georg Herwegh, Eliza and François Wille, and Clara Wolfram were constant additional attendees. The Wesendoncks came as often as they could. Liszt and the princess also enjoyed simpler evenings chez Wagner, where the princess even deigned to help Minna serve the guests. After dinner, once they had all made themselves comfortable—half sitting, half lying down—Richard read them all his libretti for *Tristan und Isolde* and *Die Sieger* (though the latter would remain unrealized in music). More intimate conversations also took place between Richard, Liszt, and Carolyne, during which Richard recounted the tale of his love for Jessie Laussot back in Bordeaux in 1850.[61]

A special highlight of Liszt's visit was a joint trip to St. Gallen, where both Liszt and Wagner had together agreed to conduct a concert of the local orchestra on November 23. They stayed at the Hotel Zum Hecht. These distinguished visitors attracted a lot of attention, and several friends and

59   BB, 126.

60   ML, 536.

61   SB IX, 60–61, here 61 (October 4 and 5, 1857). Wagner here recalled the events of 1856 in a letter written to Liszt one year later.

acquaintances awaited them at the new station—St. Gallen had only just that year become part of the expanding Swiss railway network. They were joined by the Willes, Herweghs, Theodor Kirchner, Moritz von Wyss, the architect Leonhard Zeugheer, and others. In the first half of the concert Liszt conducted his symphonic poems *Orpheus* and *Les Préludes*, while the second half featured Wagner conducting Beethoven's *Eroica* Symphony. "We will never forget this evening," enthused the local newspaper, "on which these two artistic heroes of the modern age presented such beautiful delights for us, here in our little city."[62] Wagner enjoyed finally hearing two symphonic poems by Liszt that he had previously known only from the score. It was important for his own development as a composer to hear how Liszt was able to fuse expression and content, and his *Ring* cycle benefited from the experience.

The following day they visited the famous library of the Baroque monastery in St. Gallen, then gathered for an evening party at the home of Charles Edouard Bourry, a rich local businessman and patron of the arts. Liszt played Beethoven's *Hammerklavier* Sonata, op. 106, and then they celebrated Minna and Richard's twentieth wedding anniversary by having everyone dance a polonaise through all the rooms of the house to the accompaniment of the wedding music from *Lohengrin*. It must have been quite a picture: Wagner in jocular mood, hand in hand at the front with his blissful wife, then Liszt and Princess Carolyne, and Emma and Georg Herwegh—Emma was always willing to try out anything unusual, while Georg as an old revolutionary will have found everything terribly bourgeois, but presumably put on a good face. They were followed on the dance floor by assorted St. Gallen dignitaries, all happily parading along to the music. This evening remained for Minna a high point in her life, since she was this time the joint object of celebration alongside her husband. The next day brought a festive banquet in the hall of the Hotel Zum Hecht for about forty people. The *Tagblatt der Stadt St. Gallen* reported: "Besides the most cheerful, informal tone at the table, there was also a lively intellectual discussion and a warm artistic exchange of ideas, so one might say in truth that it was an evening 'comme il faut.' The dear guests and their achievements in modern music were celebrated with passionate toasts in eloquent words."[63] Wagner naturally was unable to refrain from expanding on the time allotted for speeches in order to expound on his favorite topics. Claiming that it was better to offer no

---

62 Quoted in Fehr 1953, 70.
63 Quoted ibid., 72.

theater than bad theater, he described in detail the possible benefits of the stage for the tastes and moral fiber of the population—which seems strange when we consider that he was already planning his opera *Tristan und Isolde*, which not a few artists of the 19th century considered perfectly indecent (though he himself naturally saw no contradiction at all).

Liszt enthusiastically recommended performing *Lohengrin* at the opening of the Municipal Theater in St. Gallen (though this did not come about). Minna was seated between Liszt and Wagner, and will have enjoyed to the full their pleasurable, cheerful get-together. It was the last time that such a gathering would ever pay homage to her as the respected wife of Richard Wagner. That night there was a commotion: the Princess Carolyne had a nervous fit and got her daughter to read to her to assuage her nerves. This in turn disturbed Richard so much that he took Minna and moved into another hotel room.[64]

After seven weeks in Switzerland, Franz Liszt and Princess Carolyne finally left. Richard now found Zurich quite deserted: not only had Liszt departed, but the Wesendoncks were in Paris. The relationship between Wagner and the Wesendoncks had undergone several ups and downs this year—it seems that Richard had interpreted their repeated absences as an intentional withdrawal of affection on Mathilde's part. But mutual visits continued, and in February 1857 Minna was able to write to Mathilde Schiffner that "the Wesendoncks often come to us after dinner at 6 and it is very relaxed. I set nothing before them but tea and melba toast."[65]

The Wesendoncks were finally preparing to move into their magnificent new villa when a wonderful act of providence occurred. There was a cottage on the piece of land next to Otto's future home, and a doctor for the mentally ill was planning to buy it to turn it into a clinic. The Wesendoncks were horrified, so Otto bought up the cottage himself, and offered it to the Wagners as a lifelong rental for the same annual fee that they were paying on the Zeltweg: 800 francs. Minna was over the moon. She had never lived in such beautiful surroundings, and it seemed to her that she was finally realizing her dreams. She wrote joyfully to Princess Carolyne to tell her that she had had her eye on the pretty house with the lovely garden for years now, but had given up any hopes of ever seeing her wishes fulfilled.[66] Her next letter to Mathilde Schiffner was written on pink paper as a sign of her ebullient

---

64   Ibid., 68.
65   Minna to Mathilde Schiffner, February 23, 1857 (RWA).
66   February 6, 1857, in Fehr 1953, 375.

mood. She thanked her friend for an ornate handkerchief she had sent: "I can quite well judge from the fine, painstaking work that this lovely handkerchief won't have been cheap," she wrote, before telling Mathilde of the good news. Richard, with his sensitive hearing, had been on the lookout for a home that might offer him the peace and quiet he needed, so when Otto made his offer they immediately cancelled the lease on their Zeltweg apartment, and found someone else to take it on for 900 francs a year. "In five weeks," she wrote to Mathilde Schiffner, "that is, already before the Easter holidays, we shall be moving out in time to see all the blossoms and leaves as they sprout, right from the start. What bliss."[67] After her departure from Dresden and the deep disappointments that had been the result, it now seemed that happiness beckoned, along with justified hopes for better times.

---

67 Minna to Mathilde Schiffner, February 23, 1857 (RWA).

Chapter Eight

"Alas, now all our happiness is gone ..."

The Wesendonck Scandal, 1857–58

What bliss! At last, a great turning point seemed to have arrived. The country cottage for which Richard and Minna had so often longed, and which they had so often dreamed about, now became a reality. It was their sixth place of residence in Zurich and for Minna a double stroke of luck: she would now also have a garden of her own where she could grow vegetables and make full use of whatever she harvested. She also had reason to hope that Otto Wesendonck's patronage would mean an end to their dreadful financial difficulties. The pretty half-timbered cottage had a magnificent view of the lake and itself exuded peace, quiet, and an elegant ambience. Minna bubbled over with joy in her next letter to Mathilde Schiffner: "Although I have a terrible cough and sniffles again at the moment, the thought of being able to breathe in the pure air of the garden and its flowers on that little hill makes me feel already fresh and healthy. We could hardly find anywhere more beautiful and healthier. Richard says so too."[1] Since it was originally built as a summer cottage, a heating system had to be installed for the colder months. There was no space for individual stoves, so a heating room was set up, with pipes leading into the different rooms. There were three rooms on the ground floor, the same number on the floor above. A small gable room was set up for guests, and Minna was already looking forward to receiving Mathilde Schiffner there: "I think it will be so wonderful, if God grants me enough life, to drink a cup of coffee or tea with you on my balcony, enjoying the most magnificent

---

1   Minna to Mathilde Schiffner, February 23, 1857 (RWA).

Figure 8.1. The "Asyl" where Minna and Richard lived in Zurich, 1857–58.
Baugeschichtliches Archiv, Zurich.

view of the snowy mountains, the lake, and the city—which does not look at all bad from there."[2]

Richard reserved the upper floor for himself. His living area comprised a small study with a wonderful view of the upper lake and the Alps of Canton Glarus, then a music room, a salon, and a veranda. Minna's quarters were to be on the ground floor, a few steps above the garden. Here, she had her own realm. Minna and Richard thus had separate quarters, and she would be able to shield Richard from seeing guests when it did not suit him. But a lot still had to be done before they could move in. In his autobiography, Richard mentioned "the perennial differences between my wife and myself as to this and that,"[3] meaning his numerous requests for renovations and alterations to the house. He wanted to have "everything freshened up for our new home," wrote Minna, "and that has really kept me on my toes, since I unfortunately have to see to everything myself unless I want to end up with ten times as much trouble because things have been set up wrongly or forgotten." Minna

---

2   Ibid.
3   ML, 545.

commissioned a seamstress to mend, alter, and shorten the curtains where necessary. The furniture covers had to be dyed, the rooms wallpapered, and many a trip taken to the "trimming maker"—a specialist in ornate fabrics such as braids, laces, and tassels. But since the bills were only due at the end of the year, their finances were spared for the time being. Minna also did a lot of sewing herself. But the strain of everything now took its toll. She caught a cold, and on Easter Sunday—when she had planned to work on a hat for Natalie—she had to go to bed with a fever, a sore throat, and chills. The doctor applied leeches.

For good or ill, Richard had to take on Minna's tasks in their move from the old apartment to the cottage. He got their maid, Therese, to bring him boxes, and simply threw in laundry and clothes to empty the closets—their replacement renters on the Zeltweg were now urging them to move quickly. When the latter moved in on the appointed day, the Wagners ultimately had to stay in a hotel for ten days before moving into their house. Minna hired a cleaning woman to help with their arrival in the new place, and she got annoyed with Natalie and Therese, who in the meantime had "only been making food and brewing coffee for themselves, not caring about anything but arguing about us."[4] When Minna had recovered from her cold and went to the house, she found the boxes still standing around. The relationship between mother and daughter remained difficult. Minna was firmly in charge of the household, but Natalie still believed that they were sisters, and would not be told what to do.

By the end of April, the Wagners were finally able to move in, though bricklayers and carpenters were still coming and going, it was cold and damp, and the heating was not yet working. The Wagners' health had suffered in the past weeks, but they recovered as the weather improved. Richard's study was comfortably furnished. His standing desk for composing was there, as was his sitting desk for writing texts and letters, and there was a chaise longue in the center of the room if he wanted to rest. The music room was in easy reach for him to try out any passages at the piano. Now and then, he would interrupt his work to lie down a little. He was not available to see anyone in the mornings, and Minna made sure to keep any visitors from him. If he needed relaxation of a more physical kind, he could walk around in their park-like garden.

The garden was already well tended, and it now provided Minna with an agreeable occupation. She took pleasure in creating a vegetable

---

4   Minna to Mathilde Schiffner, June 7, 1857 (RWA).

garden—something in which she already had experience. The mild climate also meant that southern fruits were able to grow there, such as apricots, peaches, and grapes. Richard's mood improved rapidly after moving in, which also cheered up Minna. He could not stop praising "the most splendid weather, the most magnificent house, the divine air."[5] The "angelic peace" that had descended even seemed to extend to the servants. Therese was as if transformed. She now worked industriously and was even friendly.

Work on the stucco and wallpaper in the stately home next door was finished by July, which meant that the Wesendoncks too were finally able to move in. Mathilde was now the mistress of a spacious house, and she set about hosting evening gatherings that were stimulating for all concerned. She knew how to entertain in style, and her feel for aesthetics and harmony meant that her household exuded calm and spaciousness. "She was the soul of it all. The carriages, horses for riding, newspapers, books, baths, excellent meals with exquisite wines, music, interesting people who came from everywhere and liked to stay: all this made the villa a paradise for any guest."[6] It was thus an environment that corresponded perfectly to Richard's needs.

In his memoirs, the composer and commentator Richard Pohl offered a comparative assessment of Minna and Mathilde. The latter was

> beautiful in appearance, possessed of a feminine, graceful, and poetically mind-ed nature, and she exerted an obviously stimulating influence on the Master. Compared to her, Wagner's wife Minna could not help but be put very much in the shade—she had aged rapidly and was by nature rather sober, good-natured, but plain. In Wagner's presence, his wife was mostly silent. When you met her alone, she spoke openly from the heart. She could not understand at all how her husband could work for years on projects that had not the slightest chance of being realized. She had absolutely no hopes for the *Nibelungen*. She would have much preferred him to write works that could be performed everywhere and would also achieve pecuniary success. You could see at first glance that these two natures could not harmonize together, and it was not difficult to predict that their conjugal life would sooner or later end in separation.[7]

But what Pohl in retrospect found inevitable was by no means certain at this time. Richard was incredibly inspired, for his creative work enabled him to project his erotic longings for Mathilde onto an idealized, spiritual plane

5   Ibid.
6   Kopf 1899, 281.
7   Quoted in Golther 1914, XIII.

Figure 8.2. Mathilde Wesendonck, ca. 1850. Wille Archive, Mariafeld.

while his practical needs in life were being cared for by Minna. His long walks and hikes in the surrounding countryside were designed to provide him with ideas that could serve as a starting point for his composing. His unrealizable love for Mathilde was thematized in the *Ring*, *Tristan*, and later also in his *Meistersinger*. She was his Sieglinde, his Isolde, and his Eva—a quite remarkable return on his emotional investment. In the *Meistersinger*, Wagner only added Hans Sachs's stoic renunciation of Eva after he had finally realized—both intellectually and emotionally—that a union with Mathilde would always remain impossible (and in his letters to her, he indeed intimated his reasons for altering the libretto).[8] And since Richard knew that Mathilde grasped his musical language, he felt that she understood him completely.

Wagner christened this new house his "Asyl" (refuge). In the summer of 1857, Eduard Devrient came to visit and was the first to "inaugurate" the guest room. At lunchtime, Minna also had to cater for the Wesendoncks, Alexander Müller, Gottfried Semper, and Georg Herwegh—she thus had to organize food for eight people. Richard had requested a particularly opulent meal in order to impress his former Dresden colleague, though Minna was unhappy about it on account of their lack of money. Devrient described the visit to his wife Therese back home.

> He is possessed of a thoroughly odd nature, as you know, always passionately in the grip of new impressions, ideas, designs, and prejudices. He makes far too much of his physical condition, his water cures, his new doctor, etc. One gets a feeling of insecurity regarding the elegance of his charming house and the opulence of his hospitality, and this feeling is further intensified by the behavior of his wife, who enjoys everything but whose expression suggests that it cannot last long after all; or perhaps she is shying away from making use of it all. She herself seems uncomfortable and runs the house more like a servant than a housewife.[9]

After their meal, they all walked out into the upper garden, then tea was served. At dinner, Devrient read two acts from Shakespeare's *Julius Caesar*. As a former actor, Minna will no doubt have listened with greater interest to the monologues of their famous colleague than to those of her husband to which she had been subjected for decades on a daily basis. Devrient also noted again just how exhausting Richard could be:

---

8   See Rieger 2011, 87–90. For more detail, see Voss 1996, 284ff.
9   Devrient 1909, 287.

Wagner speaks at infinite length but restlessly, repeating individual words to the point of torment, and breaking off just as many paragraphs. Like Liszt. Since he wants to use all his thoughts and the fruits of his reading immediately in the course of speaking, he digresses wildly, becomes ever more incomprehensible the more words he utters, and his listeners become quite dizzy from it.[10]

Devrient sent his wife greetings from Minna: "She is a very diligent hostess, who only worries me because of the grandiose meals she organizes."[11] When their household was dissolved a year later, their wine cellar was stocked with three hundred bottles of wine—testament enough to Richard's luxurious needs in matters of food and drink.

The first few months in the Asyl flew by. They occasionally went to the theater together—to see Shakespeare's *Othello*, for example—or to concerts, such as the guest performance in Zurich given by Clara Schumann on December 7, 1857, which both Mathilde and Richard attended. Clara was at something of a loss as to what to make of him, and she was unable to find him sympathetic, despite his friendly manner.[12] Minna often went out with Emilie Heim, the wife of Ignaz, a local choral conductor, who later wistfully recalled this happy time: "And how often you called for me last winter to go to the theater."[13]

The Wagners and Wesendoncks were in near-daily contact with each other now. This also meant that Richard could see Mathilde on a regular basis without it being noticed. When Hans and Cosima von Bülow arrived in Zurich for four weeks in late August 1857 as part of their honeymoon travels, Hans made music every day, and Mathilde Wesendonck also came over to listen. Thus Richard's present wife, his future wife, and his adored muse all sat side by side in apparent harmony. They read literature together, such as works by Calderón, though Minna stuck to novels by Walter Scott. Emma and Georg Herwegh, Gottfried Keller, and other guests often dropped by. Bülow was usually highly critical of those around him, but on this occasion he wrote that he "had not experienced such pleasurable moments since time immemorial."[14] He was overjoyed to be able to get to grips with the works of a friend and kindred spirit, far away from the stultifying atmosphere of the

---

10   Ibid., 284.

11   Ibid.

12   Litzmann 1920, III, 29.

13   Burrell, 322 (letter of March 30, 1858).

14   Bülow 1909, IV, 109 (September 4, 1857).

Figure 8.3. Cosima von Bülow, photograph by Louis Held, Weimar 1857.
Nationalarchiv der Richard-Wagner-Stiftung, Bayreuth.

Stern Conservatory in Berlin where he taught the piano. Wagner admired Bülow's prodigious skill, his secure musical intuition, and his quite incredible memory. For his part, Bülow was one of the first to recognize the potential that lay in Wagner's new compositional style. He wrote to Julius Stern about *Der Ring des Nibelungen*: "Nothing comparable or even approximating it has ever been written—never at all—not in any art or language […] it is true redemption from the dung of the world."[15]

Minna reported back to Mathilde Schiffner about their visitors, and she also mentioned that Richard had finished the libretto for *Tristan und Isolde*. She regretted that he had interrupted his work on the *Ring* for this purpose—the tetralogy remained for the moment incomplete—and was worried about their future sources of income: "*Tannhäuser*, which always brought in some money, has now pretty much made the rounds of all the theaters, so we can hope for no more revenue from it."[16] She had no idea of the creative impulse that was driving Richard to the very peak of inspiration as a composer—all thanks to his love for Mathilde—nor could she have any intimation of the future impact that his latest works would have on the history of music and opera.

Numerous notes in Richard's hand testify to his frequent contact with the Wesendoncks: "Children, won't I get to see you a little today? I'm in a better state than yesterday." And another time: "It seems to me as if we'd forgotten to invite you properly on Sunday evening: please allow me to make up for what I missed! You know it's going to be a Sulzer party. I also have to inform you that tea will be drunk at 7 o'clock." And yet another time: "Will you come over a little for the last act of the *Walküre*? I—hope so."[17]

When Richard Pohl visited from Weimar, Wagner was full of hope and in a happy mood. During walks they took together, Wagner talked about the misunderstandings that existed with regard to his writings. Pohl found the atmosphere in Wagners' house highly stimulating. One evening, Wagner played and sang the end of Act 2 of *Siegfried*—the forest murmurs and the Woodbird—then began to talk about the libretto of *Tristan und Isolde*. He spoke about the transition from Act 2 to Act 3, for which he had not yet found a satisfactory solution.[18] Minna will have got to know every detail

---

15   Ibid., IV, 114f. (September 19, 1857).

16   Minna to Mathilde Schiffner, October 29, 1857 (RWA).

17   The M. Wesendonck archives in Stadtarchiv Zürich (shelfmark 84 VII).

18   Fehr 1953, 99f.

of these works, for she was there in the room when Richard explained his operas, night after night, measure by measure.

Wagner was living in an environment that was aesthetically and erotically inspiring; his domestic concerns were being administered excellently; he was in the midst of a magnificent landscape; and he had a female admirer next door who was deeply devoted to him. It all seemed too perfect to last. And the more time passed, the clearer it became to Richard that his love for Mathilde would not find fulfillment. The elation that he enjoyed in her presence was liable to switch into its opposite, and depression would seize him. He revealed to Marie, the daughter of Princess Carolyne, that it was his interactions with Mathilde that both gave him comfort and at the same time tormented him. "What is going on in me cannot be put into words: only this one thing I can intimate, namely that the world is passing away before me, more and more every day, and that I sit, sighing, on the narrowest boundary between life and death [...]. And is my art, this eternal game with my agony, still supposed to be able to please me? How long shall this deception last?"[19]

Over time, it began to pall on Otto that Richard had begun to dominate the daily routine in his villa. Whenever he came to visit, he would be specific about his wishes regarding the heating, the lighting, and even the time that meals were taken. Worse still, Mathilde liked to acquiesce to whatever Richard wanted: "in many things [...] consideration was shown to me that seemed to encroach upon his rights as master of the house," he wrote with mock cluelessness in his autobiography, several years later.[20] Mathilde had to maneuver between these two men while also trying to cope with Minna's suspicions. None of this was easy, but she also found it inspiring to be the catalyst for Richard's immense creative urge. This in turn made her feel condescension for Minna, who was "only" a housewife, cooking Richard's food and fixing his clothes, but less concerned with the spiritual and intellectual dimensions of his creative work. For her part, Minna felt belittled, and she once complained to Frau Wesendonck about her haughtiness. "But then she asked me to forgive her again, and now I am good to her again on account of Richard."[21] It is unclear what caused this particular little quarrel, but it is clear that both women were endeavoring to keep the peace for Richard's sake.

---

19   SB IX, 45 (after September 24, 1857).
20   ML, 552.
21   Minna to Mathilde Schiffner, October 29, 1857 (RWA).

The fact that Mathilde and Richard apparently agreed on mutual sexual abstinence in their marriages put an additional strain on each couple and on the relationship between them all. After it was all over, Richard wrote to his sister Clara that Mathilde had "gradually compelled her husband to do as she wished until he was at a point of giving up completely." But this only intensified Otto's feelings of jealousy, which his wife tried to allay—claimed Richard—by being completely open with him. "The only thing that made this success possible for her was the depth and nobility of her disposition, which was far removed from anything selfish, and which gave her the strength to reveal herself to her husband to the extent that when she finally threatened him with suicide, he had no choice but to abstain from her."[22] Such asceticism on all sides only served to intensify the already oppressive, sultry atmosphere, and we can surely believe Natalie when she wrote about this time to Mrs. Burrell, many years later:

> Immediately after moving into that small, unhappy house next to the Wesendoncks, Minna was banished from the bedroom that she shared with Richard. This was the very first time in her 22-year marriage that this had happened. [...] It is a fact that Mathilde very often went up to Wagner in the mornings dressed in her charming, elegant morning attire, and stayed with him in his room for a very long time. Minna found it beneath her womanly dignity and pride to go up to see Wagner's visitor under such circumstances."[23]

Given that the doors will have been unlocked, it is hardly likely that any intimate contact could have occurred. However, in his later letters to Mathilde, Wagner indeed recalled moments of tender affection between them.

There is a poem in Mathilde's cycle *Mignon*, published in 1874 in her book entitled *Gedichte, Volksweisen, Legenden und Sagen*, that supports these claims that she and Richard had sworn themselves to abstinence:

Habe oft Dich bitten wollen	I often wanted to ask you
um den höchsten Augenblick.	for the supreme moment.
Doch ein unerklärlich Bangen	But an inexplicable trepidation
schaudernd hielt das Wort zurück.	made me shudder and hold back the words.

---

22   SB X, 27–32, here 27–28 (August 20, 1858).

23   Burrell (German edition), 675; the English version is in Burrell, 528.

Einmal folgen meiner
  Neigung
wollt' ich, einmal selig sein,
Einmal an der ganzen Fülle
höchsten Erdenglücks mich
  freu'n!

Und so faßt' ich mir ein Herze,
schlich zur Nacht an deine Thür,
Wußte, daß sie unverschlossen,
wollt' mich bergen drin vor Dir!

Als zur Treppe ich gekommen,
ein Geräusch gebot mir Halt,
Denn ich sah, den Gang hin-
  schreitend,
eine weibliche Gestalt.

Leise drückt sie an der Klinke
deiner Tür und huscht hinein,
Bald d'rauf schallen Deine
  Tritte
und der Riegel schiebt sich ein.

Unerhörte Qualen wühlten
da mein ganz Empfinden auf
Und des Herzens Puls, getroffen
an der Quelle, stockt' den Lauf.

Bleiern lag's auf mir wie
  Sterben,
keine Rettung wußt' ich
  mehr,
Und ich wälzte mich am Boden,

Just once, I would gladly have
  followed my desires,
to attain bliss just once,
to enjoy the fullness, just once,
of the ultimate joy that Earth can
  offer!

And so I took heart,
and crept up to your door at night,
knowing that it was unlocked,
wanting to hide in there from you!

When I came to the stairs,
a noise made me stop,
because I saw, walking along the
  corridor,
the figure of a woman.

She softly turned the handle
of your door and darted inside.
Soon afterwards, your footsteps rang
  out
and the latch fell.

Undreamt-of torments set
all my emotions in turmoil,
and my heart's pulse, wounded
at its source, stood still.

A leaden weight lay upon me, like
  approaching death;
I no longer knew where to turn for
  help.
And I rolled on the floor

Schmerzlich zuckend, hin und her.	in painful convulsions, to and fro.

Da erklang das Lied des Harfners	Then the song of the harpist sounded
aus der Kammer unterm Dach,	from the room underneath the roof,
Und ich stürzt' zu seinen Füßen,	and I threw myself at his feet,
Blieb die Nacht in Jammer wach!	remaining awake the whole night in my misery![24]

The reaction of the narrator here is reminiscent of the "hysteria" that was supposedly rampant in the 19th century, which was often rooted in the enforced sexual abstinence of women during that especially prudish era. But if the poem does indeed depict a real occurrence, then it suggests that Richard did not abide by their agreement to avoid sexual relations in their respective marriages.

The stream of visitors to the Wagners' house did not stop. As a result, Minna was completely occupied with housework and her large vegetable garden. Richard's moods fluctuated between despair and elation. His progress with the score of *Tristan* helped him to cope with the stresses of his life. In this work, erotic love is depicted as a compulsion that brings man and woman together by severing them from their rational faculties.

Richard took delight in visits from his adored muse whenever she came over to chat with his guests or to listen to the topics he wanted to expound upon. And it gave him special pleasure to explain his work to her, because she understood precisely that his sublimated desires were directed at her. There was no one else to whom he liked to talk so much, and he also told her why: "With men, it's not at all possible: with them—despite all ties of friendship—the main thing is not to come out of your shell; to assert your personal opinion; and to let yourself be touched by as little as possible. That's just the way it is: man lives from himself."[25] Mathilde, however, was utterly there for him, and he drew her as closely as possible into his work. On September 18, 1857, he presented her with the finished autograph of the libretto for *Tristan*. A year later, Wagner told his sister how Mathilde had been overwhelmed, and had declared to him that she must now surely die.[26] In 1861,

---

24   Wesendonck 1874, 46–47.
25   Golther 1914, 206f.
26   SB X, 27–32, here 28 (August 20, 1858).

he wrote to Mathilde to say: "The fact that I wrote 'Tristan' is something for which I shall thank you with all my soul in all eternity".[27] Years afterwards, by contrast, Wagner himself called Tristan and Isolde "a couple in the fullest blaze of sin"—but this ambiguity was a conscious compositional act on his part and an integral aspect of the work.

Exactly one month after this memorable September 18, Wagner and the Wesendoncks were invited to the Willes. Richard and Mathilde celebrated their "Tristan" anniversary in secret. During a walk, Otto offered his arm to Eliza Wille, which gave Richard the opportunity to do the same to Mathilde. He was blissfully happy.

When he finished the music for the dialogue between Brangäne and Isolde in the third scene of the first act of *Tristan*, Wagner wrote to Mathilde: "Today, 'Morold struck, and I healed the wound so that he became well again' went excellently today—I have to play it for you afterwards!"[28] The connections to their own predicament were obvious, for Isolde agonizes over having to live near her secret lover, and Brangäne asks her: "Where did the man live who did not love you? Who saw Isolde and did not blissfully succumb to her?"[29] Mathilde's devotion to him made him happy and inspired him, and his work helped him to bear the torment of her proximity.

Between November 1857 and May 1858, Wagner composed five songs for female voice to texts by Mathilde. It was an exceedingly rare occurrence for him to set a text that he had not written himself, so she was well aware of the honor bestowed. Her next birthday, on December 23, 1857, provided Richard with another occasion to express his love. He arranged a morning serenade for her in the vestibule of her villa as a birthday surprise. Especially for the occasion, he took their song "Träume" (Dreams)— already finished in its version for voice and piano—and arranged it for violin solo and ten-part chamber orchestra. It was followed on that morning by a wind ensemble playing excerpts from *Rienzi* and *Tannhäuser*. By a lucky coincidence, Otto Wesendonck was away on business at the time. The event was a huge success.

As usual, Minna saw everything in a more practical light, albeit with a touch of irony, as she reported to Mathilde Schiffner:

---

27 SB XIII, 337–40, here 340 (December 21, 1861).

28 SB IX, 60 (October 1857).

29 On the sketch with this passage, Wagner wrote: "In the Asyl/first motif/May 16, 1857." Westernhagen 1973, 179.

It was 7 o'clock in the morning and everything went well and sounded well so as to wake her from her sweet dreams. I did my part inasmuch as I made all the musicians a great cup of coffee, provided them with butter sandwiches etc. since they were all there on empty stomachs and the way here is always long, especially when you have to blow your instrument afterwards. The fun cost us dearly, we had to have the music stands and instruments brought out here, and even if it was only a courtesy, I at least had to give the organizer of this little band of musicians a monetary gift of a few 20-franc pieces. I didn't think I had to open up my purse any more than that.[30]

Richard had given her two dresses in advance "so that I might appear respectably at the Wesendoncks'."[31] But Minna was afraid of the large bills that always arrived just after New Year; the costs of renovating the house had still not yet been paid.

The giving of gifts at Christmas 1857—the very last Christmas that the two couples would spend together—was superficially a harmonious occasion. Nevertheless, the underlying tensions were palpable. Minna was increasingly aware of the attention that Richard was paying to Mathilde, and of his obvious need to spend a lot of time with her. She was also bitterly aware of the chasm that existed between the Wesendoncks, who were wealthy and could afford whatever they wanted, and her own compulsive frugality. The Christmas tree was even more lavish than in the previous year. There were toys galore, and Minna gave each child something too, which cost a considerable amount "because nothing shoddy was allowed, and such things are expensive here."[32] Mathilde gave Otto several large copperplate engravings, while he gave her diamond-studded coral buttons and several silken dresses. Minna was given a collar and sleeves of muslin, decorated with lace and blue ribbons. "Richard was given another cushion, this is now the fourth since we have been acquainted. Of course, Mrs. Wesendonck does not take the trouble to make them herself, she buys them, for her circumstances make giving gifts simple and easy."[33]

Richard was delighted with the gifts he received from Minna. She had bought him two small busts, one each of Schiller and Goethe, a golden watch key (since he had lost his own), two bottles of eau de cologne, and a pair of fine socks that he had specifically requested. What particularly prompted him

---

30 Minna to Mathilde Schiffner, January 3, 1858 (RWA).
31 Ibid.
32 Ibid.
33 Ibid.

to merriment was a small rug that Minna had embroidered with swans as a witty allusion to his *Lohengrin*. Was Wagner's amused reaction perhaps more a sign of despair? After all, he was trying to revolutionize the whole genre of opera, but here his efforts were reduced to swans embroidered on a carpet. If his amusement was meant ironically, Minna didn't notice. But it speaks for her that she also made sure there were ample presents for their maid Therese and their manservant who were waiting next door in the dining room. Therese was engaged and soon to be married, so she received a black woolen shawl, lace sleeves, a collar with white ribbons, white gloves, and aprons. Their manservant was given six pairs of socks, warm gloves, a tie, and a scarf, and both received their annual salary. Even the dog received the gift of a new collar, while the parrot was given a golden nut. And Minna enjoyed all the attention she received.[34]

Richard completed the composition sketch of the first act of *Tristan* on the last day of the year, and he had his servant bring it to Mathilde, together with a poem that adopts the poetic style of his libretto, and features several references to its content:

Hochbeglückt,
Schmerzentrückt,
frei und rein
ewig Dein –
was sie sich klagten
und versagten,
Tristan und Isolde,
in keuscher Töne Golde,
ihr Weinen und ihr Küssen
leg' ich zu Deinen Füssen,
dass sie den Engel loben,
der mich so hoch erhoben!

[Blissfully happy, removed from pain, free and pure, eternally yours—What troubled Tristan and Isolde, their failures, tears and kisses, I offer in chaste, golden tones, and lay it at your feet, that they might praise the angel who lifted me up so high!]

If Minna had happened to read this, matters would have escalated immediately. In those days between Christmas and New Year, the untenability of his situation must also have dawned on Richard, for he sent a cry for help to Franz Liszt:

---

34 Ibid.

I am at the end of a conflict that involves everything that can be sacred to a man: I must make a decision, and each choice that lies before me is so terrible that I must make it with the only friend by my side whom Heaven has bestowed on me [...] I have to discuss my entire situation with you so that I might have the full approval of my only friend in whatever measures I take.[35]

This can only mean that Richard was planning to leave Minna and run off with Mathilde. Not least in light of his failed elopement with Jessie Laussot, he was aware of the audacity of such an undertaking. Minna would never have acquiesced easily in such an end to their marriage. Richard was hoping to find a solution that would cause the least misery, and decided to travel to Paris first to sound out Liszt. If the latter had given his support to the idea of separating from Minna, Richard would probably have gone straight to Otto and insisted that he divorce Mathilde. Did he perhaps even believe that Otto might provide his wife with alimony generous enough for her and Richard to pursue a lifestyle befitting her station? It is more likely that Richard gave not a thought to the financial consequences of his possible actions.

It is possible that a rift might have already occurred between Otto and Mathilde in the wake of her receiving the above-quoted poem, the libretto, and the composition sketch for *Tristan*. The audacity that Richard demonstrated here is astonishing—not just in his words, which left no doubt about the object of his desire, but also in the fact that he offered them openly to Mathilde. His poem's emphasis on "chastity" was hardly going to reassure Otto, and it is quite conceivable that he had already issued Richard with a warning in December, without Minna suspecting anything. In fact, Wagner made a passport request to his friend Franz Hagenbuch (now a cantonal councilor) on December 26, which is proof enough that Wagner was planning to leave Switzerland at short notice. Liszt was worried:

Franz your friend is with you, dearest Richard [...] Write me soon to tell me what you are intending to do. Is your wife staying in Zurich? Are you thinking of perhaps returning there later? Where is Mme W. –? The Lady Kapellmeister [Carolyne zu Sayn-Wittgenstein] has had an excellent idea, about which you will soon learn more. As soon as she has received an answer, she will write to you. Stay calm—God be with you.[36]

35　SB IX, 112–13 (January 9–12, 1858).
36　Kesting 1988, 541 (January 15, 1858).

Regrettably, whatever idea had occurred to Princess Carolyne has not been preserved in written form. Liszt's words reflect his inner agitation; he clearly recognized the seriousness of Wagner's situation.

The power struggle between Richard and Otto now became unbearable whenever Richard entered the Wesendoncks' villa. Otto found Richard's monologues threatening, and went on the verbal counterattack. Richard later got his own back with a malicious aside in his autobiography:

> His obvious worry that everything in the house would soon be adapted more to my needs than to his gave him that characteristically emphatic manner whereby a person of relatively little culture throws himself forcibly into every conversation, driven by his fears, with much the same effect that the snuffer has on the candle.[37]

It is not difficult to imagine the situation. Richard took to usurping every conversation, only to be interrupted by Otto in turn, who endeavored to trump his rival by offering economic headlines about his business successes in North America. Mathilde was obviously unable to resolve the conflict between the two men and was situated agonizingly between them. If there was any ultimate obstacle to Richard realizing the object of his passion, it was Otto, not Minna.

Something had to give, that much was clear, and Richard now found a good excuse to escape the charged atmosphere at home. On January 14, 1858, he left his Asyl and traveled via Strasbourg to Paris. He told Minna that he had business in the French metropolis in connection with settling his author's rights for France. But he made no secret in conversation with his close friends that this was a mere pretense. Minna was the one to suffer now, because the accrued bills for the past year landed on her lap. By his own admission, Richard had taken "the last pennies from her business coffers" with him. Otto had spent the past four years paying off the considerable debts that Richard had accrued and so could hardly be begged for more at present. So Richard borrowed instead from Gottfried Semper, "that poor family man." He also asked his friend Ferdinand Praeger in London for money, and wrote anxiously to Minna from Paris: "The fact that I have left you behind like this worries me more than you think."[38] He also approached Franz Liszt for help, though his request was phrased more like a command:

---

37   ML, 555–56.
38   SB IX, 140–42, here 141 (January 21, 1858).

"Well, I expect you to help me. My embarrassment is great."[39] Richard was even planning to ask his niece Johanna to organize an advance on his next royalties from Berlin. Liszt saved the day once again by having his son-in-law, Émile Ollivier, pay Wagner 1,000 francs in Paris. Minna was so frightened by their money shortage that she began sending Richard suggestions for how he might make some—such as recommending him to haggle as quickly as possible with lots of opera houses to get them to perform his early opera *Rienzi*.[40]

Despite all these worries, Richard continued to report back to her as faithfully as ever about all his undertakings. While he complained about Minna's behavior in letters to his friends, at the same time he adopted a conciliatory tone to Minna herself: "Keep loving me—despite all my faults and ignominy. We simply have to go through it all with each other; and, basically, things are going quite well now, even if I regrettably have more fame than money."[41] Had Richard resigned himself to the fact that he would never have a life with Mathilde? Or was he feigning normality to Minna in order to reassure her? He described the details of his business affairs to her, but reserved the right to refrain from going into too much detail, "in order to save for us both the pleasure this time of having a lot to tell each other by word of mouth, which is always spoiled by long-winded letters that leave you nothing really more to say when you arrive home." This hardly sounds like a broken marriage. Richard even allowed himself a joke when he claimed that he had fallen in love with the widow of the composer Ferdinand Hérold, despite her gray hair and her 50 years. When he finally succeeded in transferring money to Minna, she wrote back to express her astonishment, which in turn offended him: "My God! Whom do you take me for? I won't deny that at times and under certain circumstances I have a tendency to profligacy; but you have never known me to be indifferent to the embarrassments that arise for you as a result of this." All the same, he had to admit that he had kept certain financial matters secret from her: "I borrowed the other 100 francs from Semper, which I now tremblingly confess to you."[42] So once again, he made it impossible for her to develop any real trust in him. But in any case, she had no idea of the turmoil inside him at this time.

---

39   SB IX, 123 (January 16, 1858).

40   SB IX, 136 (Richard to Hans von Bülow, January 18, 1858).

41   SB IX, 124–26, here 126 (January 17, 1858).

42   SB IX, 164–65, here 165 (January 29, 1858) and 160–61, here 160 (January 28, 1858).

To celebrate Richard's return, Minna was planning a small banquet to which Georg Herwegh, Gottfried Semper, the Wesendoncks, and Hermann Müller were all invited. Richard was going to bring oysters with him. But the date fell through because he left Paris later than planned. He closed his last letter with bitter humor: "Adieu! Good old Madame! Stay good to me till then, and then you can badmouth me again if I behave badly. You're wonderfully welcome! Your much-loved husband."[43] It was clear to him that things could not go on like this, and after his return he wrote to Eduard Devrient to tell him that his life would now have to change. One possible solution he had in mind was a return to Germany. Running away from unpleasant things had often enough been his solution in life.

In March 1858 Otto Wesendonck was due to celebrate his 43rd birthday. Richard organized a serenade in his honor in the Wesendonck villa—no doubt as a pacifying measure on Mathilde's recommendation. He conducted an orchestra of thirty musicians in a selection of individual movements from Beethoven's symphonies, and afterwards, the high society of Zurich—sixty-four people in all—dined at large tables.[44] Richard was presented with an engraved ivory baton designed by Gottfried Semper, which he demonstratively showed to Minna (who was sitting on a sofa next to the wife of the first violinist Wilhelm Heisterhagen). Despite the bourgeois ambience, Richard was unable to enjoy the event properly, as he later recalled in his autobiography: "This festivity affected me in a melancholy way, as if it constituted some kind of symbolic high point of a life's relationship, and indeed as if its actual capacity had been overtaxed and the string of the bow pulled too taut."[45] That might have been how things seemed to him in retrospect, but the real drama was in fact yet to come.

On April 3, 1858, Wagner completed the first act of *Tristan*. Two days later, he felt frustrated because Mathilde had postponed seeing him on account of meeting her Italian teacher, Francesco De Sanctis. On the evening of April 6, the Wesendoncks visited the Wagners, but the evening developed into an argument between Mathilde and Richard about the character of Goethe's Faust in the play of that name. The next morning, Richard wanted to send Mathilde the orchestration sketch for the Prelude to *Tristan*. He entrusted it to a servant, along with a letter written in an exalted tone.

---

43 SB IX, 169–70, here 170 (February 1, 1858).
44 There is a list of the guests in Fehr 1953, 386f. The beautiful hall on the ground floor of the villa—today the Museum Rietberg—is still in existence.
45 ML, 562; see also Fehr 1953, 121.

Minna had already become suspicious, and claimed that she had been whispered things from several sides that she did not want to believe. But then she noticed how Richard always went to the villa when Otto was not at home. The daily exchange of letters had by now increased beyond what was normal. Soon afterwards, Minna herself described what happened in a letter to her confidante Mathilde Schiffner. Madame Wesendonck took to writing notes to ask:

> if Mr. Wagner had slept well, and that he should come over, the winter garden was heated. Yes, she even came herself, but forbade my maid to disturb me, I stupidly stayed downstairs and left her undisturbed. On the 6th they were both with us in the evening. On the 7th I noticed that Richard was strangely restless, he came out every time the doorbell rang and had a large roll of paper in his hand that he wanted to send to Mrs. Wesendonck. But he would not let go of it when I wanted to take it for him. He was very embarrassed and tried to hide it etc. All this perplexed me a little.[46]

When Richard handed the roll of paper to a servant to deliver to Mathilde, Minna intercepted him and told him to hand it over. She then discovered a letter hidden in it (known today as the "morning confession"). She was less interested in those sections of the letter in which Richard expounded on Gretchen in *Faust* and Isolde in his opera in order to explain to Mathilde the redeeming power of love. No, Minna's interest lay in the letter's more direct expressions of his own love for Mathilde:

> In the morning I became reasonable again, and from the depth of my heart could pray to my angel; and this prayer is love! Love! My soul rejoices deeply in this love, the source of my redemption! Then came the day, with its miserable weather; the joy of being in your garden was denied to me; I could not get on with my work. Thus my whole day was a struggle between melancholy and longing for you, and every time I felt a real longing for you, our tedious pedant [Francesco De Sanctis] kept on coming between us, he who had stolen you from me, and I couldn't help admitting to myself that I hated him.

After several pages of literary discourse, Wagner closed with the wish that he might meet Mathilde in the garden later that day.[47]

---

46   Minna to Mathilde Schiffner, April 30, 1858 (RWA).
47   Burrell, 369–72, here 369. Original in SB IX, 228–31, here 229 (April 7, 1858; the date was added after the fact by Minna).

Richard later played down the content of his letter, claiming in his auto-biography that he had sent the *Tristan* sketches "accompanied by a little note in which I calmly and earnestly described my prevailing state of mind at this moment."[48] But Minna found nothing calm or earnest about his letter: she saw a love affair. She promptly confronted Richard, who only tried to convince her that her jealousy was foolish and that it would be detrimental to her heart if she insisted on getting so upset. To calm herself down, Minna asked her bosom friend Emma Herwegh for advice. Emma herself had long, painful experience of such matters, and recommended that she seek a per-sonal conversation with Mathilde Wesendonck. She had successfully pursued this same strategy, she said, when her husband Georg had fallen in love with Marie d'Agoult. Minna waited for a week, and then approached Mathilde and told her:

> that I did not want to play the role of traitor, but also that I was no longer prepared to remain a spectator either, and that I could not bear for the best of men [i.e., Otto] to be deceived, and so on. Now this person herself wanted to play the offended party, until I told her of the letter and its contents [...] She promised me everything, that she would stop this familiarity, and that I had to believe her, because I am here.—Richard promised me the same, and forcefully tried to persuade me of the purity of his relationship for good and bad, how ridiculous![49]

Richard might well have believed that his self-imposed sexual abstinence somehow legitimized him into making his erotic desires "invisible," and that he could therefore speak of his relationship with Mathilde as something "pure." He might even have been able to convince himself and others of this supposed purity. But Minna was of a different opinion.

Minna wrote to Emma Herwegh to tell her that she had now spoken with Mathilde, who had reacted kindly, but had then discussed everything with both her husband and Richard. This was not what Minna had wanted, for she would have preferred to settle the whole matter with Mathilde alone. "My husband is no longer entering that house, whether out of strength or weakness I cannot tell."[50]

If Mathilde had concealed this incident from her husband, then she would have been put in the position of a party with something to hide. That

---

48   ML, 562.
49   Minna to Mathilde Schiffner, April 30, 1858 (RWA).
50   June 14, 1858, in *Das Forum* 1/31 (1914), 142f.

was an impression she certainly did not want to convey. Now Otto learned that there had been far more intensive communications between their houses than occurred on their evening get-togethers. This merely fueled his latent jealousy. Minna would have been willing to accept Mathilde playing the role of adored muse because she knew that the respective living arrangements of the two families would have made it impossible for Richard to attain erotic fulfilment in such a relationship. She was also convinced that Mathilde would not be prepared to leave her husband. "Of course, she preferred to remain the rich lady instead of choosing a poor devil instead."[51] By informing her rival that she was aware of her relationship with Richard, Minna was able to relieve herself of the humiliation that betrayal brought with it. Otto had hitherto tolerated his artist neighbor worshipping his wife in words and music. But the "affair" between Richard and Mathilde had now descended for both parties to the level of a banal marital conflict, which made it impossible for any further, unbiased contact between the Wesendoncks and the Wagners. The resulting situation was highly embarrassing for all those involved. Otto had endured his wife's growing rapture with extreme self-control, but he had exhausted his emotional energies. All four of them had shown great self-discipline up to now, but once things were brought into the open, the appropriate consequences had to be drawn.

Looking back on these events after the fact, Minna wrote to Jakob Sulzer and told him what Wagner had said to her:

> "I love [Mathilde] Wesendonck, we are passionate about each other and she cannot bear for us to be together any more, she can't stand you, she's jealous of you, etc." What's more, Mad. W. visited my husband secretly and forbade my servant who opened up for her to tell me that she was going upstairs [...] It's very often the case that men have an affair with some woman or other, so why should I not tolerate it too; I knew no jealousy.[52]

We may well doubt Minna's last assertion, but it is clear that she had not wanted to set the ball rolling that now inevitably ruined the happiness of their Asyl. She later repeated the above story in a letter to Cäcilie Avenarius, claiming that Richard had called her to his room to tell her that she had to leave because Mathilde was jealous of her: "in short, she would not allow us

---

51   Minna to Mathilde Schiffner, April 30, 1858 (RWA).
52   Fehr 1953, 165 (April 24, 1859).

to be together any longer, and so on. Denials or distortions do not help here, I still have it in black and white."[53]

Since Minna claimed to the end of her life that Richard had indeed tried to persuade her to give him up at Mathilde's insistence,[54] some dispute of this kind must surely have taken place. For Minna, the scandal that resulted in her leaving the Asyl brought her not just emotional humiliation, but economic and social catastrophe. She was already acquainted with the pattern from Dresden, nine years earlier. Back then, too, her husband's behavior had destroyed their existence. Now their hard-won house, garden, circle of friends, economic well-being, and reputation all threatened to slip through her fingers again. Given this situation, it is hardly surprising that Minna's heart condition now deteriorated. Richard also knew how Minna's body reacted to emotional stress, and so he sent her on a cure.

Years later, when Richard was homeless and living briefly as a guest chez Eliza and François Wille, his anger at Minna's lack of understanding broke through, and Eliza herself recorded what he said:

> Everything could have gone well between my wife and me! But I had spoiled her hopelessly and given in to her in everything. She did not realize that a man like me cannot live with his wings tied! What did she know of the divine rights of passion, which I proclaim in the flaming death of the Valkyrie who has been cast out of the grace of the gods! It is this sacrificial death for love that brings about the twilight of the gods![55]

Wagner was never going to win over many sympathizers with such a perspective, no matter how essential it was to his creative work. His relatives and friends took Minna's side because it was obvious that she was the betrayed party. Even his sisters stuck to her. Female solidarity functioned best in times of need, because every bourgeois woman in the 19th century was threatened with misery and poverty if her husband either failed to provide, left her, or died. Clara Wolfram was outraged at her brother's behavior and unhesitatingly sided with Minna, as we can read in a letter she sent to her on June 3, 1858: "You poor, sorely tried woman; no, by God, I would never have dreamed that it would come to this with Richard's good heart; I can only

---

53   November 4, 1861 (Staats- und Landesbibliothek Dresden).

54   See, for example, her letter to Cäcilie Avenarius of January 25, 1864, in Geck 2021, 140–45.

55   Wille 1982, 63.

believe that he has gone mad!"[56] She suggested to Minna that she should sell their piano or some other piece of furniture in Zurich and use the money to travel to her, then they could sit down and plan her future.

But what might this future look like? Clara first made a list of what she thought was out of the question. Minna could not go back to the theater, as the theaters were at this time too run-down, she said. What's more, she would have had to learn very different character parts than had previously been her specialty, as she was now much older. And her private theater wardrobe was long gone in any case. Instead, Clara suggested that Minna could perhaps run a small business, citing the example of a widow she knew who had run a small dress shop since her husband, a doctor, had died at a young age without leaving her any kind of fortune. "This business increased; she expanded it, after a short time it became the foremost dress shop; then she remarried and sold the business with a profit of several thousand thalers."[57] Clara was convinced that Minna, who was gifted in dealing with people, could manage such an enterprise without needing much capital, and she advised her to settle in Dresden. "I firmly believe that the financial return would be considerable—Richard's debts are not your worry. You are so respected, so well liked: I am sure the aristocracy would come running to you, even if there were a hundred such shops."[58] Minna did not take up her suggestion, however, because she firmly believed that she and Richard would ultimately resolve their differences. She was almost certainly also afraid of embarking on any financial adventures.

Richard did not want to leave the field of battle for familial sympathy to his wife without a fight. So he began writing appeasing letters in his defense, including one to his patron Julie Ritter. He explained away Minna's cure as a consequence of her poor health. He mentioned the possibility of her spending the coming winter back in Germany, but claimed it was merely on account of her loneliness and a lack of independence in her character: "she is unable to amuse herself sufficiently and needs external distractions."[59] Such excuses would have enraged Minna. He also wrote to explain himself to Clara, who now had to weigh up two different versions of the truth. However, he was unable to conceal his relationship with Mathilde entirely from her, since he

---

56 Burrell, 372–74, here 372.

57 Ibid., 373.

58 Ibid.

59 SB IX, 266–69, here 267 (May 11, 1858). Wagner wrote in similar fashion to Cosima von Bülow's sister Blandine Ollivier: see SB IX, 275 (May 14, 1858).

knew that Clara trusted Minna. He told Mathilde Wesendonck about what he had written to his sister:

> I hinted to her [Clara] what you have been to me for six years and still are: what heaven you prepared for me, and with what sacrifices and struggles you protected me; and how this marvel of your noble, high love has now been so crudely, clumsily offended. I know she understands me: she possesses an enthusiastic nature in a somewhat ragged shell. I had to give her a little clarification. But how my heart and soul trembled when I wrote this, as I described your high, noble purity with delicate features!—To be sure, we shall forget everything, get over everything, and only a feeling of elation shall remain: an awareness that a miracle occurred here that Nature weaves only once over the course of centuries, something so noble that it had never perhaps been achieved before. Leave all the pain behind! We are the happiest! With whom would we want to change places?[60]

It was typical of Richard's art of living that he was able to transform even suffering into elation. By idealizing his love for Mathilde, he wronged Minna yet again, because the sphere she now represented, whether she wanted it or not, was the reverse of what Richard considered "high, noble purity"—in other words: base, ignoble, and impure. When he describes these events in his autobiography *My Life*, the vocabulary he uses underscores this assessment: Minna had subjected his letter to Mathilde to a "trivial interpretation," she had been moved by "silly jealousy," and he had been compelled to cope with the ill effects of her "unpleasant" behavior. Minna had furthermore indulged in a "crude misinterpretation" of his "purely friendly relationship" with Mathilde, and had "threatened" and thus "offended" her.[61] Richard's letters continued this strategy of describing Minna and Mathilde by means of contrary characteristics. His love for Mathilde was based on "tenderness," "purity," and "unselfishness;" she herself was "far removed from anything base or common." In contrast, Minna was "jealous," "scornful," "belittling," "hurtful," "crude," "mean," and "coarse."

Richard continued to weave the legend of Minna's guilt in his letters to Liszt. While stating that she had been compelled to endure "a terrible period," he went on to say that she had "rushed into her misfortune as if driven by a

---

60   Golther 1914, 87 (diary entry of August 21, 1858). Years later, Wagner similarly described his love for Cosima as something that happens once in a thousand years.

61   ML, 562–63.

demon, and dragged everything down with her."[62] He hoped that their current separation would do her good: "This poor woman so completely lacks the necessary understanding to allow space for such a noble, awe-inspiring act of resignation."[63] Minna in fact saw no reason to show any such understanding. She simply felt deceived and cheated. It was hardly going to be possible for them to establish any form of trusting coexistence again, and a separation would have been a clean break. But they both lacked the courage and gumption to do it. In fact, they would even try living together again from 1859 to 1861.

The Wesendoncks had meanwhile left for Italy in an effort to recover from the turbulence at home. Minna and Richard were also in urgent need of rest. Richard sent Minna to take the waters at Brestenberg Castle, which is situated some 15 miles west of Zurich on the shores of Lake Hallwil. It was run by one Dr. Adolf Erismann, who had studied hydrotherapy thoroughly and had purchased the castle in 1844 because the numerous springs on its premises made it ideal for setting up a clinic. Minna stayed there from mid-April to mid-July. This also muddied up Richard's financial situation, because each day at the clinic cost six and a half francs.

Minna struck Erismann's son as a woman with beautiful and even facial features. He also noted that she brought along a parrot in a cage that was larger than she was.[64] The cure did not agree with her. At 5:30 in the morning, a woman came to wrap her in a wet towel. This was removed after ten minutes, then the woman washed her down with cold water from a well, and rubbed her warm again with a dry cloth. Then Minna had to go walking for an hour, she drank three glasses of water and was given milk and bread for breakfast. At 10:00 she took a cold foot bath, then she had to walk a little again, and at half past ten it was time for a half-hour hip bath at 18 degrees, during which she had to hold a wet, very cold sponge against her heart. The sponge had to be exchanged for a fresh cold one every five minutes. Then she had to go walking for another hour, and had to drink water. The whole procedure was repeated in the evening at half past five. It is astonishing that Wagner could approve of such a treatment, given that he himself had experienced the damaging consequences of water cures. Minna's description matches an account handed down by Natalie in which she criticized the doctor for prescribing ice-cold showers. According to her, Minna almost died of

---

62 SB X, 72–76, here 75 (September 27, 1858).

63 Ibid.

64 Fehr 1953, 124f.

Figure 8.4. The Brestenberg Spa, mid-19th century. Eva Rieger Collection.

a heart attack as a result,[65] and even Richard admitted to Liszt that "I was terribly worried about her; for two months I actually had to be ready for the news of her death, any day."[66] This statement in itself is disturbing, not least because it suggests an unconscious desire for that eventuality.

Minna was unable to get any distance to what had happened, and the events of the previous weeks kept running through her head, as she wrote to Emma Herwegh:

> Next Thursday I will already have been here for 9 weeks, and still my poor heart beats and rages as if it wanted to jump out. I also have bad nights, during which I have to spend 2–3 hours pacing up and down in my room [...] This suffering is terrible, and I would not even wish it on my enemy. Sometimes I want to go mad, but I always keep myself and my heart in check so that hardly anyone notices what I am suffering [...] It is really despicable how disgracefully R. is behaving towards his wife, whom he has made so ill, God help me.[67]

Richard wrote twenty-eight letters to Minna in Brestenberg, and they lay bare his efforts to put things right and save their Asyl. Time and again,

---

65   Burrell, 527–28, here 528.
66   SB IX, 325–29, here 328 (July 2, 1858).
67   June 14, 1858, in *Das Forum* 1/31 (1914), 142f. See also Rieger 2006.

however, Minna became agitated about the events of early April. Richard was driven almost to despair by it. He replied impatiently, and with a good dose of black humor:

> This, dear Minna, is the day on which I have decided—not to enter into a hydrotherapy institute, but a madhouse, for that seems the only remaining place where I belong! With everything I say or write, even if I mean it as well as I can, I end up causing nothing but misfortune and misunderstandings. If I remain silent about certain things, then I make you suspicious and distrustful, as if I wanted to deceive you; if I then write seriously, openly, and at the same time— or so I think, ass that I am—fundamentally reassuring—then I learn that I am hatching some ingenious wickedness intended to put you six feet under! But at the same time, I'm told I have to be a man! Well, I don't want to be *a* man, I want to be *your* man: Just tell me always exactly how I should speak, think, and look at the things of the world. I will always act exactly as you want, and speak, think and see nothing that does not suit you. Will that satisfy you? Also, you must always tell me what I should compose, write and conduct: I want to follow you in everything, so that you can no longer doubt me for a moment [...] Or should I finally do it like Sulzer before he married, and hate "women" altogether, and only wish that there should only be men left in the world?[68]

Richard took her to the spa, visited her there at least three times, and also picked her up again at the end of her treatment. They seriously considered adopting a child. They invited their old friend Ernst Benedikt Kietz, who still lived in France, to come and live with them, and Richard even promised to make him their universal heir. Regardless of whom they considered sharing their lives with—whether a child or an old friend—it seemed to Richard a good idea to distract Minna. He left their dog with her, though he would have preferred to keep him in the Asyl, because he too needed comfort during this time. He reported back to her about their garden, which in her absence was being tended to by their servant, and where the strawberries, asparagus, and beans were flourishing. These were all attempts to bring some semblance of normality back into a life that had been completely derailed. Georg and Emma Herwegh also promised to come and visit Minna, and each of them also wrote to Minna at Brestenberg.

During Minna's cure, the 17-year-old wunderkind pianist Karl Tausig came to Zurich for a two-month visit. Richard put him up in a nearby guest house, and spent every day with him. "His breakneck piano playing makes

---

68   SB IX, 244–46, here 244 (April 27, 1858).

me tremble," he commented. He also had his work cut out with his young charge, because Tausig ate too much candy, claimed that he was not hungry, and would proceed to consume the rusks in Richard's house anyway. Tausig could be charming too, however—after Minna's return, he was happy to play dominoes with her in order to let Richard have his early afternoon nap undisturbed.

Richard's letters to Minna were affectionate, but a different tone prevailed whenever they were in the same room together. She tormented him with her constant reproaches, but this only made him resort to unfair verbal attacks in return. On May 29, she made a brief visit back to the Asyl and they had a major argument. They both now realized that they would have to separate, at least temporarily. Minna wrote: "Richard poured out his bile against me until two in the morning."[69] His description of the evening is somewhat different. He claimed that he had told Minna they must separate:

> The earnestness with which I dwelt on our past life together appeared to shake her sufficiently on this occasion, particularly at the realization that she was responsible for the potential collapse of our last and painfully constructed chance of a respectable life in financial security, so that I heard her here, for the first time in our life, utter a gentle and dignified lament. For the first and only time she gave me a sign of affectionate humility by kissing my hand when I withdrew from her late in the night. This touched me very much and quickly awakened in me the hope for a decisive transformation in the character of the poor woman; and that in turn induced me to hope for a satisfactory continuation of the kind of life we had recently made for ourselves.[70]

Richard could not bear any criticism regarding his affair. When he tried to convince Minna that the blame for recent events actually lay with her, he was merely confusing cause and effect. It had become a repeat of their Dresden situation of nine years earlier. When Minna moved into the Asyl, it was the fulfillment of her fondest dreams and had finally given her a sense of having entered a stable phase in life. Now, however, she faced the prospect of a life of loneliness, surrounded by strangers, in different, cramped accommodation and—worst of all—plagued again by a lack of money, for there was little hope of Otto continuing Richard's allowance, which along with Julie Ritter's grant constituted their main source of income.

---

69   Fehr 1953, 145 (June 14, 1858).
70   ML, 566.

All this while, Richard was keeping every door open. A letter he wrote to Mathilde on July 6, 1858, reveals how he had continued to believe that she would leave Otto until just a few days before Minna returned home:

> When I told your husband a month ago of my decision to break off all personal contact with you [...] I was not yet completely honest in this. I just felt that only a complete separation or a complete union would make our love safe from the terrible tribulations to which we have seen it subjected in recent times. Thus the feeling that our separation was a necessity confronted the possibility—in thought, though not in volition—of our union. In this lay the cause of the awkward tension that we two could not bear. I went to you, and it stood before us, clear and definite, that that other possibility contained a sin that could not even be thought of.[71]

Richard later described to Cosima how he had tried to persuade Mathilde to flee with him: "I proposed that I should leave my wife, Mathilde her husband, and that we should marry. She replied: that would be a sacrilege [...] deep down, subconsciously, I wasn't serious!"[72] We may ignore his last remark, for it was surely intended only to assuage Cosima. For Mathilde, to run away from her marriage would have also meant giving up her children, and tantamount to a sacrilege against love, however much she might have desired Richard. He was desperate for her to assume the radical attitude with which he had endowed Isolde, but that was something that Mathilde simply could not do.

On July 15, 1858, Richard fetched Minna from Brestenberg. She was still not well. But he implored her to try and get along with Mathilde. Once again, their entire existence was at stake. But how was she supposed to endure this, emotionally and physically? She could not perceive Richard's relationship with Mathilde as anything "pure" just because it had not been consummated, when it was so clearly intensely erotic in nature. And the next scandal was in any case just around the corner. For the moment, however, things seemed to be going well. The musician Wendelin Weissheimer came to visit the Wagners, and something akin to a cheerful atmosphere was established.[73] But the good mood subsided quickly. Richard's servant Friedrich had decorated the front door of the Asyl with a garland of honor upon Minna's return. This delighted her, and she insisted on leaving her floral welcome over the

---

71   SB IX, 333–36, here 333–34 (July 6, 1858).
72   CWT I, 653 (March 14, 1873).
73   Weissheimer 1898, 28.

door for as long as possible. But Mathilde understood this as an intentional, public affront. She was indignant with Richard and complained about his behavior to both Otto and Hans von Bülow, even demanding that Minna should leave. According to Richard's report to his sister Clara, "the most outrageous scenes and torments" now ensued, and he became exhausted by having to "make allowance now for the one, then for the other."[74] A letter he sent to Eliza Wille contains the first criticism of his muse that he ever committed to paper, complaining that Mathilde did not want to understand that his behavior was determined by the consideration he had to show to Minna. Mathilde, he wrote, was tormenting him with "childish, senseless reproaches" about his relationship with Minna, and she had also spoken to Hans von Bülow in a similar fashion. This all made him painfully aware "that she is barely able to appreciate what I am suffering for her sake."[75] Just how much these events affected him is shown by a dream he had forty years later, which was faithfully recorded by Cosima: "I was between Minna and Mme. Wesendonck, the latter was making atrocious advances to me in order to annoy Minna, always looking at her. Well, neither of them, I thought, and tried to get away."[76]

Immediately after her return from Brestenberg, Minna had to cope with visitors. These included Hans and Cosima von Bülow once again. They both deeply revered the composer, and given that he felt so often misunderstood, he basked gladly in their admiration. They kept quiet in the mornings because Richard was working on *Tristan*. Hans von Bülow later apologized to Richard for Cosima, who had felt too awestruck to speak. "She is always afraid that you will think her childish and far too insignificant to be able to love you and understand you,"[77] he wrote. Hans and Cosima also witnessed a heated argument between the Wagners, much to the latters' subsequent embarrassment. When the Bülows seemed about to leave, Minna got Richard to ask them to stay all the same.

The Bülows were far from the only visitors. Karl Ritter, Karl Klindworth (Liszt's student who had spent time with Richard in London), and even Cosima's mother, the Countess d'Agoult, all made an appearance this summer. These guests variously from Berlin, London, and Paris all sensed the underlying tensions and the overall ominous mood. Hans compared it to

---

74   SB X, 27–32, here 30 (letter to Clara Wolfram, August 20, 1858).
75   SB IX, 351–53, here 352 (July 28, 1858).
76   CWT II, 292 (January 16, 1878).
77   Moulin Eckart 1927, 410 (early September 1858).

the oppressive sultriness just before a thunderstorm. But there were positive moments, such as when Klindworth played brilliantly from the piano scores of *Rheingold* and *Walküre*, with Richard in top form singing all the roles.[78] Minna had her hands full, and like everyone else involved, she too was suffering from the current situation. Her friend Mathilde Schiffner apparently suggested that she bore some of the blame for her marital rift, because Minna defended herself in her next letter: "You know only too well, if you ask me properly, how difficult it is for me to be separated from him for even one day, even more so now with the uncertainty of whether I will see him again, and if so, when [...] If it were up to me, I can assure you, it would certainly not happen." She continued later in the letter:

> Richard's honor simply cannot tolerate staying here now, since the husband, I don't know how, has also found out about the relationship. When I returned, I was vehemently bombarded and threatened by my husband who wanted me to resume relations with that woman. I therefore relented and was ready to make this enormous leap, that is really everything possible that a woman in my position could do. But the husband and ultimately this woman too don't want it, that's how she is. My husband screamed at me, furious that I am staying, only R. alone should live here, but he can't. This, dear friend, is how things stand, it's not my fault.
>
>   R. has two hearts. He is entangled on the other side and attached to me out of habit, that is all![79]

Wagner's biographers long propagated the legend that Minna was the sole culprit in the catastrophe of 1858. Her "ugly jealousy and tactless behavior toward Mathilde" were perpetuated in the literature, and she was declared to be "insensitive."[80] The romanticization of a man's love for a compliant woman and muse is a topos of Western culture that was long taken for granted in cultural history. To be sure, Richard had lucid moments when he was honest enough to allow for a different perspective, and then he refrained from assigning Minna the role of guilty party. He later confessed to Mathilde Wesendonck: "Now the last thorn is out of my soul. You must have looked for it in the wrong place: it was not my wife, but your husband who drove me away from you."[81] And to Mathilde Maier he wrote in 1863: "Inevitably,

---

78   Bülow 1909, III, 192.
79   Minna to Mathilde Schiffner, August 2, 1858 (RWA).
80   Lippert 1927, 94.
81   Quoted in Herzfeld 1938, 262.

my unhappy wife is the one who must atone for this catastrophe."[82] He alternately blamed Otto, Minna, and Mathilde, seeing himself as the victim and never as the one who had actually triggered the tragic events. The fact that Hans von Bülow wept as he said goodbye to the Asyl was perhaps an expression of insight into the chaos from which no one would emerge unscathed.[83] Nevertheless, this chaos resulted in the composition of one of the most extraordinary works in the history of opera. In Richard's own words to Franz Liszt: "Since I have never enjoyed the actual happiness of love in my life, I want to create a monument to this most beautiful of dreams."[84] His early letters to Minna give the lie to this statement, for they indeed celebrate the "happiness of love." It was in fact unfulfilled yearning to which he erected his monument. "Tristan is not really concerned with Isolde herself, but exclusively with what she means to him."[85]

---

82 SB XV, 256 (September 8, 1863).

83 SB X, 50–52, here 51 (September 5, 1858). Richard wrote to Hans: "Why did you weep when you said goodbye?"

84 SB VI, 298–99, here 299 (December 16, 1854).

85 Maschka 2013, 48.

Chapter Nine

The Bitter End, 1858–59

Before Wagner turned his back on Zurich, he urged Liszt to come and visit him. But his friend could not oblige as he had to attend the celebrations for the three hundredth anniversary of the University of Jena. Representative duties of this kind were always important to him, in contrast to Richard, who wrote that "I found it very bitter that I could not have you here during this major catastrophe of my life."[1] Did he want Liszt to try and convince Mathilde that she should leave Otto, despite her recent, clear refusal? Or had he wanted Liszt to provide some guarantee of financial security, were she to take such a step? Since Princess Carolyne had disregarded all bourgeois norms by leaving her first husband to go and live with Liszt, Richard will have been sure that he could count on their sympathy.

Minna was devastated. She confided in her good friend Sulzer—who had already stood by her during the Laussot affair—and told him of the "disastrous fate" that had now befallen her and that had made her "the unhappiest woman under the sun."[2] The origin of all this evil was perfectly obvious to her: Mathilde Wesendonck. After Richard decided to give up their Asyl, Minna wrote a farewell letter to her hated rival: "Before my departure I must tell you with a bleeding heart that you have succeeded in separating my husband from me after nearly twenty-two years of marriage. May this noble deed contribute to your peace of mind and your happiness." She enclosed a copy of the letter from Richard that she had intercepted back in April, presumably hoping that it might provide for a greater understanding of her behavior since then. She continued:

> unfortunately, I had to discover only too soon that you abused my confidence and made a very ordinary piece of gossip out of it. You repeatedly incited my husband against me and even accused me unjustly and carelessly before your

---

1   SB IX, 358 (August 11, 1858).
2   Fehr 1953, 398 (September 1, 1858).

good husband. On my return after an absence of three months, my husband told me that I had to resume seeing you. After several excessive scenes I gave in, aiming to place a cloak of forgetfulness over what had happened merely to forestall the abominable gossip that was supposed to have arisen and, quite frankly, to secure our Asyl. But in vain. It was in any case too late. You did not want it, and you were right, and it is the only thing for which I can thank you.[3]

Minna concluded by expressing her desire that Richard should now resume his work. She was being constantly tormented by all that had happened. Years later, Richard recalled how Minna had on one occasion threatened to abandon herself to drink,[4] and he might well have meant this particular time.

Richard now began writing a diary for Mathilde in which he recorded his most secret desires and emotions. He described in it his departure, which was as traumatic for him as it was for Minna. The night before he left, he dreamed that Mathilde had wrapped her arms around him and kissed him gently. He woke up, and felt sure that she was in the room with him. Unable to sleep, he waited until 5 a.m., then got up to watch the sun rise over the mountain. He felt as if all his hair was turning white. Downstairs, Minna offered him tea:

> It was a terrible, miserable hour.—She accompanied me. We went down into the garden. It was a splendid morning. I did not look around.—At our last farewell, my wife burst into tears and lamentation. For the first time, my eyes remained dry. Once again, I urged her to display mildness and nobility and to seek Christian comfort. But her old, vengeful ferocity flared up again in her.— I had to admit to myself: She is irredeemable! But—I cannot take revenge on this unfortunate woman. She herself must pass judgment.—So I was terribly serious, bitter, and sad. But—I could not cry.—So I left. And behold!—I do not deny it; I felt better, I felt I could breathe freely.—I departed into solitude: that is where I am at home; there, in that solitude where with every breath I take I am allowed to love you![5]

Minna's perspective was naturally different. She sensed clearly that his thoughts were with the other woman, and she wrote of how their farewell almost rent her heart. It was as if they were parting forever. As they both walked down the garden, he no longer looked at her, and instead kept

---

3   Burrell, 374–75.
4   CWT II, 1035 (October 28, 1882).
5   Golther 1914, 86.

looking over at the Wesendoncks' villa "until I took him by the hands and gently made him turn towards me with the words: Richard, look at me!"[6]

Minna remained in Zurich for two more weeks. The stress of it all made her ill: she came down with a severe throat infection and a high temperature. Richard traveled first to Geneva, then via Lausanne (where he met Karl Ritter) to Venice. Minna, by contrast, had to set about dissolving their household. Richard found this superfluous, but she would not listen to him, and wanted to put everything behind her as quickly as possible, so she pushed ahead. She had a number of their effects packed in boxes and put into storage, but sold the larger items through an advertisement in the local paper: one large, gold-framed mirror, a card table, an adjustable dining table for 14 people, 12 chairs, a wine cabinet with 300 bottles, bedsteads, feather mattresses, silk-covered sofas, armchairs, and carpets. All these testify to a distinctly elevated standard of living on the Wagners' part.[7] But her decision proved unwise, because her advertisement both alerted their creditors to her changing situation and provided fodder for the gossips in town about events on the Wesendonck estate.

After his departure, Richard immediately sought contact with Minna again. A telegram he sent shows how concerned he was for her: "How did yesterday go? Your health? I'm tolerable. Still uncertain. Answer at my expense 25 words. Wagner." He sent a second telegram that same day, advising her to leave soon, and a letter from him followed the next day. He tried to evade her reproaches, urging her to be calm, and begged her to resign herself to circumstances. He wanted peace and reconciliation and suggested that they should each go their own way in an effort to regain their strength.[8] Minna, however, was unable to shake off what had happened; events weighed too heavily on her for that. She often failed to find the right tone in their ensuing correspondence, which only annoyed him all the more. She did find some relief, however, in insisting on her moral superiority to Mathilde. Although she keenly felt the chasm that existed between her and her better-educated competitor from the high bourgeoisie, Minna refused to let class differences define her. She began a letter to Richard, discarded it, began it again, and finally sent off a third version: "Our little house has become a house of mourning, though things are quite merry not far from me [i.e., in the Wesendonck villa], which, I would say, really offends *me*, but this too I

---

6   Herzfeld 1938, 261f. (August 21, 1858).
7   There is a copy of the actual advertisement in Fehr 1953, 144.
8   SB X, 23–25 (September 18 and 19, 1858).

shall soon see no more." She remained convinced that Richard would soon yearn for the comforts of the domesticity she had provided: "I'm not a noble woman at all, but better than many others [...] forgive an unhappy, offended woman." She informed him that she had put their furniture in a warehouse because she had not found any room nearby with steps broad enough to allow his sofa and large boxes to be brought inside. "May God protect you and enlighten my once good husband!" she concluded.[9]

But one final humiliation awaited Minna when she finally left the Asyl on September 2, 1858. She ordered a coach to the railway station and set off with their servant Friedrich, Fips the dog, and Jacquot the parrot. But on the way, their coachman turned off along a different road, ignoring Minna's protests, and took them instead to the courtyard of the coach company where they were met by Jakob Furrer, the company manager, holding a list of the coach trips that Richard had taken but had not paid for. He threatened to keep Minna there until she paid the outstanding bills, would not let her get out, and forced her to give up part of the travel money that she had with her, and urgently needed. This story promptly made the rounds in the city. Richard was beside himself when he heard of it, and wrote Furrer a sharp letter: "Without having sent any invoice, reminder, or notification of any kind to me or my wife [...] you fall upon her in your courtyard, insult her in front of your servants, threaten to take her luggage, and even lay hands on it until the frightened, helpless woman, without being given any invoice, had to pay a sum demanded by you."[10] He threatened legal action unless Furrer apologized to Minna.

Cosima von Bülow wrote Minna a sympathetic letter, inviting her to their home in Berlin. Minna declined with thanks, explaining that she was so upset that she could only expect relatives to take her in at present. She also postponed a trip to Dresden where she was invited to stay with the Tichatscheks. Her nerves were worn out. Richard's music had once been "the dearest thing in the world" to her, but now she was unable to listen to any music at all. Earlier in the year, after the catastrophe had begun to unfold, Cosima had written to their mutual friend Emma Herwegh about her view of the rift:

> I see only sadness and ordinariness in the conflicts of a relationship that arose from vexation, complacency, and need of money. Like you, I pity Mrs. Minna, without going so far as to blame Richard, who—driven equally by his need for

---

9   Burrell, 375–76.
10   SB X, 78–79, here 78 (September 28, 1858).

an ideal and for tranquility, and incessantly wearied by monotonous drudgery in his life—has tried to wrest a little happiness from this colorless, wretched creature [i.e., Mathilde Wesendonck], who is just as incapable of leading a simple, straightforward life as of breaking with her former obligations in order to give herself to love and to support her beloved. Let us hope that the balance will be restored easily and without too big a scandal.[11]

Despite all her sympathy for Minna as the deceived party, it remained obvious to her that a woman should submit to the wishes of her lover.

Minna did not go to Berlin until the following spring, and we have no reason to suppose that she and Cosima might have met there. She probably sensed that Cosima had adopted a critical attitude towards her, supported no doubt by Richard's claims that his wife was the guilty party, but nourished too by Minna's own mistrust. Richard believed that Minna was on a mission of hatred towards anyone who was sympathetic to his plight. He wrote to Alwine Frommann early the next year that Minna "was, and continues to be, engaged in constant, often quite malicious, even horrid hostility towards people who are well-disposed to me; she seeks to denigrate me here and there, namely among women with an unbelievable ingenuity for slander. [...] She continually has all manner of things to report to me about the Bülows, for example!"[12] What Minna actually wrote to him about the Bülows has not survived; but in any case, there is an extant letter from her, written a few years later, in which she described Cosima as "a kind, intelligent lady."[13]

In his letter to Alwine Frommann, Richard also wrote about his disenchantment with the world and how he wanted to turn his back on life out of disgust with people and with the general hustle and bustle. As long as he had felt compelled to make a name for himself in the world and had been occupied with practical things, Minna had also been able to participate in his life. But now that he wanted nothing to do with the world, she could no longer follow him. Instead, she stuck to her adoration of his early works up to *Lohengrin*. The notion that Richard was turning his back on the world was fictitious—after all, he would resume his political meddling just a few years hence when he moved to Bavaria under the protection of King Ludwig II. And he also expected Minna to love him with a fidelity that could somehow ignore everyday hardships and would be nourished by sheer faith in his genius. But this could never be expected of a partner who at the same time

---

11   Quoted in Fehr 1953, 135 (June 21, 1858).
12   SB X, 292–303, here 300 (February 8, 1859).
13   Burrell, 561.

had to assume responsibility for his material care. Unlike Minna, Mathilde Wesendonck and Cosima von Bülow were indeed capable of recognizing the outstanding significance of Richard's more recent works. But Mathilde wisely rejected any union with Richard, because it would have meant living both in poverty and without her children. We may assume that Cosima, too, would have rejected Richard's contradictory demands, had she been faced with the same choices in life as Mathilde at that time.

Richard's attempts to emphasize the differences between him and Minna, and thereby convince others of her co-responsibility for their marital disaster, were doomed to failure. Everyone's sympathies were with her. The wife of the first oboist of the Zurich orchestra, Elise Fries-Steiner, confirmed that all those who knew of Minna's fate sincerely felt sorry for her.[14] Hermann Müller, a former Saxon lieutenant who had also left Dresden for exile in Switzerland, wrote to Minna to express his sympathy, calling her "you who have suffered for several years."[15] The singer Emilie Heim also corresponded cordially with Minna, telling her all the Zurich news (about concerts, operas, plays, and guest singers).[16] Emma Herwegh pitied her, as did Wagner's sisters, who felt more sympathetic towards her than towards their brother. Almost all the women who knew the Wagners were critical of Richard's behavior. So he pursued his efforts to get at least their male friends on his side. To Liszt, for example, he wrote of his passion for Mathilde: "The love of a tender woman made me happy: she was able to cast herself into a sea of suffering and agonies in order to tell me: I love you! What she had to suffer can only be appreciated by those who know all her tenderness.—Nothing was spared us; but in return—I am now redeemed, and she is happy because she knows it."[17] By transfiguring his relationship with Mathilde in this manner, Richard was situating it in an ideal world that implicitly elevated him above the common, everyday life in which Minna was supposedly at home.

Wagner had now settled into the Palazzo Giustiniani on the Grand Canal in Venice, where he was renting a large study with a bedroom and anteroom on the second floor. For her part, Minna first wanted to recuperate with relatives, then find a small apartment in Dresden. On September 2, she traveled via Lindau to Zwickau, where she stayed with her sister Charlotte and her husband, Adam Tröger. Her appearance had changed so much that

---

14   Ibid., 516–17.
15   Ibid., 525–26.
16   Ibid., 540.
17   SB X, 107-110, 108 (October 19, 1858).

Charlotte almost did not recognize her. Adam, a doctor, set about treating her organic heart condition straightaway, insisting that she must stay with them for at least six weeks. Her poor health was aggravated by nervous irritability. For years she had also suffered from insomnia, and this had now worsened. A doctor had treated her for gout back in 1853 and had prescribed hot baths and showers, though Richard claimed in a later letter to Minna's Dresden doctor Anton Pusinelli that these had aggravated her condition "to the point of insanity. She then became acquainted with laudanum, which she was carelessly advised to take in small doses against insomnia; since she enjoyed no success with it, she exaggerated the doses up to several times twenty drops at a time."[18] Richard referred to Minna's opium intake several times after her treatment of 1853, also in his correspondence with her after the Wesendonck catastrophe, so it seems clear that she had continued to take this dangerous opiate.[19]

Minna's brother-in-law had clearly recognized the seriousness of her condition, for when Richard inquired about her state, he received a worried reply. Richard now wrote to Hans von Bülow that Minna was suffering from constant presentiments of death, and this scared him: "No one should die of grief because of me: I cannot allow that!"[20] he told Hans. Her mind played through her recent experiences obsessively, and her physical and emotional reserves were spent. In October, she moved to Chemnitz to lodge with Clara and Heinrich Wolfram. Princess Carolyne invited Minna to join her and Franz Liszt at the Altenburg in Weimar, but Richard did not approve, so she declined their offer.

Minna's confidante Mathilde Schiffner was the only person able to rescue her from her depressive mood, and she all but begged her tó come. Now, with her relationship with Richard at its lowest point, it seems that Minna needed to be reassured of her few remaining friendships. With Mathilde, she could discuss everything: "O, how infinitely I am looking forward to our reunion, come, yes, please! Kläre [Clara Wolfram] has written to me that you can also stay with her, how nice! Then we'll be able to have a gossip and a chinwag. If you could only arrange to stay for a long while, we shall live the life of the gods."[21] She also asked Mathilde to look out for a small, ground-

---

18   SB X, 126–27 (November 1, 1858).

19   See Wagner's letters to Minna and Liszt respectively in SB IX, 297–98, here 298; and 325–29, here 328.

20   SB X, 70–71, here 71 (September 27, 1858).

21   Minna to Mathilde Schiffner, September 15, 1858 (RWA).

floor apartment for her in Dresden, which ought to comprise a living room, a bedroom and a kitchen: "Richard will fetch me as soon as his amnesty is through, which will probably take a long time.—That's why I will be staying there for so long," she wrote.[22]

Despite all his letters stating the contrary, Richard kept dreaming of a union with Mathilde Wesendonck, as is obvious from how he was plunged into disappointment when he learned that Mathilde was determined to "undertake renunciation," whatever we might imagine this to mean precisely. "When I thought of you," he confided to his diary,

> then parents, children and duties never crossed my mind: I knew only that you loved me, and that everything sublime in the world had to be unhappy [...] And I am gripped by a wrath that makes me want to say: And you are prepared to sacrifice everything to them who know nothing of you, comprehend nothing of you, but want everything from you?[23]

It grieved him to think that she was willing to put her family duties first, while he, the creator of worlds in sound, was so much in need of her.

Once Richard's dreams of happiness with Mathilde were shattered, he turned his attentions back to Minna, instead of pushing for a definitive separation. He told Joseph Tichatschek in all seriousness that Minna was busy settling down in Dresden, and that he too intended to return to there. "In that way, we would still be able to spend our old age comfortably together [...] I have nothing against Dresden, and I would actually feel a stranger everywhere else."[24] He wrote in similar fashion to Liszt. Minna also learned that he was still inwardly bound to her. "Pusinelli should take you in hand, so that when I come to knock on the door of that happy house in Dresden, I find there a perfectly healthy, revitalized, good woman, and then this time we shall set off on our undisturbed, quiet old age."[25] But Hans von Bülow, having witnessed a heated argument between the Wagners in Zurich, was taken aback by this change of tone and wrote to Karl Ritter to tell him so: "[Wagner] seems to be yearning for his wife (!!!), who whines to him about her imminent end and thereby naturally prompts him to renewed pity— no matter how trivial her methods might happen to be."[26] Richard finally

---

22   Minna to Mathilde Schiffner, September 9, 1858 (RWA).

23   Golther 1914, 92f.

24   SB X, 76–78, here 77 (September 27, 1858).

25   SB X, 101–103, here 102–103 (October 10, 1858).

26   Moulin Eckart 1927, 3 (October 10, 1858).

wrote to Minna that she should without doubt count on seeing him again at Easter, if he managed to get a full amnesty for Saxony. Then they would hunt for a place where she could offer him a permanent home for life.[27] This manner of thinking was simply part of Wagner's mentality: he compulsively began dreaming of rebuilding things, just after everything had been torn down. This quirk of his would prove a blessing to posterity because it enabled him to maintain an uninterrupted flow of creative energy. But it could make those around him suffer.

From Chemnitz, Minna traveled on to Dresden, where she stayed with Joseph and Pauline Tichatschek. Pauline was very fond of her and had secretly arranged an interim solution for her in the form of a small, two-room apartment on the ground floor of a house at Marienstrasse 9. She had thought of everything. Minna found eggs, flour, bread, and butter in the pantry, plus wood and coal. This made her very happy, because her brother-in-law had been unable to give her any kind of monetary advance, and she had hardly any money left. She was suffering from a dilation of the heart, and her health was now dependent on having a pleasant environment and harmonious rest. Once again, a sense of female solidarity made itself felt: "All my women friends have remained faithful to me, they are pampering me and spoiling me to their hearts' content," she wrote to Sulzer from Dresden.[28]

After Richard's departure from Zurich, his correspondence with Mathilde Wesendonck halted for a while. Eliza Wille acted as a mediator as best she could, but without success. Richard's first letter to Mathilde from Venice was returned unopened. She had refused to accept it, probably in order to prove to Otto that a complete break had indeed been effected. However, she sent gifts, and kept up contact in this way.

On October 13, 1858, little Guido Wesendonck died. It was Otto who informed Richard, presumably because Mathilde's grief made her unable to do so. Before the end of the month, however, she sent him her diary. His longings flared up again, now intensified by the acute pain of separation. He wanted to set out immediately so that he might be close to her. Presumably she had told him of her suffering at his departure. Richard now asked Eliza Wille to arrange a meeting at her home in Mariafeld at Christmas. But she felt out of her depth, and handed over their correspondence to her husband. François Wille now wrote a few lines to Richard whose sarcasm could hardly be surpassed. He wrote that Eliza had been

---

27   SB X, 57–61, here 60 (September 14, 1858).
28   Fehr 1953, 148 (December 15, 1858).

alarmed and tormented by your letters; by the whole manner in which you are harrying her and inflicting on her a role against which she in vain protests and that makes her feel anguished, ashamed, and infuriated. And that says something, given her great weakness, her good nature, her capacity for self-sacrifice, and her special admiration for you [...] But of course, you are also a disciple of Schopenhauer and of Buddha and can endure a whole night of renunciation, purification from egoism, and forgiveness, in order thereafter to follow the commands of desire, ruthlessly and mercilessly. And with your artist's imagination you paint everything that flatters the "will," and in order to satisfy your whims you are willing to conjure up the purposeless, hopeless torment, destruction, scandal, and disgrace that you had just abandoned.[29]

But not even these harsh words could quell Richard's yearning for a reunion with Mathilde. In the spring of 1859, he resumed contact. When he learned of Minna's poor health through his brother-in-law, he wrote in the diary that he would later give to Mathilde:

Help me also to bear the terrible burden that lies on my heart. Yesterday I received a detailed report on my wife's illness from a reliable doctor. She seems beyond recovery. The development of an edema in her chest is imminent; she will be subject to increased, perhaps protracted suffering that will be ever more agonizing, with death her only prospect of release. The only thing that can alleviate it and make it bearable is the greatest possible quiet, and staying far from any moral agitation.—Help me to care for this unhappy woman![30]

We can only imagine Mathilde's probable astonishment at this exclamation, because Minna's illness would have taken a turn for the worse, not the better, had Mathilde actively stepped in to help her. But Richard was presumably begging for emotional support. Or was he in fact keen to inform Mathilde about what he assumed was Minna's imminent death, as he would then have been free for his beloved? In his letters to Minna, however, he continued to hold up the prospect of a renewed life together. This pattern repeated itself regularly. Richard painted the past in gray, he passed over the present with silence, but painted the future in shimmering, rosy colors.

After her stay with the Tichatscheks, Minna planned to move into the house where she had once lived with Richard. Healthwise, she continued to suffer. Being in company was bad for her nerves, so she rarely went out. Palpitations meant she was often unable to sleep, and she struggled to

29   Fehr 1953, 402f. (November 6, 1858).
30   Golther 1914, 125f. (November 1, 1858).

breathe. Stairs were especially difficult on her. Worse still were her fits of nervousness and anxiety. In order to take her mind off things, her doctor advised her to go to the theater, because he understood that psychosomatic issues were accelerating her organic heart condition. She also visited the singer Wilhelmine Schröder-Devrient, who had contributed so much to making *Rienzi* a success and was now mortally ill. Minna wrote that she looked "as if she had been pulled out of the grave," and hoped that she might yet endure a quick death: "She has fallen away from God, herself, and all men," wrote Minna to Cäcilie Avenarius, "and nothing of her greatness has remained to her but the greatest bitterness; in a word, she is an unhappy woman, at the sight of whom your heart turns over in your body."[31]

Minna began having problems with the local police in Dresden, and she realized that it was not going to be easy for the wife of a wanted criminal to settle in the city again. Richard accordingly proposed that she should come to Venice. They also discussed the possibility of Karlsruhe as a meeting place.[32] He became exasperated and asked if there was really no one to assist her in her dealings with the authorities. She agreed with everything he wrote, but remained skeptical, suspecting that his concern for her did not signify any new blossoming of love, but was bound up primarily with his own convenience. In a letter to Mathilde Schiffner, she wrote: "Who will guarantee me in future that he won't prove himself weak in this matter in his older years, and that he loses this passion, which is very often the case with old men. Then I'll have to go through the same thing all over again."[33]

Minna's assurances that she was not in a hurry to get back with Richard were nevertheless as contradictory as his that he wanted to move back in with her one day. In reality, she hoped that her husband would get his amnesty, and then return to Dresden. In an effort to speed up the process, she went of her own accord to August von Lüttichau, Wagner's former boss and nemesis, to find out the status of a possible reprieve. Richard even encouraged her in her actions—but was he really serious in this? Lüttichau demonstrated a sense of decency towards Minna by giving her free tickets to all performances at the Royal Court Theater. But she made no headway with an amnesty. She also tried to convince Lüttichau to organize a performance of *Lohengrin*, though in this she found Richard unenthusiastic because he had a low opinion of the kapellmeister Karl August Krebs who would have to conduct it.

---

31 April 15, 1859, to Cäcilie Avenarius. Schröder-Devrient died on January 26, 1860.

32 SB X, 134–37, here 136 (November 14, 1858).

33 Minna to Mathilde Schiffner, September 24, 1858 (RWA).

Figure 9.1 Minna Wagner in Paris, 1859. Nationalarchiv der Richard-Wagner-Stiftung, Bayreuth.

Minna sent Richard a photo of herself, which he placed on his worktable next to a portrait of his father, and he wrote back to say that it was his favorite gift. "The eyes and your gaze are quite exquisitely appealing. You have something in them that suits you very well; something gentle, melancholic, not restless. Perhaps this is also due to your suffering, you poor woman!"[34] These small signs of affection will have touched her. As a wedding-anniversary-cum-Christmas present, Richard sent her a coat, the making of which he supervised himself, "specially made, and [I] chose the material" (he did love choosing fabrics), plus a black satin dress, which he got Karl Ritter to take to her. And he promised he would never ask for it back to use as padding in his dressing gowns (as had apparently happened in the past).[35] In return, Richard asked her to send him some genuine Parisian snuff and a pretty bag for small cigars, which she gladly did, using Karl as an intermediary again. When Richard also got Natalie to procure a night lamp as a Christmas present for Minna, he asked her to have it decorated with the words "he is a good man after all" as a joke, recalling how Minna had trained their parrot to call "Richard is a bad man."[36] When Minna thanked him for it, he commented: "May you have little need of the night lamp. But if you do need it when you wake up, just think: he is a good man after all! Then you will soon fall asleep again."[37]

Just as in previous years, Richard endured psychosomatic symptoms whenever he quarreled with Minna. On one occasion, he described the reaction that a "terribly agitated letter" from her had triggered. He felt ill, lost all appetite, could not keep anything down, became feverish, and felt miserable.

Time and again, Minna brought up the matter of his professional career and expressed her regret that he no longer conducted. But Wagner resisted all such suggestions. If he had remained a conductor in an opera house, he said, his inner resistance to the task, coupled with the hassle and fuss that rehearsals and performances brought with them, would have made him ill. But this claim of his stands in contradiction to his assurances that it had only been Lüttichau who had made his job in Dresden so unbearable: "Oh, if that man back then had treated me a little more gently, as befits an artist of my kind, how much would have been different, or would not have happened!"[38] All

---

34 SB X, 175–78, here 176 (December 10, 1858).
35 SB X, 152–54, here 153 (November 20, 1858).
36 SB X, 174 (December 9, 1858).
37 SB X, 200–203, here 203 (December 25, 1858).
38 SB X, 137–42, here 142 (November 14, 1858).

Minna could do was to make sure that she did not take all his contradictory statements too seriously.

"Now it's a full quarter-century that we have known each other and rolled our eyes!—A beautiful time—: what will things be like after another quarter-century??—I think by then I will have my amnesty."[39] This letter from Richard of May 12, 1859, is relaxed in tone, obviously in an endeavor to play down the crisis that had taken place between them. Most of the letters he wrote in this year were addressed to Minna. His correspondence with Liszt, once so lively, had diminished noticeably. Richard still wrote often to Mathilde, and these letters provide impressive documentary evidence of his progress with *Tristan*. But his thoughts were also with Minna, and his letters to her reveal just how preoccupied he was with the injustices she had suffered on account of the events of the previous year. He himself had no guilty conscience about anything—such matters were largely foreign to him—but he was well aware of the emotional wounds that Minna bore. And since he also knew how she suffered physically from emotional stress, he was also worried about her state of health. Her severe heart palpitations had meanwhile relented, but she still suffered from insomnia, and complained of difficulty breathing and of persistent coughing spasms. Pusinelli recommended that she take a long cure in the summer.

Richard's letters to Minna over the course of this year cover a wide variety of topics, and he resumed his well-worn habit of writing about everyday matters. He listed the meals he was eating: his preferred dish was veal chops with spinach, with either fish beforehand, or chicken or game afterwards. Every evening, his servant fetched him a glass of lemon ice cream.[40] Minna in turn reported how Wilhelmine Schröder-Devrient, whom she met frequently in Dresden, had been critical of the libretto for *Tristan*, calling the third act nothing but "dying all round," which outraged Richard: "Well, I see many other things in it, and the practicality of its performance has also been well considered [...] Can't she comprehend art as art, without judging it always from the perspective of theatrical routine?" he asked.[41] Eager to distract Minna, he described the water-carriers in Venice and reported on the gondoliers' chorus, whose singing he could hear from his balcony. In St. Mark's Square one day, he heard the march from *Tannhäuser* being played by a brass band. He was annoyed by the sluggish tempo, so he revealed himself as the composer of the work and showed the musicians how to play it correctly. They then played the overture to *Rienzi* in his honor, and he listened to it as he and Karl Ritter ate dessert and drank a half-bottle of champagne in a nearby restaurant.[42]

The style of Richard's letters to Minna is naturally diametrically opposed to that of his letters to Mathilde. Thus he writes to Mathilde: "I sat at the grand piano; my old golden pen stretched the last piece of web over the second act of *Tristan*, and then, hesitant and lingering, it drew the fleeting delights of the first reunion of my loving couple."[43] To Minna, in contrast, his only comment about *Tristan* was: "Over the turn of the year, *Tristan* will go like warm bread."[44] But it was not just the style of his letters to the two women that was different. Sometimes, the actual content of them was also contradictory. Minna could not get the idea out of her head that Mathilde had been the reason for the opera's composition, and she felt that Richard was undermining the bourgeois laws of marriage by writing it. But he assured her that the opera had nothing to do with his own experiences: "You can truly write nothing, especially in drama, unless it stands outside you, so that you can see it facing you, as it were. If you are in it, then you are incapable of writing clearly."[45] Mathilde, of course, was told a different story:

> The wonderful relationship that connects me to [...] Tristan is something you will easily grasp. I say it openly, because it is a phenomenon that belongs to the consecrated spirit if not to the world: never has an idea entered into experience in such a determined way. Just how much these two [the idea and the experience] predestined each other constitutes such a fine, wonderful relationship that any common understanding could only imagine it in the most meager, distorted way.[46]

Mathilde understood his words immediately, and it was his love for her that continued to spur him on to complete the opera.

Richard left Venice in late March 1859, when Saxony demanded that the local authorities cancel his residence permit for the city. So he returned to Switzerland, lodged at the Hotel Schweizerhof in Lucerne, and continued working on the last act of *Tristan*. Composing usually kept him at his desk

---

42   SB X, 117–21, here 119 (October 28, 1858).
43   SB X, 241–48, here 241 (January 19, 1859).
44   SB X, 117–21, here 120 (October 28, 1858).
45   SB X, 234–41, here 239 (January 16, 1859).
46   SB X, 241–48, here 242–43 (January 19, 1859).

from the morning until 4 p.m. He then went for a long walk, drank tea, and read the newspapers at 8 p.m., wrote letters, and by 10 p.m. was so sleepy that he could not even read in bed. The solitude that he had embraced did not suit him particularly, but it was well-nigh ideal for making progress on his opera. His grand piano had arrived from Italy, along with a foot rug from Minna. The famous swan rug also arrived that had been her Christmas present for him during the time when they were still friends with the Wesendoncks. Wagner spread it out in front of the divan because it had now grown on him.

Richard's correspondence with Mathilde continued, albeit on a level that could not arouse any suspicions in Otto—who was still an important adviser for him in financial matters. Richard even summoned up the courage to get Otto to purchase his scores, for which a princely advance was paid. It was almost certainly Mathilde who convinced him to take this step. After all, she had renounced all close contact with Richard for the sake of Otto and their children, and Otto clearly felt able to demonstrate his appreciation.

Although Minna and Richard endeavored to keep the gory details of their separation secret, all manner of rumors leaked out, including false ones. Eduard Devrient—who admittedly was not overly fond of the composer— noted that Wagner had "got rid of his wife in the most hurtful way, because she was too ill and too much of a hindrance to him. After that, [Otto] Wesendonck in turn got rid of this unfaithful friend of the house who had meanwhile laid ever tighter snares around his own wife. Given that degree of selfishness, everything seems permissible."[47] This defamatory version of events had emerged among the Zurich gossiping crowd. Two years later, Devrient met Wagner himself again, who told him (or, rather, Devrient's daughter) a very different story: "At Marie's he went all soft and spoke of his wife's heart disease that had supposedly been the real cause of the rift with Wesendonck in Zurich, and the reason why he left the place." But this latest fiction was not well received: "This kind of treatment has earned him the highest degree of loathing on the part of my womenfolk."[48]

Richard was afraid that news of what had happened might spread— and when it did, it merely made people more sympathetic towards Minna. As a result, they each had differing interests that sometimes bore strange fruit. Four months after he left Zurich, Richard was still providing their old friend Sulzer with a downplayed version of the truth, blaming Minna's

---

47   Kabel 1964, II, 301 (February 6, 1859).
48   Ibid., 379 (April 18, 1861).

heart condition for his departure ("the state [...] of my wife [...] become so worrying to me that we had to consider a thorough change in our living arrangements").[49] But Minna wrote to Sulzer with her own version just a few days later, since she appreciated him as a loyal family friend:

> It will not have remained entirely unknown to you that in recent times I had to endure the worst insults on the part of my weak, vain husband, instigated by an inexperienced, happy, heartless woman devoid of conscience. Unfortunately, it is so often the case, with very few exceptions, that men live with women in the most intimate friendship, and they conceal their [outside] relationships with a certain sensitivity; but he screamed in my face in the most vulgar, crude manner, that that woman could not stand me, was jealous of me, and definitely wanted our separation, etc. [...] I have become so miserable that my friends and relatives hardly recognized me; I need peace and quiet for a long time, if I am to regain only a small part of my health.[50]

But even now, her old Saxon humor had not left her completely: "I almost wish that he might try things out with his girlfriend for a while. Perhaps that would be a good cure for his illness."[51]

Ultimately, however, Minna was anxious to ensure that the reasons for their separation did not become fodder for the chattering classes. Vulgar gossip upset her, since preserving a certain bourgeois decency was essential to her well-being. Richard also became annoyed when these embarrassing events were still the topic of conversation among relatives and friends a year later. He believed that all this gossip was only making Minna more and more agitated, and he wrote to Pusinelli to warn him:

> I am particularly afraid of a certain [Mathilde] Schiffner, a seamstress, a good, affectionate creature, who has remained in our family as a kind of heirloom. Please deal with her properly when you get the opportunity. However well-meaning she might be, my wife needs to be discouraged, not supported, in her truly foolish ideas about me and my domestic affairs, which become completely distorted as soon as people speak about them.[52]

---

49   SB X, 168f. (December 3, 1858)
50   Fehr 1953, 148f. (December 15, 1858).
51   Ibid.
52   SB X, 149–50, here 150 (November 18, 1858).

Also in his dealings with Liszt, Richard similarly adopted a tone of paternal benevolence toward Minna that would have been more appropriate for dealing with a child:

> She is pampered and cared for by me like a child conceived on a honeymoon. In return, I have the satisfaction of knowing that she is also thriving; her terrible illness is noticeably improving; she is getting back on her feet and hopefully will also become somewhat sensible in her old age. As a result, only recently— just when I had received your *Dante* [Symphony]—I wrote to her to say that we had been through hell; may purgatory now be good for her, since then at last she might have a little piece of paradise too.[53]

Given all the stories about her that Richard was repeating to everyone, it is difficult to get an accurate picture of Minna's true condition. Her own letters were later destroyed—either Richard or Cosima was the culprit—so we only have those documents that Natalie hid from them. Just one letter from Minna to Richard is extant from this time. It survives in a draft version, written in Chemnitz in late October 1858, and deserves to be printed unabridged here. In it, Minna reacts to his accusations that Clara is a bad influence on her.

Dearest Richard!

This will be my last letter to you from here. A week from today I shall be traveling to Dresden with dog, bird, and Natalie, whom I expect here next Tuesday with Jacquot, and we shall immediately move into my little flat with the old Fräuleins Rottdorf, 9 Marienstrasse, which suits me very well. Good Pauline Tichatschek wrote me a few days ago that she had my little apartment fixed up quite prettily; she had had it supplied with all necessary implements for my convenience, even with some kitchenware, which I probably shan't need, since I don't care to do any cooking for myself alone. I was really very pleased with the good lady; at least one person cares for me. I shall see whether I may keep the furniture during my stay there, for it would, of course, save me great expense if I needn't have my things brought from Zurich. I had written to Pauline Tichatschek that I would have my belongings sent, and forced her to betray the surprise she had prepared, which made me very sorry for her sake.

I was pleased and surprised to receive such a quick answer to my letter; here I must be considerably closer to you than in Zwickau, for there I often received your letters only on the sixth day, while here they come on the fourth day. The dear lady also wrote to me that the forgotten 50 louis d'or would be

---

53   SB XI, 67–71, here 70 (May 7, 1859).

sent to you from Hanover; the intendant and the musical director were present again at the ninth performance, for which no tickets could be obtained after 10 o'clock in the morning. The directors would be real fools if they should throw away their chance of good profits by not performing *Rienzi*. You are right to tease me about it; with my extreme modesty I really felt funny myself for mentioning the gift of *Rienzi* only jestingly, so I was glad that you took it that way; I'll not do it again.

And now, my dear Richard, your enclosure to Clärchen [Clara Wolfram] and the threat to write to Mathilde [Schiffner] oblige me to assure you most solemnly that the good creature is innocent; she does not know anything about the last affair; she had written to me while I was still in Zurich, quite shocked, and with the most fervent sympathy for us, whether it was true that we were going to be divorced (from which may God ever protect me) because you wanted to marry a rich and very courted baroness; a certain Frau Kälberle, who had spent the summer in Zurich, had spread this pretty news in Dresden. I wrote at once to Mathilde that nothing of this ugly gossip was true, which made her most happy; she knows nothing more, so she will be very astonished to get a letter from you. Anyhow, my dear Richard, you must not imagine that the true reason for your departure from Zurich is not known; don't consider what I tell you about this matter as a reproach; I myself appear to people far more quiet than I am inside: at the utmost a tremor may be perceived in my voice, but certainly I shall not give away anything; even to Clärchen I would not have admitted anything if she had not already known everything before my arrival. Her eldest son had brought the pretty tidings from the singing club; I had to tell you this in answer to your unjust accusation, though I should have liked to keep it from you. Some day, when the time comes, I shall tell you the news from Dresden, but as you will see it did not come from Mathilde at all. Believe me, I have no external cause to tear my wounds open; people see that quite well and avoid talking about it. These [wounds] bleed freely in any case; they were too deep; you may even believe that I pray God to make me forget them, but unfortunately it has been in vain so far; when once they shall have healed I also shall be saved. You have made me very miserable by all the offenses and insults which I have had to suffer on account of your liaison. You know very well that no word against you nor anything has passed my lips as to *that former* Bordeaux affair, but then I was not made to suffer as much as during the last one.[54]

Despite all the suffering she had endured, this letter also reveals affection, a continuing interest in his operas, and a spark of the humor that Richard liked so much about her. But she remained firm in the face of his

---

54   Burrell, 526–27.

criticism. Given that she had already revealed details of the events in the Asyl to Mathilde Schiffner back in April 1858, her assurance here to the contrary was an outright lie. However, she had confided "this abominable secret to [Mathilde's] soul under the greatest secrecy" and had asked her to burn her letter after having read it. She wanted to protect Mathilde, but at the same time needed her as a sympathetic ear for her troubles. Richard did not understand that his insistence to Minna that she should remain silent was hardly helping matters—almost every one of his letters to her contains an injunction of this kind. On the contrary, she had to be able to talk about what had happened with people who could be discreet.

In April 1859, Minna traveled to Berlin and saw a performance of *Lohengrin*. She had previously tried in vain to get an assessment of the production from Hans von Bülow, who apologized about this to Richard: "I should actually have written about *Lohengrin* to your wife. By Jehovitsch—I just had no time to do it. Please apologize to her for me—I assumed that Frommann would have taken care of the matter."[55] Minna's own report did not seem to encourage Richard, but in any case he did not think much of the quality of the performances in Berlin, and did not mention them in his letters to her. But he also got her to deal with certain business matters for him. Back in 1844, he had published his operas at his own expense with the Dresden court music dealer Carl Friedrich Meser. To this end, several friends had lent him money—including Anton Pusinelli and Hans Kriete. After fleeing the city in the wake of the 1849 Uprising, he had ceded literary ownership of the operas to his creditors. Now he was afraid that he might be defrauded, and he accordingly cursed "s[hit]-pants Kriete" in a letter to Minna (in German "hosensch[eisser]"[56]—Richard felt free enough to use vulgar expressions of this kind in their correspondence). He authorized her to admonish his Dresden creditors personally about any intention on their part to sell on the publication rights to his operas.

Richard's chastisements continued unabated, nonetheless. In May 1859, he wrote to her: "Above all, I see to my regret that a feminine vanity that might easily be excused is constantly keeping you in the dark about what is actually meant by love."[57] To be sure, they each understood something different by it. For him, love meant being completely accepted by a woman who would give everything to be there for her man. For Minna, love meant

55   Moulin Eckart 1927, 43 (February 5, 1859).
56   SB XI, 46–49, here 48 (April 24, 1859).
57   SB XI, 88–95, here 88 (May 18, 1859).

loyalty and devotion on both sides. She saw this as having been destroyed by Richard's affairs, though it was the concomitant indignities that she found so difficult to bear. Two weeks later, Richard returned once again to the matter of the gossiping "seamstress madam":

> Old maids like her have nothing of the world in their hearts but gossip, and gossip again, in one form or another; what else is left for them but to worry about other people, since they have no one to call their own who concerns them. And this applies to everyone, whether a seamstress or an artist; they all have something suspicious and suspecting about them, and they have their mouths everywhere. They know something that isn't right about everyone, things at which people would turn up their nose. You will disagree:—But I don't care![58]

This verbal abuse merely prompted Minna to reply in kind, and then he in turn had to apologize for the harshness of his remarks.

These arguments between them were further fueled by Richard's preface to his "Autobiographical Sketch," published sixteen years earlier, but which Minna had now uncovered (or had been given by someone). This text described his life up to 1842, and it mentioned their marriage with a single, somewhat derogatory sentence: "I married there in the fall of 1836, under the most disagreeable external circumstances."[59] His next autobiography, "A Communication to My Friends" of 1851, is not much different: "I was in love, got married in an impetuously selfish manner, tormented myself and others under the unpleasant impression of a domesticity devoid of possessions, and thus fell into that kind of misery whose nature it is to ruin absolutely everyone." And a little later, he wrote: "My domestic afflictions increased."[60] Although this presumably referred to his financial worries, Minna was bound to find such remarks hurtful. She tried to make Richard understand that it was his behavior at the time that had caused her to turn away from him inwardly, and he actually agreed with her: "I happily believe you that I was a bad fellow." When she now started rubbing his nose in the old Laussot affair again, it was his turn to be annoyed, though he also admitted: "I can't hold it against you entirely for now giving me a whiff of dear old Bordeaux in return."[61]

---

58   SB XI, 113–19, here 115 (May 31, 1859)

59   SSD I, 12.

60   SSD IV, 256.

61   SB XI, 108–10, here 110 (May 30, 1859).

Richard was annoyed that she was so concerned about saving money. To celebrate his birthday in absentia, she had drunk cheap sparkling wine from Lössnitz that had made her ill, and he reminded her of how they had once both got badly drunk from it when they were younger: "To the end of my days I shall not forget how that stuff made us fall to the ground, heavy as lead."[62] Her frugality repeatedly provoked him, not least because it served to demonstrate how inadequately he was providing for her. When she sent him an elegantly embroidered folder lined with purple velvet as a gift—which he liked very much—she spoiled it by enclosing a note in which she told him he could put it back in its wrappings and leave it unused if he wanted. To Richard, this was as if she were intent on annulling a love token, and it ruined his pleasure in it. He got his own back by indulging in exaggerated criticism of her women friends.

But still they remained unable to break away from each other. When Minna visited the little spa town of Bad Schandau on the banks of the Elbe, just south of Dresden, in June 1859, he wrote to her: "If I were allowed, I would gladly come to lovely Schandau," and insisted: "Believe me, I long for nothing more earnestly in this life than to close it with you in peace, quiet, and contentment."[63] They both dreamed of a new life together at the end of the year—Richard, because he first and foremost needed a functioning household in order to work undisturbed; Minna, because living for Richard remained her unique purpose, despite everything. She became convinced that finishing the composition of *Tristan* also meant the ultimate end of his would-be love affair with Mathilde Wesendonck. She wrote to Cäcilie Avenarius:

> Richard is currently still in Switzerland on the Rigi, at Kaltbad [a spa near Lucerne] in order to recover somewhat, since he recently took up work again and has finally finished his *Tristan* after two years, thank God! Even if I have no hope at all that this opera will make the rounds of the German theaters, I know that Richard would not have begun anything else before finishing this fateful *Tristan*. He first had to get the heat of passion out of his body.[64]

As always, Richard felt anxious when he did not hear from Minna for a while—especially now in Lucerne, where he was all on his own. His daily routine, as he himself described it to her, was monotonous. For days on

---

62   SB XI, 113–19, here 113 (May 31, 1859).
63   SB XI, 124–27, here 126 (June 12, 1859).
64   August 17, 1859, in Geck 2021, 44–49, here 45.

end he saw only the servants. When the weather was bad, he missed having someone to talk to because he did not even have a dog with him. All the pets had stayed with Minna. "One just wants to get one's jaw working once in a while!—thus I live only by what the mail brings me. Your letters are always so welcome to me because, first of all: they entertain me; 2, they please me with good news about your condition—and 3, their overall tone give me the peace and hope that I so very much need for our old days (my hair is going shamefully gray!)."[65]

Minna too was concerned about Richard's welfare, so she asked Emma Herwegh to persuade her husband Georg to go and visit him in Lucerne. It must have been a blow to her when she learnt that Richard had actually paid the Wesendoncks a visit in early April, supposedly to put an end to all the gossip: "I surely don't need to tell you that this does not change in the slightest my plans or our plans for the future," he wrote to Minna. "Everything remains as we agreed. Behind me—and hopefully behind you—everything is now clear, light, and bright, and there are no more mists or clouds to disperse."[66] How was Minna supposed to react to this? Was he asking her to forget all the deep hurt she had endured? It was as if he were asking her to pretend that nothing had ever happened. In fact, he visited the Wesendoncks twice more, in mid-April and in May. In June, Otto and Mathilde also visited Lucerne. So they were now seeing each other on quite a regular basis.

By the beginning of August 1859, the score of *Tristan und Isolde* was finished after an intensive period of work. Richard was aware of the perils that lay in the charged, erotic aura of the music, for already back in April he had written to Mathilde: "Child! This Tristan is going to be something terrible! This last act!!!——— I fear that the opera will be banned—."[67] On the same day that Richard completed *Tristan*, *Lohengrin* was given its first-ever performance at the Court Theater in Dresden, and Minna was there. In the early days after the Zurich scandal, she had been unable to bear hearing his music. But those initial feelings had now subsided. She was especially fond of *Lohengrin*, and she thought that the leading roles were better cast in Dresden than in Berlin. "I have to uplift and invigorate myself by listening to Richard's works, otherwise I would not be able to write a friendly letter to him (this is just between us)," she wrote to Emma Herwegh. "He certainly has an ardent admirer of his earlier works in me, I feel as if I had helped to

---

65 SB XI, 59–63, here 60 (May 2, 1859).
66 SB XI, 39–43, here 41 (April 18, 1859).
67 SB XI, 58 (April 1859).

create them, since during that time it was me who looked after him, and me alone who took all our domestic worries on my shoulders. How very different it was in our last years together."[68] Richard's early operas were a part of her own life story. She had loved listening to him when he played her his works, singing them to her, and discussing them with her. Now she was superfluous, and the music that flowed from his pen was no longer hers.

The Wagners had now been separated for over a year. Since all efforts to obtain an amnesty in Germany had been thwarted by the Saxon king, Wagner decided to move in with Minna somewhere else. He urged her to go to Bad Schandau as soon as possible in order to restore her health, but then to travel to Karlsruhe with their dog and parrot. They had already discussed the possibility of meeting there. It was not yet certain whether they would move to Paris together, or whether Richard should perhaps even go to North America. But he proposed that in the latter case, she should stay in Paris and wait for him there.[69] None of this excited her much. The idea of living a lonely life for months at a time in Paris, where she hardly knew anyone anymore, will have made her anxious—not to mention her lack of any fluency in French, coupled with their continuing lack of money. Nevertheless, she decided to acquiesce, and so agreed to join Richard in Paris. He replied: "I am convinced that you will feel quite comfortable there even without me; and we shall properly adopt Kietz: that goes without saying, since he is the youngest child of the house. You would benefit greatly if you could learn French properly."[70] It was naturally insensitive of him to demand of a 50-year-old woman that she should learn a language. Besides, as a woman, she would inevitably be more housebound and would have fewer opportunities to meet other people and practice speaking.

Richard suggested that Minna should choose a woman companion for their time together, one who might help to look after her and entertain her. His reasons for this were twofold: on the one hand, he wanted to be able to go about his business unencumbered during the day, separate from Minna; and on the other, he was afraid of the demands that her ill health might make on him. He also wanted a servant—one to sweep the rooms, polish the silverware, make the food, serve it, and wait on him, especially when he was bathing. Furthermore, this servant would have to accompany him on his trips and take care of the luggage. He began dreaming of what their

---

68   August 29, 1859, in *Das Forum* 1/31 (1914). See also Herzfeld 1938, 247.

69   SB XI, 29–31, here 31 (April 9, 1859).

70   SB XI, 39–43, here 41 (April 18, 1859).

future life as a couple might look like, and promised Minna that he would be sociable. He would gather together assorted German-speaking friends to visit them on evenings, he said, and would make sure to be at home whenever they came round.

In September 1859, Richard moved to Paris. His desire to live together with Minna had now become a certainty. "There are no serious marital differences, nor have there ever been," he had written to Pusinelli[71]—an astonishing statement in view of the many letters he had sent to friends and relatives after their separation in which he had emphasized their incompatibility. Pusinelli expressed reservations about Minna traveling to Paris again, but Richard overruled him and encouraged her to come, assuring her that she would regain her composure there. She remained skeptical, but he painted a picture of a life of prosperity, and listed all the advantages of the area where he now lived. There were wonderful possibilities for walks, and the nearby Bois de Boulogne offered good air, peace, and quiet, he said. There were many cultural offerings to enjoy, too. Above all, it would be nice and cozy for her. He would keep away from their home any visitors who might disturb them: only good friends would be allowed to come. He was naturally anticipating earning a sustainable income and was calmly confident about it—hence his conviction that he would be able to afford a comfortable household. He repeated his desire that they should engage a companion for her: "I shall spare no expense in this [...] So—obey me, and do not contradict me! It must be so!"[72] He also managed to allay one of Minna's final fears by promising never to buy either silk furniture or silk curtains (though it was a promise he did not keep).[73]

Time and again, Richard spoke of the young, educated, French-speaking woman whom he wanted to hire for her. Minna resisted the idea and became so suspicious that he had to defend himself against her mistrust: "I did not have anyone picture-pretty in mind, but someone pleasant, which one can be without even being pretty."[74] Finally, he agreed to Minna's suggestion that they should take Natalie as her companion. But when Minna suddenly changed her mind and decided not to bring Natalie after all, Wagner tried to find another woman for her—until Minna wrote to him to say that she felt this to be an attack on her independence. Her identity depended precisely on

---

71   SB X, 149–50, here 149 (November 18, 1858)
72   SB XI, 249–54, here 252 (September 25, 1859).
73   SB XI, 288–94, here 291 (October 9, 1859).
74   SB XI, 317–20, here 318 (October 24, 1859).

her fulfilling her role as a housewife who held all the strings—and this aspect of life was all the more important since Richard had barely informed her about his compositional and writing plans for years. And now, of all things, he proposed denying her a role as ruler over her own household. Doing nothing did not suit her; she was too lively and too interested in many different things.

After a long cure in Bad Schandau, Minna took on a large number of tasks, including shipping their furniture and household goods to Paris. In mid-November, she made the 29-hour trip from Dresden to Paris, via Magdeburg and Cologne, and was finally reunited with Richard. This was a gamble for both of them, because they had only grown further apart in the meantime.

Chapter Ten

"In love and fidelity, your Emma"

Emma Herwegh

At first glance, it would be hard to imagine a greater contrast between two women: on the one hand Minna, born into poverty, poorly educated, but always striving to maintain her bourgeois reputation; then on the other hand Emma Herwegh, upper-class, possessed of a broad education, and with a lively interest in politics. But there were even more matters in which they diverged. Back in 1849, Richard's politically motivated activities had cost Minna everything that she valued: her social position, financial security, reputation, and prestige. As a result, she regarded any involvement in politics as synonymous with ruin. Emma embodied the very opposite. She was convinced that action and political engagement could give meaning to her life and help her to rise above the sterile atmosphere of her well-off family. Material possessions themselves were unimportant to her.

This list of contrasting characteristics could be continued at will. And yet we also find commonalities between these two women that inculcated a sense of solidarity in Minna and Emma, culminating in friendship. Both were artistically active in their younger days. Minna had been a successful actor for several years, while Emma was excellent at drawing, dabbled in composition in her youth, and wrote elegant prose. What united them most of all was the fact that they both lived with men who had broken with social conventions and embarked upon extraordinary lives. Just like Minna, Emma too had encountered mortal danger at least once in her life. During the revolutionary uprisings of 1848, Emma and her husband Georg had hidden variously in a wheatfield and in a granary in order to evade enemy troops hunting for them. Under threat of arrest and possible execution, they managed to escape by disguising themselves as peasants. Back in 1839, Minna and Richard had crawled on their stomachs across the border from Russia to East Prussia while fleeing their creditors; they soon afterwards endured a stormy sea voyage that left them in fear of their lives. Both women also had to cope with infidelity on the part of their famous husbands, and were forced to do so in the public eye on account of the open scandals that resulted. And both women on occasion experienced bitter poverty.

The revolutionary poet Georg Herwegh (1817–75) moved to Zurich in 1851, Emma followed him there, and they joined the Wagners' close circle of friends. They regularly dined at each other's homes, and several written invitations from Richard survive from around 1854, some of which were addressed to Emma, not Georg: "Dearest lady! We are de-sister-in-law'd [i.e. Natalie had left] and are very much looking forward to tomorrow at 2 p.m."[1] Usually, the Wagners and Herweghs invited each other as a couple. But when Minna was at Seelisberg for a cure in 1854, Richard was still invited to dine with the Herweghs, and he claimed they were the only people who looked after him. At the Zurich production of *Tannhäuser* in February 1855, Richard gave the Herweghs free tickets for the middle box in the theater, where they will almost certainly have sat next to Minna. A friendly relationship gradually developed between the two women.

Emma was born into the wealthy, upper-class Siegmund family in 1817 and grew up in Berlin. She once described herself as follows to the poet Frank Wedekind, to whom she became close in old age: "Not a very full head of hair, but silky soft; a narrow forehead, an extraordinarily fine nose, ideal lips, but beauty came to an end at the chin. Then her figure: hands and feet almost artistically formed."[2] Her father was born Jewish but converted to Protestantism and raised his children thus. He was a businessman—a purveyor to the Prussian Court of elegant dresses and fabrics, with customers from the high bourgeoisie and aristocracy coming and going in his store. He indulged his daughter, and ensured that she received an unusually good education for girls of her generation. She received lessons in history, drawing, modern languages, and literature, all provided by excellent private tutors, and liked to take an active part in discussions about philosophical, religious, historical, and political subjects. She was also proficient in several languages. But nor did she miss out on sporting activities: she went horse riding and sailing, and learned to shoot. She showed a particular preference for artistic

1   SB VI, 319 (1854?).
2   Wedekind 1986, 295.

Figure 10.1. Friederike Miethe: *Emma Herwegh as an Amazon*. Dichter-und Stadtmuseum Liestal.

activities; her portrait drawings of friends and acquaintances reveal real talent and a lot of technical skill.

The sheer diversity of her talents made Emma inwardly restless and indecisive. "When I read a lovely book, it seems to me as if I have to write; when I see a picture that exudes a primal beauty of feeling and inspiring ideas, then it's painting that seems to me to be my favorite language; and at the first note of melody that emerges from a string, I again want to devote all my strivings, all my strength, to music. I am chaotic through and through," she once wrote in despair.[3] The aimlessness of life that she faced as the daughter of a wealthy family was something that she found soul-destroying: "Great tiredness.—Went sailing in the evening.—Played whist. Indisposition. Potato salad." She read the books of Bettina von Arnim (1785–1859) and envied her for the recognition that she enjoyed in Berlin's literary and intellectual circles. One of Bettina's privileges was the right to choose whether she wished to entertain or not—for she was allowed to remove herself from a gathering if the fancy took her, simply under the pretext of requiring certain hours for study purposes. Emma begrudged her this freedom, and complained that "A woman like me, by contrast, has to wait until people leave, and yet I would so dearly like to spend my time differently."[4]

In line with the limited possibilities that seemed open to the women of her time, Emma toyed with becoming either an artist or a wife. It is here that we find initial parallels to the life of Minna, though for her, acting was primarily a bread-and-butter occupation, and only secondarily a vocation. Minna refused to accept the customary condemnation of actresses as shameless women of dubious morals, and insisted on being measured by bourgeois standards of respectability. Emma, however, cared little for bourgeois norms. She felt drawn to all the arts but demanded too much of herself. Her restless mind meant she was unable to devote herself to a professional training in any specific artistic activity. What's more, Emma's father was wealthy, so she was under no compulsion to choose a profession at all—unlike Minna.

Deciding on a career path was not Emma's sole concern, however. Minna's sexual experiences had begun at 15, whereas Emma dreamed of waiting for the right man: someone who would have to be very special. She fell in love with women too, but did not equate these crushes with the "real" love that had to be bestowed on a man. Her lofty artistic aspirations had placed her in a dilemma about what future lay before her, but she felt her problems could be solved by finding an important man to whom she might submit in marriage. So when the renowned revolutionary and poet Georg Herwegh visited Berlin in 1842 while on a tour of Germany, he came as if on cue. They were engaged within a week of having met. This was again in stark contrast to Minna, who spent months unsure about whether to marry Richard, and on more than one occasion simply left him in her wake.

The moment that Emma fell in love with this "bridegroom of my heart," all talk of her becoming an artist came to an end. Minna remained deeply

---

3   Krausnick 1998, 13.

4   Quoted in Rettenmund/Voirol 2000, 24.

attached to her profession and considered it a sacrifice to give it up for Richard's sake, but the free-spirited Emma—of all people—happily subordinated all she did to her duties at the side of her man. Georg and Emma married in March 1843. They moved to Paris half a year later, and their son Horace was born there that same year. Emma's generous dowry meant they were able to run a large household and maintain a genteel lifestyle. Their salon became a dignified venue for discussions on political and literary topics, and they entertained illustrious guests including the Countess Marie d'Agoult, Franz Liszt's former partner. Herwegh had already tried unsuccessfully to have an affair with Karl Marx's wife Jenny, but he had more luck with the countess. This plunged Emma into crisis. She tried repeatedly to find a way to cope with this painful situation so that it might become more bearable: "I know, Georg, you love me like no other being could, I feel you must love me because I am completely absorbed in you, I want nothing but you."[5] To Emma, her love for Georg had been decided by providence and so was indestructible. This act of idealization was probably an unconscious reaction, but nevertheless a clever strategy. Nor did Emma hesitate to tussle with her rival, to whom she wrote: "Since my Georg loves me, I think there must also be something in me that you might like,"[6] which must have irritated and perplexed the countess. Emma's prudent behavior—fed by her determination to do battle for her own role as wife—was probably what caused a cooling of Georg's feelings towards the countess, and ultimately led him back to Emma. Her diary from this period reveals that she suffered most when he felt pity for her. She wanted him to recognize her as an equal partner.

Minna reacted badly to Richard's political enthusiasms in 1849 and urged him to avoid indulging in senseless activism. Emma and Georg, by contrast, were both willing to risk their lives for the dream of a fairer, democratically legitimate social order. The corrupt King Louis-Philippe of France was ousted from his throne in 1848, and this event was soon after followed by an uprising in Berlin, with battles on the streets. Germans living in France became infected with the revolutionary ideas around them. They elected Georg Herwegh the President of the "German Democratic Society," an association of professional revolutionaries, former soldiers and volunteers from different countries who all wanted to fulfil their long-held dream of a democratic republic east of the Rhine. Georg and Emma together penned a revolutionary address of solidarity with the French people. But they did not just want to

---

5   Quoted in Krausnick 1998, 52.

6   Quoted ibid., 56.

be writing political pamphlets and declarations. They wanted to demonstrate their own credibility and take an active part in the struggle. So Georg led a small army called the "German Democratic Legion" to aid the revolutionaries in the Grand Duchy of Baden, just across the border from France, where the local insurgents were fighting under Friedrich Hecker. Emma was all aflame for his plans and decided to accompany her husband in his fight for freedom. She wore black cloth pants, a black velvet blouse, and a leather belt in which she kept pistols and a dagger, and the ensemble was so ideal for the purpose that she was often mistaken for a young man. Emma certainly did not lack courage. Women bearing arms (nicknamed "shotgun women") were a threat to the social status of men and consequently attracted a lot of aggression. But Emma endured the hardships of snow and rain without complaint, marched in the front line, and helped prepare sandwiches for the men when they reached their night quarters. She also took an active part in the discussions among the leaders and on one occasion even gave an inspiring speech to the troops. Hecker had been hesitant to call on Herwegh's legion for help, so Emma bravely took on the duties of a messenger, traveling alone by rail, carriage, horse, donkey, and on foot across the enemy lines. She established contact with Hecker, then traveled back to her own group. But they did not succeed in meeting up with the revolutionary troops in southern Baden.

During a short battle in Niederdossenbach, the legionnaires took flight in the face of numerically far superior Württemberg troops. The strength of the enemy also caused Herwegh's own group to scatter. Afterwards, Emma and Georg hid in a wheatfield while the enemy troops passed by. They were rescued by a farmer who sheltered them in his granary and later provided them with simple clothing so that they could escape across the border to Switzerland, mingling with the country folk. They were very lucky to have happened on an understanding farmer, because armed women were generally ostracized, and many people bore a vicious resentment towards "Herwegh and his damned wife."[7] Georg Herwegh was afterwards accused of having fled from the battlefield as soon as the fighting began. The next year, 1849, Emma wrote a pamphlet in which she described the legionnaires' participation in the failed Baden Uprising from her point of view, her primary purpose being to clear her husband of accusations of cowardice, not to achieve any kind of fame as a writer.

To Emma, women writers were mere "bluestockings." She believed that it was not for women to rise above men artistically, or to appropriate fields

---

7   Craig 1988, 217.

of activity that ought to be reserved for the opposite sex. Her internalization of the typical ideological convictions of her time, according to which women were to be excluded from artistic creativity, stood in stark contrast to her political principles and actions. She was inspired by the politics of freedom, and happily committed herself to new ideas. When she heard of peoples aspiring to liberate themselves, as was the case in 1848–49 in France, Germany, Poland, Italy, and elsewhere, her enthusiasm took over and she promptly ignored all the restrictions that were traditionally imposed on women. "Our time does not just need men, but women too. Women who like men feel all the glowing yearnings for freedom [...] Together we shall unite in hurling lightning bolts into the world, oh, and I want to prove to them what a woman can do when she puts aside her own ego."[8] She also had violent fantasies: "If the Russian government together with [Tsar] Nicholas had stood in front of my window, then bang bang, those fellows would have been blown up, and the white Lithuanian eagle would have hovered high in the air," she wrote after shooting exercises to which a friend had taken her.[9] She believed that a woman should put aside her own desires in pursuit of greater ideals, and implicitly also to the benefit of her male partner—not in the usual sense of submitting to bourgeois femininity, but in submitting to the necessities of the political struggle.

Contemporaries such as Otto von Corvin accepted Emma as she was, and found her more practical-minded, more energetic, and more fearless than her husband Georg. Emma smoked cigars—she was a chain-smoker, claimed Gottfried Keller—and during the legion's long march she had worn pants and pistols like a man; but she by no means saw herself, as some did, as a kind of Amazon. "She never feared for herself, nor cared for herself, only for her husband [...] despite her manly courage, she did not lack the gentler virtues either. She was a splendid wife and a tender mother."[10]

In 1848, Emma's father suffered major financial losses during an economic crisis, and he was forced to cut her allowance significantly. The luxurious furnishings of the Herweghs' Paris apartment had to be sold off. Georg, like Wagner, was incapable of earning sufficient money to satisfy his needs, and so he began paying regular evening visits to the exiled Russian socialist Alexander Herzen and his wife Natalya. When Herzen and his wife went to

---

8   Quoted in Krausnick 1998, 28.
9   Quoted in Craig 1988, 211. Tsar Nicholas I of Russia ran an authoritarian, repressive regime.
10   Quoted in Krausnick 1998, 47.

Geneva in June 1849 under fear of police surveillance, Herwegh followed them, and in September Natalya became his mistress. In 1849–50, while Emma was still in Paris, Natalya Herzen traveled with her two sons to Nice, and the Herweghs then joined them there.

At first, Emma probably no more suspected anything than did Alexander, but Natalya was unable to bear the tensions between them all, and so confessed everything to her husband. They initially attempted a *ménage à quatre*, and Emma held on, convinced that Georg and Natalya would soon end their relationship. But the situation dragged on thus for an agonizing two and a half years. When Natalya became pregnant, no one knew which of the two men was the father. Despite her inner turmoil, Emma was the one in all this who managed to keep her wits about her, and who endeavored to mediate between them. She had resolved to tolerate the pact into which they had entered, rather after the manner of George Sand. All the same, her capacity for self-denial and suffering in these circumstances is quite astonishing. She repeated to herself time and again that Georg would return to her alone, and she was ultimately proved right. In February 1852, Natalya wrote a farewell letter to Georg—probably dictated to her by her husband. Three months later, she was dead from pleurisy. Alexander Herzen blamed Georg for her sudden death and made their affair public. The scandal soon spread far and wide, and the salons now had a prime subject of gossip. Emma even felt compelled to defend herself against the scandalmongers in a letter to the editor of the *Neue Zürcher Zeitung*.[11]

Herwegh now moved to Zurich, while Emma remained in Nice with their sons Horace, Camille, and Marcel. Her friends urged her to seek a divorce, but this was unthinkable to her. In Zurich, Herwegh met Wagner, and for several years Georg was one of his closest friends. Their relationship seemed unbreakable. It was Georg who acquainted Wagner with Schopenhauer's philosophy, which was to have a major impact on his thinking and his work. They also decided to invite Ludwig Feuerbach to Zurich, though in this they were not successful. Herwegh's son Marcel later wrote:

One day, Wagner discovered [Schopenhauer's book] *Parerga und Paralipomena* on Herwegh's table, opened it, and burst out laughing. He had come across the chapter on women. "He must have known Minna!" he exclaimed, and read on eagerly. On his way back, he stopped at the Meyer and Zeller bookstore to order everything that had been published by Schopenhauer up to that point. From that day on, [Schopenhauer's philosophy] became his new pet project,

---

11   Ibid.

though he abused it so much through his overenthusiastic advocacy that he literally frightened off his best friends.[12]

Richard had opened the book at its infamous chapter "About Women," in which the philosopher presents his private misogynistic views in the guise of universal wisdom: "The very sight of the female form teaches us that woman is destined neither for great intellectual tasks nor physical work."[13] He adds that women are "childish, ridiculous, and short-sighted, in a word, through-out their lives they are big children: a kind of intermediate stage between the child and the man who is the true human being." The female sex is to Schopenhauer unaesthetic because it has no real understanding of the arts. It was quite possible that it was the following passage that reminded Richard so gleefully of Minna: women, wrote Schopenhauer, "always only ever see what is closest to them, they adhere to the present, assume that the appearance of things is the thing itself, and prefer the trivial to the most important mat-ters." One can well imagine that Richard's laughter would have amused nei-ther the novelist Eliza Wille nor the highly educated Emma Herwegh. Even Mathilde Wesendonck, who wrote her first poems in 1857 and later insisted that Wagner had "awakened" her,[14] would have been dismayed.

Georg Herwegh also influenced his friend in another matter. He had been educated in both linguistics and the natural sciences and had mastered not only the ancient, Classical languages but also the most important modern ones. He was able to communicate perfectly in French, Italian, and English. Wagner was not so proficient, however, and also spoke with a heavy Saxon accent. Herwegh loved to read dictionaries, claiming to prefer them to the best novels. Wagner, eager to profit from this knowledge too, soon became the terror of all around him by developing a mania for doggedly divining etymological roots for all manner of words. Minna accused Herwegh of driv-ing her husband quite mad. Richard's etymological extravagances would end in awkward marital arguments, most of which were pacified by Jacquot the parrot, that extraordinary bird that could whistle five bars of Beethoven's 9th Symphony and that delighted in squawking its familiar refrain of "Richard Wagner is a bad man!"[15]

---

12   Herwegh 1932, 46f.
13   Schopenhauer 1950, 650.
14   Eichmann-Leutenegger 2002, 85.
15   Herwegh 1932, 46f.

For his part, Georg Herwegh benefited from his friend's musical expertise. His own artistic creativity had dwindled away, and he lived more or less from the poetic reputation that he had earned in his youth. When Emma moved to Zurich to join him there in 1853, their social life together resumed. She enjoyed meeting their intellectually interesting friends, and their home was soon filled with exiles from Germany, France, and Italy. She loved taking part in discussions until the early hours, and it was thanks to her that the men around her—some of them professional revolutionaries with widely differing allegiances—did not fall out with each other for good. Since the scandal with Natalya Herzen, the phlegmatic Georg had lacked the energy to reinvent himself and establish a new sphere of activity. But Emma was bursting with a desire to work. With her inexhaustible energy, she actually resembled Richard.

The Wagners were naturally among the regular guests chez Herwegh, and this is how the two wives got to know each other. This circle of friends, focused on the Wagners, Herweghs, Willes, Gottfried Keller, and Gottfried Semper, met alternately in the apartment of one or the other of them. Franz Liszt and Princess Carolyne did not fail to visit the Herweghs when they came to Zurich, and in 1853, Richard was envious that the princess showed a greater interest in Emma than in him. Liszt, Herwegh, and Wagner took a mountain hike that summer and swore brotherhood as they drank from the three springs that bubble forth on the Rütli meadow. When Franz and Carolyne came to Zurich again in the fall of 1856, they visited the Herweghs in their home on the Rämistrasse and Liszt charmed everyone with his playing, despite their out-of-tune grand piano.[16]

By 1859, Emma's fortune was finally exhausted, and they struggled to keep their heads above water. She translated from the Italian to earn a little money, though it was never enough. In 1866, shortly after Minna's death, Emma had to auction off all their household goods, their paintings, and their valuable library in Zurich to satisfy their creditors. She had acquired the reputation of a "well-known eccentric woman,"[17] though this did not bother her. When Georg died of pneumonia in Baden-Baden in 1875 at the age of just 58, Emma had his coffin taken across the border to Liestal in Switzerland, for he had been adamant that he should be buried in republican soil.

---

16   ML, 541.
17   Quoted in Krausnick 1998, 101.

Given their so very different opinions and personalities, how was it that Minna and Emma became such good friends? Both had grown up at a time when notions of "ideal" femininity were still very much rooted in the late 18th century. The establishment of the bourgeois family in around 1780–1800 was accompanied by efforts to determine gendered characteristics that were specifically "female." The ideas propagated at the time are along the lines of those described by Christian Ludwig Beck's pronouncements of 1786:

> God has commanded woman to submit her will to that of man. [...] But if woman should believe that she was put into the world for her own sake, merely to enjoy and amuse herself at the expense of the male sex [...] then she is forgetting her destiny and is guilty herself of a wickedness that will condemn her to the fate of a stockfish: one whose head is removed and cannot be enjoyed without being tenderized.[18]

Whether from a pedagogical, philosophical, or anthropological point of view: women were characterized as naïve, natural creatures whose sole duty was to be there for their husbands. Both Minna and Emma were aware of these norms, yet each chose to live their life according to their own plan. Emma was certainly aware of the more egalitarian concept of gender as represented by the Enlightenment belief in natural law and that was upheld to some extent by several early Romantics. But while she adopted an ostensibly "masculine" demeanor through her fighting spirit and demonstrative acts of courage, she remained conservative with regard to her relationship with Georg, as we can discern from her favorite adage in life—one that she claimed helped her, especially in times of emotional exhaustion, and which she also shared with Minna:

> Do not complain, whatever may happen, so long as you have those around you in this world who are closest to you; take heart then; your worries are only on their account, and in order to get rid of these worries, you would have to bury everything for which you care to live—enough![19]

This suggests that she indeed sometimes found it difficult to stand by her man, even though this was the path she had chosen in life. After Richard's affair with Jessie Laussot, Minna wrote to Richard: "Duty only develops from love, especially for a woman, and I have always borne the worst of times with

---

18 Quoted as in Dülmen 1992, 40f.
19 Burrell, 329 (September 29, 1858).

love, courage, and even with a smile."[20] This was a view of life that she and Emma shared.

Minna had dreamed of a quiet, bourgeois life as the respected wife of a respected kapellmeister. Emma, on the other hand, wanted to break out of her boredom and devote herself to a great mission in life—and this meant offering her full support for Georg's political activities. Minna took her role of wife and homemaker very seriously and wanted to rise up in society at Richard's side. Her disappointment was all the greater when her husband became a wanted criminal, because this made her tumble down the societal ladder that she had only just managed to ascend. Emma was utterly indifferent to society, and at times was wanted by the police herself. She had started her life in the upper echelons of society, but had found it dull. Money was unimportant to her. Both women fell, and had far to fall. But for both of them—despite all their protestations that they were untainted by jealousy—the greatest blow of all was the infidelity of their respective husbands.

The friendship between Emma and Minna began in 1853, when the former moved to Zurich to join Georg. The relationship between the two women was marred only by the frequent lack of money in both their households. There is an extant, undated note from Emma that runs: "My dear Minna, forgive me if I'm bothering you, but things are really worse than bad. Do you still have a few francs? I haven't got a cent, and can't get anything before tomorrow evening."[21] Such requests were a burden on Minna, since she had to be extremely thrifty with the little housekeeping money that Richard was able to provide. At times, Emma's begging habit even threatened to ruin their friendship. Minna even began complaining to Mathilde Schiffner that she was loathe to see Emma and did not want any letters from her. "She's always asking me for money and virtually snatches it from my purse [...] I know better how to spend my money than to squander it through sloppy housekeeping; she has already wrangled many a franc from me."[22] But however poverty-stricken the Wagners were, Minna did not stop sharing what she had. This is evident from Emma's comments after the embarrassing incidents surrounding Minna's departure from the Asyl, when she was ordered by the local coach company to pay Richard's accumulated debts. "It was a stroke of luck that you still had enough to pay them despite being so depleted!" wrote Emma sympathetically:

---

20   Burrell, 290 (May 8, 1850). Emphases removed.
21   Burrell (German edition), 652; English version in Burrell, 505.
22   Minna to Mathilde Schiffner, June 15, 1856 (RWA).

When I heard it, I felt a shock, as I immediately thought: now you're in trouble at the end, because you had still shared what you had with me. If something like that had happened to me, I would either have had to stay there, or I would have left my things behind. What a fine state of affairs to be in! When it comes to such matters, I don't believe that there is another woman in Zurich who has been so initiated into the miseries of life as the two of us have—dear, good Minna!

As a keen observer of the Wagners' marriage, Emma had also recognized Richard's psychological dependence on his wife: "Now you'll see if I am right when I prophesied that your Richard would not manage to bear things without you." But she was cautious, too: "One cannot advise another in matters that delve so deeply into one's individuality, because every word that comes from the mouth of a third party, however kind it might be meant, can at best only be superfluous."[23]

As far as the Wesendonck matter was concerned, Emma took Minna's side. She recorded her opinion of the scandal in a letter to Princess Carolyne:

This drama is one whose genre is difficult to categorize, but I confess that of the four people who are the actors in it, this poor Minna deserves the greatest sympathy. She has invested all her capital (you know: the most beautiful girl in the world, etc.) and exhausted all her strength in the service of her "lord and master," and now she is in the process of being sacrificed to an idol. What shenanigans! May fate be milder to her than people are![24]

At this point, Emma was herself in very bad health, and she also told the princess that she was running gauntlets of her own—presumably yet more humiliations on account of debts.

Richard did not like it when women appropriated traditionally masculine behavior, as Emma did. But nor did he have a high regard for Minna's women friends in general. "I don't have much respect for your many other correspondents. What you women concoct among yourselves is not much use as a rule, and your father was quite right when he didn't want you all to learn to write,"[25] he wrote to Minna. By April 1859, Emma was utterly impoverished, and Richard became highly critical of both Herweghs. This offended Minna, for Emma's support had meant a lot to her, especially after

---

23　Burrell, 329 (September 29, 1858).
24　Herwegh 1933, 115.
25　SB XI, 76–80, here 80 (May 12, 1859).

the Wesendonck affair. Richard called her "a shameless, dishonorable beggar and swindler. The very thought distresses me that I might ever again live in the same place as these people, and in the event of attaining the tolerable prosperity for which I hope, I would be exposed at any moment to Mrs. H.'s plundering."[26] His assessment was diametrically opposed to that of Fanny Lewald, however, who visited the Herweghs and wrote afterwards: "One has to concede that both are possessed of a noble nature. Emma Herwegh shows such deep love, such unconditional devotion, that this alone makes her beautiful and significant."[27]

Wagner kept on twisting the knife in his criticism of Emma, whose self-confidence had been bothering him for a long time.

> I shall be truly so open, dear Minna, as to call your present intimate friendship with this woman a great weakness, and to count it against you as such. And even if I had nothing more than my thorough dislike for this woman, then I might nevertheless hope that you might hold back a little in your relations with her, out of sheer consideration for me, given that I do not force upon you those for whom I feel affection [...] Enough—they are and remain a ragtag bunch, useless and without purpose, unapologetically plundering every friendship, living only for the day, and shamelessly exploiting all their friends [...] I hope, dearest Mutz, that [Emma] Herwegh has not yet grown so close to your heart for what I say here to upset you seriously.[28]

Richard's logic here is downright perverse because Minna had not the slightest intention of forcing anything or anyone on Richard. He rightly suspected that he had hurt her, and she issued a prompt, indignant reply that made him backtrack quickly. "Don't put too much emphasis on my last remarks,"[29] he wrote. But it was too late; he had written them already.

Nor did it suit Richard that Cosima von Bülow (later the second Mrs. Wagner) was friendly with the Herweghs. He once spoke disparagingly about Emma in the presence of both Bülows, which displeased Cosima. Richard accordingly retracted his remarks in a letter to Hans,[30] and later reiterated his backpedaling in a letter to Cosima herself (at a time when he and Cosima were still on polite, "Sie" terms):

26   SB XI, 29–32, here 30–31 (April 9, 1859).
27   Quoted in Krausnick 1998, 66.
28   SB XI, 29–32, here 31 (April 9, 1859).
29   SB XI, 34–36, here 34 (April 14, 1859).
30   SB IX, 134–37, here 135 (January 18, 1858).

In order for you to visit me in trust, dear child, I must tell you that I am ultimately quite fond of the Herweghs. He in particular is the dearest male person
to me here [...] We often invite his wife too, and I always politely offer her a
cigar, and look away when she smokes rather gracelessly. Just between us: she
is a thoroughly well-behaved, highly intelligent, very talented woman, and an
incomparable friend. God! If only I had a wife who could procure me money
the way she does for her husband![31]

Although he had previously castigated Emma's repeated begging (not a little surprising, given his own virtuosity in this field), Richard here praised
her persistence in contrast to Minna, to whom any form of begging was
repugnant. His use of diametrical pairs of opposites—"ragtag bunch" and
"incomparable friend," demonstrates Richard's vacillating opinions; in reality, his dislike prevailed. Emma sensed this herself. When he once asked her
if they were close friends, she replied: "Dites des ennemis intimes, ce sera
plus exact" (let's say intimate enemies, that would be more exact).[32] She
once contemptuously referred to him as a composer without a heart who
acted like a hysterical woman.[33] So while she utilized feminine attributes to
describe him, he denigrated her by describing her as masculine; both epithets
were extremely offensive at the time.

During the Wesendonck crisis, Emma was Minna's closest confidante. It
was to her that Minna turned for advice after intercepting Richard's "morning confession" to Mathilde, and she followed Emma's recommendation
that she should speak to Mathilde directly. Emma had probably anticipated
some form of womanly solidarity, hoping that such a step would convince
Mathilde to limit her future visits to the Asyl. After all, Emma had two
serious marital crises behind her that she had been able to resolve by demonstrating restraint and patience. She had no idea that Mathilde would
discuss everything with her husband. In retrospect, her advice proved to
have been a mistake, and merely accelerated the fracture in relations that
was in any case imminent.

After Minna left Zurich, her correspondence with Emma centered on
traditionally female matters. Minna had lent two maid's caps to a washer-
woman in Zurich and had forgotten to ask for them back. She now asked
Emma to see to it, and also to purchase a veil for her. In the following years,
the subject of illness naturally began to dominate their letters. After moving

---

31   SB IX, 206–208, here 207 (March 1, 1858).
32   Craig 1988, 220.
33   Quoted in Krausnick 1998, 91.

back to Dresden, Minna wrote to Emma how people had welcomed her cordially for her own sake—and in this, she could rely on Emma to understand
her. In Dresden, Minna was no longer just the wife of the famous composer,
but was judged on her own merits. There also seems to have been a crisis in
Gottfried Semper's marriage at this time, for Minna wrote to Emma shortly
after the Wesendonck debacle: "I also ask you to greet the Sempers for me,
I wonder how the wife is doing? Oh, God, we poor [women] always have
things to bear."[34] When Emma on one occasion planned to travel to Berlin,
they had the idea that she might want to meet Alwine Frommann, the friend
of the Wagners. Alwine had let Minna know that she would in any case be
in touch when *Lohengrin* was given again at the Berlin Court Theater, and
Minna told Emma that it would be doubly pleasurable to her to see the
opera together. Emma also greatly admired Wagner's music, and the joint
visit indeed came about.

As for Georg and Richard, they became estranged over time. Wagner's
readiness to kowtow before the powerful did not go down well with
Herwegh, nor did Wagner's open commitment to German nationalism after
the establishment of the Wilhelmine Empire. A rift ensued. When Ludwig
II visited Wagner in Tribschen incognito, Herwegh wrote a mocking poem
about it. And when Wagner was finally able to celebrate a triumphal success in the Konzerthaus in Berlin in 1872—by which time Minna was no
longer alive—Herwegh reacted with another poem, this time mocking
Wagner as the emperor's lackey. Richard retaliated with name-calling in a
rhyme of his own, describing Herwegh as a "Pied Piper" and a "democratic
ballad-monger."

The heartfelt affinity between Minna and Emma remained until Minna's
death. When Minna failed to hear from her friend for a while, she immediately became worried: "If I had the money, I would come to you instead of
having to write, which is an imperfect medium. Perhaps I'll win the lottery.
They say: whoever has no more luck in love will have it in gambling. Then I
will see you!—Until then, keep me dear to you, a little. Give my best wishes
to your excellent husband! With sincerest kisses from your Minna."[35] They
no longer discussed the respective infidelities of their husbands, but the uni-
fying bond between them remained—something that Pauline Tichatschek,
another woman betrayed by her husband, once expressed in a letter to
Minna in words that could hardly be bettered: "We have to bear it all alone,

---

34   Letter of September 18, 1858 (RWA).
35   December 15, 1861, in *Das Forum* 1/31 (1914).

and only when you find a fellow sufferer—as I am—then you can feel what the other suffers. This is why, my dear, beloved Minna, we shall be united for the rest of our lives."[36] Emma also knew what it meant for a woman to subordinate her life to her husband, and later summed up Minna thus: "The world will never know everything that this good, faithful proletarian soul did for her husband."[37]

---

36   Burrell, 552–53, here 553 (December 8, 1860).
37   *Das Forum* 1/31 (1914), 142.

Chapter Eleven

"Neither wife, housekeeper, nor friend"

Dresden, Paris, Biebrich, 1860–62

When Minna finally read Richard's 1851 autobiography "A Communication to My Friends," it aggrieved her for months that he had described their marriage as a failure. She wrote to Emma Herwegh that this new upset, of which Richard was again the cause, was taking its toll on her heart. "Ought I not to lose all trust if I am promised that I should now experience only good things, i.e., no more insults, only for that promise to be broken time and again after having just been made? No, my good Emma, it takes a very special character to be able to forget all this—and to get healthy again."[1] Under these conditions, cohabiting with Richard was going to remain difficult.

Richard remained convinced, however, that Paris was the most suitable place for Minna to live. He had meanwhile taken a liking to a small, pavilion-like house at 16 rue Newton, not far from the Arc de Triomphe. It would shield him from all unwelcome noise, though it was really far beyond what he could afford. He generously paid the rent for three years in advance, undertook to pay the costs of any necessary repairs, and also paid for luxurious interior furnishings. If his decorator's testimony is to be trusted, Richard's bedroom was furnished especially lavishly. The ceiling was covered in puffed silk and was divided up by garlands of roses, all held together in the middle by a bouquet of roses. The alcove for the bed was bordered by arches emblazoned with more rose garlands. There was a curtain on the back wall, and the other walls of the alcove were covered with more puffed silk, a mirror embedded in its folds in each case. A mirror also hung

1   Letter of August 29, 1859, in in *Das Forum* 1/31 (1914).

from the ceiling. Wagner could thus see himself reflected on all sides when he lay in bed. He had also treated himself to an armchair upholstered in the most precious silk brocade and eiderdown.[2] As with every new apartment that he decorated, his aim was to compensate for all the world's impositions upon him, while at the same time providing himself with the inspiration he needed for his creative work. It is remarkable that he shunned all sentimentality as a composer, but loved the height of saccharine kitsch in real life. He wrote to Mathilde Wesendonck that he had arranged for his bedroom to be papered with plain, pale violet paper with green stripes,[3] which sounds far more innocuous than what his decorator recorded. In any case, these new furnishings included some 150 items that together cost 2,186 francs. Otto Wesendonck had transferred money to him to fund his stay in Paris, but it was rapidly disappearing.

Richard set up a small music room on the upper floor and installed his beloved Erard grand piano there, with a desk cabinet next to it. The room next door was made into a salon for Minna. Most of the furniture, carpets, curtains, and other household furnishings came from what had remained after the sale of their household effects in Zurich.

In their letters, Minna and Richard had often enough pondered trying to live together again. Minna remained skeptical—and her instincts would ultimately prove astute. Initially, however, things looked positive. Wagner was planning a series of concerts in Paris with excerpts from *Tannhäuser*, *Lohengrin*, and the Prelude to *Tristan und Isolde*, all featuring outstanding German singers such as Jenny Bürde-Ney, Joseph Tichatschek, and Albert Niemann. The preparations were laborious, but the concerts finally took place in late January and early February, 1860. The hall was packed—though the numbers were deceptive, because numerous complimentary tickets had been given away. This fact was hidden from Minna, who was delighted with the full house. She wrote to her friend Mathilde Schiffner, listing everything that had been performed, and assuring her that no other composer had ever been received with such rapturous applause. Even the orchestral musicians had cheered him after every piece. "The press is writing most nobly, often almost enthusiastically, without being bribed at all, not like Meyerbeer does it, and not like the journalists in Dresden who oppose their

---

2   Report by Clemens Mathieu in *Süddeutsche Monatshefte* 11 (1931), quoted in Otto 1990, 218.

3   SB XI, 357–60, here 359 (November 11, 1859).

own countryman."[4] This reference to Wagner's rival was something she had clearly adopted from her husband, who was ill-disposed towards his former patron, and always suspected that he and others were contriving against him. Minna continued:

> Despite the big, beautiful theater becoming ever more crowded each time, so that for the last two [performances] there were no more tickets available several days beforehand, still the costs are so terribly high that Richard will have to pay extra instead of earning something for all his sweat and toil. But the benefits will come as soon as his operas are given here. They are already being demanded, but regrettably have still not been translated [...] Richard himself is so impatient that he wants the best singers in Germany to come to him next May in order to perform his *Lohengrin* and *Tristan* at last, though after having seen the efforts invested in these concerts, I hope and pray that it doesn't come about. I also think that the time is too short till then to get all the décor ready, and *Tristan* alone would not be advisable. As you know, I am against this opera, perhaps unjustly.[5]

Richard yearned to hear his own compositions, but Minna judged their prospects primarily from a practical, economic perspective. She was precisely informed about their finances, as we can see from the list she made of his concert expenses. Renting the concert hall cost 8,000 francs; lighting and infrastructure 1,100; the orchestra 7,000; and the choir 3,000. Advertising costs were extra. So they had to sell a lot of tickets even to have any hope of coming close to covering Richard's expenses.

Mathilde Schiffner must have suspected that quarrels might erupt between the Wagners, because Minna corrected her afterwards, though not without a touch of bitterness in her tone:

> You are greatly in error, dearest friend, if you believe that I often quarrel with Richard, as is probably the case with various other people. God preserve me from that, no, that is another matter with us. Not a word passes my lips about what happened on his side, there is no grumbling or grousing, it's the so-called courtly tone that I hate, and which now exists between us. There is no more trust, no more warmth, both of which we used to have. We remain silent about everything and we don't have any comfy discussions, which were often a good thing.[6]

---

4   Minna to Mathilde Schiffner, February 10, 1860 (RWA).
5   Ibid.
6   Ibid.

It was by maintaining this distance from his wife that Richard was able to create the calm he needed to be able to function. He was afraid of reverting to their earlier, fruitless quarrels, and Minna too was keen to avoid any argument. So she likewise held back, and they both resorted to a cold attitude of self-control. But it was precisely this atmosphere between them that made her suffer. She believed trust and warmheartedness to be the most important prerequisites for a good marriage, and it was these two qualities that Richard now denied her. He was also desperate to avoid any reproaches from her about the past. So he went about his business and she often did not see him all day except at dinner. Sometimes he also disappeared in the evenings, but she stopped asking where he went. She thought she knew it anyway, because she became convinced that he was visiting Blandine Ollivier, the sister of Cosima von Bülow. She ultimately drew up a bitter inventory of the current state of their marriage, and shared it with Mathilde Schiffner:

> I am not a wife here, which is fine with me because the love necessary for it is absent, and I don't have to be subjected to his ill treatment. Nor am I a housekeeper—I don't get the money for that. Nor am I a friend, for that I lack the necessary trust—unworthy persons have robbed me of it. So what reason do I have to like things. Perhaps the silk dress that I have to wear as the wife of the famous R.W. But for that I lack the vanity, and this is hardly something that I'm going to acquire in my old age since I didn't possess it in my young years either.[7]

Minna regretted not having listened to Pauline Tichatschek, who had advised her against going to Paris. Inwardly, too, she had been reluctant to come.[8]

Minna did find some comfort in writing to her women friends, and she also received affection in return. When Pauline Tichatschek visited the Brockhaus family, she wrote to Minna on December 8, 1860, that Luise had "said that she is very sorry for you, since life with Richard must be very hard, but you must have patience with him since he can't live without you."[9] Pauline then alluded to her own husband, who had fallen for a dancer, which she said she accepted "in bitter silence."[10] Such expressions of solidarity did Minna good, since she felt she was not alone in suffering her husband's infidelities. She also learned from Pauline that her niece Johanna Wagner (now

7   Ibid.
8   Ibid.
9   Burrell, 552–53 (December 8, 1860).
10   Ibid., 553.

Johanna Jachmann) had surprised her husband Alfred with a chambermaid and was considering a divorce.

How different was all this from her time in Paris twenty years previously! Back then, Minna had been indispensable to Richard's sheer survival—and that of their circle of friends—but now her function was to be the representative wife of the composer. That was something with which she was not comfortable. In the past, she had endeavored to remove all obstacles from Richard's path to give him the space and time he needed for his creative activities. She regarded that as a legitimate task for her—one that provided her with a degree of prestige and respect. But it was precisely this that was now denied her. Her remark "I am not a wife here" probably also alludes to the cessation of physical intimacy that Richard had apparently decided upon. This, too, was bound to have an adverse effect on her, since it meant there was less and less to bind them to one another.

Minna's suspicions that Blandine and Richard were enjoying more than friendship were probably not unfounded, not least because rumors to this effect were already circulating in Paris. She must have voiced her suspicions aloud, because Blandine's husband Émile wrote her a stern letter requesting that she desist in future.[11] Alarm bells always rang in Minna's head whenever Richard was in the vicinity of enthusiastic ladies (whether married or not). It also struck her that Richard refused her requests for tickets for her friends, whereas he was happy to urge whole boxes of seats on Blandine.

Minna had long since become accustomed to Richard's flamboyant dress sense at home. Eduard Devrient, the director of the Grand Duke of Baden's Court Theater in Karlsruhe, met Wagner there in March 1861 when he stopped off on his way from Paris to Vienna. Devrient recorded their encounter as follows in his diary:

> I visited Wagner in his guesthouse. This poor man, who, as he tells me himself, has acquired nothing at all in recent years and spent an immense amount of money in Paris, all funded by his friends, whom he must surely be eager to repay—this poor man sat in his green velvet dressing gown lined with purple satin, wearing Turkish pants of the same fabric and a broad, brown velvet beret that was perched clumsily on his head and comically set off his pointed, lawyer-like face. I did not leave him in the dark about his meagre prospects for

11   "I want to tell you that Ollivier has written a very severe letter to Mme. Wagner, who, it seems, has been spreading very unpleasant gossip about Blandine." Thus Liszt in a letter to the Princess Carolyne zu Sayn-Wittgenstein, in Wallace 1927, 104.

procuring extraordinary monetary sacrifices from the Grand Duke, neither for a performance of *Tristan*, nor even for the honorary stipend that he requested (well, demanded actually) in order for him to live and compose in happy domesticity and do whatever he pleases and ignore what doesn't please him. Naturally, he would do so in velvet and satin and in the luxurious comforts that I know from his time in Zurich.[12]

Devrient just could not understand that Richard needed luxury as a stimulant for his creativity. Nor could he comprehend that Richard was intolerant in artistic matters because he was simply demanding when it came to performances of his works, and did not want to contradict what he had long stipulated for "model performances" back in his Zurich writings. When Wagner attended *Tannhäuser* in Devrient's theater in Karlsruhe in March 1862, he criticized every little thing. Devrient commented on this in his diary afterwards:

> Return visit to Wagner. He criticized Brulliot in the second act yesterday for appearing somewhat earlier than he should have done, and also criticized similar trifles without listening at all. From all this he extrapolated the supposed fact that the whole theater is in a mindless state. How can such a man live only by expressing contempt for everything that exists, while exalting himself on his own throne? [...] This unfortunate fellow spoils things with everyone who means him well.[13]

Minna would have agreed with Devrient in this, and would have seconded his closing remarks too. Wagner, he concluded, was one of those men who did not want to serve the world, but who instead expected the whole world to be at their beck and call, "under penalty of the fiercest contempt and enmity."[14]

Minna did not much like the French way of life. "Everything is geared to outside pleasures such as driving, riding, theater, mistresses, soirées, etc."[15] She found it telling that the word "gemütlich" (comfortable or cozy) did not exist in French. Yet the metropolis had changed since the large-scale rebuilding program instigated by Napoleon III. The darkness, the narrow streets, and the dirt from the time when the Wagners had first settled there had largely disappeared. But she seemed not to notice the city's architectural

---

12   Kabel 1964, II, 382 (March 8, 1861).

13   Ibid., 401 (March 10, 1862)

14   Ibid., 405 (May 31, 1862).

15   Minna to Mathilde Schiffner, February 10, 1860 (RWA).

transformation, because she stayed mostly at home. The only variety in her life came when Richard took her out. But in the space of half a year, they attended just seven plays (thanks to free tickets they had been given). Minna could no longer stand his monologues; they simply upset her. Nor did they have much more to say to each other. When Richard started planning a trip to Vienna, Minna even thought of taking on a small apartment of her own in Paris, should he extend his period of absence from the French capital.

Once a week, Wagner held an evening salon that proved very popular. Regular guests included the composers Charles Gounod, Stephen Heller, and Camille Saint-Saëns, plus the writer Jules Champfleury and the Czech painter Jaroslav Čermák. Minna did not find these evenings especially appealing because she understood too little French. However, she did grow fond of Franz Liszt's mother, and visited her frequently. Otherwise, she usually stayed in her room on the upper floor, and got her mail brought to her by their servant. She had resolved to leave immediately and return to Switzerland if Richard were to embark on another erotic adventure. "I will not go to my homeland," she wrote to Emma Herwegh in March 1860; "I would have to be ashamed of myself, since everyone had advised me not to travel here and made all manner of predictions to me."[16]

The situation was an unhappy one for both of them. Richard kept Minna at arm's length in order to protect himself, but she still became aware enough of their financial situation to get anxious. She wrote to Natalie in May 1860 to complain that lots of people were turning up to dine with them, but Richard only provided her with irregular housekeeping monies. She accordingly had nothing left to spend on herself, though she still managed to look decent, she said. She also urged Natalie to be industrious and neat, and told her that she "mustn't swan around like those saucy sluts in Zwickau."[17]

It was not until Richard traveled to Brussels in March 1860 that their old familiarity returned—though only on paper. He wrote her whimsical poems in which he reported on his experiences and gave advice along the lines of "don't eat too much cabbage."[18] It was probably just such signals of their old attachment and affection that made it difficult for her to detach herself, and kept her bound to her husband. He managed to be more affectionate when far away than he was in everyday life. Back home in Paris, pointed remarks from Minna would upset him and provoke him to angry outbursts; these

16   Letter of March 24, 1860, in *Das Forum* 1/31 (1914), 155.
17   Burrell, 554 (letter of May 8, 1860).
18   SB XII, 98–99, here 99 (March 23, 1860).

Minna in turn interpreted as his truculence. But his letters from Brussels also suggest that he no longer had any desire to keep her informed about his compositional work, as had once been his habit, and which Minna had enjoyed so much. *Tristan* had undone all this.

What made Richard suffer most was the fact that living away from his German homeland meant he only rarely heard his works. Experiencing them live was in turn a stimulant to further creativity, as he knew full well. He wrote in this regard to Agnes Street-Klindworth:

> I cannot devote myself to my art, nor even think about it: I cannot hear nor think a single note of it […] My poor wife is withering away through agitation and sleeplessness: she really needs a spa cure;—but nor can I send her on one. I hear nothing, and I experience nothing but thoughtlessness, dullness, failures, defeats, haggardness, shrugging shoulders.[19]

That same day, he also wrote to Malwida von Meysenbug: "My older operas are now completely exhausted, my new ones are being hindered, I have enormous losses, and—no one to help me!"[20] This is tragic when we consider the satisfaction he was able to attain in his work after King Ludwig II's patronage finally freed him from existential cares—not to mention the huge sums that his works later earned, and still earn today, almost two hundred years later.

Anton Pusinelli had advised Richard to send Minna to a spa cure in Bad Soden in the Taunus region, just outside Frankfurt am Main. It was difficult for Richard to drum up the necessary money, but at the last moment he found a wealthy benefactress in the shape of Marie von Kalergis (later Princess von Muchanoff). She had met Wagner seven years earlier in Paris in the company of Liszt, and now gave him 10,000 francs in compensation for the expenses that his concerts had incurred. This enabled Minna to leave immediately for her cure. Now Wagner was also in a position to see to his outstanding correspondence—he had recently even lacked the money for stamps.[21]

It was becoming increasingly clear to Richard that life in Paris just did not suit Minna; it would have been better to leave her in Dresden. His initial conviction that she might be able to recover her health by living quietly in Paris had been shattered. He wrote to Julie Ritter, explaining that Minna's energetic temperament meant that she got agitated about all manner

---

19   SB XII, 202–203, here 203 (June 22, 1860).
20   SB XII, 199–201, here 199 (June 22, 1860).
21   Glasenapp 1977, III, 266.

of things and could not find any peace. Minna in turn wrote to Mathilde Schiffner that Richard "has been complaining a lot lately that I am always on his back. Our rooms are separated by a large salon, and I also avoid being seen by him, I evade him whenever I can, but then don't know where to hide."[22] She wanted to cash in the coupons for some bank stocks she held, but had to keep this secret from Richard, "otherwise the money would be gone in a day." She now invited Mathilde Schiffner to visit her in Soden at her expense: "Just don't worry about me, I am a much too sensible, calm woman, I have learned to overcome many things, and will continue to do so."[23] It pleased her that for once she was not a recipient of charity, but was able to be generous herself to a friend.

Richard wrote to their old Dresden friend Ferdinand Heine to tell him that Minna was taking the waters in Bad Soden, as her doctor had recommended:

Overall she feels tolerable, even though my last adventures in life were not of a kind that always allowed her to be in a good mood and patient with me. Things are just hard for me, very hard, and the only thing that cheers me up, oddly, is that from afar, people always look at me as if I were someone who doesn't know what to do with all his happiness and well-being.[24]

For her part, Minna reported back to Mathilde Schiffner in a good mood:

After traveling constantly yesterday until 1 o'clock by fast train, I immediately walked around to look for a nice apartment where we can both live. I then actually succeeded in finding one to which I can invite you without hesitation. You can sleep with me in a rather spacious room, the living room is something special, but snoring is not allowed. So you will stay with me. What I'm paying for it is no concern of yours, everything else will sort itself out.[25]

Her Parisian misery was well behind her now, and she was determined to forget it:

We can stroll around together, the scenery everywhere is beautiful. Come, please, so that you may stay here for a long time. Oh, how I'm looking forward to having you here! I can't even contemplate the possibility that you won't come, it would be too sad for me, I have thought of everything so nicely, and

---

22   Minna to Mathilde Schiffner, June 22, 1860 (RWA).
23   Ibid.
24   SB XII, 216–17, here 217 (July 10, 1860).
25   Minna to Mathilde Schiffner, July 1860 (RWA).

we shall go on excursions, goodness, the gods would even rejoice at how happy we good children are.[26]

In this summer of 1860, Richard was finally given a partial amnesty that applied to all the German states except Saxony. He was thus able to pick up Minna after her cure in Bad Soden. He took her first to visit his brother Albert in Frankfurt, then to Baden-Baden, where he also paid his respects to Princess Augusta of Prussia and thanked her for helping him get his pardon. Wagner then persuaded Minna to go on a spontaneous steamboat trip on the Rhine with him. But she was naturally annoyed when he ordered two single rooms in a loud voice,[27] for she became anxious about anything that intimated to others the rocky state of their marriage. All the same, she presumably enjoyed the days they spent together. Did she already suspect that it would be their last ever joint vacation? Then they went back to Paris, where Minna celebrated her birthday down in the dumps after catching a bad cold while waiting almost two hours for Richard at the Tuileries Garden. She also got severe pains in her arm. Their maid Therese had procured a beautiful bouquet of flowers and placed it on the breakfast table, and Minna had initially assumed it was a gift from Richard. But he then had to tell her that he had spent everything on their trip, and so was unable to buy her anything at all. Minna summed up her feelings of bitterness in a letter six days later to Mathilde Schiffner, in which she claimed to have told him: "For one franc here you can get a large bouquet that would undoubtedly have given me great joy on Sept. 5, more than any gifts I was promised. And how often is a 5-franc piece simply cast away without giving anyone any joy?"[28] However charming and affectionate he might be in his letters, and however often he demonstrated his concern for her welfare, Richard was also equally able to be forgetful and indifferent in everyday life. Minna sensed that their earlier bonds of dependence, love, and affection had been destroyed. She was naturally unaware that she herself had played a part in their destruction when she had refused to follow Richard into exile after the Dresden Uprising. He, however, was unable to exist without unconditional loyalty. These were psychological boundaries between them that affected them both but could no longer be dismantled.

---

26   Ibid.
27   Letter to Cäcilie Avenarius, quoted in Herzfeld 1938, 285.
28   Minna to Mathilde Schiffner, September 11, 1860 (RWA).

Minna's distress at his behavior towards her—his well-nigh dismissive fri-
gidity—was only one side of the story, however. When it came to his music,
she still longed for his success as much as he did, and took a keen interest in
how he and his music fared. Several performances of *Tannhäuser* were now
scheduled at the Opéra in Paris, and she was looking forward to them. The
rehearsals dragged on for months, and Richard also fell seriously ill with a
typhoid fever, through which Minna nursed him for many weeks. Before the
first full rehearsal, Minna wrote to Natalie that Richard had "dropped the
beautiful overture for his *Tannhäuser* and added instead a jumble of Venus
spookiness."[29] She feared that this erotic expansion of the opening scene—
the "Bacchanale"—might jeopardize the opera's chances of success. Since
Richard no longer discussed his work with her, she could not understand
what had prompted him to make these changes and additions to his score.
Richard had written to Mathilde Wesendonck to explain that "back then,
when I wrote *Tannhäuser*, I was unable to realize rapture—what I should
almost like to term 'feminine ecstasy.'" So he had now cast everything aside
and drafted the scene anew: "truly, I am shocked at my cardboard-backdrop
Venus from back then!" He was presumably trying to explain to Mathilde
that only she had been capable of awakening in him the emotional, sensual depths necessary for him to ascend to a higher plane of compositional
maturity.[30] Minna much preferred the original version. Perhaps she also suspected that this new version, in which triangle, castanets, timpani, cymbals,
and tambourine evoke an exotic, passionate sound world, was in some way
bound up with Mathilde.

Minna invited her "good, dear son" Ernst Benedikt Kietz to attend the
dress rehearsal. She could sit next to him, she wrote, and point out all the
beauties of the score, for she knew every note of the opera well. She referred
to herself as his "old mother-by-adoption," and loved assuming a maternal
role with him: "You'll stay for dinner, and I'll carry you to the rehearsal, as a
good mother takes her little son. [...] Just come, the arms of your parents-
by-adoption are wide open to embrace their dear son."[31]

Richard had campaigned for months to get his *Tannhäuser* performed at
the Paris Opéra, but the scandal the production now occasioned exceeded
anything that had gone before it. The members of the Jockey Club—a
Parisian, high-class gentlemen's club whose members held several boxes at

---

29   Minna to Natalie Planer, February 10, 1861 (RWA).
30   SB XII, 263–69, here 266 (September 30, 1860).
31   Burrell, 385–86 (February 19, 1861).

the Opéra—had prepared themselves to engage in loud protests on the evening. Whistles at the ready in their kidskin gloves, they heckled and laughed at the chaos that resulted. However, a large number of those in the audience then began a counter-protest that was similarly raucous, and fisticuffs almost broke out. The singers had to pause for up to a quarter of an hour at a time before they could continue with the performance.

The writer Malwida von Meysenbug has left us a vivid account of the events at the Opéra. She had gone into exile in London after the abortive revolutions of 1848, had moved to Paris in 1859, and visited Wagner there. She went to England in 1860 to teach, but traveled back to Paris along with her foster-daughter to attend the premiere of *Tannhäuser*. She was enthralled by Wagner's music, and by his theories for improving humanity through culture. Malwida described the various groups that had lined up in advance to oppose Wagner: the press, because he did not bribe the critics; the "claque" (the Opéra's organized group of professional applauders), whom Wagner regarded with contempt; and those opposed to him on political grounds because the production had been actively promoted by Princess Pauline Metternich. She was a close friend of the French Empress Eugénie, but also the wife of the Austrian Ambassador to Paris, which meant that the work was immediately assumed by many to be foreign to the French national temperament. Meysenbug went on to describe the gentlemen of the Jockey Club: "What did these distinguished libertines care for the performance of a chaste work of art that celebrates the victory of sacred love over sensual intoxication?" Malwida had correctly understood the moral of the plot, though she failed to mention the impact of the music, for the sounds that Wagner conjured up for the sinful world of the goddess of love are far more compelling than the renunciatory utterings of his virtuous Minnesänger. After venting her wrath over the innate vulgarity and boundless depravity of the young men in the club, she described how chaos broke out in parts of the audience after the Bacchanale, during the transition from Venus's grotto to the Thuringian Forest. The performance was able to conclude, but only amidst general tumult.

Wagner wanted to withdraw the score, but was persuaded otherwise by his circle of friends, and so allowed a second performance. His pessimism proved accurate, however, for the struggles in the audience became even more bitter. Malwida sat in a box with Minna, next to one full of Frenchmen who were whistling, shouting, and hissing. She was outraged, and insulted them vociferously in French, calling them a rabble of street urchins: "In this manner, I continued speaking so loudly that Frau Wagner became alarmed

and whispered to me: 'My God, you are too bold, you'll get into trouble.'"
But this did nothing to deter Malwida. On the contrary, she began address-
ing the troublemakers directly: "Gentlemen, even if you will show no consideration for anyone else, then at least take note that the composer's wife is
sitting here next to you."[32] But this only helped for a brief while before they
resumed their hubbub.

Richard decided not to attend the third performance on March 24, but
sat it out at home in peace with Minna. Perhaps he also did this out of consideration for her current state of health. He did not want her to become
too agitated, as this would only put even more strain on her already weakened heart. Her condition had indeed deteriorated under the impact of these
events. She now began suffering from severe palpitations and a heavy cough.
The performance itself proceeded as noisily as the previous two. Afterwards,
several friends met in the foyer of the Opéra and then drove to the Wagners'
apartment. Richard and Minna were sitting comfortably, drinking tea.
Richard smoked a pipe and demonstrably remained calm while his friends
reported on the evening's chaos—though Malwida noted how his hand was
shaking. He now decided to withdraw his opera altogether.

For Minna, the whole experience was harrowing. Hans von Bülow had
understood the state of things correctly when he wrote, horrified, to Richard:
"Your poor wife! How she must have suffered! We have been thinking a lot
about her and would have gladly expressed our sympathy. But how could we
find words of consolation, of reassurance?"[33] The gloating comments in the
press will have shocked Minna, for she attached more importance to maintaining a good reputation than Richard ever did. His own inner turmoil also
had an impact on her as his wife. She wrote to Natalie to tell her about the
scandal and, like Malwida, expressed especial indignation towards the gentlemen of the Jockey Club:

> The so-called Jockey Club are the rich, frivolous gentlemen who have their
> mistresses in the ballet, nearly all employed without any salary, with whom
> they amuse themselves after the ballet, behind the scenes, and this in the most
> indecent manner. These gentlemen were furious when they arrived at the the-
> ater, which they usually do only during the second act, and from then on,
> the row started. They had bought whistles and whistled as soon as someone
> applauded. I did not go to the third performance. I suffered too much from
> those waggish tricks, but it is said to have been a regular *war*. All the ladies,

32   Meysenbug 1905, III, 292.
33   Moulin Eckart 1927, 448 (March 20, 1861).

the princesses and the highnesses, got up and applauded, and pointed their fingers toward those two stalls. The whole impartial public shouted "*à la porte les Jockeys*" [throw the Jockeys out of the door], etc. The Emperor was there all three times, but he could do nothing, they are legitimists [royalist opponents of the Emperor]. Richard has withdrawn his score.[34]

Wagner experienced the complete opposite in May 1861 in Vienna when he attended a festive performance of his *Lohengrin*. This was the first time he was able to hear his work in its entirety. He sat in a box in the second tier. The audience recognized him and greeted him with seemingly never-ending, thunderous applause. A few days later, Vienna also performed *Der fliegende Holländer*, and the tributes and acts of homage continued. At the dress rehearsal, he was led onto the stage to rapturous acclaim from the participants. Everyone made an effort to impress the composer to the utmost, which made Richard weep with emotion. These ovations were repeated at the performance itself. He reported everything to Minna with satisfaction, because he knew how much his successes meant to her:

> I had hidden myself in a box in the stalls so that no one could see me. But that didn't help. After the overture, I had to go onto the stage to express my thanks, then 3 times after each act, and 5 or 6 times after the last act, when I also had to say a few words again. The audience was unbelievably warm and lively; and there were princes and counts in the boxes. Everyone shouted and applauded along. Well, now I really have a story to tell![35]

But not even this success was enough to solve Wagner's financial problems. The *Tannhäuser* scandal had damaged his reputation, and he was simply unable to organize sufficient performances of his works in Germany for as long as he was outside the country himself. As a result, he was unable to earn the royalties he needed. The sudden death of their little dog Fips in June 1861 seemed to Richard to signify a final rupture in his life with Minna. He decided to give up their house in Paris and to send Minna on a cure for the time being. He did not know yet where he might end up himself. In July, their complete furniture was packed up—his Erard grand piano being the sole exception. He wanted Minna to move to Dresden. "For my part," he wrote to Mathilde Wesendonck in July 1861, "I am no longer thinking of settling down. This is the result of my most recent, difficult, infinitely

---

34   Burrell, 378.
35   SB XIII, 136–37, here 136 (May 20, 1861).

laborious experiences! I am not destined to tend to my muse in the bosom of cozy domesticity."[36] When Minna and Richard said their farewells in their increasingly empty apartment, it was unpleasant for both of them. After Minna arrived at her spa, he wrote to her from Paris that he was "in a very depressed mood on account of this constant repetition of the same, restless fate". But this was an assessment that applied to both of them.[37]

Minna had set off for Bad Soden on July 11, accompanied by their parrot. Back in Paris, Richard wrote to Malwida von Meysenbug resignedly about his current state of exhaustion. He had wasted two years, he said: two years lost for art. He set off for Weimar, interrupting his journey for a day to visit Minna at her spa. He found her in the company of Mathilde Schiffner, the friend who had become indispensable to her.

Richard became convinced that his wife should go back to Dresden. Her doctor Pusinelli was there, she had an extensive circle of friends and acquaintances in the city, and she had always felt at home there. So he spoke to her and convinced her that it was for the best. He, however, was keen to return to Vienna to sound out his possibilities for work there. He promised Minna that he would in the future send her 1,000 thalers a year under any and all circumstances.

After her cure, Minna spent several weeks in Weimar, then followed Richard's advice and returned to Dresden. This meant repeating the process of packing up, unpacking, and setting up home again—all accompanied by the same old sense of upheaval, as she confirmed in a letter to Emma Herwegh with a dash of sarcasm: "At present, I have once again been drifting around from place to place for 5 months, devoid of any home, which is just what I need at my advanced age."[38]

Richard remained contradictory in his statements about whether he actually wanted to live with Minna again. On the one hand, he was insistent that he could well imagine a situation in which they could get along splendidly with each other; but on the other hand, he was equally convinced that this depended on his getting a secure position in life, and on finding a pleasant place where they might settle down for good. His assessment of their situation was accurate: the serious crises that had arisen between them had always been at a time when he had given up either a secure job (as in Dresden in 1849) or a comfortable domestic situation (such as when he had made it

---

36 SB XIII, 166–67, here 166 (July 12, 1861).
37 SB XIII, 170–72, here 170 (July 16, 1861).
38 December 15, 1861, in *Das Forum* 1/31 (1914).

impossible for them to remain in the Asyl in Zurich, nine years later). Each of these instances had plunged Minna into new, unfamiliar circumstances against her will. Her resulting disappointment inevitably met with energetic opposition on his part, for he knew well that his nervous restlessness left him no other course of action. This incompatibility between them had repeatedly reared its head, and he knew it was something that he had to put behind him, once and for all.

Minna celebrated their silver wedding anniversary on her own, depressed. Richard wrote in his diary: "24 Nov. Minna's silver wedding anniversary,"[39] thus exempting himself from the occasion. She wrote to Emma Herwegh to tell her that he had given her a golden bracelet "and a whole year's sabbatical"—meaning that he had provisionally packed her off to Dresden without him. Since she was the wife of a former revolutionary, she was initially denied permanent residence in the kingdom of Saxony and needed a special permit to live in Dresden. She was presumably granted half a year at first, because in December 1861 she wrote to Emma: "I will stay here until next April. The gods alone know where my wanderings shall take me!" And just as she knew who had "seduced" her husband in the May Uprising back in 1849—August Röckel—so she also knew clearly now what was to blame for her current misfortune: "This is all thanks to *Tristan*."[40]

Meanwhile, Richard was looking for a new female partner, and his beloved Mathilde Wesendonck remained the object of his erotic longings. In late 1860, she had been the recipient of an outburst of emotion from him that stands out among his letters, in which he otherwise endeavored to maintain some form of normality:

> O, my child! Where shall I find my one and only consolation?—I once found a heart and soul that understood me completely in these moments, and to whom I became dear because they too understood me and were able to understand me! You see, it is to this soul that I flee, and like someone weary unto death I shall let my limbs sink down, and lower myself into the soft ether of this friendly being. All my experiences, the unheard-of emotions, sorrows, and sufferings from the past will be dissolved, like dissipating storm clouds, into a refreshing dew that shall wet my burning forehead: then I shall feel refreshed, and shall finally enjoy peace, sweet peace: I am loved—and recognized![41]

---

39 BB, 135.
40 December 15, 1861, in *Das Forum* 1/31 (1914).
41 SB XII, 304–06, here 306 (December 23, 1860).

But immense disappointment beckoned less than a year later. The Wesendoncks invited Wagner to join them in Venice, only for him to realize that Mathilde was pregnant again (their son Hans would be born seven months later, in June 1862). This child was a watershed: Richard understood that Mathilde would for the coming months—no, years— be absorbed by all the concerns of pregnancy, birth, and infant nurture. Richard wrote to her afterwards, full of sadness: "It is only now that am I completely resigned! One thing I had never given up, and thought that I had onerously won it back: to find my Asyl once again, and to be able to live near you once more.—A reunion of one hour in Venice was enough to destroy this last, dear delusion of mine!"[42]

A few flirtations with the opposite sex served to brighten up his mood. In January 1862, he spoke to his friend, the composer Peter Cornelius, about his "doll," which was his name for Seraphine Mauro, the attractive niece of his Viennese friend Josef Standhartner. "It wouldn't bother me at all if the girl came to me, and was to me exactly what she could be to me, given her pretty little nature.— But how to find the 'terminus socialis' for it? Oh, heavens!—it's such an absurd shame!"[43] He simply had no understanding for the moral indignation that would result in their bourgeois environment, were his "doll" to give in to his desires.

These months were among the most difficult of Wagner's life. He had no female partner with whom he might plan his future, his financial situation was once again more than precarious, his marriage was wrecked, and there were no wealthy patrons waiting in the wings for him. He had resigned himself to many things, and was bitterly disappointed that none of the high-ranking aristocrats in Germany was willing to liberate him from his peripatetic life. He gave vent to his bitterness in a letter to Hans von Bülow: "For 25 years I have been married, recognized, loved, admired; [...] but here I am, hanging around in guest houses and imagining myself to be an opera composer!"[44] He wrote similarly to his sister Cäcilie, complaining of how he was without a family, a home, and an income. Out of desperation, he invited Peter Cornelius to move in with him. Cornelius was eleven years his junior, and Richard did not even try to disguise his intention to appropriate the younger man completely: "I would consider you as if belonging to me, like my wife; everything—happiness and misfortune—will be shared equally

---

42   SB XIII, 350–52, here 350 (December 1861).
43   SB XIV, 42–44, here 43 (January 9, 1862).
44   SB XIII, 227–29, here 229 (September 24, 1861).

and in common; everything will be quite self-evident [...] Understand me right. You will do what you do, and I'll do what I do, but always like two people who actually belong together, like a married couple."[45] Cornelius was astute enough to turn him down and avoid his stultifying influence.

One last, dramatic attempt to reunite with Minna took place in February 1862, when Richard decided to settle in Biebrich, just outside Wiesbaden. In his typically vague manner, he had praised Biebrich to her as a pleasant place to live, and had held out the prospect of possibly living together again. He went out apartment-hunting with the aid of his publisher Schott, and found something suitable in a large summer house. He waited for his furniture to arrive from Paris, and wrote to tell Minna that she could use whatever furniture he did not need. She had understood that the complaints in his letters were because he lacked help in his domestic life, so when their furniture arrived at the German customs office, Minna spontaneously decided to go to Biebrich and help him out. Richard was delighted. In a letter she wrote to Cäcilie, Minna mentions that he had even wept tears of joy when she went to him. Both of them were keen just to be nice to each other.

But their good mood did not last long. The next morning at breakfast, Richard received a letter from Mathilde Wesendonck. This opened up old wounds and put a nervous strain on both of them. Minna poured out her heart to Natalie afterwards: "All peace was at an end before I had said a *single* word. He raved and shouted without any reason, telling me that this is not my business, he can correspond with anyone he likes, etc."[46] Richard's raving and shouting made Minna feel as if she were somehow to blame for this outburst, which upset her even more. A day later, they went to Darmstadt together with the Schott family, where they all attended a performance of *Rienzi* given by Albert Niemann's traveling opera company. They returned to Biebrich the next day.

> As we were seated at breakfast, another voluminous letter from that hussy W. arrived. But again I didn't add a word about it. My Richard, however, started talking himself into a really savage fury, then I only said: 'Well, it is certainly a peculiar coincidence.' Those words he mockingly repeated, as streetboys do. I said that he could abuse me as much as he wished, I wouldn't answer anything; so he actually continued ranting for three-quarters of an hour.[47]

---

45   SB XIV, 42–44, here 42–43 (January 9, 1862).
46   Burrell, 408–9, here 408 (March 6, 1862).
47   Ibid.

Their fierce dispute shows just how much their nerves were on edge. But things were about to get even worse. The next day, the boxes with their furniture had to be opened and unpacked at the customs office. An official told them that one box had arrived in the mail a few days earlier. Minna opened it, assuming that it would contain sheet music with customs duty to pay on it. But no: "There it was again from that awful woman: an embroidered cushion, tea, Eau de Cologne, pressed violets. Now a new scandal was to be expected, nor did it fail to come. I don't want to repeat what I had to hear again, although I begged and implored him not to shame me in front of people."[48]

They both now grasped that their marriage was utterly and irreparably shattered. Richard's overly irritable reaction to Minna's reproaches, and Minna's projection of anger onto Mathilde, were merely the external signs of their innate incapacity to continue. Minna arranged the furniture in Richard's rooms as swiftly as possible and traveled back to Dresden five days later. She had not given up hope that Richard's love for Mathilde would wane—a hope that had been nourished by his occasional, ambiguous remarks in this regard. Richard wrote to her in May, mentioning Biebrich as merely a provisional arrangement for him, and announcing that he would be moving in with her in Dresden that coming November—though he also immediately emphasized that this, too, could only be temporary. It is noteworthy that he omitted any mention in his autobiography of the letters from Mathilde Wesendonck that had arrived so infelicitously, though he did at least admit to Minna that he had behaved inappropriately towards her: "I must deeply lament the strange coincidences that were responsible for clouding our mood during our brief reunion; most of all, however, I regret realizing how extraordinarily irritable and restless is my temperament."[49] It was well-known that Richard could become hurtful when angry. "In his passionate irritability he was capable of any injustice," wrote Eduard Hanslick,[50] and Ferdinand Praeger remarked in similar fashion on this character trait of Wagner's: "He [...] spared the feelings of none by an incisive criticism which cut to the core, and yet an over-sensitiveness made him writhe under the slightest censure."[51]

---

48   Ibid., 408–9 (slightly amended: Burrell gives "filthy woman," which is somewhat too strong; replaced with "awful woman").

49   SB XIV, 98–103, here 98 (March 11, 1862).

50   Hanslick 1894, II, 9.

51   Praeger 1892, vii.

Richard also wrote to Cornelius about his regret over the incident. The latter was on friendly terms with Minna, and it seems likely that a conversation with her had prompted him to attempt some form of mediation. But Richard now confided that it was impossible for him to continue living together with her. "My heart bleeds: and yet I realize that I must fight all softness of my heart with force, since my only salvation lies in being firm and open."[52] He admitted that he yearned for a homely atmosphere and had hoped to regain this by moving back in with Minna. He described to Cornelius how he had felt when she entered the room: "My heart opened up, and my emotion and great joy must have shown her straightaway how things were with me."[53] He saw that she seemed refreshed, and realized that she was thriving, away from his restless lifestyle. But they did not find much to talk about. Minna seems to have ceased her willingness to listen to his monologues, for she began telling Richard details of her own life in Dresden, which he found boring. In his letter to Cornelius, Richard mentioned the gift from Mathilde that had unfortunately reached him on the same day that Minna was unpacking their boxes. "Unable to see my relations with that woman other than in a repugnant, trivial light, she was unwilling to understand any of the explanations that I gave her purely for the sake of reassuring her, and instead sounded off in that vulgar fashion of hers that then made me lose all composure again [...] this whole insane edifice thus stands there again, bright and unshaken!"[54] After ten days of hell, said Richard, he had to come up with a plan so that this would never happen again. He wanted to send back to Dresden the belongings that he didn't need in Biebrich, and would ask Minna to reserve a room for him in her apartment. He would not even rule out spending a few weeks there at a later date. But essentially, he wanted to live away from her. He was aware that he would thereby bear the financial burden of running two households when he could barely maintain one, and the decision was not easy for him to make: "I deeply pity others who are suffering. It is horrible to me to know that someone is suffering because of me!"[55] But he was convinced that she no longer loved him. At the close of his letter, he was overcome by the misery of being alone, and he lamented: "Oh God! Now my tears are overwhelming me, and I say: if only there were a friendly, feminine being who might gently take me in!! I am

52   SB XIV, 89–94, here 89 (March 4, 1862).
53   Ibid., 90.
54   Ibid., 91.
55   Ibid., 93.

now closing my mind to that! And thus I think that all the sufferings of my wife are avenged!"[56] After having so emphatically thematized the redemption of man through woman in his works, he, of all people, would now have to live alone.

Shortly before this chaos ran its course, Richard had sent Mathilde Wesendonck a copy of the libretto to *Die Meistersinger von Nürnberg*. After having met the Wesendoncks in Venice, he had finally grasped that he would never possess Mathilde. So he had revamped the plot of his new opera by having Hans Sachs sacrifice his interest in Eva in order to emphasize how he, Richard, had renounced Mathilde.[57] By sending her the libretto he was effectively confirming to her his own act of renunciation. But not only was Mathilde out of reach: with Minna now gone, he also had lost the partner who had always helped him to settle down after each of his aimless wanderings, and had each time provided him with a sense of homely domesticity.

In late March 1862, Minna's doctor Anton Pusinelli prepared an expert opinion on her state of health. His conclusions affected Wagner personally, since Pusinelli stated that it was the upheavals after the Dresden Uprising of 1849 that had triggered her heart condition. In his opinion, she had possessed a strong constitution before her departure. But nine years on, the healthy, strong woman he had once known was no longer recognizable; she was now physically and emotionally a wreck.

> I had not expected such a glaring expression of severe inner affliction. [...] I found proof of an organic heart disease [...], a completely irregular pulse, constant respiratory distress, a trembling, quivering voice, her face pale and possessed of an anxious, almost frightened expression, and then there was her constant restlessness that she was powerless to conceal; all this and other things confirmed my diagnosis [...] her condition at that time seemed to be almost hopeless. I immediately prescribed medicines and a special diet, and together with her subsequent whey and bathing cure in Schandau, these had a favorable impact and considerably reduced her complaints, all the more so because her long-desired return to live in her fatherland had a beneficial effect on the patient's mind. But none of this was able to relieve her deep-rooted condition. It was to my regret and against my will that the sick woman left here again in the fall [of 1859], at the request of her husband, and she exchanged the beneficial quiet of her stay here for the excitement of Parisian life. Nor did the consequences fail to materialize that I had feared. The news I received thereafter was

---

56   Ibid.
57   See Voss 1996, 284f.; Rieger 2011, 88–89.

not comforting, and revealed her deep longing for her home. After two painful summers, the patient finally returned here in the fall of 1861.[58]

Pusinelli believed that the positive effects of Minna's earlier stay in Dresden (in 1858–59) had been almost completely negated, and it took considerable efforts on his part to return her to the condition she had been in before leaving in 1859.[59] Pusinelli thus clearly implies that living with Richard had made Minna ill.

It is not a little ironic that this report—which essentially documents the incompatibility of Richard and Minna—was what helped Richard to get his long-yearned-for amnesty in his home region of Saxony. Minna drove the process onwards and asked him to write a letter to the king. He wrote it, sent it to Minna, and she forwarded it. Richard's amnesty now became an act of mercy to his sick wife. On April 1, 1862, Minna received word of the decision in Richard's favor that meant he could now travel to his native Saxony without fear of punishment. But the news for which he had hoped for so many years now came too late to please him properly. Dresden just was not attractive to him anymore.

Richard asked Pusinelli to inquire cautiously whether or not Minna might agree to a divorce, but Minna brusquely rejected any such notions: "If he wants a complete divorce, then I say: No," wrote Minna to Pusinelli. "He should be patient and wait until God separates us. Separation?—he has already separated from me, since I have been pushed around alone in the world for years now. He can come to Dresden if he wants, he shall always find asylum here."[60] Richard knew that she feared divorce would be seen by society as an act of disgrace, so he swiftly took everything back. He even claimed in his letters to her that he had never in fact considered divorce, and blamed it all instead on her poor doctor.[61] The distrust that Minna already harbored towards whatever Richard said was merely intensified by these claims, for she knew full well that any notions of divorce would never have originated with her doctor alone.

In Richard's subsequent letters to her, a pattern emerges that is similar to what had happened after their rupture in the Asyl in Zurich. Richard reported on opera performances and other daily events, thereby maintaining

---

58   Lippert 1927, 172ff.

59   Ibid.

60   Herzfeld 1938, 315 (June 16, 1862).

61   SB XIV, 192–93, here 192–93 (June 27, 1862).

some semblance of normality; but it was not enough. Minna's physical afflictions made her irritable, and at times even unjust towards him. She became increasingly abusive and accused him of pushing her out into an alien world. When an invitation from her sister Amalie arrived from Russia, she used it to demonstrate to Richard just how much others still cared for her. This in turn offended him, though he was unable to do anything about it. He wrote to her, resignedly: "Whoever finds letters from you to me will read in them how my wife calls me and my behavior towards her 'heartless,' 'crude,' and 'mean.' So this will probably also appear in my biography.—I cannot change it now!"[62]

Early July 1862 saw the arrival of Hans and Cosima von Bülow in Biebrich. Hans assisted on the piano while Richard rehearsed the title roles of Tristan and Isolde with Ludwig and Malvina Schnorr von Carolsfeld. Both Hans and Cosima were overwhelmed by the extraordinary music and wrote veritable hymns of praise to it in letters to Liszt in Rome. When they left Biebrich, Richard accompanied the Bülows as far as Frankfurt am Main, where Richard allowed himself a prank that in retrospect took on a deeper meaning. He asked Cosima to sit on a pushcart that was standing empty in a square, and she agreed without hesitation—though out of consideration for Hans, Richard refrained from actually pushing her around in it. It was at this point that we find the first use of the familiar second-person pronoun "du" in correspondence between Richard and Cosima. Her obedience to him made Richard aware of her unconditional devotion—a devotion that culminated in a sexual relationship between them two years later.

Minna went on another cure in June 1862, this time to Reichenhall in southern Bavaria (just across the border from Salzburg). Shortly before her departure she had sent another awkward letter to Richard—he told his sister Clara that it read as if written by a madwoman. All his hopes were now pinned on her present spa therapy. Hans von Bülow—who believed that a final separation between the two was the logical step to take—wrote rather maliciously to Karl Klindworth in August that "His wife has settled in Dresden, from where she has betaken herself to Reichenhall in Tyrol for several weeks for a new luxury cure. In one respect, then, your cherished wish for him is being fulfilled: Separation from Madame."[63] But Bülow's mocking reference to Minna as a woman of leisure and luxury is an injustice

---

62   SB XIV, 156–59, here 159 (May 21, 1862).
63   Moulin Eckart 1927, 10 (August 5, 1862).

Figure 11.1. Clara Wolfram, Richard Wagner's sister. Eva Rieger Collection.

on his part, and the tables would soon enough be turned when his own wife abandoned him for the friend whom he adored so much.

In July 1862, Richard once again asked his former patron Otto Wesendonck for a loan, this time to fund Minna's final resettlement in Dresden. Otto refused; but since a note of thanks for renewed help exists from Richard, sent a few days later, Otto had presumably reconsidered in the meantime—perhaps at the request of his wife. Wagner now also had the idea of asking Otto for permission to publish the songs he had written to poems by Mathilde, during the time of his intense infatuation. Wesendonck agreed, and Schott promptly offered to pay Richard to publish them.

In their correspondence, Richard and Minna stuck with matters that they could both cope with, emotionally and otherwise. In August, a dog bit Richard's thumb so badly that he could not work, at which Minna wrote to him from Reichenhall:

> It frightened me at first that the awful, ungrateful Leo bit you, I hope it won't get bad. I'd rather have taken the bite myself because such wounds heal quickly with me. The stupid animal doesn't even deserve to be fed scraps of bread as you probably used to do; just be careful with him, you never can trust these old malicious bulldogs. You'd do me a favor if you'd tell me in two words that your poor hand is all right again.[64]

All the same, there were still moments in her letters when Minna was seized by a desperate rage and went on the attack against Richard. Her reproaches wore him down. In a letter of December 27, 1862, he was clearly at the end of his tether:

> Oh, my good Minna! You should also be concerned to make things easier for me! You ought to soften your complaints, even when they are justified (and they are with regard to your most recent hardship!). But you are eternally subject to delusions about me and my life, and nothing seems to be able to wrest you from them. Just believe that I am leading an utterly *miserable* life, daily, hourly—and am never, *never* cheerful! [...] Of all my worries and hardships, my worries about you remain the ones that gnaw at me most.[65]

Richard had to conduct a concert in Leipzig in November 1862, and took the opportunity to visit Minna in Dresden, just 60 miles away. He

---

64   Burrell 411 (August 4, 1862).
65   SB XIV, 368–69, here 368 (December 27, 1862).

expressly asked her not to come to Leipzig herself, because he wanted her to avoid any excitement. Besides the *Tannhäuser* Overture, Wagner gave the first-ever performance of the Prelude to *Die Meistersinger*, and Bülow also played Liszt's A-major Piano Concerto. The concert was poorly attended and financially unsuccessful. He then traveled to Dresden. Clara Wolfram was visiting Minna when Richard arrived, so their meeting remained friendly. Minna had made a carpet with "SALVE" ("welcome" in Latin) embroidered on it in capital letters, and had placed it in front of her apartment door where Richard had to cross it. She had prepared a bedroom and a living room for him, and in one room she had arranged for his red silken curtains from Paris to be fitted. There was also some furniture left over from their time in Zurich, along with the old mahogany desk that Wagner had used in Dresden over a decade earlier. The Ritter family had acquired it after he fled, and had meanwhile returned it. These touching recollections of their past domestic ambience made it evident—without the need for any verbal explanations—that Minna wanted to provide a home for him in Dresden, despite all their quarrels. She still considered herself his legitimate wife. Did she really still entertain hopes that he might return to her? Richard was touched by the care she took, but it had long been clear to him that there was no way that he could ever resume his old life. Back in April, just a month after his full amnesty had finally been granted, he had taken care to explain that he would not be returning permanently to Dresden, and he left it up to her to decorate her apartment after her own taste. That alone should have made her realize his intentions, because Richard usually participated gleefully in furnishing and decorating his living quarters. But he also knew how to nourish her hopes by holding out a vague prospect of establishing a home for himself in Dresden after all.

Their conversations about money will no doubt have been the most difficult for both of them. The maintenance payments that Richard had promised had recently failed to materialize again, which meant Minna had to go into debt. His fame was growing year by year, but even in the spring of 1863, shortly before his 50th birthday, he proved once again unable to keep up his payments to her. The visit that Richard made to Minna in late November 1862 was in fact the last time that he ever saw her.

The Wesendonck episode remained for years a source of hurt to Minna. It never ceased gnawing at her. For Richard, however, the memory of it faded over time. When he looked back in later years, his once passionate love for Mathilde had fallen by the wayside. To Cosima, he played down Mathilde's sometime significance in his life. "She was very sweet" "She helped me nicely with my work" "She gave back nicely what one gave her" "It was a relationship that should not have been tested."[66] This makes it sound as if Wagner had engaged in nothing but a mischievous flirtation, though it was a malicious distortion of the truth. For her part, Mathilde had embarked on a career as a writer just a few years after the conflict of 1858 and had developed a certain routine as an author. Her works included the dramas *Gudrun* (1868), *Edith or the Battle of Hastings* (1872), *Frederick the Great* (1871), *Odysseus* (1878), *Alcestis* (1881), and others. On one occasion, she sent Richard a volume of fairy tales she had published, but he declared scornfully: "These are tales she tells her children."[67] To him, she had simply joined the ranks of women who had betrayed him because they had not loved him enough.

Despite everything, Mathilde behaved extremely generously towards the Bayreuth Festival. She became one of the major patrons of its scholarship foundation, and stipulated that it should be further endowed after her death. She was outraged that Houston Stewart Chamberlain's large-scale biography of Wagner all but passed over Richard's relationship with her, and she had a correction printed in a music journal. Once, in conversation with the Frenchman Louis de Fourcaud, she even let her feelings get the better of her, declaring that "Wagner soon pushed me aside; I was in Bayreuth only as a visitor, barely recognized, practically unknown—and yet I am Isolde!"[68]

Cosima recognized Mathilde's importance, however, and in 1900 she thanked her warmly for sending her books; she called Otto Wesendonck a tender, noble man, and was grateful for the kind reception that Mathilde had shown her son Siegfried when he had visited them.[69] But Cosima was eager for certain things to stay unsaid. Already back in 1878, she had written to Mathilde about this, but in her typically rapt, tortuous prose in which meaning seems enveloped in some strange code. She wanted to ask Mathilde to remain silent about what belonged in the past, but it turned out thus:

> If I confide to you this deeply profound [...] emotion, and not merely this, but if even I, too, should declare it through my silence, then it is because I believe I know that you will wholly grasp that you, in your own silence, acknowledge the truthfulness of this silence, that you will understand it through your con-

---

66　Cosima Wagner on "Wagner's relationship to Mathilde Wesendonck," in Mack 1980, 404 (January 1896).

67　Ibid., 405.

68　Cabaud 2017, 4.

69　Mack 1980, 520, 652.

sent, and that you will be able to maintain it almost to the point of deception, which, to be sure, is already inherent in almost every act of speech.[70]

But Mathilde will presumably have lost little time thinking about the later Wagner, and will instead have recalled the man who had loved her, and who as late as 1861 was still able to write to her: "The fact that I have written *Tristan* is something for which I shall thank you from the bottom of my soul for all eternity!"[71]

Minna was meanwhile concerned about the future of her daughter, who was staying with the Tröger family in Zwickau and was helping out in the household. She was glad that Natalie was out of the house, but still felt obliged to ensure that she got on in life. Women of the bourgeoisie in the 19th century were expected to submit to certain forms of (self-)discipline, and it is clear that Minna had internalized this manner of thinking: she was insistent that her daughter be neat, clean, and eager to work. She had been worrying for years about where Natalie might end up. Already back in 1843, in a letter to Cäcilie Avenarius, Richard had expressed mocking doubts that Natalie might ever be able to learn French: "That is a result of erroneous, wishful thinking, and it would be clear to her if she were only willing to subject her letters written in German to cold-blooded scrutiny."[72] Minna knew all about women's limited opportunities for career advancement, so when Malwida von Meysenbug held out the prospect of procuring a position for Natalie as a governess, Minna sent money to pay for lessons so that Natalie might learn the basics of music (playing the piano), drawing, French, and history. In addition, wrote Minna, Natalie should display good manners so that she might move easily among high society; and she should also dress well. She advised Natalie to take up sewing or knitting during the breaks in her studies so that she might get some relaxation.[73] Minna did not want to trouble Richard with all these worries, but she only ended up being unkind to Natalie too: "First of all, old child, you must finally become independent,

---

70 Letter from Cosima Wagner to Mathilde Wesendonck (January 14, 1878) in the M. Wesendonck archives in Stadtarchiv Zürich (shelfmark 84 VII). Translator's note: I have here eschewed any attempt to couch the meaning of this paragraph in simpler language, and have endeavored instead to be as faithful as possible to the tortuousness of the original.

71 SB XIII, 337–40, here 340 (December 21, 1861).

72 SB II, 236–41, here 237 (April 8, 1843).

73 Minna to Natalie Planer, May 7, 1860 (RWA).

or do you want to stay in this childishness forever and continue your lessons for years to come?"

Minna remained unable to admit to being Natalie's mother, not least because it would have meant admitting her own youthful transgressions. Bourgeois women of her time were only granted limited freedoms when it came to expressing imagination, creativity, or sensuality, nor were they allowed any freedom in their relationship with their own bodies. So it should not surprise us that Minna's letters to Natalie include criticism of the young women of Zwickau who supposedly dressed in a manner beyond the bounds of decency—she called them "Plumpsäcke"[74] ("ungraceful sacks"). On another occasion, she told Natalie that "I wouldn't dance with such embarrassing creatures even if I were a man, much less [take] one of them as my wife."[75] Minna suspected that Richard's money situation meant that he would be unable to support Natalie properly in future, and she wanted to ensure that her daughter was financially secure. There was no social welfare at the time, and even working as a governess could be a risky undertaking, given that such jobs offered no retirement plan. But at least a post as a governess would have enabled Natalie to keep herself for a few years. When Minna suggested that Natalie take on a two-year apprenticeship in Bern, Richard objected because he judged her character to be "lackadaisical and devoid of energy." He thought it would be better if she were given an opportunity to train closer to Minna in Dresden. It remains unknown whether or not Natalie accepted the position with an English family that Minna found for her through a friend. When Natalie wrote to her about a man who was keen to court her, Minna began to grow impatient. With a sense of pragmatism that bordered on the mean, her only concern was to provide for her daughter, and she was far from sensitive about Natalie's self-esteem: "If your Turk [*sic*] has not declared himself by autumn, he will never do it. Then you shall come to me and it will be all right [...] You are a bit too old for T., nor is it a great stroke of luck to get a man who earns 320 thalers. Don't be fussy, my good Natalie, and don't make such ugly faces, otherwise you won't even get this poor devil. I would fit you out as well as I can and see to things to the best of my ability."[76]

---

74   Ibid.
75   Minna to Natalie Planer, October 2, 1859 (RWA).
76   Minna to Natalie Planer, March 6, 1862 (RWA).

Chapter Twelve

"That weak, blind man ..."

The End of a Marriage, 1863–66

After his separation from Minna, Richard felt terribly lonely:

> I am always alone, with—servants. Me! No woman at my side! No educated person with whom I might converse at home! [...] Neither king nor emperor can offer me anything if things aren't right at home! I cannot find any rest. Now I am again looking for a woman who might keep my things in order: it comes and goes, I cannot decide. Am I cursed that I can't get any help in this?[1]

In the spring of 1862, Richard made the acquaintance of the 29-year-old Mathilde Maier at a soirée held by his publisher Schott in Mainz. They were apparently introduced by Wendelin Weissheimer, a friend of her family who also knew Wagner well. He told Wagner in advance about her, and later described their meeting in boorish terms: "When she came, he was sitting in one of the side alcoves of the salon that were cordoned off by heavy curtains. I led her there, pulled back the curtain a little and said: 'Herr Wagner— Fräulein Maier,' then I pushed pretty Mathilde inside and closed the curtain behind her again."[2] Mathilde, however, recalled their encounter rather differently, and in a way that sounds more credible. She wrote that Wagner had been depressed and so did not want to be introduced to anyone. He had actually already left the gathering, but had returned because of a storm raging outside. He went to a room adjoining the party, where Weissheimer and a neighbor from Mathilde's table took turns to keep him company. Mathilde

---

1 SB XVI, 242 (to M. Maier, June 22, 1864).
2 Weissheimer 1898, 92.

claimed that she had passed a message to Wagner in jest that she was expecting him to join her. He agreed, and indeed went to sit at her table.[3]

Richard enjoyed the admiration Mathilde bestowed on him, and he saw in her a possible future life partner—one who could manage his household, of course, but who could also help to fulfill his emotional needs and share in his intellectual life. His letters to her do not exude the ecstatic rapture that we find in his correspondence with her namesake Wesendonck, but Wagner would have dearly liked to have this other Mathilde as a lover and even as a wife—if only Minna were no longer on the scene. To be sure, he had meanwhile acquired a woman to act as his domestic help, cook, parlor maid, and servant all in one, and whose husband also worked for him in a multiple capacity as servant, gardener, and janitor (Anna and Franz Mrazék). But in early 1863, he nevertheless asked Mathilde Maier to abandon all her bourgeois prejudices and move in with him—though he did admit to his "sweetheart from Mainz" that there was no hope of marriage as long as Minna was alive.

Mathilde Maier came from a middle-class family. Her father had been a notary, and she lived with her mother, a sister and two aunts in Mainz. A letter she later wrote to Nietzsche has survived in which she discusses his book *Human, All Too Human,* and which leaves no doubt as to her intellectual capacity.[4] However, it was impossible for her to accept Richard's entreaties because she could not risk the scandal that would have ensued in the bourgeois circles in which she moved. He was unable to comprehend her reticence, and tried to cajole her and her mother into acquiescence. To no avail. All the same, his infatuation repeatedly got the better of him— "I love you so deeply!"—but again his "dearest, most blissful sweetheart" turned him down.[5] He felt wounded. If she were to get married, she would have to leave her mother; so why not do it anyway for him, without marriage? He offered her the option of living on the upper floor of his Vienna apartment.

Oh God, God, always making these considerations for miserable, petty bourgeois concerns—despite being loved so much! How could anyone love even more? You can see how things are! I've been struggling for so long about how to write to you calmly about all this, but now my patience is at an end—it's so disgraceful that I should always have to cope with everything alone! I just can't,

---

3   See Scholz 1930, V.

4   Published in ibid., 273ff.

5   SB XVI, 156 (May 10, 1863).

Figure 12.1. Mathilde Maier, photograph by Wilhelm Rudolph. Nationalarchiv der Richard-Wagner-Stiftung, Bayreuth.

can't anymore: a decision has to be made now, and I fear that you will lose me if you can't help me in everything. Talking and letters won't work.[6]

It was she who was responsible for his distress, he told her. "My need cannot be dismissed: it has to be stilled!"[7]

Mathilde's independent spirit irritated Richard, and it prompted him to assign her ironic, masculine nicknames such as "the little duke" or "dear nephew." He endeavored to assert his own higher, masculine authority by referring to himself as "the good uncle" or "Uncle Richard," and calling her his "dear child" or "my dear little girl." "I want a dear woman at my side, even if it's a child!" he wrote, and the ambivalence in his language clearly annoyed Mathilde. A manuscript copy has survived of a reply she sent him, in which she takes Richard to task over the linguistic distance that he maintained between them:

> In your last letter, you intimated that the tone of my own letter did not agree with you, and yet it is the same tone that you adopted at the start and have consistently upheld. Please try and recall whether there was not some paternal tenderness in all the friendliness that you have shown me; a certain something that came very much from on high and could well have wounded my vanity, had I not felt too sincere a pleasure in seeing you a little more cheerful. Because you know that when I saw you for the very first time, a deep sense of pain in your being made an indelible impression on me. I would have dearly liked to gather together all the pleasures of the world if only they could have helped me excise that pain for just a moment. When we met again, I suddenly found that I possess in myself (i.e., as you perceived me) the means to please you a little. I should gladly give up your knowing me if I was not sure that what I am is as dear to you as that which you assumed me to be (for I am not that cheerful, carefree child). As a result, I forgot that it was all based on a lie—and if not a deliberate one, then at least one that was tolerated.[8]

Mathilde consciously assumed the childlike role that Richard had originally assigned her, but at the same time she required him to see through this role-play, and thus refrain from regarding her as a child in real life as well. The second half of her letter is just as illuminating, if in a different way:

> God knows why you now, all of a sudden, declare me to be "of age". Now I can no longer continue with the deception; for now I am responsible for myself.

---

6   SB XVI, 177 (May 26, 1863).
7   SB XVI, 242f. (June 22, 1864).
8   Scholz 1930, 271f. (undated, presumably May 1862).

Even at the risk of becoming nothing at all to you, I must now destroy the image you have made of me and to which I have lent little more than my face [...] It weighs me down, I cannot bear it that you should think me more than I am. I shall only say it straight out: as far as narrow-mindedness is concerned, I am as cowardly as most women. Not up to a point where I would lie for it, but up to the point of hiding. I was not like this when I was younger, but life has ruined me. Two reasons might perhaps serve as my excuse: first, I have a mother to whom nothing in the world is as dear as I am, and who suffers terrible grief if I do something that can be misinterpreted. I love my mother unspeakably and cannot bear it when she suffers, especially if I am the cause of it. My second reason is that I do not have enough contempt for people; some of the narrow-minded are in fact people of whom I am very fond.[9]

Richard was demanding more from her than she could offer in return. A life as a common-law wife would have alienated her from society for ever, to be regarded by one and all as an "easy woman." When she refused to comply, he blamed it on her overly rational arguments—for although he was friends with women intellectuals, he ultimately required them all to submit to his wishes. He grumbled: "Ah yes! I always say: just look at everything she knows, how she's always right! And how she's also managed to discern that she would become indifferent to me if she were always with me! No, she is too clever! There is nothing that can be said against it, for she is the judge in this."[10] But Richard nevertheless maintained his respect for her, and even years later he still took the trouble to keep her informed about his concerts and opera performances—and she for her part often traveled to attend them.

Richard made other attempts to find a partner at this time, but they also failed. He developed an interest in the actress Friederike Meyer, the sister of the singer Luise Dustmann-Meyer, though she proved unable to extricate herself from her previous lover. She had "become completely devoted and trusting," Richard wrote to Hans von Bülow:

and I gladly tried to show myself worthy of this spirited, highly talented girl. But now she seems to be mired in the most repulsive relations with Guaita. Her character, her utterly shattered state of health, and the theatrical career that has thereby been interrupted, mean she is in the sad position of being unable to break completely with her admirer.[11]

---

9   Ibid., 271f. (undated, presumably May 1862).
10   Ibid., 17 (June 1862).
11   SB XV, 84 (February 16, 1863).

Carl von Guaita was the artistic director of the Municipal Theater in Frankfurt am Main and a professional pillar of support for Friederike Meyer. As a result, she rebuffed Wagner just as Mathilde Maier had done.

In late 1862 and early 1863, Wagner conducted several concerts with excerpts from his works in Vienna. He was suffering from a painful catarrhal illness at the time, and so abandoned his plan of inviting Minna at short notice. Money worries forced him to undertake a concert tour to St. Petersburg and Moscow in the spring of 1863. This finally brought him a profit: 6,000 roubles and 4,000 thalers respectively. He immediately took on expensive lodgings in Penzing (today part of the 14th borough of Vienna). He had the dining room, work room, study, tea room, bedroom, and dressing room lavishly wallpapered and decorated with fabrics, as was his want. The tea room, for example, was decorated in smooth green with stripes of purple velvet and gold trim in the corners, and the armchairs and divans were reupholstered. But things were not good: without a wife by his side he found it difficult to work, and the months passed without him being able to devote himself to composition—the field in which he knew full well that he was extraordinary.

More and more, Minna began to misunderstand individual sentences in his letters, which meant he had to embark on protracted explanations about what he had originally intended to say. Her distrust disturbed him and hurt him, and he admonished her to hold back. He told her that being near to Vienna was essential to him, and that this was why he had taken a summer apartment in Penzing. He wanted to work there in complete seclusion. He told Minna that his peace and quiet now took precedence over everything, and for this reason, too, he did not want Minna with him. Her state of health was becoming ever worse. She often became extremely agitated and suffered from insomnia, and then took digitalis, quinine, or morphine to cope better.[12] She later also suffered from coughing fits with violent chest pains and coughed up blood.[13]

Good friends advised Richard to marry a wealthy woman so that he might put his financial worries behind him, once and for all. But it was clear to him that Minna would never agree to a divorce. To Editha von Rhaden, a lady of the Russian Court in St. Petersburg, he wrote that no advantage in the world could induce him "to inflict the ignominy of a divorce—with all the

---

12   Letter to Cäcilie Avenarius (February 16, 1864) in Geck 2021, 152–56, here 154.

13   Letter to Cäcilie Avenarius (March 17, 1865) in ibid., 193–94, here 194.

appalling, necessary negotiations required for it—on that poor woman; the only injustice she ever committed was to allow herself to be married to me."[14] Such statements on his part reveal a softer, empathetic side to his personality, and also reveal why he avoided trying to effect a complete separation from Minna.

As always when he had a lot of money in his pockets, Wagner did not look too closely at how he spent it. At Christmas 1863, the gifts he gave his friends were so excessive that even they were embarrassed. The composer Peter Cornelius reported to his sister Susanne that Wagner had given him a heavy overcoat, an elegant gray dressing gown, a red scarf, a blue cigar bag (with lighter), beautiful silk scarves, splendid gold shirt buttons, a copy of the book *Struwwelpeter*, an elegant ink wiper with a gold motto on it, fine bow ties, and a meerschaum cigar holder with his initials on it.[15] Although Richard was perfectly able to do his sums—just a few years earlier, he had drawn up a list for Sulzer of all the income to be expected from performances of his works at different theaters—his money just melted away. Was it the pleasure of handling beautiful things while he was shopping, or did he feel a need to maintain his friendships by giving material gifts? Why did the fear of bankruptcy not compel him to budget better? The strife he had endured with Minna had so often resulted from his inability to plan ahead and to make provision for the future—all of which were fundamental maxims of the Protestant system of ethics. But in any case, he derived more pleasure from buying nice things and giving them to others than he did from transferring money to his wife.

In early 1864, the noose tightened. He took up new debts in order to cover older ones, landed with loan sharks, and was being increasingly harassed by his creditors. When he learned from his brother-in-law Heinrich Wolfram that Minna was in bad health, he burst into tears: "All I wanted to achieve by living apart was to avoid us rubbing each other up the wrong way [...] I can't get my head around it and am constantly crying! I cannot say how that unhappy woman makes me lament! [...] A catastrophe with Minna would ruin me now forever. Oh, may she prosper and calmly leave all other adversities to me!"[16] This was another example of his capacity for compassion, born of his heightened sensibilities—though we cannot know whether the emotion he displays here was merely born of the moment, or

---

14   SB XVI, 58 (March 14, 1864).
15   Scholz 1930, 138 (January 11, 1864).
16   SB XVI, 45f. (February 16, 1864).

Figure 12.2. Anton Pusinelli and his wife, photograph by Ch. Hahn, Dresden 1871. Nationalarchiv der Richard-Wagner-Stiftung, Bayreuth.

more deeply felt. Minna's presence now would have been unbearable to him, but he still felt inwardly bound to her on account of the decades they had spent together.

A prison sentence now beckoned because of his debts, so his friends advised him to flee Vienna before his creditors could get their hands on him. He tried to raise money, but without much success (depending on how one calculates his debts, they would today be the equivalent of some 60,000 US dollars). Wagner's reputation was seriously damaged by his flight. His critics gloated over his disgrace, his assorted love affairs prompted further ridicule in the city, and even Eduard Hanslick wrote with apparent relish about what had happened: "He rented a pretty villa in Penzing, had it furnished and decorated to his taste, took a delightful ballet dancer there with him whose task was to welcome his guests, and then, one day—he was gone."[17] Heinrich Esser reported back to Wagner's publisher, Schott: "If he begins a love affair in every city where he happens to be staying, this is a private matter and none of my business,"[18] though this was not a little malicious, and unfair to boot. Wagner had no idea how to raise the money he needed to send to Minna, so he once again wrote to the influential Russian lady in waiting, Editha von Rhaden in St. Petersburg, asking her to persuade the Grand Duchess Elena Pavlovna to transfer 1,000 thalers to Minna at Walpurgisstrasse 16 in Dresden. His letter amply demonstrates his intense sympathy for Minna's fate—though he also adds a tactless remark to the effect that the princess would not have to keep up her payments for very long, given the seriousness of Minna's illness.[19] When he received no answer, Wagner wrote again three weeks later to repeat his request: "[I] lack any assurance that my wife will be provided for; oh, if only you could console me about this!"[20] Everything seemed to be going downhill, and he even began to entertain thoughts of suicide.

Wagner was now without any permanent residence. He turned to his old patron Otto Wesendonck, asking if he might take him in. Otto refused point blank. Wagner now traveled via Lake Constance to Switzerland anyway, stopping off in Zurich before making his way to Mariafeld, the villa of François and Eliza Wille situated high up among the vineyards on the eastern banks of Lake Zurich—the same house that held so many happy memories of the

17 Hanslick 1894, II, 9.
18 Quoted in Gregor-Dellin 1980, 510.
19 SB XVI, 57ff. (March 14, 1864).
20 SB XVI, 95 (April 3, 1864).

times when he and Minna had both been guests there back in the 1850s. The master of the house was not at home, so Eliza received Richard alone. She was a gracious hostess, ensured that he was able to rest, and even assigned him a servant to see to his needs. After working, he would sit with her and brood over the past. He complained bitterly about his wife, who had never understood that he could not live "with his wings bound,"[21] as Eliza later recalled. Wagner continued this train of thought in the letters that he wrote to Eliza shortly afterwards: "It has become my punishment and my fate to have spoiled my own wife by overindulging her to such an extent that she ultimately lost her ability to behave fairly towards me. And we've seen the consequences of this."[22]

This view of Minna as little more than a child was one that Richard repeatedly expressed at this time. In her own letters, Minna in turn complained about his rudeness and his fits of rage. Since she consistently came up against a wall of incomprehension on his part, she too kept repeating the same accusations. She never managed to shake off the impact of the Wesendonck business, carrying the scars of it to her deathbed. To Minna, Mathilde alone bore the blame for everything, as she again confirmed in a letter to Cäcilie Avenarius:

> But what could I do about the fact that the woman found my husband so handsome and so interesting that she prized apart our longstanding, happy marriage of almost 22 years, so that he hated me as the one who hindered his happiness and still hates me? I told both him and her that I did not want to be an obstacle to them, so that they could belong to each other. But she preferred to remain the rich merchant's wife and did not want to become the wife of a poor artist. Why didn't these two people accept my offer at the time?[23]

This twist on what had happened was unfair to Mathilde Wesendonck, but it made things a little more bearable for Minna in retrospect.

While Minna stuck to her opinion that Richard had acted out of vanity and weakness, he by contrast continued telling everyone that his wife had been incompatible with him, and their marriage excruciating. This too was a distortion, but it helped Richard to justify their separation. All the same, when his mood was mellower, his mind kept straying back to the injustices that Minna had endured in their marriage, and he admitted the wrongs on

---

21 Wille 1982, 63.
22 Ibid., 81.
23 Geck 2021, 91 (January 25, 1864).

his part. When Minna's sister Charlotte died, he sent a note of sympathy and added: "Poor Minna! Fate brought you to one of the strangest of men. Every day I experience more and more just how little I am actually understood and how alone and abandoned I stand! What a wonder that you too should have to suffer so much because of it."[24]

Richard's money worries were now so urgent that he had to ask Minna's doctor Pusinelli to give her an advance, which he did. Richard also told him that his debts meant he would have to marry a rich woman, though he would need Minna to agree to a divorce first. Pusinelli knew from experience that broaching this topic with Minna would upset her unduly. Minna found it degrading to have to accept money via Pusinelli, especially since he had eight children of his own to support. She was also hurt that Wagner had written an almost brazen letter to Pauline Tichatschek in late April, urging her to help him with money for Minna. He claimed that he would be able to repay her for everything later. Minna had only heard in a roundabout fashion about Richard's desperate need for money, but she had her verdict ready: "Richard is pushing me onto my doctor and women friends such as [Pauline] Tichatschek, who he thinks should keep me until next winter. That's why he wrote only to them and sent his regards through them too. He thinks that this means he's seen to my needs regarding the rent, servant, and income."[25] She had meanwhile heard that he had employed a cook and a servant in Vienna—the latter supposedly dressed in splendid livery with silver shoulder tassels.

Just when he was utterly exhausted, his nerves at an end, and with no prospect of being able to pay off his debts, Wagner learned out of the blue that the young King Ludwig II of Bavaria had been searching for him for two weeks. On May 3, 1864, Wagner happened to be in Stuttgart when the Bavarian Court Counsellor Franz Seraph, Baron von Pfistermeister, arrived and asked to speak to him. The newly crowned king was an enthusiastic adherent of Wagner's music and wanted to do everything he could to support him. Wendelin Weissheimer later described how tears ran down Wagner's cheeks as he packed his suitcase, trying as best he could to squeeze in his green silk dressing gown robe that kept spilling out—a sight that his friend never forgot.[26] Before this complete reversal, Richard had really begun to believe that everything was coming to an end. But just one day later, he was already meeting his young patron at his city palace, the Residenz in Munich.

---

24   SB XVI, 44 (February 15, 1864).

25   Letter to Cäcilie Avenarius (May 6, 1864) in Geck 2021, 163–66, here 165.

26   Weissheimer 1898, 268.

He responded to Ludwig's rapturous admiration in high spirits, though there is admittedly something artificial about the description of his current state that he penned to Eliza Wille: "Oh, at last a love affair that does not bring suffering and torment with it! But will I be able to renounce the 'feminine' completely? I tell myself with a sigh that I almost wish it! One glance at his dear picture helps me again! Oh, this sweet boy! Now he is surely everything to me—world, wife, and child."[27]

At one stroke, everything looked different. After Richard's conversation with the king he was able to pay off his debts in Vienna, and he wrote to Pusinelli to say that he could now pay off his debts to him too, and also resume regular maintenance payments to Minna. The king provided him with the salary of a high-ranking court official (a "Ministerialrat," a ministerial counsellor, at 4,000 florins per annum), and over the course of the next few weeks Wagner received six times this amount again, simply as a gift. And things continued thus. In today's terms, the sum he received would amount to over half a million US dollars, and it constituted roughly a tenth of the royal budget.[28] Richard was careful not to mention any of this to Minna for several weeks, however. Shortly after his first meeting with Ludwig II, she had written in despair to Cäcilie about how she hoped she might win the lottery: "The last time the lottery was drawn I asked God on my knees to let me win something decent—then I would know what I had done—but again, sadly, nothing came!"[29]

Soon, however, Richard realized that the adoration of his young, enthusiastic but melancholy king was not enough. Together with his servants, Anna and Franz Mrazék, he moved into a villa just outside Starnberg, the lakeside town some 15 miles south of Munich. He missed Minna and the logistical expertise that she had acquired when moving apartments, and he finally realized what a burden it was to move:

> My loneliness is terrible […] the desolation of my household, the necessity of dealing with things for which I am really not made, and doing so only by myself: this paralyzes my spirit. I have now had to move again, to set up a household, worry myself with knives, forks, bowls, pots, bed linen, etc. Me, a glorifier of women! How they are so kindly leaving their errands to me.[30]

---

27 SB XVI, 201 (May 26, 1864).
28 Gregor-Dellin 1980, 527f.
29 May 6, 1864 (Staatsbibliothek Berlin).
30 SB XVI, 255 (June 30, 1864).

Richard now tried once again to win over Mathilde Maier. He had the seemingly bright idea of writing to her mother to propose adopting Mathilde as his daughter, and then marrying her once Minna had died. "Do I have to assure you that Mathilde would be in good and noble hands with me, protected against any suspicion, any taint, and in fact in the most emphatic, vigorous manner? Or perhaps it would be possible, without wishing to nourish any sacrilegious desires, to await the death of my wife and in such a case to ask for the hand of your daughter?"[31] Apart from the sheer tactlessness of his suggestion, he had clearly been quite unable to imagine himself in Mathilde's shoes. As she had already tried to explain to him before, her reputation would have been ruined for good, had she acquiesced in any of this. It did occur to him, however, that the consequences for Minna would have been catastrophic, had Mathilde's mother taken the trouble to write to her for further information. He probably recalled what had happened many years earlier when Jessie Laussot's mother had contacted Minna and thereby thwarted his plans to elope with Jessie. So he admonished Mathilde to ensure that her mother must not contact Minna under any circumstances. Fortunately, she was a level-headed young woman who suspected that everything could only end in disaster, so she simply did not let the letter reach her mother at all.

One week afterwards, in late June 1864, there was yet another dramatic turn in Richard's life. Cosima von Bülow came to visit him at his villa above the Starnberg Lake, accompanied only by her two daughters. Hans had sent them on ahead, and did not arrive for another week. Cosima and Richard now began a sexual relationship that resulted in their daughter Isolde. Richard had supposedly "sealed a vow" in Berlin with Cosima a few months earlier, on November 28, 1863, "to belong to each other alone."[32] However, he could not count on Cosima leaving Hans for him—after all, she was the mother of his two small children. So he had hedged his bets by continuing to court Mathilde Maier. But after his Starnberg encounter with Cosima, he informed Mathilde that it would have greatly embarrassed him, had she nevertheless agreed to move in with him. Her arrival would have been "a source

---

31　SB XVI, 247 (June 25, 1864).

32　ML, 729. Was perhaps this supposed event of November 1863 an intentional act on Wagner's part to shift the date of their relationship forward by several months, in order to mention Cosima in his autobiography as his new partner? His autobiography otherwise closes with his call to Munich by Ludwig II. See also BB, 27, 39 and 139.

Figure 12.3 Cosima and Richard Wagner, photograph by Fritz Luckhardt, 1872. Wikimedia Commons.

of nameless, quite unbearable torment to my heart."[33] Mathilde Maier will have been puzzled by what this sentence meant, and could only later have understood that Cosima had in fact decided in favor of Richard. After that, Wagner's letters to Mathilde became less frequent, though they remained in contact, and she later belonged to the small circle of friends who were allowed to borrow one of the few privately printed copies of his autobiography *Mein Leben*, which in itself was a sign of his trust.

On Richard's advice, King Ludwig had offered Bülow the post of pianist to the king, and he began work later this summer. Hans probably suspected that Richard was the real father of Cosima's daughter Isolde, but he played along with their charade. In the years hereafter, his behavior became a mixture of attempted chivalry and depression with aggressive episodes. These months were emotionally stressful for all those involved. Liszt joined them too in August 1864. He had reproached his daughter in Karlsruhe about her affair with Richard and hoped to be able to save her marriage to Hans. Liszt left at the end of August, and Hans and Cosima left shortly afterwards. Richard was now separated from Cosima for seven weeks, which tormented him.

Peter Cornelius arrived at the end of 1864; the king had appointed him, too, at Richard's insistence, for he wanted an assistant. Cornelius had resisted for a long time because he feared for his independence, but then acquiesced. He began visiting Wagner at noon for work, and would not get home again until the evening. In a letter to their mutual friend Josef Standhartner, Cornelius described a day he spent with Wagner chez Cosima. First, Wagner read aloud from texts that fascinated him at the moment, then the whole first act of *Tristan und Isolde* was sung. After barely half a cup of tea for refreshment, Richard moved on to *Parsifal* and recounted the entire plot. Wagner constantly talked about himself, read from his works or sang them, wrote Cornelius.[34] This gives us a good idea of Wagner's hypnotic yet enervating abilities and his inexhaustible urge to self-presentation that compelled all others to submit to his will. Cornelius was unable to recognize that Wagner actually needed to perform for an audience in order to attain an inner balance after the hard work of composing. But his account also gives us a clear insight into what Minna must have experienced during their marriage.

In August 1865, Hans and Cosima traveled to Budapest to hear the world première of Franz Liszt's oratorio *Saint Elisabeth*. It was also an attempt to

---

33   SB XVI, 262f. (July 19, 1864).
34   Quoted in Gregor-Dellin 1980, 539.

distract Cosima from Richard, who felt her absence keenly, and suffered dreadfully from this second, long, enforced break. It tormented him that this intellectually challenging, highly musical woman was ready to belong to him, but was now taken away. He was no longer willing to engage in resignation or renunciation such as had helped him cope in the case of Mathilde Wesendonck. And when Cosima did not hesitate to express to Richard her jealousy of Mathilde Maier while she was herself away with Hans, Richard became aggressive: "And all this, while you are swimming in joy and delight over there, but I am languishing here in clouds of fog; sick, gloomy, and wasting away!—Very nice!—I'll remember this—and 'You'll be surprised'!—I hope a sensible letter will come very soon, otherwise it's over!" But then his longing for her burst out, as if he were a desperate child: "Cosima must always be with me—always with me: there is no other way." Or: "Stay with me, don't go again. Tell poor Hans openly that I can no longer cope without you. Oh heaven, if only you could quite calmly be my wife before the world!"[35]

Richard now moved into a house on the Brienner Strasse in central Munich and furnished it with every conceivable luxury. This merely provided further fodder for the city gossips. Minna would hardly have been able to come to terms with his new life; he had plunged into a very different world indeed. His sensibilities had been further refined, and his aesthetic and sensual needs could now be satisfied in many different ways. He could afford anything he wanted, and so began business dealings with a dressmaker whose task it was to fulfill his desires for beautiful fabrics. On one occasion he ordered satin samples in numerous colors, then decided on dark pink with ribbons in pale yellow and orange. He wanted a lightly quilted, flowered duvet, richly ornamented with bows, and he also ordered shoes, "with beautiful rose bouquets embroidered on white, light gray and yellow satin. The shoes must be padded and beautifully fashioned."[36] Although Richard had to wear silk because of an allergy to cotton,[37] such excess would have alienated Minna as it went far beyond the extravagances on his part that she had endured herself.

---

35 Letters of August 18 and 20, 1865, in BB, 41–42 and 46–47.

36 SB XVI, 381 (1864, no date), 334 (October 10, 1864) to Bertha Goldwag.

37 "he suffered [...] from occasional attacks of erysipelas. [...] His skin was so sensitive that he wore silk next to the body [...]. Wagner could not endure the touch of cotton, as it produced a shuddering sensation throughout the body that distressed him." Praeger 1892, 251–52.

In May 1865, Richard invited Anton Pusinelli to the premiere of *Tristan und Isolde* in Munich—but asked him to keep quiet to Minna about it.[38] That was a wise step, because this work remained suspect to Minna until the day she died—this "union of grandeur and refinement, sensuality and sublime depravity," as Thomas Mann described *Tristan* in 1931, the "most supreme and most dangerous of Wagner's works."[39] Richard also invited his sister Clara, though "with just one condition! Not a word about it to Minna!"[40] The first performance—which was preceded by over twenty rehearsals—took place on June 10, 1865. The majority of the reviews were negative, though they admitted that Wagner was pursuing his musical goals with great perseverance and seriousness.

It was perhaps inevitable that Richard should become involved in political intrigue in Munich. It was just too tempting to exert his influence on his sensitive young king. Ironically, his biggest work, *Der Ring des Nibelungen*, deals with the dangers of power and what happens when one tries to prolong it; but Richard could not help misusing the trust he enjoyed with the king in an effort to use royal authority to improve the world after his own fashion. There is also a correlation here to the way in which he propagated Schopenhauerian redemption through renunciation in his work and had exhorted its virtues in his relationship with Mathilde Wesendonck. But all notion of renunciation was promptly cast aside when it came to his physical relationship with Cosima. "This supposedly brilliant, triumphal fairy-tale episode, the friendship with the king [...] proves in retrospect to have been the most sordid, shameful, scheming intermezzo, regardless of whatever view of it one takes," wrote Martin Gregor-Dellin.[41] Just as in Dresden, Richard once more acted impulsively and unwisely. Unjust attacks on him in the press led him to launch a counterattack against men in the king's cabinet and the Crown Office. This could not be tolerated. Members of the nobility, the cabinet and the Crown Office had already fought against his appointment in the first place, and now they saw their chance to remove him altogether. Public disputes arose on account of his luxurious lifestyle, his influence on the young monarch, and rumors of his relationship with Cosima. The king had no choice but to order him to leave the Bavarian capital. Although his

---

38   SB, XVII, 143 (May 6, 1865).
39   Thomas Mann, "Wagner und unsere Zeit," quoted in Zelinsky 1976, 193.
40   SB XVII, 134 (April 26, 1865).
41   Gregor-Dellin 1980, 523.

banishment was cushioned by an annual salary of 8,000 florins, it neverthe-less made Wagner relive his old trauma of being cast out of his homeland.

Meanwhile, Minna was enjoying visits to the theater in Dresden thanks to getting free tickets, and her circle of friends continued to stand by her. The respect that she received there was balm to her soul. At Richard's insis-tence she had begun renting a larger apartment, and his letters continued to convey the impression that he would at some point, eventually, move back to the city. In order to save money, Minna furnished and sublet some of her rooms. She now sensed that Richard wanted to leave the past behind and was cultivating a new lifestyle that had nothing in common with her anymore. A letter she wrote at this time to Ernst Benedikt Kietz, her friend from the old days, conjures up a nostalgic picture of their Parisian past together and also shows her sense of humor:

> If you should already have counted me among the deceased, try in your heart to restore an old friend to life, for—despite everything—I still belong to this earth. [...] But since I have the sneaking suspicion that your coming may be delayed for a little while longer, I would in the meanwhile like to know how you are, whether you are married and the father of several dozen children, etc. I ask you to give me some news of yourself *soon*. May you gather from my request that I don't belong to that miserable race of people who trample down the past with their feet and that I always remember dear old friends with a grateful heart, not only those of the *good* old days, but also those of the earliest, really *bad* days. How terrible they were and still how happy compared to the present. How the world was open to us then—what yearnings, what hopes![42]

Minna learned about Richard's present life through the press—her acquaintances and friends probably showed her the latest articles and cari-catures. She knew the *Augsburger Allgemeine* and *Punsch*; the latter magazine had published a satire on "The Morning Life of a New German composer," and often published caricatures of Richard. He had become alien to her. Her letter to Kietz continues in a manner that shows both a certain pity for her husband, and also a slight trace of contempt:

> You probably read in the papers nearly a year ago about his enormous good fortune; namely, that the young King, who is very musical and at the same time enthusiastic about Wagnerian music, had him located in Zurich and sum-moned to the court, offered him a life free of worries so that he could work un-encumbered; which, however, has not yet materialized. Your fine, dear friend

---

42 Burrell, 415–17, here 415–16.

Pecht and some other eccentric, frivolous riffraff move around him and the papers are making fun of it, as, for example, in the *Augsburger Allgemeine* Nos. 50 and 55. Even *Punsch*, which appears in Munich, reports the funniest absurdities about Richard's life and luxury, which can have very bad consequences, considering German standards.[43]

Minna had naturally also learned about Richard's love affair with Cosima. The scandal—for that was how the press described it—will have troubled her, but she nevertheless remained silent about it. Her immediate circle of friends was now most important to her. She kept up many old ties, such as her friendship with the singer Jenny Bürde-Ney, whom she invited to visit her at home. She also invited Cäcilie Avenarius to Dresden—a visit that Cäcilie much enjoyed, as she confirmed afterwards in her letter of thanks. They reminisced about their experiences back in Paris, twenty-five years earlier, when Richard and Minna had suffered such deprivation. And shortly before she died, Minna wrote to Cäcilie as if she wanted to reassure herself of her love: "I don't think I could bear it if you were to withdraw only a small part of the love you have bestowed on me. Oh, never do it, but let me enjoy the warmth of your love for me, and be happy in it." When Cäcilie lamented that she missed having women friends around her, Minna wrote back in praise of female solidarity:

> I can understand that you lack a dear female companion, for what can one discuss with men? Either they are absent-minded or in a bad mood. I wish I could send you a few of my women friends. Since they know I am ill, they are exceedingly kind and good to me, never leaving me alone for an evening, and often 4 to 5 of them have been here [...] Men do not come into my realm at all, only the doctor and my tenant, who does not count, and whom I often do not see for three weeks at a time.[44]

After Minna's death, Cäcilie praised her hospitality to guests, her kindness and goodness of heart, and added that she had been a "major focal point" in her life. Perhaps Minna sometimes recalled Richard's mocking insistence that "what you women concoct among yourselves is not much use;" but none of this bothered her any longer. She was now busy creating an environment for herself that suited her. There were several women

---

43   Ibid., 416–17.

44   To Cäcilie Avenarius, December 17 and 25, 1865 (Staats- und Landesbibliothek Dresden).

friends who enjoyed her confidence, and with whom she could converse unselfconsciously, and they were a comfort to her in the last months of her life.

Minna's parents, her only brother, and two sisters all died before her. She had one sister left—Amalie von Meck, who lived in Russia—and Natalie, of course, who joined Minna in Dresden in early January 1865 to help her out around the house, and who also earned a little money from giving piano lessons on the side—though only for 5 pfennigs an hour, as she did not consider herself a trained teacher. Otherwise, life for Minna became increasingly lonely. She felt her physical decline ever more acutely, and asked Richard to issue her a power of attorney so that she might dispose of everything in her possession as she saw fit. He granted her this wish, and she bequeathed everything to Natalie. But her last will and testament maintained the fiction of Natalie being her sister, despite this meaning that the will could have been contested. Even when she was nearing her end, Minna still could not bring herself to tell Natalie the truth. But nor were relations easy at home. There was trouble again, just like back in Zurich, because Natalie became good friends with Minna's maid: "They ate, drank, and laughed together in the kitchen, but none of them came when I rang the bell, and I could have expired quite comfortably, unnoticed, in my little room."[45]

On May 15, 1865, Wagner received news that his wife was at death's door in Dresden. Subsequent dispatches brought news of a temporary improvement, and she would in fact live on for several months. In years gone by, bad news about Minna would have triggered health problems of his own, but now it barely touched him because he had long committed himself inwardly to Cosima. For her, he wrote ecstatic lines whose content (not to mention literary quality) Minna would have found laughable. She had never been party to such high-flown imaginings:

O my Cosima!
Today I'll come to you! I could not
be happy here, because I know my beautiful wonder woman[46] is there!
O Cosima! O Ludwig! You are beautiful!—United
with you,[47] how mighty, how beautiful I am!

---

45 To Cäcilie Avenarius, December 17 and 25, 1865, in Geck 2021, 216–21, here 219.

46 764 Wagner writes "schönes Wunderweib."

47 765 Wagner uses the plural form of you, "Euch."

Pray for poor Hans!
Greetings! Greetings! My woman!
I am redeemed—I am happy![48]

At last, Richard had reached his goal—this poetic euphoria was merely a reflection of his current blissful state of mind. He had succeeded once more in finding a musically educated woman of the upper classes who loved him—but unlike Mathilde Wesendonck, Cosima was actually prepared to leave her husband for Richard.

In late July 1865, Richard traveled to Dresden with Hans von Bülow in order to pay his last respects to the singer Ludwig Schnorr von Carolsfeld—his first Tristan—who had died at just 29, but he made no effort to meet Minna when he was there. She, however, remained unable to distance herself from him, despite all her criticism. Time and again she returned to him in her letters to Cäcilie Avenarius. When Cäcilie wrote to her that Richard must be unhappy, after being banished from Munich in the fall of 1865, Minna was indignant: "I cannot quite understand how being banished on a salary of 8,000 florins can make you unhappy. To be sure, this sum is admittedly mere pocket money to Richard. But I and many others would be delighted to be banished for ever to wonderful Switzerland with such a lovely amount of money." All the same, just what Richard still meant to her also shines through: "I have long since buried my husband, who was otherwise a good man. But my heart broke as I did so, and as long as I live, I shall mourn for him."[49]

Three weeks before Minna's death, an essay was published in the *Volksbote* newspaper in Munich, claiming that Wagner was living in luxury while his wife languished in poverty. Richard insisted that Minna write a corrective statement, which she did, and it was indeed published: "I hereby declare it to be true that I have up to now been sent maintenance payments by my absent husband, Richard Wagner, which have enabled me to live without cares. It gives me particular satisfaction to be able to use this present declaration to silence at least one of the many slanderous statements directed against my husband."[50]

---

48   BB, 99 (November 18, 1865).
49   To Cäcilie Avenarius, December 17 and 25, 1865, in Geck 2021, 216–21, here 220.
50   Quoted in Tappert (1901–02), 1409.

But Wagner's opponents would not stop. It was rumored that the letter had not been written by Minna, but merely signed by her. In order to find out the truth, the editor of the newspaper made contact with a "high-ranking person" in Dresden after Minna's death. The answer they got was this:

> Richard Wagner's wife died a few days ago. She had been living here for a considerable length of time, separated from her husband, but in bitter poverty, and I also heard at the time that she had received support from city funds. It thus seems reasonable to suppose that the declaration published in the newspapers was a result of blackmail, or the result of a brief instance of maintenance received from her husband. As I have said, the grave has been closed over this poor woman, and further discussion cannot lead to anything. The above, however, may be stated as fact today.[51]

Wagner's supporters—presumably Pusinelli—then got the city's poor-relief authorities to certify that Minna had never claimed help from them. The truth lies somewhere between these two extremes. Minna had often enough feared losing her maintenance and had been compelled to take out loans on occasion. But it was equally true that Richard had never severed the connections between them, neither financial nor otherwise.

Just a few days before Minna's death, Richard had been dictating his memoirs to Cosima and had reached as far as his marriage to Minna. As he wrote to his sister Luise Brockhaus, he was able to recount his younger years in a cheerful tone, and even unabashedly recalled his youthful indiscretions. "From then on [...] my life became serious and bitter, and I fear that this cheerful tone will now leave me—my marriage is coming! No one knows what I suffered because of it!"[52] Richard thereby played his part in encouraging a pejorative assessment of his first marriage—one that can be traced through biographical writing on Wagner down to the present day. It was all forgotten how, back in 1849, he had for months on end harried and begged Minna to follow him into exile in Switzerland; forgotten, too, were the decades of intimate, familiar correspondence between them. And the fact that Minna had created the domestic circumstances under which he was able to compose his early operas and plan the later ones was now actively suppressed.

In December 1865, Minna took ill with a catarrhal throat infection. An old kidney complaint also returned. She was leaving her house on the arm

---

51   Staats- und Landesbibliothek Dresden, Ms. Dresd. App 2725, 14.

52   SB XVIII, 30 (January 1, 1866).

of Mathilde Schiffner one day when she almost fell at the first step and was suddenly so weak that she could barely walk at all. She initially seemed to recover, but remained frail. One day before her death, she began another letter to her beloved Cäcilie. She had been to the opera house for the first time in months and had seen *Fernand Cortez* by Spontini. She had fond memories of the work, for Richard had seen a performance of it in Berlin back in 1836, and it was this experience that had led him to compose his own first successful opera, *Rienzi*, which she loved so much. But her letter remained unfinished; Minna died on the night of January 25, 1866, at the age of 56. Her death certificate states that she had suffered from an acute pulmonary edema. A post-mortem examination of the body found an abnormally enlarged heart, just as the doctors had suspected.

Anton Pusinelli immediately sent Richard a telegram. He followed it up with a letter giving a detailed account of what had happened. The news of Minna's death reached Richard just as he was in the midst of a major crisis of his own. He had left Munich at the end of 1865, after having been hounded out of the city, and had withdrawn to the area around Geneva to spend Christmas there with his servants. His renewed homelessness and separation from Cosima were difficult for him to bear. In January, a fire broke out in the house in Geneva where he was lodging, though it did no serious damage. While repairs were being made, he went to the south of France to look for a suitable place for him and Cosima to live, and it was while he was in Marseille that Pusinelli's message reached him. Time was in any case too short for him to travel to Dresden for the funeral, and he wrote back: "I assume that your friendly concern will mean that the body of my poor, unhappy wife will receive the same honor in my name that I would have shown, had she had passed away happily at the side of the husband she had made happy. It is in this spirit that I ask you to organize her final resting place."[53] He thanked everyone who had shown Minna love and honor at the last. To Natalie he wrote to say how the sad news of Minna's death had reached him when he was far away, and that there was nothing he could say about it: "I myself am living only thanks to an awareness that I am still destined to create important works: this alone gives me the strength to bear the outrageous tribulations to which my life is constantly subjected, and from which in recent years I was keen to spare Minna. By sparing her thus, I felt reassured myself."[54] This comes across as thoroughly sincere.

---

53   SB XVIII, 57 (January 26, 1866). ·
54   SB XVIII, 104 (April 2, 1866).

Minna was buried in the Old Cemetery of St. Anne. Pusinelli ensured that she had a dignified burial. Her coffin was covered with opulent flowers and palms that had been given by well-wishers, and five carriages followed the coffin to the cemetery. The officiating priest sat in the first, along with Natalie, Luise Brockhaus, Pusinelli, and Pusinelli's son Karl, who was Minna's godchild. Her Dresden circle of acquaintances, friends, and family members paid their last respects. These included Joseph and Pauline Tichatschek—who had procured and furnished an apartment for her in Dresden upon her return—Ferdinand Heine, in whose garden the Wagners had so often relaxed, Gustav Kietz, who had been an eager lunch guest chez Wagner, Otto Kummer, the sculptor Ernst Hähnel, and the concertmaster Franz Schubert. Mathilde Schiffner was also there—Minna's most intimate, long-lasting friend who had been privy to all her joys and sorrows. The procession moved slowly through the cemetery. At the graveside, brass players from the royal orchestra played a lament, and a choir sang a chorale.

When Cosima Wagner learned in 1887 that the grave had been badly damaged by the weather, she arranged for it to be restored, which was surely a conciliatory gesture on her part.[55] When the grave was due to be leveled in 1920, Siegfried Wagner requested an extension for another forty years. The cross at the grave disappeared over time. In 1991, on the 125th anniversary of Minna's death, the Bayreuth Foundation covered the cost of a new marble cross. Today it bears the number 4 in row L 6.

One wonders what might have gone through the minds of the mourners at Minna's funeral. Did they perhaps remember her as a person in her own right, or did she enter the collective memory merely as the wife of the famous composer? Richard was still in Geneva, moping on account of his separation from Cosima. A few weeks after Minna's death, he noted the following:

Der Tag bricht an. –
Oder ist's die Nacht? –
Dort modert meine Frau –
dort siecht die Geliebte!—Und hier? –
Frühling!

[The day is dawning. – Or is it night? – There my wife rots away – There my beloved languishes! – And here? – Spring!]

---

55   See her letter to Natalie in Burrell, 444–45, here 444 (July 31, 1887).

Does he mention Minna's death here in order to heighten the sense of pain caused by his current separation from Cosima? Or is he instead placing Minna on the same level as Cosima, his "hohe Frau" (high lady)? These are questions that cannot be answered. By this time, he had long since united his life with that of his new partner and could bear anything except the thought of losing her. Life for Wagner could not exist without love. From *Die Feen* (1833) to *Parsifal* (1882), his stage works are permeated by this longing for love: by a yearning for a motherly, caring partner that sprang from a deeply rooted emotional need. It was of life-determining importance to him to show in his art how love is a natural commandment: one that determines every-thing. His own bonds to women demanded loyalty and devotion from them, even beyond death.[56] This rigid dependence, which at the same time bore within it feelings of aggression toward independent, self-willed women, had also shaped his relationship with Minna in the first years of their marriage. His early letters to her reveal a form of manic dependence, and this trait was later transferred onto other women. Richard's relationships with Mathilde Wesendonck and Cosima von Bülow were each idealized as sublime, excep-tional affairs that in the latter case culminated in a sense of blessed salvation: "O, my Cosima! We will be happier than mortals have ever been, for we Three [he here included King Ludwig] are immortal. Death cannot break our bonds [...] O Cosima! Now only the works remain to be created."[57] Now, finally, Richard felt that fate had rewarded him richly, and the years that followed Cosima's divorce from Hans were the happiest he ever knew.

Minna would have shaken her head at such elevated vocabulary. Nevertheless, there were moments now and again when Richard became aware of how his lifestyle had destroyed their marriage, and he acknowl-edged what he had inflicted upon her. When she once told him about a performance of *Lohengrin* that had deeply moved her, he wrote back: "Take these uplifting impressions of which you tell me, and ponder that whoever achieves what I do can reward others for their own sacrifices only through performances like this. So love my *Lohengrin*; it is one of the few things that I can offer you!"[58] That sounds honest; and indeed it was. He knew that he could not change if he wanted to continue producing his extraordinary works. But even when he placed his works at her feet, as it were, she was very aware of just how much she had contributed to them, at least until the

56   See Rieger 2011.

57   BB, 98 (November 13, 1865).

58   SB XI, 189 (August 16, 1859).

time of his flight from Dresden. As she had written to Mathilde Schiffner, a few months after joining Richard in his Swiss exile, she was delighted "that everything he created was achieved in my environment alone; and the fact that I understood him was proved to me when he used to read me all his libretti and play his compositions scene by scene to me—just me alone—and discussed them with me."[59]

Richard was aware of the potentially explosive nature of his letters to Minna, so he tried to get them back from Natalie. "If Minna should happen to have given away these letters, I shall deal with such an unlawful act by any legal means available, should this become necessary; I shall insist on these papers being handed over," he wrote to her.[60] Natalie sent him some, but had no intention of giving them all away, and later sold the rest to Mary Burrell. Shortly after Minna's death, Richard finished the score of the first act of *Die Meistersinger*. In the following April, he moved into Tribschen, a genteel, spacious house in an idyllic spot on the banks of Lake Lucerne that still stands today. It was here that he spent the next six years of his life, together with Cosima. After Cosima's divorce, she and Richard were married on August 25, 1870, in a Protestant church in Lucerne.

But at night, Minna lived on. Richard once dreamed that the staircase in his house had disappeared, and he had called Minna to come and help him. Another time she had run away from him, whereupon he ran after her. Cosima heard more than once how he would call out "Minna" in his sleep. Then he would dream that Minna had abandoned him in Dresden, even though it was he who had fled, not her. His subconscious was perhaps dealing here with their inner, emotional separation—the rift that had arisen because of his political activities. He also repeatedly dreamed that he could not send her money. And in yet another dream, he came home and told Minna that he had been to Tichatschek's, "whereupon she [was] furious, and I withdrew, saying to myself: I'm going to sleep in the hotel and tomorrow I'll go to the lawyer. Then I said to myself: This has to end, and she [threw] billiard balls at me."[61] There were also moments when Richard sensed that it was dishonest to blame Minna for all their shortcomings, and in 1859 he wrote to their Berlin friend Alwine Frommann with a sincerity that is truly

---

59   Minna to Mathilde Schiffner, mid-May, 1850 (RWA).

60   November 27 (presumably 1868), in Burrell, 576–77.

61   CT II, 457, 519, 803 and 898 (December 4, 1879; April 11, 1880; October 5, 1881; and February 26, 1882).

impressive: "I cannot overlook for a moment the fact that it was my nature and my life that ruined the woman."[62]

In his new life, Richard tended more and more towards a reactionary view of what he saw as German national superiority. But at the same time, he suffered from his dependence on King Ludwig. He wrote to Röckel in a moment of pride and self-awareness: "If there were a trace of German spirit in Germany, of respect for what is great and noble, then it would not require such artificial detours to place a man like me meaningfully between a prince and the people."[63] But while he failed in his political goal to mediate between the King and his subjects, Richard at least attained his own, personal goals by being able to quench his yearning for love. With Cosima's help—she kept uninvited guests away from him and provided for him in every way—he completed his *Ring des Nibelungen*, which consolidated his worldwide fame, and whose topicality has remained undimmed to this day.

For all his dependence on women, Richard nevertheless became increasingly convinced over the next few years that they were an inferior species, thus legitimizing male dominance as the natural way of things. In 1881, he wrote:

> When mixing the races, the blood of the nobler male is corrupted by the ignoble female. The masculine suffers, character perishes, and the females gain so much that they can take the place of the males. (Renaissance) The feminine thus remains mistress of redemption: here art reigns, there religion; the immaculate virgin gives birth to the Savior.[64]

If he had read this to Minna, she would surely have protested. Minna was never going to acquiesce in the complete subordination of the self as was preached by Cosima (though Cosima often used subterfuge to get her own way anyway). "I will gladly give up anything," Cosima confided downheartedly to her diary; "it seems to me that it is my natural destiny to leave everything behind, and to want nothing." Although she attained with Richard the happiness that she had desired, she was still unhappy in many ways, and at times she could not contain herself: "My birth. Oh, if only I could erase it and thus end all the suffering that it brought." And: "Deeply aware

---

62 SB X, 297 (February 8, 1859). Minna was still alive at this time; Richard presumably meant the ruin of their relationship.

63 SB XVIII, 242f. (November 2, 1866).

64 BB, 243 (October 23, 1881).

that I have only one task: to make life easier for him."[65] When Richard once lamented to Cosima that he had never acquired a lover "directly from nature, for myself, but always via another," referring specifically to Minna and Cosima herself (and implicitly, perhaps, to Mathilde Wesendonck too), this wounded Cosima terribly. "Oh how I wish with all my soul, all of it, that a spotless being might consecrate itself to him!—Even if such a remark pains me, my feelings of happiness can still predominate, because he says it on account of being so free and sure of me that he can pour out everything of himself, and everything from him is good!"[66] As a young kapellmeister, Richard had by no means thought of Minna's "spotlessness" when he courted her.

Cosima, however, was more suited to the role of "high lady," and she became involved in the history of Wagner's reception, helping him to assume cult status. Nor was she alone, for even Hans—who liked to think in hierarchical terms—had metaphorically laid himself reverently at Richard's feet in a letter he wrote back in 1859: "one looks friends in the eye, but with you, people look up [...] I would—in all seriousness—be inclined to become your boot cleaner and commission agent, but I am not brazen enough to claim to be called your friend."[67] Minna was a successful, independent actor, and would never have accepted this for herself. She was happy to take on tasks that made her husband's life easier. She also cleaned his boots when there was no money for a maid, but at the same time she confidently regarded herself as a co-creator of his early works. For this she gave her life. She wanted to be recognized, respected, and loved, but was not ready to let herself be absorbed in adoration of her partner. "The years with Minna encompass the entire becoming of the Master [...] Mathilde [Wesendonck] only triggered the creative urge once again. Cosima accompanied Wagner as he matured and harvested. The Wagner of the thirteen mighty music dramas grew at Minna's side."[68]

---

65   CWT I, 51, 616, 69 (February 7, 1869; December 24, 1872; March 10, 1869).
66   CWT II, 1041 (November 8, 1882).
67   Moulin Eckart 1927, 436 (August 24, 1859).
68   Herzfeld 1938, 246.

References

Primary literature

Bülow, Marie von, ed. (1909): *Hans von Bülow: Briefe und Schriften*, vols. III and IV. Leipzig: Breitkopf & Härtel.

Burk, John N., ed. (1950): *Richard Wagner Briefe. Die Sammlung Burrell.* Frankfurt am Main: S. Fischer Verlag.

Burk, John N., ed. (1951): *Letters of Richard Wagner. The Burrell Collection.* New York: The Macmillan Company.

Burrell *see* Burk

Devrient, Eduard (1909): *Briefwechsel zwischen Eduard und Therese Devrient.* 2 vols. Stuttgart: Carl Krabbe Verlag.

Ermatinger, Emil, ed. (1916–18): *Gottfried Kellers Leben, Briefe und Tagebücher.* 3 vols. Stuttgart and Berlin: J. G. Cotta.

Das Forum 1/31 (1914): "Richard Wagners erste Frau an Emma Herwegh," 142–156.

Geck, Martin, ed. (2021): *"Und über allem schwebt Richard." Minna Wagner und Cäcilie Avenarius: Zwei Schwägerinnen im Briefwechsel.* Hildesheim: Olms.

Golther, Wolfgang, ed. (1914): *Richard Wagner an Mathilde Wesendonk. Tagebuchblätter und Briefe 1853–1871.* 44th ed. Leipzig: Breitkopf & Härtel (first published 1904).

Hanslick, Eduard (1894): *Aus meinem Leben.* 2 vols. 3rd ed. Berlin: Allgemeiner Verein für Deutsche Litteratur.

Heintz, Albert (1896): "Richard Wagner in Zürich. Ein Gedenkblatt zum 13. Feb.," in: *Allgemeine Musik-Zeitung* 14/2, 92–94 (M. Wesendonck's reminiscences).

Herwegh, Emma, ed. Horst Brandstätter (1998): *Im Interesse der Wahrheit.* Lengwil: Libelle.

Herwegh, Marcel (1932): *Au Banquet des Dieux. Franz Liszt, Richard Wagner et leurs amis.* Paris: Peyronnet.

Herwegh, Marcel (1933): *Au Soir des Dieux. Des derniers reflets Wagneriens à la mort de Liszt (1847, 1883–1886).* Paris: Peyronnet.

Kabel, Rolf, ed. (1964): *Eduard Devrient. Aus seinen Tagebüchern.* 2 vols. Weimar: Böhlau.

Keller, Gottfried, ed. Carl Helbling (1951): *Gesammelte Briefe in 4 Bänden*, vol. II. Bern: Benteli.

Kesting, Hanjo, ed. (1988): *Franz Liszt–Richard Wagner. Briefwechsel*. Frankfurt am Main: Insel.

Kietz, Gustav Adolph (1907a): "Die Zeit der ersten *Rienzi*-Aufführung in Dresden," in: *Richard Wagner-Jahrbuch* II, 426–27.

Kietz, Gustav Adolph (1907b): *Richard Wagner in den Jahren 1842–1849 und 1873–1875*. Dresden: Reissner.

Kopf, Josef von (1899): *Lebenserinnerungen eines Bildhauers*. Stuttgart and Leipzig: Deutsche Verlags-Anstalt.

Lesimple, August (1884): *Erinnerungen*. Dresden and Leipzig: Heinrich Minden.

Litzmann, Berthold, ed. (1920): *Clara Schumann. Ein Künstlerleben nach Tagebüchern und Briefen*. 3 vols. Leipzig: Breitkopf & Härtel, first published 1902.

Mack, Dietrich, ed. (1980): *Cosima Wagner. Das zweite Leben. Briefe und Aufzeichnungen 1883–1930*. Munich & Zurich: Piper.

Meysenbug, Malwida von (1905): *Memoiren einer Idealistin*. Berlin and Leipzig: Schuster & Loeffler.

Moulin Eckart, Richard Graf Du, ed. (1927): *Hans von Bülow. Neue Briefe*. Munich: Drei Masken Verlag.

Otto, Werner, ed. (1990): *Richard Wagner. Ein Lebens- und Charakterbild in Dokumenten und zeitgenössischen Darstellungen*. Berlin: Buchverlag Der Morgen.

Pecht, Friedrich (1894): *Aus meiner Zeit. Lebenserinnerungen*. 2 vols. Munich: Verlagsanstalt für Kunst und Wissenschaft.

Praeger, Ferdinand (1892): *Wagner, as I knew him*. New York: Longmans, Green, & Co.

Praeger, Ferdinand (1892): *Wagner, wie ich ihn kannte*. Leipzig: Breitkopf & Härtel.

Röckel, August (1912): *Aus dem Grabe eines 48er Revolutionärs*. Leipzig: Gohlke.

Roner-Lipka, Berta (1986): "Erinnerungen," in Werner G. Zimmermann, ed.: *Richard Wagner in Zürich*. Zurich (170. Neujahrsblatt der Allgemeinen Musikgesellschaft Zürich), 7–17.

Sattler, Bernhard, ed. (1962): *Adolf von Hildebrand und seine Welt. Briefe und Erinnerungen*. Munich: G.D.W. Callwey.

Scholz, Hans, ed. (1930): *Richard Wagner an Mathilde Maier (1862–1878)*. Leipzig: Weicher.

Uhlig, Theodor, ed. Rudolf Louis (1913): "Briefe von einer Schweizer-Reise mit Richard Wagner," in *Süddeutsche Monatshefte* 2, 603–18, 693–700.

Wagner, Cosima, ed. Martin Gregor-Dellin and Dietrich Mack (CWT): *Die Tagebücher*. 2 vols. Munich and Zurich: Piper, 1976–77.

Wagner, Richard (1905): *Richard Wagner an Minna Wagner*. 2 vols. Berlin and Leipzig: Schuster & Loeffler.

Wagner, Richard (SSD): *Sämtliche Schriften und Dichtungen*. 16 vols. 6th ed. (Volksausgabe). Leipzig: Breitkopf & Härtel, [1911].

Wagner, Richard (SB): *Sämtliche Briefe*. 26– vols. Vols. 1–9 ed. Hans-Joachim Bauer, Klaus Burmeister, Johannes Forner, Gertrud Strobel, and Werner Wolf. Leipzig: Deutscher Verlag für Musik, 1967–2000. Vols. 10–25 and 27 ed. Martin Dürrer, Margret Jestremski, Isabel Kraft, Andreas Mielke, and Angela Steinsiek. Wiesbaden: Breitkopf & Härtel, 1999–.

Richard Wagner, ed. Martin Gregor-Dellin (1969): *Mein Leben*. Munich: List (first published 1963).

Wagner, Richard, tr. Andrew Gray, ed. Mary Whittall (ML): *My Life*. Cambridge, New York etc.: Cambridge University Press, 2009 (first published 1983).

Wagner, Richard, ed. Joachim Bergfeld (BB): *Das braune Buch. Tagebuchaufzeichnungen 1865–1882*. Munich and Zurich: Atlantis Musikbuch Verlag, 1988 (first published 1975).

Wallace, William (1927): *Liszt, Wagner, and the Princess*. London and New York: Kegan Paul

Wedekind, Frank, ed. Gerhard Hay (1986): *Die Tagebücher. Ein erotisches Leben*. Frankfurt am Main: Athenäum.

Weissheimer, Wendelin (1898): *Erlebnisse mit Richard Wagner, Franz Liszt und vielen anderen Zeitgenossen nebst deren Briefen*. Stuttgart and Leipzig: Deutsche Verlags-Anstalt.

Wesendonck, Mathilde (1862): *Gedichte, Volkslieder, Legenden, Sagen*. Zurich: Kiesling.

Wesendonck, Mathilde (1874): *Gedichte, Volksweisen, Legenden und Sagen*. Leipzig: Dürr.

Wille, Eliza (1982): *Erinnerungen an Richard Wagner. Mit 15 Briefen Richard Wagners*. Zurich: Atlantis Musikbuch-Verlag (first published 1894).

Zelinsky, Hartmut (1976): *Richard Wagner—ein deutsches Thema. Eine Dokumentation zur Wirkungsgeschichte Richard Wagners 1876–1976*. Frankfurt am Main: Zweitausendeins.

Zinsstag, Adolf, ed. (1961): *Die Briefsammlungen des Richard Wagner-Museums in Tribschen bei Luzern*. Basel: Zinsstag.

Zolling, Theophil (1899): "Richard Wagner's erste Frau. Mit ungedruckten Briefen von Minna Wagner-Planer," in *Die Gegenwart*, 40–42.

Secondary literature

Becker, Wolfgang (1962): *Die deutsche Oper in Dresden unter der Leitung von Carl Maria von Weber 1817–1826*. Berlin: Colloquium.

Bekker, Paul (1924): *Wagner. Das Leben im Werke*. Berlin and Leipzig: Deutsche Verlagsanstalt.

Bélart, Hans (1912): *Richard Wagners Liebestragödie mit Mathilde Wesendonk. Die Tragödie von Tristan und Isolde.* Dresden: Reissner.

Brendel, Franz (1854): *Die Musik der Gegenwart und die Gesammtkunst der Zukunft.* Leipzig: Hinze.

Brinkmann, Reinhold (2001): "Lohengrin, Sachs und Mime. Nationales Pathos und die Pervertierung der Kunst bei Richard Wagner," in Danuser and Münkler, 206–21.

Busch-Salmen, Gabriele (1991): "…eine reiche und vornehme Wiege … Pompöse Wohnansprüche Richard Wagners," in Monika Fink *et al.*, ed.: *Musica privata. Die Rolle der Musik im privaten Leben. Festschrift Walter Salmen.* Innsbruck: Helbling, 215–39.

Cabaud, Judith (2017): *Mathilde Wesendonck. Isolde's Dream.* Milwaukee: Amadeus Press.

Craig, Gordon A. (1988): *Geld und Geist. Zürich im Zeitalter des Liberalismus 1830–1869.* Munich: Beck.

Dahlhaus, Carl (1975): "Wozu noch Biographien?" In *Melos/Neue Zeitschrift für Musik* 1/2, 82.

Dahlhaus, Carl and John Deathridge (1984): *Wagner.* London: Macmillan.

Danuser, Hermann and Herfried Münkler, ed. (2001): *Deutsche Meister—böse Geister? Nationale Selbstfindung in der Musik.* Schliengen: Edition Argus.

Drüner, Ulrich (2016): *Richard Wagner. Die Inszenierung eines Lebens.* Munich: Blessing.

Dülmen, Andrea van, ed. (1992): *Frauenleben im 18. Jahrhundert.* Munich: Beck/ Kiepenheuer.

Eichhorn, Ulrike (2012): *Richard Wagner in Paris 1839–1842.* Berlin: Eichhorn.

Eichmann-Leutenegger, Beatrice (2002): "'Sprich, warum dies bittere Scheiden?' Mathilde Wesendoncks dichterisches Werk," in Langer and Walton, 85–89.

Erismann, Hans (1987): *Richard Wagner in Zürich.* Zurich: Verlag Neue Zürcher Zeitung.

Fehr, Max (1934 and 1953): *Richard Wagners Schweizer Zeit.* 2 vols. Aarau and Leipzig: Sauerländer. Vol. I 1934; vol. II 1953.

Fetz, Bernhard and Wilhelm Hemecker, ed. (2011): *Theorie der Biographie. Grundlagentexte und Kommentar.* Berlin and Bosten: De Gruyter.

Gartmann, Joos (1985): *Die Pferdepost in Graubünden.* Disentis: Desertina.

Gerhard, Ute (1983): "Die Anfänge der deutschen Frauenbewegung um 1848. Frauenpresse, Frauenpolitik und Frauenvereine." In Hausen, Karin, ed.: *Frauen suchen ihre Geschichte.* Munich: Beck, 196–220.

Glasenapp, Carl Friedrich (1977): *Das Leben Richard Wagners.* 6 vols. Reprint. New York: Da Capo Press (first published Leipzig 1905–11).

Gregor-Dellin, Martin (1980): *Richard Wagner. Sein Leben. Sein Werk. Sein Jahrhundert.* Munich and Zurich: Piper.

Gutman, Robert (1968): *Richard Wagner. Der Mensch, sein Werk, seine Zeit.* Munich: Piper.

Hanke, Eva Martina (2007): *Wagner in Zürich. Individuum und Lebenswelt.* Kassel: Bärenreiter.

Hartmann, Ludwig (1902): "Minna Wagner," in *Breslauer General-Anzeiger*, June 12.

Herzfeld, Friedrich (1938): *Minna Planer und ihre Ehe mit Richard Wagner.* Leipzig: Goldmann.

Kapp, Julius (1951): *Richard Wagner und die Frauen* Reprint. Berlin: Max Hesse (first published 1912).

Kapp, Julius and Hanns Jachmann (1927): *Richard Wagner und seine erste "Elisabeth" Johanna Jachmann-Wagner.* Berlin: Dom-Verlag.

Klein, Christian, ed. (2002): *Grundlagen der Biographik. Theorie und Praxis des biographischen Schreibens.* Stuttgart and Weimar: Metzler.

Kloss, Erich (1908): "Richard Wagners erste Gattin," in: *Dramaturgische Beilage zur Deutschen Bühnen-Genossenschaft* 43, July 3.

Knust, Martin (2007): *Sprachvertonung und Gestik in den Werken Richard Wagners.* Berlin: Frank & Timme.

Krausnick, Michail (1998): *Emma Herwegh. Nicht Magd mit den Knechten.* Marbach: Deutsche Schillergesellschaft.

Kühnel, Jürgen (1986): "Wagners Schriften," in Müller and Wapnewski, 471–588.

Kummer, Friedrich (1938): *Dresden und seine Theaterwelt.* Dresden: Heimatwerk Sachsen.

Langer, Axel and Chris Walton, ed. (2002): *Minne, Muse und Mäzen. Otto und Mathilde Wesendonck und ihr Zürcher Künstlerzirkel.* Zurich: Verlag Museum Rietberg.

Lippert, Woldemar (1927): *Richard Wagners Verbannung und Rückkehr 1849–1862.* Dresden: Aretz.

Maschka, Robert (2013): *Tristan und Isolde.* Kassel: Bärenreiter.

Maurer Zenck, Claudia (2000): "Komponierte Weiblichkeit—Rollenprofil der Isolde oder: Als Frau Isolde zuhören," in Vill, 95–123.

Müller, Ulrich and Peter Wapnewski, ed. (1986): *Richard-Wagner-Handbuch.* Stuttgart: Alfred Kröner.

Newman, Ernest (1933): *The Life of Richard Wagner*, vol. I. London: Cassell.

Rettenmund, Barbara and Jeannette Voirol (2000): *Emma Herwegh. Die grösste und beste Heldin der Liebe.* Zurich: Limmat Verlag.

Rheinberg, Brigitta van (1990): *Fanny Lewald. Geschichte einer Emanzipation.* Frankfurt and New York: Campus Verlag.

Richardson, Joanna (1986): *Judith Gautier. A Biography.* London and New York: Quartet Books.

Rieger, Eva (2006): "'Der Hypochonder bald kurirt, wenn ihn die Welt brav cujonirt': Minna Wagners Krise im Schweizer Kurhaus Brestenberg," in *Heimatkunde aus dem Seetal 79*, 13–18.

Rieger, Eva (2011): *Richard Wagner's Women*, tr. Chris Walton. Woodbridge: Boydell Press (originally published as *"Leuchtende Liebe, lachender Tod": Richard Wagners Bild der Frau im Spiegel seiner Musik*. Düsseldorf: Artemis & Winkler, 2009).

Rieger, Eva (2018): "Replik auf Udo Bermbach," in *wagnerspectrum* 14/1, 255–70.

Rieger, Eva and Hiltrud Schroeder (2009): *Ein Platz für Götter. Richard Wagners Wanderungen in der Schweiz*. Cologne, Weimar etc.: Böhlau.

Rose, Paul Lawrence (1992): *Richard Wagner und der Antisemitismus*. Zurich and Munich: Pendo.

Schopenhauer Arthur (1950): *Sämtliche Werke*, vol. II. Wiesbaden: Brockhaus.

Schwabe, Günther (1988): "Mathilde Wesendonk (1828–1902)," in Wilhelm Janssen, ed.: *Rheinische Lebensbilder* 11. Cologne: Rheinland-Verlag, 235–56.

Stümcke, Heinrich (1905): *Die Frau als Schauspielerin*. Leipzig: Rothbarth.

Tappert, Wilhelm (1901–1902): "Minna Wagner, geb. Planer," in: *Die Musik* 1, 1401–1411.

Unseld, Melanie (2009): "Musikwissenschaft," in Christian Klein, ed., *Handbuch Biographie. Methoden, Traditionen, Theorien*. Stuttgart: Metzler, 358–65.

Urner, Klaus (1976): *Die Deutschen in der Schweiz*. Frauenfeld: Huber.

Vill, Susanne, ed. (2000): *"Das Weib der Zukunft". Frauengestalten und Frauenstimmen bei Richard Wagner*. Stuttgart and Weimar: Metzler.

Voss, Egon (1996): *"Wagner und kein Ende." Betrachtungen und Studien*. Zurich and Mainz: Atlantis Musikbuch-Verlag.

Walton, Chris (2007): *Richard Wagner's Zurich. The Muse of Place*. Rochester, NY: University of Rochester Press.

Westernhagen, Curt von (1962): *Vom Holländer zum Parsifal. Neue Wagner-Studien*. Zurich: Atlantis.

Westernhagen, Curt von (1973): *Die Entstehung des "Ring." Dargestellt an den Kompositionsskizzen Richard Wagners*. Zurich: Atlantis.

Zehle, Sibylle (2004): *Minna Wagner: eine Spurensuche*. Hamburg: Hoffmann und Campe.

Index

Eastman Studies in Music

Ralph P. Locke, Senior Editor
Eastman School of Music

Additional Titles of Interest

Analyzing Wagner's Operas: Alfred Lorenz and German Nationalist Ideology
Stephen McClatchie

Berlioz in Time: From Early Recognition to Lasting Renown
Peter Bloom

Brahms's "A German Requiem":
Reconsidering Its Biblical, Historical, and Musical Contexts
R. Allen Lott

Canonic Repertories and the French Musical Press: Lully to Wagner
William Weber, with Beverly Wilcox

Claiming Wagner for France: Music and Politics in the Parisian Press, 1933–1944
Rachel Orzech

Lies and Epiphanies: Composers and Their Inspiration from Wagner to Berg
Chris Walton

Musical Analyses and Musical Exegesis:
The Shepherd's Melody in Richard Wagner's "Tristan and Isolde"
Jean-Jacques Nattiez
Edited and translated by Joan Huguet

Richard Wagner's Essays on Conducting: A New Translation with Critical Commentary
Chris Walton

Wagner and Venice
John W. Barker

Wagner's Visions: Poetry, Politics, and the Psyche in the Operas through "Die Walküre"
Katherine R. Syer

A complete list of titles in the Eastman Studies in Music series
may be found on our website, www.urpress.com.